I0235309

JASCHA HEIFETZ

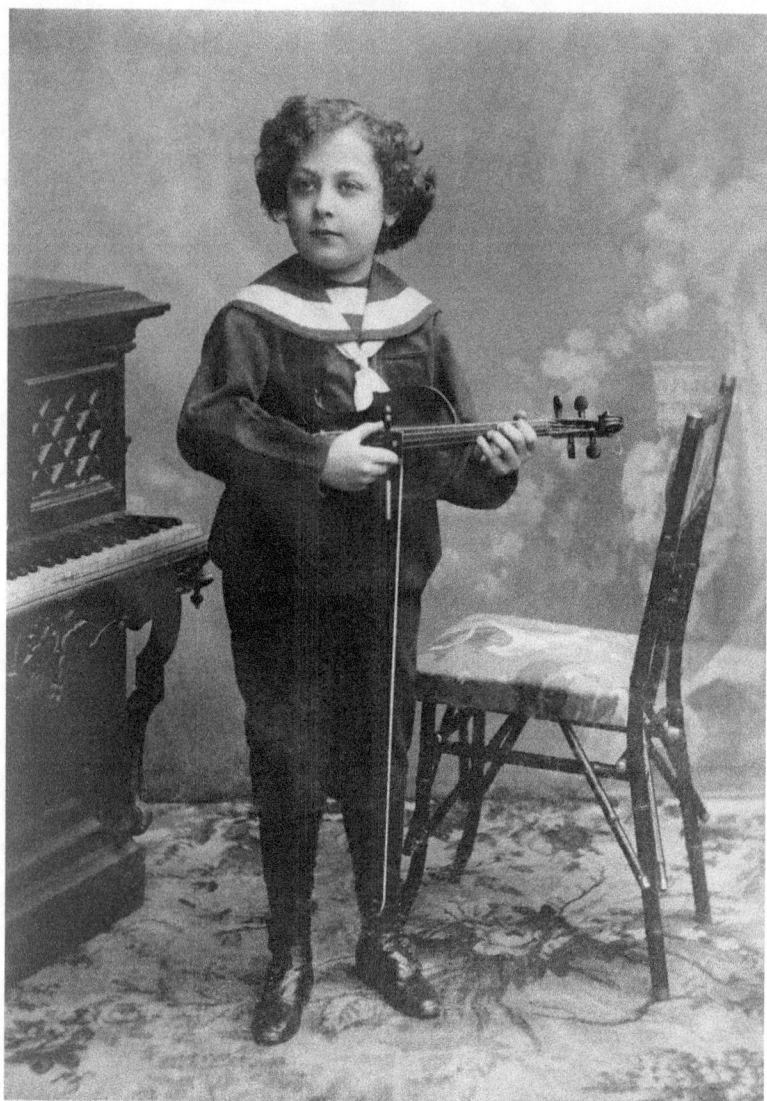

RUSSIAN MUSIC STUDIES   *Malcolm Hamrick Brown, Founding Editor*

JASCHA HEIFETZ

Early Years in Russia

GALINA KOPYTOVA

WITH THE COLLABORATION OF
Albina Starkova-Heifetz

TRANSLATED AND EDITED BY
Dario Sarlo & Alexandra Sarlo

INDIANA UNIVERSITY PRESS   *Bloomington & Indianapolis*

This book is a publication of

INDIANA UNIVERSITY PRESS
Office of Scholarly Publishing
Herman B Wells Library 350
1320 East 10th Street
Bloomington, Indiana 47405 USA

iupress.indiana.edu

Telephone orders   800-842-6796
Fax orders   812-855-7931

© 2014 by Indiana University Press
This work appeared originally in Russian
as *Jascha Heifetz in Russia: From the
History of the Musical Culture of the
Silver Age* by Galina Kopytova (Russian
Institute for the History of the Arts).
© 2004 Kompozitor, St. Petersburg.

ALL RIGHTS RESERVED

No part of this book may be reproduced
or utilized in any form or by any means,
electronic or mechanical, including
photocopying and recording, or by
any information storage and retrieval
system, without permission in writing
from the publisher. The Association of
American University Presses' Resolution
on Permissions constitutes the only
exception to this prohibition.

☉ The paper used in this publication
meets the minimum requirements of
the American National Standard for
Information Sciences—Permanence
of Paper for Printed Library
Materials, ANSI Z39.48-1992.

MANUFACTURED IN THE
UNITED STATES OF AMERICA

Library of Congress
Cataloging-in-Publication Data

Kopytova, G. V., author.
  [Iasha Kheifets v Rossii. English]
  Jascha Heifetz : early years in Russia /
Galina Kopytova with the collaboration of
Albina Starkova-Heifetz ; translated and
edited by Dario Sarlo and Alexandra Sarlo.
    pages cm. — (Russian music studies)
  "This work appeared originally in
Russian as Jascha Heifetz in Russia
: from the history of the musical
culture of the Silver Age by Galina
Kopytova. ? 2004 Kompozitor, St.
Petersburg."—Title page verso.
  "The present edition in English is more
than a translation of the original. With
the support and approval of the author, it
has been updated with new research and
sources and has been adapted to an English-
speaking audience"—Editors' introduction.
  Includes bibliographical
references and index.
  ISBN 978-0-253-01076-6 (cloth : alkaline
paper) — ISBN 978-0-253-01089-6 (ebook)
  1. Heifetz, Jascha, 1901–1987. 2. Violinists—
Biography. 3. Heifetz, Jascha, 1901–1987—
Appreciation—Soviet Union. I. Starkova-
Heifetz, Albina, author. II. Sarlo, Dario,
editor, translator. III. Sarlo, Alexandra,
editor, translator. IV. Title. V. Series:
Russian music studies (Bloomington, Ind.)
  ML418.H44K6713 2013
  787.2092—dc23
  [B]
                                              2013034077

1 2 3 4 5   19 18 17 16 15 14

Dedicated to the memory of Robert Heifetz

CONTENTS

AUTHOR'S PREFACE

THE IDEA FOR A BOOK about the childhood of Jascha Heifetz (1901–1987) did not arise overnight, and the story behind the book is notable in and of itself. In the middle of the 1980s, I was conducting research in the personal archive of the violinist and music critic Viktor Grigoryevich Valter (Walter) (1865–1935) in the Russian Institute for the History of the Arts. The documents and materials were fascinating, but nothing stood out as particularly significant. At that time, I did not know a surprise was hidden in a particular folder that a previous owner had labeled, "unidentified." In that folder I discovered correspondence addressed to Valter—letters and telegrams signed by a certain R. Heifetz and his son Joseph. Judging by the postage stamps and the address of the sender, these letters were written from Vilnius, Lithuania in the summer of 1911 and from Loschwitz, Germany, near Dresden, in the summer of 1913. A tiny but enthusiastic voice rang out from the stillness of the archive: "Much Respected Viktor Grigoryevich! I am on vacation now, and only practicing violin and piano a little bit. I am now studying the Tchaikovsky Concerto and the Handel Sonata. . . ." My immediate impression that these words belonged to the great Heifetz was confirmed only when I reached the very last piece of correspondence in the folder, which was signed, simply, "Jascha."

In 1991, for the ninetieth anniversary of Heifetz's birth, I published this discovery from the Valter archive in the magazine *Sovetskaya muzyka;* my four-page article led to a fortunate meeting.[1] In 1993 Robert Heifetz, the eldest son of the great violinist, sought me out in Russia. His desire to learn as much as possible about the Russian years of his father's life served as a further inspiration. Robert continued to support the project enthusiastically and ensured that it could be completed. Robert's wife, Albina Starkova-Heifetz, also took an active part in the creation of this "Russian" biography of Jascha Heifetz. She devoted much effort, time, and love to the book, and worked alongside me in various archives, collecting and piecing together information about members of the large Heifetz family, as well as reading and editing the manuscript at every stage. She is the full co-author of this biography, and the original Russian publication was made possible with her generous financial support. Without the inspiring influence and practical assistance of Robert and Albina, this book would not exist.

The great violinist Jascha Heifetz lived a long and brilliant life that spanned nearly the entire twentieth century. As fate would have it, his biography is divided into two parts. He lived in Russia for the first sixteen and a half years of his life, and spent the remaining seventy years in the United States. Despite the difference in length, both periods of his life hold equal significance. The Russian years encompass his childhood and early youth—the stages of his initial growth and development and the years in which his performance style took shape. The American period saw Heifetz rise to a level of supreme mastery of performance—a level that profoundly influenced the art of the violin in the twentieth century. Heifetz himself defined the major milestones of his life in the following succinct manner: "Born in Russia, first lessons at 3, debut in Russia at 7, debut in America in 1917."[2] The very beginning of this extraordinary life was in Russia.

The political realities of the past century—both the era of Stalinism and the years of the Cold War—played a significant role in the division of Heifetz's life into these two separate stages. Western writers offer only general impressions of Heifetz's Russian period, and likewise, Soviet musical studies display only a restrained interest in his American years. The fact that Heifetz emigrated from Russia to a foreign country after the 1917 February Revolution proved to be an ideological obstacle for Soviet writers. All the same, they did write about him. Lev Raaben's 1962 book, *Leopold Auer: A Sketch of His Life and Career*, is the only work to include documentary evidence concerning Heifetz's student years at the St. Petersburg Conservatory. Toward the end of the Thaw, Raaben also published the only Russian text dedicated entirely to Heifetz, a biographical essay entitled "Jascha (Joseph Robertovich) Heifetz," which he included in his book *The Lives of Remarkable Violinists*. This twelve-page essay describes Heifetz's life and career and dedicates three and a half pages specifically to the early Russian period of his life and his subsequent 1934 return to the Soviet Union on tour. The next publication about Heifetz came out in Russia a quarter century later. The article, published in the 1997 encyclopedic dictionary *The Russian Abroad: Golden Book of Emigration, the Encyclopedic Biographical Dictionary* by Vladimir Grigoryev, gives a comprehensive account of Heifetz's career. Nevertheless, the work suffers from a large number of factual inaccuracies including incorrect dates connected with the early period of his life. Other Russian-language materials on Heifetz include translated memoirs and several magazine publications, including a 1988 article by Igor Oistrakh in *Sovetskaya muzyka*, entitled "To the Memory of Jascha Heifetz."

English-language literature about Heifetz is more extensive and varied, but there remains no complete biographical study worthy of a musician of such stature. Artur Weschler-Vered's 1986 book, *Jascha Heifetz*, monitors the trajectory of Heifetz's career with an emphasis on his 1953 tour of Israel. Herbert Axelrod's book *Heifetz* has been published in three editions since 1976 and deserves some attention. Along with material from reviews and memoirs, the book includes numerous photographs illuminating Heifetz's life, including some from the early Russian period. Heifetz also often figures in the memoirs of musicians based in the United States, including violinists Albert Spalding and Nathan Milstein, pianists André Benoist and Samuel Chotzinoff, cellist Gdal Saleski, and musicologist Boris Schwarz. Others who wrote about Heifetz include Dagmar Godowsky, Samuel and Sada Applebaum, and Roger Kahn. Furthermore, several articles about Heifetz appeared in the pages of *The Strad* magazine. To coincide with the centennial of Heifetz's birth, two of his former students published books dedicated to the last years of his life—*Jascha Heifetz Through My Eyes* by Sherry Kloss and *Heifetz as I Knew Him* by Ayke Agus. Despite the lack of a full-length biography of Heifetz in either the country where he was raised or his second homeland, interest in his life and work remains high, and Heifetz's significance for all lovers of the violin remains indisputable. This is true for those old enough to have heard Heifetz perform as well as younger generations, who have learned about Heifetz's work through his legacy of audio and video recordings.[3]

The present book is dedicated to Heifetz's childhood—from his birth in Vilnius to his young life in Russia and his eventual arrival in the United States in 1917. While I have drawn on all the major Russian and English sources of Heifetz material of both a scholarly and biographical nature, the book is based largely on primary documents from the Russian period of Heifetz's life.

This documentary narrative is based upon unique archival documents, written and oral recollections of Heifetz's descendants and relatives, and hundreds of reviews that appeared in the Russian and foreign press in the early twentieth century. It tells the origin story of the great violinist, and about the people who influenced him and whom he himself influenced. It is a portrait of a musician set within the context of a young and terrible century.

Over the years of work on this book, many wonderful people connected with its creation have passed away. Moscow Conservatory Professor Vladimir Grigoryev (1927–1997) was a violinist and music critic whose research became the starting point in the process of uncovering Heifetz's Russian family connections. Yelizaveta Khakina (1921–1999) was a brilliant translator of Yiddish, and Margarita Heifetz (1921–1999), a professor at the St. Petersburg Conservatory, related her story of meeting Heifetz long ago in 1934. Jascha Heifetz's eldest son, Robert, a bright, intelligent, and wonderful individual, passed away on April 7, 2001. At the time the manuscript was in the publication process in Russia, news came from New York of the deaths of two more people close to Heifetz—his cousin Anna (Anyuta) Sharfstein-Koch and his niece Anne Chotzinoff Grossman.

I am deeply indebted to Heifetz's descendants and relatives outside of Russia for their help and for the materials they have given to me, and I wish to express my sincere thanks to them: Josefa Heifetz, Jay Heifetz, and the late Suzanne Parry. I am equally grateful to members of the Russian Heifetz family: Professor Aleksandr Nemirovsky, Irina Averyanova, Ilya Lamov, the late Lilya and Leonid Heifetz, and Ilya Heifetz.

I would also like to thank Lev Axelrod, Yelena Goncharova, Olga Dansker, Igor Dmitriev, Lyudmila Kovnatskaya, Olga Manulkina, Aleksandr Mussel, Maria Perekalina, Galina Retrovskaya, Ivan Sablin, Nadezhda Tarshis, Aleksandr Frenkel, Yevgenya Khazdan, Natalya Chekmareva, Karina Balasanian, Irina Grigoryeva, Pavel Sedov, Genrikh Agranovsky, Galina Baranova, Alisa Ilyina, Thomas and Olga Aigner, Igor Voskresensky, Mark Horowitz, Sherry Kloss, John and John Anthony Maltese, Vera Maksakova, Andrey Mizura, Jascha Nemtsov, Gerhard Neubauer, and Erik Stenstadvold.

A number of years have passed since the original publication of my book in Russia, and I am now delighted to see it reach a new audience. I would like to thank Dario and Alexandra Sarlo, who initiated this translation project, and wish to express my most sincere gratitude for their efforts in producing this new edition of my book. Dario and Alexandra's ardent enthusiasm and self-sacrificing work helped to overcome all the difficulties related to a project of this scale. Our years of collaboration on the English-language edition have united us in our common admiration of the genius of Heifetz.

My sincere hope is that readers of this edition will learn not only about Jascha Heifetz's remarkable childhood, but also something about the country and atmosphere in which he spent his formative years.

Galina Kopytova
St. Petersburg, Russia
Summer 2012

EDITORS' INTRODUCTION

JASCHA HEIFETZ WAS FAMOUSLY reticent when questioned about his childhood, and he made no attempt to write an autobiography. It is not surprising, therefore, that Heifetz's earliest years have long been considered something of an uncharted and mysterious period in the life of the great violinist. With this edition of Galina Kopytova's biographical narrative about Heifetz's childhood, an important chapter in music history is presented to the English-speaking world.

Galina Kopytova's original book was published in Russia in 2004 by the Kompozitor publishing house in St. Petersburg. The book brought the story of Heifetz's remarkable childhood to a Russian audience proud of the prodigy who spent his formative years in Russia. It received positive reviews, and a second printing appeared two years later.

The present edition in English is more than a translation of the original. With the support and approval of the author, it has been updated with new research and sources and has been adapted to an English-speaking audience. Additional photographs have been discovered, the maps of St. Petersburg and Vilnius have been redrawn, and the family tree has been expanded. All documentary sources have been translated directly from the originals (French, German, Yiddish, and Norwegian), and those in English have been transcribed directly. Wherever possible, references to accessible English-language sources have been provided. To maintain the focus on Heifetz's childhood, a chapter on Heifetz's 1934 tour of the Soviet Union in the original biography was omitted.

In the reference notes and selected sources, we have generally followed the system of transliteration endorsed by the Library of Congress and the British Library, but without the superscript arcs above the letters for those Cyrillic characters represented by two Latin letters in the strict Library of Congress/British Library system. In the body of the text, however, we have been more flexible, opting to simplify some additional aspects of the Library of Congress transliteration system and to use familiar spellings of well-known Russian names. For example, we use Tchaikovsky rather than Chaikovskii, and Koussevitzky rather than Kusevitskii.

The Russian Empire of the late nineteenth and early twentieth centuries encompassed a variety of nations and ethnicities. Consequently, this work includes names of Polish, Lithuanian, Yiddish, Georgian, and other linguistic origins. Many of the characters in this book moved between countries and eventually became known by names that differed from the original versions. Wherever possible we have spelled common names in familiar variants, or according to how the individual was known; in some cases, we have transliterated names of various ethnic origins from their Russian versions.

Heifetz's parents named him Joseph, which would have been pronounced Yosif in Russian. In various personal documents from the 1920s, Heifetz wrote his name as "Joseph," and this same variant appears in the English-language literature; we also use that spelling. The name Jascha (pronounced Yasha) was used as a diminutive of the name Joseph, and it is with this diminutive that the violinist became known. Among family and friends in Russia, however, other diminutives were also used, including Jaschenka, Jasinka, and Josifka.

The names of the immediate Heifetz family members have been kept in the forms they themselves adopted after immigrating to the United States: Ruvin, Anna, Pauline, and Elza. An exception to this rule is in quoted materials where diminutives are often used—Elza becomes Elinka, Elzinka,

Elzutka, and Elzochka; Pauline becomes Polinka, Polya, Pesya, and, in the hands of her musical brother, she is Polka-mazurka.

The city of St. Petersburg, the setting for much of this book, underwent many political and social upheavals during the early twentieth century, and as a result, the name of the city changed to Petrograd in 1914 and Leningrad in 1924. The correct name has been given according to the historical context. In relation to towns, cities, and other geographic locations that formed part of the former Russian Empire, we have opted in the majority of cases to use commonly known or current names (for example, Vilnius instead of Vilna), except in quoted material.

In February 1918 the Bolshevik government implemented a calendar reform that brought Russia in line with the West at a cost of thirteen days. Events in Russia before the reform are dated according to the Julian calendar (Old Style, or OS); events outside of Russia are dated according to the Gregorian calendar (New Style, or NS). Where there is potential for confusion, both dates are provided.

We wish to thank Carolyn Brown, Mary Lou Reker, and the entire John W. Kluge Center staff at the Library of Congress for providing an environment conducive to this project. Since then many people have assisted in the production of the new edition, including Ayke Agus, Albert and Joan Benoist, Stephanie Bothwell, Graham Down, Elena Fomicheva, Martin Gilbert, Lisa Grossman, Frank and Evelyn Higham, Mark Eden Horowitz, Alexander Ivashkin, Ron and Laura Ivey, Sherry Kloss, Patricia Krafcik, Henry and Rudolph Lea, Matthew Mallen, John and John Anthony Maltese, Anna Melyakova, Astra Michels, Daiva Navarrette, Thomas O'Donnell, Paul Olefsky, Estela Olevsky, Roger and Patricia Stockton Plaskett, Laurence Richter, Esther Rider, Martin and Angelika Riskin, Marna Sapsowitz, Adam Sarlo, Mario and Andrea Sarlo, Hartmut Schütz, Janine Schütz, Irina Sharkova, Arthur Vered, James Warren, and Daniel Wiktorek. We wish to thank those at Indiana University Press who worked with us throughout this project, including Jane Kupersmith, Malcolm Hamrick Brown, and Raina Polivka. We extend our gratitude to those who translated reviews and documents from French, German, and Yiddish: Irene Auerbach, Tom Jeffers, Clarisse O'Donnell, Robert A. Rothstein, and Fiammetta Tarli. Finally, we wish to thank those who have provided support for this project, including Zina Markevicius and the Lithuanian Assistance Foundation, Mari Haig, Navroz Karkaria, Henry and Rudolph Lea, and Kenji Yoshimoto.

Dario and Alexandra Sarlo
Philadelphia, United States
Summer 2012

LIST OF ABBREVIATIONS

The following is a list of archival collections consulted during research on this book and the abbreviations adopted when referencing them in bibliographic citations:

ST. PETERSBURG

TSGIA SPB   Tsentral'nyi gosudarstvennyi istoricheskii arkhiv Sankt-Peterburga (Central State Historical Archive, St. Petersburg).

KR RIII   Kabinet rukopisei Rossiiskogo instituta istorii iskusstv (Manuscript Office of the Russian Institute for the History of the Arts).

OR RNB   Otdel rukopisei Rossiiskoi natsional'noi biblioteki (Manuscript Division of the Russian National Library).

OR SPBGK   Otdel rukopisei i arkhiv Sankt-Peterburgskoi gosudarstvennoi konservatorii imeni N. A. Rimskogo-Korsakova (Manuscript Division and Archive of the N. A. Rimsky-Korsakov St. Petersburg State Conservatory).

Muzykal'naia biblioteka Sankt-Peterburgskoi akademicheskoi filarmonii imeni D. D. Shostakovicha (The Music Library of the St. Petersburg D. D. Shostakovich Academic Philharmonic).

Fonogramarkhiv Instituta russkoi literatury (Pushkinskii dom) Rossiiskoi akademii nauk (Phonogram Archive of the Institute of Russian Literature [Pushkin House] of the Russian Academy of Sciences).

Tsentral'nyi gosudarstvennyi arkhiv kinofotofonodokumentov Sankt-Peterburga (Central State Archive of Film, Photo, and Audio Documents of St. Petersburg).

MOSCOW

RGALI	Rossiiskii gosudarstvennyi arkhiv literatury i iskusstva (Russian State Archive of Literature and Art).
GARF	Gosudarstvennyi arkhiv Rossiiskoi Federatsii (State Archive of the Russian Federation).
RGAF	Rossiiskii gosudarstvennyi arkhiv fonodokumentov (Russian State Archive of Audio Documents).
TSA FSB	Tsentral'nyi arkhiv Federal'nyi sluzhby bezopasnosti Rossiiskoi Federatsii (Central Archive of the Federal Security Service (FSB) of the Russian Federation).

VILNIUS

LVIA	Lietuvos valstybes istorijos archyvas (State Historical Archive of Lithuania).
LLMA	Lietuvos literaturos ir meno archyvas (Lithuanian Archive of Literature and Art).

WASHINGTON, DC

JHC LOC	The Jascha Heifetz Collection, Library of Congress.

NEW YORK

The New York Public Library.

Sources taken from the Russian collections are listed according to standard Russian archival terminology: f[ond] = a unified collection of archival materials; op[is'] = an inventory or list of files in a fond; d[elo] = a file, an item, or a unit in a fond, or a basic unit of classification in a fond; ed[initsa] khr[aneniia] = similar to a delo, a unit of archival storage comprising a single document or a collection of related documents, or a file; l[ist] = folder, folio, leaf, or sheet; s[tranitsa] = page; ob[orot] = verso, overpage, or overleaf of a sheet.

Vilnius, 1904. Adapted from *Evreiskaia entsiklopediia*, vol. 5
(St. Petersburg: Brockhaus & Efron, 1908–1913), 572–573.

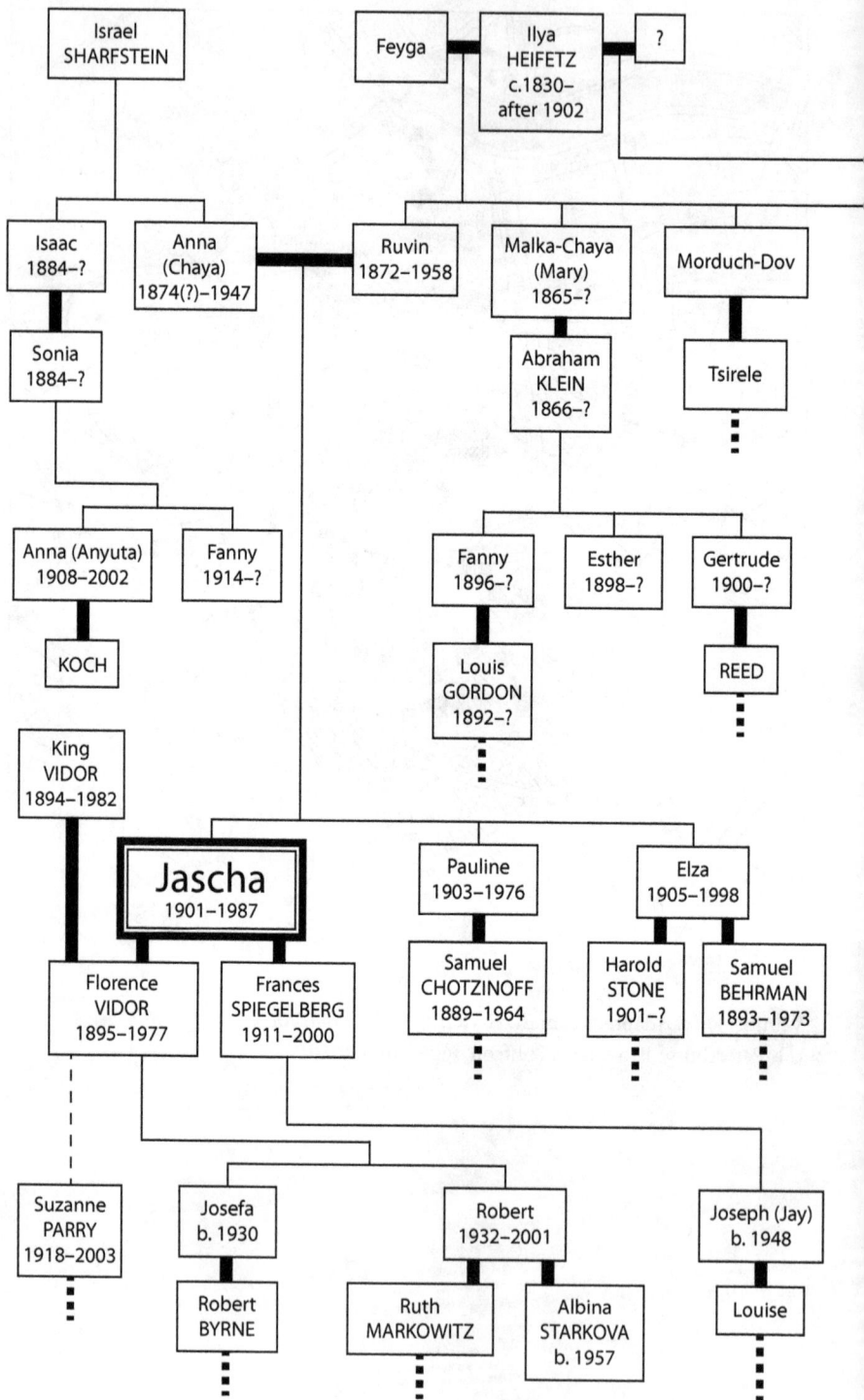

Israel SHARFSTEIN

Feyga — Ilya HEIFETZ c.1830–after 1902 — ?

Isaac 1884–?

Anna (Chaya) 1874(?)–1947 — Ruvin 1872–1958

Malka-Chaya (Mary) 1865–?

Morduch-Dov

Sonia 1884–?

Abraham KLEIN 1866–?

Tsirele

Anna (Anyuta) 1908–2002

Fanny 1914–?

Fanny 1896–?

Esther 1898–?

Gertrude 1900–?

KOCH

Louis GORDON 1892–?

REED

King VIDOR 1894–1982

Jascha 1901–1987

Pauline 1903–1976

Elza 1905–1998

Florence VIDOR 1895–1977

Frances SPIEGELBERG 1911–2000

Samuel CHOTZINOFF 1889–1964

Harold STONE 1901–?

Samuel BEHRMAN 1893–1973

Suzanne PARRY 1918–2003

Josefa b. 1930

Robert 1932–2001

Joseph (Jay) b. 1948

Robert BYRNE

Ruth MARKOWITZ

Albina STARKOVA b. 1957

Louise

The Heifetz Family Tree. Jascha Heifetz's branch of the tree is shown in full.
The remaining branches are shown in proportion to their representation
in the text of the book. Marriage indicated with a thick line.

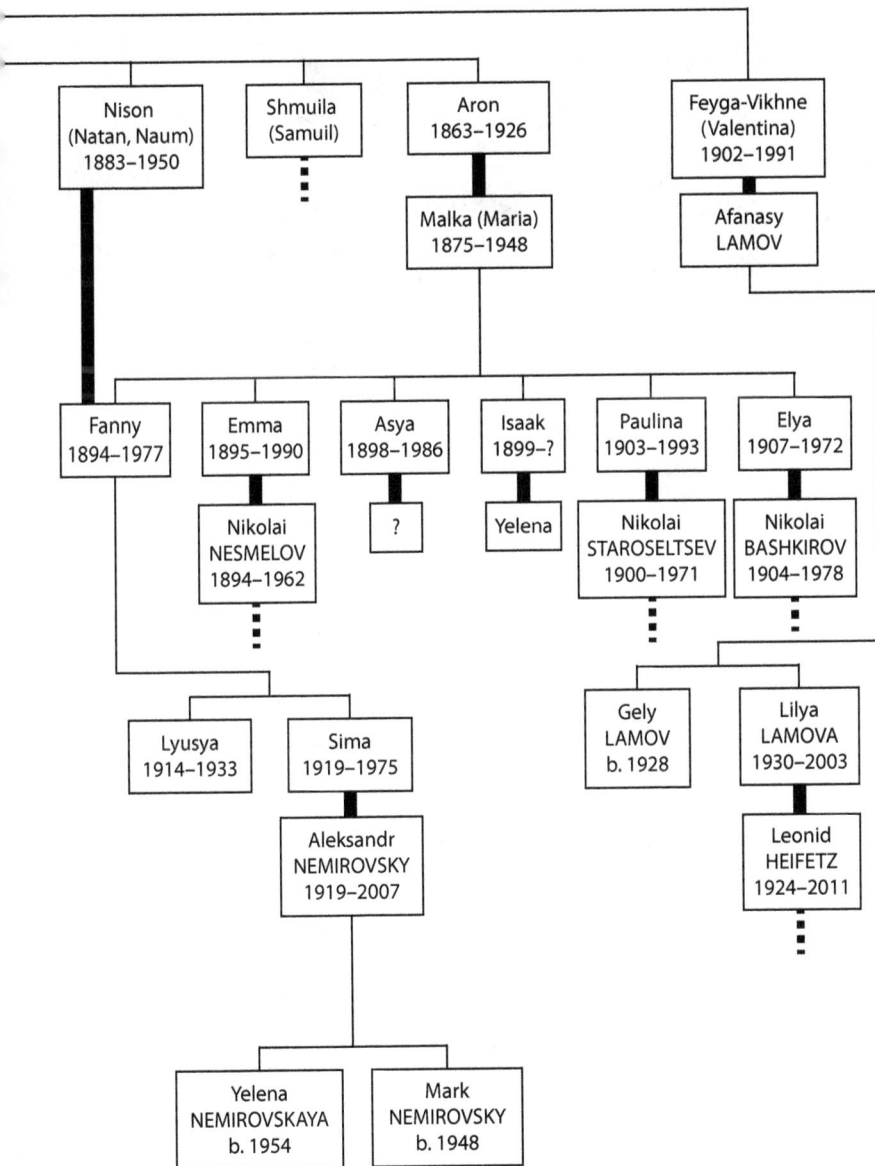

| Nison (Natan, Naum) 1883–1950 | Shmuila (Samuil) | Aron 1863–1926 | Feyga-Vikhne (Valentina) 1902–1991 |

Malka (Maria) 1875–1948

Afanasy LAMOV

Fanny 1894–1977 | Emma 1895–1990 | Asya 1898–1986 | Isaak 1899–? | Paulina 1903–1993 | Elya 1907–1972

Nikolai NESMELOV 1894–1962

?

Yelena

Nikolai STAROSELTSEV 1900–1971

Nikolai BASHKIROV 1904–1978

Gely LAMOV b. 1928

Lilya LAMOVA 1930–2003

Lyusya 1914–1933 | Sima 1919–1975

Aleksandr NEMIROVSKY 1919–2007

Leonid HEIFETZ 1924–2011

Yelena NEMIROVSKAYA b. 1954 | Mark NEMIROVSKY b. 1948

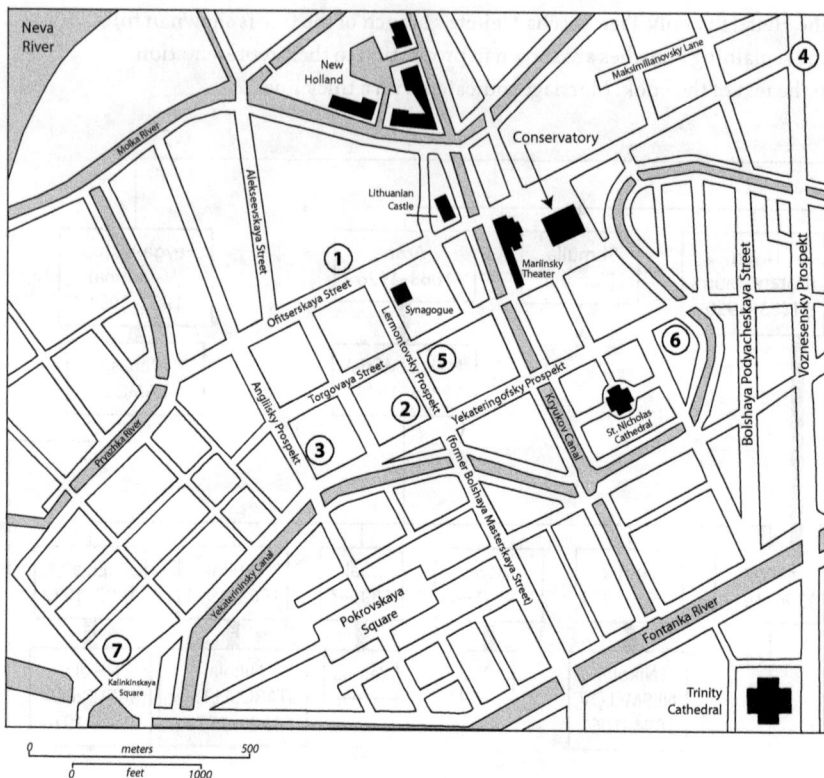

The location of the Heifetz family's residences in St. Petersburg:

1. January to April 1910: 37 Ofitserskaya Street (now Decembrists' Street)
2. From September 1910: 11/55 Bolshaya Masterskaya
   Street (now Lermontovsky Prospekt, 9/55)
3. September 1911: 40 Angliisky Prospekt
4. From October 1911: 20 Voznesensky Prospekt
5. From September 1912: 8/10 Masterskaya Street
6. From October 1913: 119 Yekaterininsky Canal (now Griboedov Canal)
7. January 1915 to July 1917: 115 Yekateringofsky Prospekt
   (now Rimsky-Korsakov Prospekt)

Adapted and expanded from a map by Martin Gilbert in Mikhail Beizer, *The Jews of St. Petersburg: Excursions through a Noble Past.* Philadelphia: The Jewish Publication Society, 1989, xxix. *Courtesy of Sir Martin Gilbert.*

JASCHA HEIFETZ

CHAPTER ONE

Early Roots of the Heifetz Family

THE HEIFETZ FAMILY TREE includes over one hundred people across five generations and family members who now reside in the United States, Australia, Israel, Latvia, and Russia. The oldest Heifetz name preserved in family memory is that of Ilya (or Elye), Jascha's paternal grandfather, who was born around 1830. Two photographs of Ilya survive in the personal records of his descendants; one is an individual portrait, and the other a group photograph featuring Ilya, surrounded by his children and grandchildren. With one photograph now located in Russia and the other in the United States, these two unique, symbolic documents unite the Heifetz clan across the world.

According to family legend, Ilya Heifetz worked as a teacher (*melamed*) in a Jewish boys' school (*cheder*) and lived with his large family in Polotsk, a provincial city in the western Russian province (*guberniya*) of Vitebsk, which is now part of Belarus. The surviving family group photograph dates from the late 1890s, when Ilya was well over sixty and his wife, Feyga, was no longer alive. An earlier photograph from the 1870s shows Jascha's father, Ruvin, as a child, with his mother and grandmother, and is stamped, "Novo-Alexandria (Poulavy)."[1] Novo-Alexandria was the name of a settlement in the Lublin province located on the bank of the Vistula (Wisła)

River, seventy-five miles from Warsaw. Formerly known as Puławy, the city was renamed Novo-Alexandria in 1846 after a visit by Empress Alexandra Fyodorovna, wife of Tsar Nicholas I. It functioned as an important trade center between Russia, Austria, and the Baltic region, and reverted to its former name, Puławy, in 1918. By the end of the nineteenth century, Novo-Alexandria had experienced a large influx of Jewish settlers; about 2,500 of its 3,500 residents were Jewish.

Ruvin Heifetz was born on March 22 (NS April 3), 1872, in either Novo-Alexandria or Polotsk. His parents, Ilya and Feyga Heifetz, raised five additional children: a daughter, Mary (Malka-Chaya), and four sons, Morduch-Dov, Aron, Samuil (Shmuyla), and Natan (Nison). At least two of Ruvin's brothers—Samuil and Natan—were born in Polotsk, one older and one younger, suggesting Ruvin was also born there. Ilya's six children were registered as belonging to the Polotsk *meshchanstvo*—the name for the lower middle, urban classes in Russia (a member of this class was called a *meshchanin*, female *meshchanka,* or plural *meshchane*).

According to the recollections of descendants living in Riga, Ruvin's oldest brother, Morduch-Dov, worked as a teacher and lived in Polotsk with his children and wife, Tsirele. His mail correspondence until the 1910s bore the address, "Polotsk. Morduch Heifetz, beyond the Dvina." During one of his visits to Polotsk with his parents, five-year-old Jascha played his tiny violin at the wedding of Morduch's daughter Feyga.

Ilya's second son Aron Heifetz (1863–1926) also lived and taught in the Polotsk region; one of the earliest surviving Heifetz family documents relates his birth:

> Certificate no. 483. It is hereby certified by the Polotsk Community Rabbi that to the Polotsk *meshchane,* lawful spouses Elye Itskov and Feyga Heifetz, in the month of September 1863 in the city of Polotsk, was born a son, who is given the name Aron.[2]

According to Aron Heifetz's employment documents, he completed six years of secondary study in Daugavpils (then Dvinsk), about ninety miles from Polotsk. He taught at a Jewish school in the village of Kreuzberg before returning to Polotsk in 1904, where during the Soviet years he became the director of School number 6. Aron and his wife, Malka or Maria (1875–1948), had five daughters and one son.

Samuil was the only son of Ilya Heifetz not connected with the teaching profession. A certificate from the Imperial Warsaw University held in family papers declares: "Shmuila Elyevich Heifetz is by the medical department of this university found worthy by examination of the title of dentist and confirmed in this title 19 November 1904."[3]

The youngest son, Nison Heifetz (1883–1950), more frequently called Natan or sometimes Naum, pursued musical studies at the Warsaw Institute of Music from 1896 to 1903. He later taught at schools in Warsaw and Yekaterinoslav (now Dnipropetrovsk), and after 1920 worked in Moscow at the Jewish Chamber Theater, the University of the Peoples of the West, and the Gnesin School of Music. He married his niece Fanny (1894–1977), the daughter of his brother Aron. During the Soviet years Fanny became a historian, defended her doctoral dissertation, wrote books on the history of the French workers' movement, and worked with historian and academic Yevgeny Tarle. In 1945, Fanny became a victim of political repression under the Soviets. Natan and Fanny figured prominently in Jascha's childhood.

By the end of the nineteenth century, the city of Polotsk, where Ilya Heifetz and his family lived, was a district center with a population of twenty thousand, 62 percent of which were Jews. The thousand-year history of the city witnessed several tragic episodes, including the Livonian war in the second half of the sixteenth century and Napoleon's 1812 invasion of Russia. For the Jewish population, the most traumatic event occurred in 1563, when Ivan the Terrible ordered the drowning of the entire Polotsk Jewish population in the Daugava (Dvina) River. Locals commemorated the day of the tragedy each year with a procession to a hill on the riverbank, the supposed burial place of the drowned victims.

Few Jews lived in Russia proper during the second half of the eighteenth century, but with the partitioning of Poland toward the end of the century, Russia acquired Belarusian, Lithuanian, and Polish territories, each with a long history of Jewish settlement. Almost immediately Russian authorities classed the Jews as a foreign element and subjected them to restrictive laws. As the more democratic western countries began to remove such limitations, however, Russia hardened its relationship to the Jews throughout the nineteenth century, a development strongly supported by the state's official ideology declared under Tsar Nicholas I, referred to as "Orthodoxy, Autocracy, Nationality." Russian Jews faced increasing restrictions, but conversion to Christianity could free them from such laws as those forbidding them from living in or acquiring property in rural areas and closing off certain trades and crafts from them. Furthermore, a series of laws sought to remove Jews from a thirty-mile belt stretching through the western provinces. In essence, state policies strove feverishly to reduce the number of Jews in Russia, either by assimilating them or by encouraging them to settle beyond the borders of the empire, after which any return became impossible.

Laws permitting Jewish settlement only in Russia's western regions, called the Pale of Settlement, led to the relative isolation of more than five million people. The Pale encompassed Ukraine, Moldova, Belarus, Lithuania, and Poland, as well as portions of western Russia proper. Furthermore, the structure of traditional Jewish life itself encouraged the separation of Jews from the rest of the population; Jewish upbringing, family relationships, and education all bore a religious character, creating a strong internal bond within the Jewish communities.

Given the traditional organization of Jewish society in the nineteenth century, Ilya Heifetz most likely worked as a teacher and taught in a Jewish boys' school with instruction in reading, writing, basic arithmetic, and prayers. For most of the nineteenth century, such boys' schools and the *Talmud Torah* (a boys' school for the poor) were the only available sources of religious education, giving even the poorest Jews a chance to study and learn about their heritage. The idea of a Jewish boys' school has traditionally evoked images of a crowded, cold, dimly lit space, where boys of varying ages studied up to twelve hours a day. Instruction was in Yiddish, textbooks and other study aids were a rarity, and teaching methods usually focused on rote learning. Most teachers tended to be elderly men from a variety of backgrounds, including former merchants, craftsmen, brokers, haulers, and synagogue servants. Generally, a teacher's own education was limited to the same type of school, and most lived meager lives with few luxuries.

From the 1840s onward, Russian authorities battled to raise the teaching standards in these schools. They began by instituting compulsory teaching exams for instructors and introduced requirements for those graduating from rabbinical schools; both approaches failed and were subsequently canceled. In the 1890s, following an unsuccessful fifty-year struggle, the authorities declared that anyone wishing to teach Jewish children religion and the Hebrew language would require a certificate from the director of a Jewish school. A certificate lasted for one year and cost three rubles; since no professional exam was required, the certificate functioned as little more than a confirmation of trustworthiness.[4] Teachers received very small salaries, and although some began teaching out of necessity alone, others were truly dedicated to imparting knowledge and wisdom to the younger generation.

Teaching is not the only profession attributed to Ilya Heifetz. After some of Jascha's earliest concerts, the Jewish press showed a heightened interest in the boy's background, reporting that his grandfathers "were Jews who led prayers and sang Sabbath hymns [at home] and in general were fond of singing."[5] Another newspaper added that "his grandfathers were cantors and singers."[6] More information about Ilya appears on a document dated 1943 that belonged to his son Natan, which reads: "Father: worker (tailor), mother: homemaker."[7] During the Soviet years, few would admit on a work-related document to having a father who did religious work. Natan's document comes from the employment records at the Gnesin School of Music, and it is possible that he listed his father as a tailor to hide the fact that Ilya was a teacher or cantor. Natan's intention was not, most likely, to distort the truth but simply to omit it. Fulfilling duties as a cantor and teacher did not necessarily prevent a Jewish *meshchanin* from working as a tailor, and so it is also possible that Ilya worked as a tailor as well as a teacher and cantor.

Judging by the photograph of Ilya Heifetz from the early 1890s when he was about sixty, he was a solidly built man with a round face and high forehead. By the time of the family group photograph in 1898, he looked significantly older, but his appearance is deceiving, since during this same period he remarried, and in 1902 his new wife gave birth to their daughter, Feyga-Vikhne, from whom originated the Leningrad branch of the Heifetz family. The name of Ilya's second wife is not recorded, but it is known that she died from injuries sustained during the Russian Civil War (1917–1922). Since Ilya had already died by then, sixteen-year-old Feyga was taken in by Aron's family, and she lived with them in Polotsk and then in Moscow, where all of Aron's six children eventually moved to pursue higher education.

Ruvin left home at the age of twenty-six, in 1898, the same year his father Ilya remarried. He was of average height, slender, and like all his brothers, he began balding early. He cultivated a mustache curled at the ends, and his right cheek carried a faint but noticeable birthmark. In Russia, and in the Russian language, Ruvin's name traditionally appears as the variant "Ruvim," which is the spelling used in the canonical translation of the Old Testament. As a result, Russian publications often refer to Jascha Heifetz with the patronymic "Ruvimovich," but his father called himself Ruvin throughout his life, and the name Ruvin (not Rubin or Reuven) appears in the majority of official documents associated with him, both in Russia and the United States.

The extent of Ruvin's early education is unknown, but he was reasonably educated. The family spoke Yiddish (by the end of the nineteenth century, 95 percent of Jews in the region considered it their native language), and it was in Yiddish that Ruvin wrote lengthy and animated letters to his family. Although Ruvin's letters in Russian contain no major spelling errors, they are full of stylistic and grammatical errors. For example, after Ruvin moved to the United States, he continued to communicate with his brother Natan in Yiddish, but after Natan's death in 1950, Ruvin wrote a letter in Russian (dated December 8) to the children of his deceased brother, since they did not know Yiddish. The letter is full of mistakes and shows how profoundly his Russian had deteriorated.[8]

Ruvin received no higher or conservatory education. Having become a proficient violinist early on, he began working in the small local orchestras which were plentiful in Polotsk and throughout the Pale. According to Lev Raaben, the author of the first Russian study on Jascha Heifetz, all those acquainted with Ruvin claimed that he had great musical talent, and that "only hopeless poverty in his youth, and the absolute impossibility of receiving a musical education interfered with the development of his talent."[9] Life was difficult for Ilya Heifetz's large family surviving on his teacher's wage, but the term "hopeless poverty" seems too extreme; many people lived in far worse circumstances. Ruvin knocked on doors in search of work; he performed in klezmer orchestras at weddings along with his brother Natan, who had received a conservatory education and played the violin. Natan explained in his personal memoirs that the first steps in his own musical development began at home: "From five years old, my mother, who had excellent musical talent and a wonderful voice, began to teach me piano."[10] It seems the family owned a piano, further contradicting the image of "hopeless poverty," and it is probable that like Natan, Ruvin also received his earliest musical training at home.

The development of Jewish folk instrumental music, known as klezmer, spans several centuries. Up to the middle of the nineteenth century, klezmer musicians worked in closed, mens' groups, passing skills from father to son. Gradually, as the demand for folk orchestras increased, youths from outside the tradition joined the groups, and according to scholar of Jewish musical folklore Moisei Beregovsky, more than three thousand professional Jewish musicians worked in Russia by the end of the nineteenth century.[11] A klezmer ensemble usually employed between three and five instrumentalists, but sometimes as many as nine or ten. A large ensemble might include a first and second violin, a viola (more frequently an extra violin), a cello or bass, a clarinet, a brass instrument (either cornet or trombone), and drums. The training process was simple. Young musicians were given a demonstration of several elementary methods of playing and then trained in the usual repertoire: dances played at Jewish wedding celebrations (*freylekhs, sher, beygele, broyges tants, khosidl*) and pieces accompanying the wedding ceremony proper that were played upon meeting the guests, at the seating of the bride, and at the time of the feast. The repertoire included additional popular dances as well as adaptations of music of other nationalities. For generations, this rich musical material was passed on by ear, but by the end of the nineteenth century, klezmer musicians notated their music.

There is no conclusive evidence as to how Ruvin learned to play the violin, but reviews of Jascha Heifetz's early concerts mention that Ruvin started the violin at the age of four.[12] At such a young age, a family member probably acted as Ruvin's first violin teacher, possibly his older brother Aron, who also played the violin.[13]

The autobiography of Avraam-Yehoshua Makonovetsky, mentioned in a publication by Beregovsky, contains a revealing example of the life of a klezmer musician; Ruvin may have followed a similar path. A native of the Kiev (Kyiv) province and practically the same age as Ruvin, Makonovetsky began playing the violin at the age of seven and soon after began two years of training with the experienced violinist Sirotovich. "I earned money for him," wrote Makonovetsky. "He taught me to play dances and I was his second violinist. He didn't use printed music or method books to train me." After leaving Sirotovich the young violinist joined a choral group in Radomyśl. "There they exploited me terribly and gave me no training," he later recalled, "but I taught myself how to play all the instruments." Unsatisfied with the education he received from the klezmer musicians, Makonovetsky taught himself the "three parts of Beriot as well as Niedziel-ski's Polish school, bought the printed concertos, duets, various good and difficult etudes."[14]

In addition to his musical training, it appears Ruvin also possessed an entirely different skill. In an extensive article entitled "Jascha Heifetz, l'empereur du violon," Nicole Hirsch describes Ruvin as "a very modest shoemaker," who also played music.[15] If that is true, Ruvin most likely spent some of his early years training in the craft of shoemaking and working as an apprentice. In any case, by his mid-twenties, Ruvin decided to settle down with his bride-to-be, Anna (Chaya) Sharfstein. Anna came "from a very poor family," and before their marriage she worked hard to support her parents and younger brother Isaac. She earned money through embroidery and lace making; the items she made went both for sale and toward decorating the family home—countless stitched table cloths, tea cloths, and other items adorned tables, backs of couches and chairs, and walls.[16] According to family recollections, Ruvin was acquainted with the Sharfstein family over the course of several years, but it was not until the spring of 1898 that Ruvin and Anna's traditional betrothal ceremony took place. When Ruvin arrived at the bride's home he followed the tradition of the time, which was for the groom to place a ring on the bride's finger while reciting the words: "Behold, thou art consecrated unto me with this ring according to the laws of Moses and of Israel." The wedding took place no less than a year after the engagement; the exact date of the wedding is found on a wedding invitation preserved in the archive of Jascha's Moscow relatives:

Izroil [Israel] Sharfstein || Elye Heifetz
and wife || and wife

most humbly request that you honor with your presence the wedding of

their daughter Chaya || his son Ruvin
with Ruvin Heifetz || with the maiden Chaya Sharfstein

Sunday March 7, 1899 (8th of Nisan) at the Baraukh station R. O. railroad.[17]

This invitation supports the family legend that Ilya Heifetz remarried, since the phrase "Elye Heifetz and wife most humbly request that you honor with your presence the wedding of *his* son Ruvin" (italics added), indicates that his current wife was not Ruvin's mother. The invitation also identifies the wedding venue as the Baraukh railroad station, which is on the Riga-Orlov (R. O.) line between Polotsk and Daugavpils, and although it is called Baraukh on the invitation, it also appears in different guides as Baravukh, Barovukh, and Borovukh.[18] Despite the confusion, all names point to a single location: a railroad station located ten miles from Polotsk.

Traditionally the bride's family hosted the wedding as well as the betrothal ceremony, and thus the address on the invitation likely refers to the home of the Sharfsteins. Celebrations began the day before the wedding and continued for a week or more. The groom's Sabbath morning prayer in the synagogue formed part of the proceedings and was followed by a gathering of the groom's circle of friends to celebrate his farewell to single life. A similar event for the bride and her friends involved music and dancing; guests brought their own refreshments and paid the musicians for each dance. On the wedding day, musicians played during the ritual seating of the bride on an overturned tub. Then, after the bride's traditional dance with the married women in the party, the men oversaw the pre-evening prayer, and the groom read his confession, pleading for forgiveness for all his previous sins. At this point the wedding ceremony proper began: the bride was led around the groom seven times and the rabbi recited a prayer over the glass of wine from which the bride and groom took a sip. After the exchange of wedding rings, the bride and groom held hands and entered the *chuppah*, a canopy supported by four poles. After another sip of wine, the marriage was completed with the smashing of the glass against the floor in memory of the destruction of Jerusalem. A wedding banquet with live music followed the ceremony, and the final part of the celebration included a dance for all the women and the bride, who then sneaked away. The men began an even more energetic dance with the groom, who also disappeared. The farewell song was played, but the celebrations often continued until dawn.

Ruvin Heifetz's new wife, Anna, was an attractive woman with blue eyes and soft facial features. Years later in the United States, her son-in-law Samuel Chotzinoff described her appearance as the "Slavic type."[19] Anna was born on April 3 (NS April 15), but the exact year of her birth remains unclear. On an official document completed in 1912, Ruvin gave his wife's age as thirty-eight, suggesting she was born in 1874, but records from the United States show that on paper, at least, Anna was still thirty-eight years old in 1920. To further confuse the matter, when Anna died in January 1947, a short obituary in *Musical America* reported her age as sixty-nine, making her year of birth 1878.[20] The most likely explanation is that Anna was born in 1874 and then reduced her age by a few years after arriving in the United States.

Anna's large, stately figure contrasted with Ruvin's thinner frame; their equally contrasting personalities seemed to complement each other, too. Anna generally appeared imperturbable and gave the impression of being dispassionate, but also purposeful and practical. Although she sometimes seemed unsmiling, she often had a cheerful and infectious laugh. Ruvin was more passionate, boisterous, and talkative. The marriage, however, was not entirely ideal, and by the 1930s the relationship between Ruvin and Anna ended, though they continued to live in the same house for a few years. After dedicating themselves to raising their children and sharing a concern for the development of their son's musical career, it appears the marriage eventually lost its direction.

Ruvin and Anna moved to Vilnius sometime between their wedding in March 1899 and the birth of their first child in January 1901. Anna's father, Israel, and brother, Isaac, also moved with them, but there is no further evidence of her mother; perhaps she died soon after her daughter's wedding. Israel Sharfstein worked in Vilnius as a hauler. He owned a horse and wagon and transported wood and water. Printed reports of the time suggest that Israel also had some musical talent, just like Jascha's paternal grandfather Ilya.[21]

Anna's brother, Isaac Sharfstein, was much younger than she. He was born in March 1884 and was still a youth at the time of his sister's marriage. The brother and sister developed a strong relationship and Anna fulfilled the roles of both sister and mother to Isaac. She sewed clothes for him, helped him with his studies, advised him on jobs, and held unquestionable authority in his eyes. Isaac's trajectory shadowed that of his sister and her husband—he moved with them from Polotsk to Vilnius, from where he and his family followed the Heifetzes to Petrograd and eventually to the United States.

CHAPTER TWO

1901–1906: Vilnius

FOLLOWING THE THIRD PARTITION of Poland in 1795, the city of Vilnius (Vilna)—once the capital of the Grand Duchy of Lithuania—was annexed by the Russian Empire. By the end of the nineteenth century, Vilnius was a large provincial capital in the Russian Empire and played an active role in Russian life as a center for trade, industry, and culture. By the early twentieth century, remnants of the city's history included the magnificent palace of Kazimierz Sapieha, which was later turned into a military hospital; Gediminas Castle and the ruined towers on the Castle mount; the cathedral bell tower; and the Lithuanian crest above the city gates. Vilnius resembled most other Russian cities of this period, even though only one-seventh of its population was ethnically Russian. As a result of nineteenth-century russification, storefront signs and advertisements were converted to Russian, and authorities assigned standard Russian names to city streets.

Half of Vilnius's 150,000 inhabitants were Jewish, and in many respects the city functioned as the unofficial capital of the Pale of Settlement. There were fewer Jews in Vilnius than in the two other major Jewish centers of the Russian Empire—Odessa and Warsaw—but Vilnius's centuries-old role as a cultural and religious center gave it a prominent position for Jews in Russia's northwest region. From 1573 onward, the Great Synagogue in Vilnius became the focal point for an expanding Jewish population, and the Jewish ghetto expanded further under Władysław IV's 1633 regulations allotting Jews certain trade and craft rights. Even with these new regulations, Jews were allowed to settle only in the area near the synagogue on Zhidovskaya Street (later Yevreiskaya Street).[1] Several streets were closed to accommodate the ghetto's expansion within the borders of the historical center. Some areas within these boundaries continued to remain off limits to Jewish settlement, including Ostrobramskaya Street with its Christian church that often held processions.

The Jewish ghetto in Vilnius was devastated several times during its four centuries of existence. During ruinous pogroms of 1592 and 1635, the synagogue was destroyed, money was stolen from the community, and thousands of Jews were expelled or killed. Military incursions included an attack by Cossacks under the reign of Tsar Aleksei Mikhailovich (1645–1676), Swedish invasions in the seventeenth and eighteenth centuries, and the arrival of Napoleon's troops, who in 1812 turned the Jewish cemetery into a stockyard, destroying thousands of gravestones.

When Vilnius fell under Russian jurisdiction in 1795, the Jewish population believed the new political climate would improve their living conditions, and in celebration they instituted an annual "Lighting of the Lamps" ceremony at the synagogue on the 15th of Av (OS July 30). Although these hopes went largely unfulfilled, some positive developments did follow: Jews were permitted to study in the medical faculty of Vilnius University; Emperor Alexander I spent three thousand rubles on a new building for the Jewish Hospital Brotherhood; and finally in 1861, limitations on Jewish settlement in the city were lifted, and the ghetto was abolished by law.

Important scientific, scholarly, and literary figures from the Jewish community of the entire northwest region poured into Vilnius; association with the so-called "Lithuanian Jerusalem" and the Yiddish term "Vilner" connoted an educated and liberal-thinking person. The *Talmud Torah* rabbinical school, another notable Jewish institution, was established at the end of the seventeenth century and transformed into a teaching institute in 1873. There were also two Jewish cemeteries: the old one in the Šnipiškės neighborhood, which closed in 1830, and a new one in the Antakalnis (then Antokol) neighborhood, housing the tombs of many famous Jewish cultural figures.

At the turn of the twentieth century, living standards among Vilnius Jews ranged from great wealth to abject poverty, but overall the standards were significantly lower than those of the city's Christian population. Many Jews worked in factories for little pay, and there were twice as many property owners among Christians, who formed less than half of the city's population. Jews, however, conducted almost all of Vilnius's trade, and by the end of the nineteenth century they owned 80 percent of all trade licenses, producing furs, gloves, stockings, and many other items.

It was into this bustling city that Ruvin Heifetz first arrived around 1899. He traveled from Polotsk with his young wife, her father, and her younger brother. Ruvin's first child was born in January 20, 1901 (NS February 2), and in accordance with religious law, the ritual of circumcision was held the eighth day after his birth. The sixtieth entry in the Vilnius register of Jewish births in 1901 reports:

> Date and month of Birth: Christian, January 20. Jewish, Shevat 13. Date and month of circumcision: Christian, January 27. Jewish, Shevat 20. Performer of circumcision: Osher Spokoino. Place of birth: Vilnius. Class of father, names of father and mother: Polotsk M[*eshchanin*], Ruvin Eliev Heifetz, Chaya Israelevna. Who was born and his/her given name: Joseph.[2]

Controversy still surrounds the exact year of Jascha Heifetz's birth. In a booklet accompanying the monumental forty-six-volume (sixty-five-CD) RCA / BMG Classics set from 1994, *The Heifetz Collection*, Heifetz's year of birth is given as 1900 with the explanation that "Heifetz's mother advanced his birth date one year when no one was looking."[3] Since some falsification of the synagogue books did occur in the nineteenth and early twentieth centuries, this situation is certainly not impossible. The motivation for falsifying a boy's age was usually to avoid the draft, but oldest or only sons were legally exempt from the draft, and since Jascha was the only son in the family, this is unlikely as motivation for reducing his age. Unfortunately there are no other dependable references to Anna Heifetz changing her son's age, thus the birth register is the only reliable evidence. Although sources like the register are sometimes inaccurate, Jascha's dates from the register in fact agree with many other official documents from the early period of his life in Russia.

Ruvin and Anna named their son Joseph after the noble son of Jacob, forefather of the twelve tribes of Israel, and from early on his family affectionately called him "Josinka," or "Jasinka," which often became "Jaschenka." According to a number of popular biographical accounts, Ruvin always knew his son would be a musician. From an early age Jascha showed a remarkable interest in the sounds he heard around him and would stop crying in his cradle whenever his mother sang, or his father played the violin. Following an interview with Heifetz in the 1920s, author Alexander Woollcott described Jascha's early development:

> Indeed, the other members of the cabaret orchestra in which (Ruvin) played the fiddle used to roar with derisive laughter when he would boast of his great plans for the baby he had at home. Whereupon, with much heat, the elder Heifetz would collar these doubting Ivans, dragging them to his home and bidding them be quiet while he showed them. Then, standing beside the crib, he would play a bit of Tchaikovsky on his own violin. Complete silence from the crib. Then, with a wink at the skeptics, he would play it a second time, but at a certain point would pluck a sour note from the strings. At that the two-year-old would let out a squawk of protest and reach through the bars to catch at his father's coat. In that gesture of musical criticism the elder Heifetz foresaw, as in a crystal ball, the rapt crowd at Carnegie Hall.[4]

During the early twentieth century, many musicians arrived in Vilnius to satisfy a growing interest in park and restaurant entertainment, and the author Moisei Beregovsky noted in particular that klezmer musicians and their children (who had more formal musical education than their parents) began seeking positions in a variety of musical ensembles.[5] There was greater opportunity for work in Vilnius than in Polotsk, which suggests Ruvin was no longer just a klezmer musician, but probably played other kinds of music. Resident musicians played in restaurants, cabarets, and *cafés chantants;* musical variety shows took place in the Hotel Palace, and in the Hall of the Assembly of the Nobility, which had a venue on Dvoryansky Lane with a resident ensemble, as well as a summer performance space in the Bernardinsky Gardens.

The summer months were filled with live outdoor music, particularly in the Bernardinsky Gardens and in the Botanical Gardens, where the director Ivan Schumann ran events for many years. Ruvin likely played in smaller ensembles such as operetta groups that were active at the time. Simultaneously many Jewish troupes performed musicals in Yiddish, providing much-needed income to local musicians. In addition, traveling opera companies arrived in Vilnius each season, and local musicians often filled any vacant spots. Although the work was inconsistent and paid poorly, violinists could just manage to survive on this income. This difficult reality contrasts sharply with Heifetz's own description of his father as the concertmaster of the Vilnius Symphony Orchestra.[6] A permanent orchestra was not established in Vilnius until December 1909, a month before the Heifetzes departed for St. Petersburg.

Some confusion still surrounds the question of where Jascha was born and where he lived for the first nine years of his life. First, unlike many famous artists, Heifetz spoke little about his childhood. Second, Vilnius suffered a number of historical cataclysms during the twentieth century, including two world wars, the 1917 Russian Revolutions, and a variety of other upheavals that led to major political changes. Each political epoch brought about its own ideological priorities, which were reflected in the city's rich history of names. The city witnessed the fall of the Russian monarchy in 1917 followed by the rise of Soviet power and the union of Belarus and Lithuania, "Lithbel." Later, Lithuania became an independent state, but its capital, Vilnius, was annexed to Poland. During World War II the city became part of Soviet Lithuania, and finally, with the demise of the Soviet Union in 1991, Vilnius became the capital of the reborn, independent Lithuanian state.

Each period brought adjustments to the city's layout and changes to street names. Old buildings were rebuilt, and many dilapidated structures faced demolition, especially in the central area of the city where the poorest Jews had resided for centuries. In light of these changes, it is no surprise that Lithuanian researchers still disagree on the exact location of Heifetz's childhood home. In 1991 Vilnius historian Genrikh Agranovsky noted the conflicting claims in the press: "The paper *Komjaunimo tiesa* from September 12, 1989 claims that this house is located on Užupio Street, but for some reason shows a photograph of a house on 27 Maironio Street."[7] Prominent Lithuanian conductor Saulius Sondeckis also wrote about the location of

Heifetz's childhood home, insisting that it was the small two-story building at 27 Maironio Street.[8]

One address known for certain is that of Jascha's grandfather, Israel Sharfstein, which is given as 3 Safyannaya Street both in the "All Vilna 1914" directory and on a 1908 postcard addressed to "Ruvin Heifetz and Family."[9] The postcard notes apartment "40," suggesting that their building was quite large. Safyannaya Street no longer exists, but at the turn of last century it ran parallel to Bakshta (now Bokšto) Street and turned onto Zarechnaya (now Užupio) Street. In its place there is now a main road called Maironio Street, formerly known as Tesos Street in Soviet times. Although there is potential for further investigation, Lithuanian researchers investigating the location of Heifetz's childhood home appear to be looking in the right area.

Judging from late nineteenth-century maps of Vilnius, Safyannaya Street was a narrow and winding backstreet stretching from Ozerny Lane to a bridge over the river Vilnia (or Vileika).[10] From there, Zarechnaya Street joined Polotskaya Street, which in turn widened into the eastward-running Polotsk highway. From the southern end of Safyannaya Street, Ozerny Lane extended to the fish market that occupied an open area not far from the river. A strong smell of fish saturated the surrounding streets, and Jascha's cousin Anna (Anyuta) Sharfstein-Koch described this odor as a particularly vivid childhood memory.[11]

Of the twenty buildings on Safyannaya Street, number 8 was a Jewish almshouse and number 18 was a Jewish religious administration building. The other buildings along the road were privately owned residences, many of which were rented out. Ownership of 3 Safyannaya Street, where the Heifetz family probably lived, changed several times in prerevolutionary years. In 1909 it belonged to Mr. Soltz, who also owned properties on Nemetskaya Street and on Obzhorny Lane. Sharfstein-Koch remembered apartment number 2 at 3 Myasnaya Street as another possible place both her family and the Heifetzes resided in Vilnius. Myasnaya Street was in the center of the Jewish ghetto and stretched from Nemetskaya Street to Steklyannaya Street. Sharfstein-Koch recalled that either the Safyannaya Street or Myasnaya Street apartment was on the second floor, and that on the first floor lived the cantor and conductor Aron Olefsky and his family.[12]

Olefsky and Ruvin Heifetz were close friends, and although Olefsky's son Maxim was two years older than Jascha, the two boys spent much of their childhood together. The close friendship between the Olefsky and Heifetz families continued a decade later in St. Petersburg, when Maxim arrived to study at the conservatory and was welcomed into the Heifetz family home. Years later this friendship was rekindled on American soil.

A unique historical atmosphere characterized the winding streets of Vilnius's Jewish quarter. The lined-glass squares of Dutch-style windows punctuated thick peeling walls, and sharp, pointed tile roofs towered above hanging wrought-iron lanterns. The cobblestone streets were narrow and uneven, and children from the Jewish quarter sailed little boats down their rainwater grooves. Half-circle arches with tile roofs stretching across the narrow streets connected the upper stories of buildings and turned the streets into tunnel-like burrows. A sea of painted signs and billboards advertised clothing, food, antique shops, tailor shops, barber shops, and countless other businesses.

From an early age, Jascha's natural affinity for music astonished his parents. He sang recognizable melodies at the age of one and a half, and by the time his sister Pauline was born in 1903, he sang lullabies alongside his mother.[13] Ruvin bought Jascha his first violin when he was just three years old, and although most children that age play on eighth-size instruments, Ruvin gave his son a quarter-size violin. Years later, Heifetz discussed this early start: "If you start playing the violin at three, as I did, with a little violin one quarter of the size of a normal violin, I suppose the violin becomes second nature in the course of time."[14] In 1928 Woollcott wrote that Heifetz "himself does not now remember a time when he could not play the violin, any more than you can now remember a time when you could not walk."[15] Ruvin was later reported to have said that the ten rubles he paid for the little violin was the best investment he ever made.[16] Jascha's teacher, Leopold Auer, also stressed the value of an early start when he wrote: "In the case of the violinist, the sooner serious study begins the better."[17] Although Auer probably meant at the age of six or seven, Jascha began the violin with his father at the age of three. An anonymous manuscript based on the words of Jascha's parents contains an account of how "the boy immediately internalized a G major scale that was demonstrated to him and played it back with astonishing accuracy on his tiny violin."[18]

Hyman Gerber (1880–1964) was a Vilnius musician who knew Jascha from birth and had close ties to the Heifetz family. Gerber described how Ruvin directed his son's early violin study, and it seems from these observations that Ruvin had inherited a predisposition for teaching, just like his father and brothers. "My father gave me my first lessons," Heifetz recalled of his childhood, but "I think that there were times I would have preferred something more playful. Let us say that my father 'persuaded' me to practice; and I am glad that he did."[19] Musicians who knew Ruvin valued his teaching ability; over the course of his life, Ruvin taught many beginners the basics of violin technique, his son being the most successful example. According to Gerber, Ruvin did not develop any particular method of his own, but used the well-established violin schools of some of the great pedagogues of the nineteenth century: "in fact he used the most old fashioned method by de Bériot, then Kayser and straight to Kreutzer. He also used Schradieck's daily studies and Hřímalý's scales."[20]

Charles-Auguste de Bériot, a representative of the Belgian school of violin, published his "Methode de violon" in Paris in 1858. A Russian edition of the work was published in 1870 by Matvei Bernard, and it became an important rite of passage for many Russian violin students. It is possible that Ruvin also studied according to the de Bériot method when he was younger, since it was intended principally for self-study. De Bériot recommended solfège for beginners and describes the correct way to hold the violin and bow. The core of de Bériot's work is divided into three parts: the first two address performance technique, and the third addresses what de Bériot describes as "style," that is, using technique to master the expressive potential of the violin.

Based largely on his own teaching experience, de Bériot attempted to instill in his students the principle that technical mastery was not a goal in and of itself. As de Bériot writes in his forward, "feverish striving for the development of technique, which has in recent years so overcome many violinists, very often takes the violin away from its truest and noblest task—to imitate the human voice. Our goal is not so much to further develop technique," he continues, "as to preserve for the violin its true character, which is to express and convey all the moods of the soul."[21] The first two exercise sections include an accompanying line for second violin, which would have allowed Ruvin to play along with his son.

Heinrich Ernst Kayser's contribution to violin pedagogy was a collection of preparatory studies entitled "Thirty-Six Etudes for Violin." Several Russian editions of the collection noted that the studies "are used in conservatories in Moscow, St. Petersburg, Cologne, Copenhagen, Leipzig and elsewhere."[22] Kayser's etudes were reprinted almost yearly after the Bolshevik Revolution, and most Russian violinists of the twentieth century studied them, including. Heifetz. As an adult Heifetz recalled that he "was able to play in all seven positions within the first year of [study] and . . . could play the Kayser Etudes also in that time."[23]

Rodolphe Kreutzer's "Forty-Two Studies or Caprices" are representative of the French school of violin playing. Jascha studied them with his father. He also studied the exercises of Henry Schradieck and the "Scales and Arpeggios for Violin" by Jan Hřímalý. Hřímalý was a russified Czech and a representative of the Moscow violin school, which differed in many ways from Leopold Auer's St. Petersburg violin school (at the conservatory) where Jascha later studied. In these early years, neither Ruvin nor his son could have recognized the differences between the two Russian violin schools; nevertheless, scales and arpeggios became a crucial part of Jascha's practice regime. Years later, when questioned on how a student should practice, Heifetz replied:

> If I had a half-hour's time to practice, I would work for twenty minutes on scales in various forms, and on trills. The next ten minutes I would work on pieces, but then I would choose the difficult passages only. Once your fingers are in shape, and your right hand is in good form, you can do the pieces as well as your technic and temperament will allow.[24]

Yelizaveta Epstein was a contemporary of Heifetz in Vilnius and later became an instructor at the Leningrad Conservatory. Her mother met Jascha one day on her way home from the store and described the scene as a "miracle." Yelizaveta told the following story based on her memories of her mother's encounter with Jascha:

In a narrow and dirty lane, where the poorest Jews then lived, she saw a tiny boy with little golden curls. He was holding a small violin and his playing immediately astonished Mama. She went up to him and asked him his name, where he lived, where he got his violin, and who taught him. The boy spoke Yiddish but did not know a word of Russian. He said that his name was Jascha Heifetz and that his father was a shoemaker. He then gestured with a finger towards his father's pitiful dwelling where the workshop door was open onto the street and his father sat industriously repairing the torn and modest shoes of his clients.[25]

As with the embellished Vilnius legend of the golden-haired wunderkind who became a great violinist, there is no doubt an element of exaggeration in Yelizaveta's account, but the Epstein story is the second independent source to describe Ruvin working as a shoemaker, repeating the claim made by Nicole Hirsch.

Heifetz's second sister, Elza, was born in early September 1905.[26] Life was tough for the Heifetz family during these years, and while Anna Heifetz stayed home caring for the children, Ruvin went out to earn enough to support his family. As an adult, Heifetz did not like to recall the circumstances in which he grew up and rarely spoke about how his family lived during these early years. Since there are so few memories from Heifetz himself, the recollections of his cousin Anyuta Sharfstein-Koch are all the more significant. She was born seven years after Heifetz and was the daughter of Jascha's uncle Isaac Sharfstein. Although Sharfstein-Koch's memories go back no earlier than the start of the 1910s, after the Heifetz family had already left Vilnius, she remembered stories her parents told her. Since the lives of her family and the Heifetz family were so intertwined, her memories following the Heifetz family's departure also shed light on the earlier years.

According to Sharfstein-Koch, the family lived near the river in a brick building with a small porch, and she remembered playing with Jascha's toys, in particular a stuffed policeman figure called Andryushka.[27] The building faced the synagogue in one direction and a big church in the other, and as with most buildings in this area, they were close together, had steps up to a porch, and no front yard. A few of these buildings had internal courtyards, including the building in which the Heifetz family lived.

Their apartment was on the second floor and included one medium-sized bedroom, a dining room, and a large kitchen. Plumbing was not installed in Vilnius until 1912, so the apartment had no running water and no electricity. The oven in the kitchen heated the entire apartment, and a gaslight hanging by a chain from the ceiling had to be lowered to be lighted. Since the oven was turned off overnight, the apartment became cold and the family relied on down-feather quilts to keep warm.

There was no separate bathroom in the small apartment; instead, an area was partitioned off in the kitchen for a toilet, and a special cleaner called a "gold nose" came to clean it every day. Sharfstein-Koch recalled that a Polish servant worked in the house on Saturdays since the Heifetzes observed the Sabbath. As in every Jewish home, the family followed the ritual "lighting of the candles" on Friday evenings, which involved placing candles on the table and setting it ready for the Sabbath feast the next day. The woman of the house—Anna Heifetz—lit the candles and then, while covering her eyes with her hands, said the *techinah*, a prayer begging for the blessing of God on her husband and children. Friday evenings also involved the preparation and cooking of cholent, the traditional Jewish stew made for the Sabbath. Meat, potatoes, carrots, beans, prunes, and other available ingredients were placed into a large and sealed cast-iron pot. The pot was then taken to a nearby baker who at the end of the workday put the cholent in a hot oven overnight. The next morning these pots were placed in front of the bakery with colored identity ribbons ready for collection. As families returned from the Saturday morning service at the synagogue, parents usually sent older children to the bakery to fetch the cholent. Since cooking on the Sabbath was forbidden, the stew was the main food eaten that day.

Newspapers reported that Heifetz's grandfather oversaw his religious education.[28] Israel Sharfstein taught his grandson the elements of religious tradition every Jewish child learned, including the Torah (Chumash), the recitation of a prayer before every meal, and respect for parents and elders. Jewish folksongs and the telling of Jewish folktales were also important aspects of early family life, and Jascha's love of folk music later connected him with Zinovy Kiselgof, an expert on Jewish musical folklore in St. Petersburg. In addition to the religious training Jascha received from his grandfather, his mother taught him many traditional Jewish songs and folktales.

Under the influence of Chasidism, a religious teaching that spread among East European Jews beginning in the eighteenth century, a spirit of mysticism entered into the folktales. Jewish folk characters differed from those in Russian and other European stories; where European stories often told of valiant knights working miracles of strength and bravery, Jewish heroes usually triumphed through their wisdom and intellect.

By all accounts, Anna Heifetz was a patient mother who reacted calmly to the pranks and sometimes mischievous behavior of her three children. These pranks were sometimes quite boisterous, and during the early years in the United States the children often ran around the house spraying each other with water and shooting bread balls at "opponents" across the dinner table.[29] This lively atmosphere was undoubtedly also part of family life in Vilnius, but it did not distract Jascha from his violin studies. Ruvin recognized his son's talent and quickly realized he needed to find him a professional teacher. As one author described later, many young musicians looked on with envy as Heifetz performed his spectacular debut in Carnegie Hall. They cursed their own fathers for not giving them such a start, and headed home after the concert vowing not to make the same mistake with their own children.[30]

Ruvin's plans for his son's musical development became apparent in May 1906, when Vilnius newspapers reported the following: "The Music School announces that applications for entrance to music classes of the school will be accepted in the school office daily beginning May 10 from ten in the morning to two in the afternoon, and from five until eight in the evening. A birth certificate and certificate of vaccination against smallpox should be attached to the application."[31] As soon as he could, Ruvin obtained his son's birth certificate from the synagogue and received the necessary vaccination certificate from the Jewish hospital.[32]

CHAPTER THREE

1906–1909: Music School

UNDER THE AUSPICES OF THE Russian Music Society
(RMO), music schools opened throughout major cities in Russia during
the second half of the nineteenth century, providing the primary source
of professional musical training. The RMO was founded in 1859 following
the efforts of the pianist and composer Anton Rubinstein; patronage from
the Tsar's family in 1869 led to its elevation as the Imperial Russian Music
Society (IRMO). Both St. Petersburg and Moscow IRMO schools quickly
gained conservatory status and became the chief centers of higher musical
education. By the start of the twentieth century, music classes and schools
under the IRMO across Russia had advanced significantly, and they became the main suppliers of teaching staff for the conservatories in larger
cities and in the provinces.

The Vilnius division of the society opened in December 1873, but
closed just a few years later. It reopened in 1898, albeit on a small scale,
and by the 1906–1907 season it counted only four actual members.[1] Short
resources placed concerts and educational work on hold until the 1906 arrival of two respected women—Baroness Alisa von Wolf, the wife of the
trustee of the Scholarly Circle of Vilnius, and Lyudmila Lyubimova, the

wife of the governor of Vilnius and a trustee of orphanages. Following the efforts of these two women, the number of society members grew initially to thirty-six, then to 130 by the next season, enabling the Vilnius division to stage an entire series of public concerts.

The music school under the Vilnius division of the IRMO began as a private music school and was run by the pianist Antonina Spasskaya.[2] Music classes under the direction of the IRMO began in 1898, and the school gained its official status in 1904. A board member of the local IRMO named Mikhail Treskin became director of the school in 1898 and served as inspector of musical arts classes. According to the official school charter, the musical arts taught at the school included piano, singing, orchestral instruments, music theory, and music history. In addition, the general curriculum included lessons in the Russian language, religion, arithmetic, geography, history, and foreign languages. By the start of the 1906–1907 academic year, only twenty-seven of the school's 193 students attended general curriculum classes, and by January the school ended the general courses to save money.

The school faced considerable financial difficulties that year, and at the end of August the main IRMO board provided the school a thousand-ruble subsidy, but it was far from enough to resolve the situation.[3] The newly formed board of the Vilnius division of the IRMO worked hard to support the school. According to the annual report, a general meeting of Vilnius IRMO members during the 1906–1907 year called for the town council to renew the thousand-ruble subsidy, which previously had come from the city's funds. The subsidy was canceled, however, because of financial volatility connected with the unsuccessful Russo-Japanese War and the 1905 Russian Revolution. With Russia in desperate need of loans from foreign banks, Tsar Nicholas II was forced into overseeing democratic reforms and created a parliament (the State Duma). Although the First and Second State Duma of 1906 and 1907 lasted only a few weeks, they nevertheless strengthened confidence in Russia in the eyes of western creditors and resulted in the reinstatement of subsidies to educational institutions such as the music school in Vilnius. Still, in 1906 there was no subsidy, and the school's budget suffered greatly. To address the problem, the general

Vilnius IRMO meeting also resolved to participate in the gatherings of the local Jewish Society's board of representatives, since, as outlined in the report, the Jewish community produced "a significant contingent of the music school's students." Orel Lipetz became the school's representative to the Jewish Society, and he also joined the trustee committee of the Vilnius *Talmud Torah*. That year, Lipetz personally loaned the music school 1,000 rubles and a further 1,750 rubles the next year.

Since the school's budget relied heavily on funds received from its students, all instrumental class fees were increased by ten rubles to cover the budget shortfall. The average tuition fee amounted to around seventy rubles, and although some students paid more, children from poorer families were often exempt. No doubt Jascha belonged to the "contingent studying at the school's expense"—significant reason why his parents decided to educate their son in a school and not privately.

The school thrived in spite of its financial difficulties. As the director and inspector of classes in the musical arts, Mikhail Treskin led the largest piano class, which contained sixty-eight students, and he also taught courses in elementary theory, solfège, and harmony. Besides Treskin, there were four other piano teachers at the school who taught an additional sixty-three students, and Mikhail Weinbren taught nine pupils in his cello class. V. Karmilov led the solo voice class of twenty-five students, and Yosif Enders directed twenty-two students in the student symphony orchestra class. The only violin teacher in the school, Ilya Malkin (1865–1953), taught a violin class of nineteen during the 1906–1907 year; "Heifitz, Joseph" appears sixteenth in the alphabetical list of Malkin's students. Although spelled incorrectly, this is the first printed mention of Jascha's family name.[4]

Jascha's enrollment at the age of just five years and seven months violated many of the IRMO's rules. Paragraph thirty-four in the Charter of Music Schools of the IRMO dictates that "those wishing to enter into the student body shall be examined in artistic and scholarly subjects, and of the latter should possess knowledge no lower than of those entering the first grade of the boys' gymnasium of the Ministry of National Education."[5] What scholarly knowledge could a five-year-old boy have? Did he even speak Russian at that time? With the aid of the enormous interest shown by Malkin, Jascha was accepted and placed directly into the third grade.

Ilya Malkin was born on November 7 (NS November 19), 1865, near Mogilev in the town of Shklov, and was registered to the *meshchanstvo* in Chaussy (Čavusy), a small town about twenty miles from Mogilev. In his conservatory record he is listed as Elya Nokhimovich-Davidovich Malkin, and in his passport, as Ilya Davidovich Malkin.[6] Malkin graduated from Leopold Auer's class in the St. Petersburg Conservatory in May 1886 and received his violin performance certificate on May 26, 1888. He lived for a period in Moscow on Filippovsky Lane, but by September 1890 returned to the St. Petersburg Conservatory. He then passed required exams in music theory, harmony, and general subjects in order to obtain his diploma and the title of Free Artist. The conservatory's artistic council certified Malkin's diploma on May 31, 1891 and awarded it on March 21, 1892.

After teaching independently for several years in Vilnius, Malkin began violin classes in the music school when it opened in 1898. Malkin and his violinist wife Basia (later changed to Bessie, then Bertha) participated in the musical life of the city and performed in chamber music concerts. Heifetz biographer Artur Vered describes a close connection between Jascha's father and Malkin,[7] and an early newspaper article reported that during these years, Jascha frequently studied with Malkin at the professor's home.[8] Malkin lived on Bolshaya Street, home to the City Theater, Hotel Palace, and many other institutions and impressive stores, and not far from where the Heifetzes lived.

Visiting Malkin's home was a treat for Jascha—the first real experience of an intellectual household. The violin teacher lived with his wife and two daughters, Maria (known affectionately as Marusya) and Margareta (Ritochka). Jascha became close friends with Marusya, exchanging letters with her for years. Malkin's conservatory diploma and Free Artist status gave him, as a Jew, the right to live freely in any city of the Russian Empire; thus, unlike many others in Vilnius, Malkin lived there by choice. In Russia at this time, Jews and those without documents were generally treated as outcasts. Malkin's situation allowed him to forget about the Pale of Settlement and *almost* become a real citizen, even if in reality no status could completely protect Jews from anti-Semitism. The coveted title of Free Artist itself did not always guarantee the rights it technically granted; the famous Russian composer and teacher Mikhail Gnesin discovered as much during a visit to Taganrog, where he was unceremoniously arrested, had his passport confiscated, and was sent back to his city of residence.[9]

Around the time Jascha entered the music school in Vilnius, Malkin set up a private teaching practice. Announcements appeared in the *Vilensky vestnik* between August 29 and September 11, 1906: "Private music school of the Free Artist I. D. Malkin (Bolshaya St., Building 58) announces entrance exams for a class in string instrument performance." It was reported on September 12, however, that "the private school of I. D. Malkin, barely having managed to open, has ceased to exist. As expected, it did not survive the competition from the respectable and established music school. Malkin will return to the school faculty to teach a violin class."[10] Ruvin wanted his son to study with Malkin, but he refrained from taking up the opportunity for private lessons with him or any of the many private teachers in Vilnius. For Ruvin, Malkin and the music school represented a stepping stone on Jascha's path to the St. Petersburg Conservatory, not just because Malkin graduated from there himself, but also because he had studied with Auer. Malkin only spent the 1885–1886 year in the Auer class, but even such a short experience with the famous professor left a powerful mark, binding him to the people and principles of the "Auer" School.

When Jascha began studying at the music school in 1906, it was located at 28 Vilenskaya Street, one of the largest city thoroughfares.[11] The *Talmud Torah*—one of five city synagogues and prayer houses—was situated along this road. The local board of the IRMO rented a fairly large building for the music school; part of it was even sublet to raise money during the school's financial struggles. The location proved less than ideal, however, and the institution later moved to a building formerly occupied by the "Rossiya" insurance society. The old school building became a private boys' gymnasium and secondary school directed by M. A. Pavlovsky, and during the Soviet years the building housed the Ministry of Agriculture. Jascha left Vilnius before the school moved to the new building; the "All Vilna" directory for 1909, the last year Jascha lived in his hometown, still names the address of the music school as 28 Vilenskaya Street. It was there that

Jascha's parents brought him in September 1906, and it was there that he first performed in public and eventually received his graduation certificate.

Three months into the academic year, Jascha made his first public appearance during one of the school's traditional evening concerts, which were usually reserved for older students. The 1906–1907 school year included five such concerts: three in the first half of the year and two in the second. According to the programs found in the annual report of the Vilnius IRMO, Malkin's students performed twelve times during these five events and played challenging pieces such as de Bériot's *La rêveuse* and *Scene de ballet*, and concertos by Accolay and Viotti. Auer described the Viotti concertos in A and E minor as pieces for "the young violinist," but they still require a considerable amount of skill.[12] A student of Malkin named Shmuel Kolotukhes performed one of the two Wieniawski concertos, which demand an advanced level of ability. In general, Malkin's students played at an impressive level.

Jascha performed in the second student evening concert, which took place on December 7, 1906.[13] Surviving the winter weather in Vilnius required heavy clothing and the willingness to navigate through snow and ice.[14] In describing his gymnasium years, the artist Mstislav Dobuzhinsky recalled the "cheerful sound of little bells—always the property of sleigh drivers (winter was always snowy, with heavy frosts)."[15] One imagines that Jascha's proud parents dressed their son in enough clothing to keep him and his hands warm on the trip to the school. The family had a few options—either an expensive cab with the sound of little bells, a horse-drawn cart costing five kopecks per person, or the most likely option, a brisk walk through the snow.

Jascha played seventh that evening, accompanied by a young girl from Treskin's piano class who accompanied all the solo numbers. Although this was Jascha's first public performance, the little boy had already played in front of family and friends at various celebrations, including the wedding of his cousin Feyga, daughter of Morduch-Dov. It seems Jascha's first public performance did not intimidate him; a review of the concert by the *Vilensky vestnik* refers specifically to the young boy's confidence:

> The second student evening held at the school of the Vilnius division of the
> Imperial Music Society passed with even greater success than the first . . .

astonishing everyone, was six-year-old wunderkind Heifitz [*sic*], who without shyness, and with much confidence, played the *Fantaisie Pastorale* by
Zanibe. [16]

Despite the misspelled surname, the incorrect age, and the wrong
composer, these few words constitute the first printed response to Jascha's
playing. This debut left a firm impression in Heifetz's own mind, and years
later he recalled: "My first appearance in public took place in an over-
crowded auditorium of the Imperial Music School in Vilna, Russia, when
I was not quite five [*sic*]. I played the *Fantaisie Pastorale* with piano accompaniment."[17] At the time of this debut concert, after three months at the
school, Jascha was still just five years and ten months old. The little-known
composer of his piece was actually Jean-Baptiste Singelée (1812–1875), a
talented violinist who "wrote many violin pieces, especially fantasias on
operatic airs, also several concertos (in all 144 published works)."[18] The
Fantaisie Pastorale was published in 1906 by the German house of H. Litolff,
in Braunschweig, but was issued in Russia only in 1928. Malkin no doubt
realized that this lyrical piece would give Jascha a chance to demonstrate
his particular talent.

During this period, Anna Heifetz's brother Isaac Sharfstein, who lived
with the Heifetzes, turned twenty-one and was called into military service.
Although the family worried greatly about him, Isaac returned safely to
Vilnius after serving the required eighteen months. Before leaving and
with the encouragement of his older sister, Isaac began training as a type-
setter and started working at the typographical office of *Vilensky vestnik*
after his return. On May 10, 1907, Isaac married a young woman named
Sonia (both she and Isaac were born in 1884), and they soon started their
own family.

Just a week after the wedding, at the end of the school year, Jascha took
his first exams. On May 13, the *Vilensky vestnik* reported: "Exams are to
take place in the music school. 18 May—violin and cello starting at 11am
(class of I. D. Malkin and class of M. T. Weinbren)."[19] A few weeks later,
the newspaper printed a review of the exams: "Very little satisfied us in this
year's violin exams; there was no particular talent to be seen, no particular
successes. A brilliant exception is the young . . . violinist Heifetz, literally

astonishing in his development and technique; the child was accepted into the IV class with a high grade."[20]

Having finished the school year successfully, Jascha enjoyed more time at home playing with his little sisters, but never at the expense of several hours of practice each day, a routine that continued throughout his life. Along with practicing scales, arpeggios, and studies, Jascha also composed. According to the unpublished manuscript *Biografia genialnogo malchika* (*Biography of a Boy Genius*), "the march and waltz composed by [Jascha] in the seventh year of his life are kept by his happy father."[21] Although the eventual fate of these early compositions is unknown, Heifetz continued to display a natural inclination toward composition throughout his life, as seen in his cadenzas, transcriptions, arrangements, and his love for improvisation.

The 1907–1908 school year began on September 3, and the *Vilensky vestnik* reported that "On Monday September 3, at 1pm, in the music school of the Vilna division of the IRMO, a prayer service will be held before the beginning of classes. Those wishing to honor the school with their presence are invited to visit at the appointed time."[22] Those of the Jewish faith were not required to participate in the prayer service, which was led by the school's religion teacher—a Russian Orthodox priest—so three-quarters of the students in effect became outsiders in their own school. Larger schools such as the Vilnius State Men's Gymnasium employed different religion teachers to cater to students of various faiths, including not just Orthodox, but Roman Catholic, Lutheran, and Jewish. This policy promoted a sense of equality among the students, but as the state religion, Orthodoxy retained priority.

The Vilnius IRMO celebrated its ten-year anniversary during the 1907–1908 season with a number of special events. The thousand-ruble annual subsidy and a one-time grant paid from the city coffers supported the events, and the city council arranged a low rate for rental of the large City Hall, enabling the IRMO to stage a series of impressive musical events in the largest concert venue in Vilnius.[23]

In October, as part of the special events organized by the IRMO, the St. Petersburg Symphony Orchestra of Count Aleksandr Sheremetyev performed twice.[24] The concert on October 16, 1907, was dedicated to Tchai-kovsky and included the Sixth Symphony, *Capriccio Italien,* Overture to *Francesca da Rimini,* and the first movement of his Violin Concerto, played by David Berthier. It is possible that at this concert Jascha heard the sound of a professional symphony orchestra for the first time. The second or-chestral concert that month included pieces by Berlioz, Beethoven, Wag-ner, and Henri Vieuxtemps's *Ballade et Polonaise* for violin, performed by Armando Zaniboni, a piece Jascha played later that year for his second-year exams.

On November 19, the Vilnius IRMO organized another concert fea-turing Ioannes Nalbandian, an assistant professor at the St. Petersburg Conservatory who later became Jascha's first conservatory instructor. Al-though the publicity poster for this performance describes Nalbandian as a "professor," in reality he earned that title only a few months after this per-formance. His concert included the Paganini Concerto in D, the Sarasate Habanera, and the Aulin Gavotte, all pieces Jascha later studied.

During the 1907–1908 school year, Malkin put Jascha forward for two public performances, both times with pieces by the composer de Bériot. Reviews of these concerts did not appear in local newspapers, but only an-nouncements about them published the day before the concerts, including the following: "12 December 1907, in the building of the music school (28 Vilenskaya Street) will be the second student evening recital. Starting at 8 in the evening."[25] Jascha performed de Bériot's Aria with Variations.

Two significant events occurred between Jascha's first concert in De-cember and his second on March 27. The first was a joyful family occasion: on January 29, Isaac and Sonia Sharfstein celebrated the birth of their daughter, Jascha's cousin, Anna (known as Anyuta throughout her life), whose recollections and memories feature throughout this book. Already in her nineties, Anyuta Sharfstein-Koch recalled vividly her Russian child-hood from her home in the United States. She inherited toys and other items from the Heifetz children, including a chamber pot with a wooden seat, and when she grew a little older, she joined in games with them, often sharing in the bumps and bruises doled out by the boisterous young boy.

The second significant event to occur in Vilnius during this period was the visit of Professor Leopold Auer from the St. Petersburg Conservatory.

Auer gave a series of successful concerts throughout the northwestern region with the pianist Wanda Bogutska-Stein, who later became his second wife, and following one concert in Kaunas (then Kovno) on February 10, a newspaper wrote that "L. S. Auer has aged, and walks with difficulty, but is as ever the king of his violin and bow, which are as obedient as ever to him.[26] The playing of this virtuoso artist is distinguished by its beauty, mellowness and strength of tone, beautiful cantilena, legato. . . . Such melodiousness of the bow, such accent, such staccato!"[27] During Auer's stay in Vilnius, Malkin arranged for his former professor to hear Jascha play. The *Vilensky vestnik* wrote that "the exceptional talent of the Heifetz child inspired delight even in such a competent and strict connoisseur as Professor Auer, having listened to him on his last visit to Vilna and having eagerly expressed the wish to take up his further musical education."[28] Although Malkin and Jascha's parents surely found Auer's visit inspirational and encouraging, it seems this meeting with the short, bald gentleman made little impression on Jascha, since he later never mentioned meeting his future teacher at the age of seven, long before his studies at the St. Petersburg Conservatory began.

On March 27, Jascha gave his second performance of the school year at the fourth student recital, playing his first major work—de Bériot's Concerto no. 7. This particular recital came to Heifetz's attention again in 1926 following a concert in Lowell, Massachusetts, when a woman named Dora Rostler, a former Vilnius resident, handed Heifetz a handwritten program she brought when she emigrated: "She had tucked it away as the souvenir of a great occasion, and when life shifted her from the Baltic Sea to Massachusetts Bay it was still among her possessions."[29] Remarkably, this fourth student recital is absent from the annual report of the Vilnius IRMO, so it is only through the handwritten program, now saved in the Library of Congress archives, that this event can be documented.

On May 17, just a month and a half after performing the de Bériot concerto, Jascha played an entirely new selection of pieces for his annual exam. A review of the school exams in the *Vilensky vestnik* reported that "it is impossible to pass over in silence the exceptional and far from childish performance of the young students Vudovich and Vizun and the miracle-child Heifetz, seven years old, who performed one of the most difficult

Dont études and the Vieuxtemps Ballade and Polonaise."[30] Malkin's choice of repertoire came directly from the Auer school; Auer suggested in his book on violin playing that after a student mastered the Kreutzer études, he should study Dont's Twenty-Four Caprices. The Vieuxtemps *Ballade et Polonaise* also features in Auer's list of recommended teaching material.[31] The result of Jascha's exam was positive: he entered the fifth grade with the highest marks.

It was typical for a violin student at the age of seven or eight to progress from a quarter-size violin to a half-size one. During an interview conducted in 1920, Heifetz told the story of how he acquired his next instrument:

> I was quite a little chap at the time, and seeing the instrument in a shop window I begged my father to buy it for me. The price asked was thirty rubles, and my father only wanted to pay twenty, deeming that to be all it was worth. I had my heart set on the fiddle, however, and I stood close to dad while the bargaining was going on, tugging at his coat-sleeve, silently coaxing him to buy it. But the dealer would not lower his price, so presently my father turned away and I followed in deep distress, beseeching him to re-consider his decision. "Well," said my father at last, "run back and offer him twenty rubles again, and if he will not take that offer him twenty-five, and if he won't take that, offer him thirty." I did exactly as I was bid. I told the man my father said offer him twenty rubles, and if he wouldn't take that to offer twenty-five, and if he wouldn't take that to offer him thirty. And it wouldn't take a particularly clever guesser to say what the man got.[32]

By the end of the 1907–1908 academic year, the school once again faced financial difficulties. The local newspaper reported that the "Director of the Vilna music school informed the City Council that the school is in a critical financial position and does not have the means to pay salaries to instruc-tors for May and April. In view of this, the director of the school requests that the council pay even just a half of the subsidy assigned by the city."[33] A letter from the director Mikhail Treskin to the St. Petersburg Prince Pyotr Svyatopolk-Mirsky, who during his time in Vilnius facilitated the founda-tion of the music school, described the difficulties facing the institution. Dated May 23, 1908, Treskin's letter reads:

> With the departure of Your Highness, the mus. [*sic*] school has suffered many difficult moments. More than once the school has been left without

any board, with all the artistic and organizational responsibility falling to me alone. Now Baroness A. G. von Wolf (*née* Barbi)—famous singer and wife of a trustee of the school district—heads the board, but the baron is leaving Vilna on another assignment. Such is, clearly, our fate....[34]

With Baron B. E. von Wolf's assignment to diplomatic service in Italy, the board of the Vilnius division of the IRMO lost the significant support of the Wolf family. Following a general meeting, Baroness von Wolf became an honorary board member, and her place as division head was taken by her assistant Lyudmila Lyubimova, the wife of the governor of Vilnius.

Suspended salaries and other budgetary troubles forced the school's teachers to seek additional income. In a letter to the composer Maksimilian Steinberg (1883–1946), Malkin revealed that he had begun searching for extra summer work earlier that year. Steinberg had been born in Vilnius, and his well-connected father worked as inspector of the Vilnius Jewish Teachers' Institute. Steinberg graduated from the St. Petersburg Conservatory that same spring of 1908 and was connected to the conservatory hierarchy through his marriage to Nadezhda Rimskaya-Korsakova, the daughter of the great composer. Steinberg visited Vilnius in February and called on his former teacher, Malkin. Not finding him home, Steinberg left a card. Malkin sent a reply to Steinberg in St. Petersburg, dated February 14, 1908:

> Dear Maksimilian Oseevich!
> I received your card and very much regret that we were not able to see each other in person. I want to ask you something, dear Max... I would very much like a conducting position for the summer at one or another of the resorts or parks, and while I am aware that requests of this kind come frequently to the conservatory, if you in any case would not refuse to say a word for me to Glazunov or Rimsky-Korsakov, then I would hopefully find a position.... My wife and daughter send their greetings and thank you for keeping us in your thoughts. I wish you the very best and remain forever deeply affectionate and respectful.
>
> I. D. Malkin
> Address: Sirotskaya St. bldg. 21, apt. 4. Malkin[35]

Steinberg's response to Malkin is unknown, but it is possible that something did come of the letter, since Malkin turned again to Steinberg two years later for help when sending Jascha to the conservatory. Malkin's letter also reveals that along with teaching and performing, he also pursued work as a conductor.

The new 1908–1909 academic year brought positive news for the school's financial situation. In a letter from St. Petersburg dated September 6, 1908, the IRMO's main board secretary, V. Nápravnik, informed Treskin that in the coming session of the State Duma, a petition for an increase in the state subsidy of IRMO music institutions would be submitted through the Ministry of Internal Affairs. To support this, it was suggested they approach certain music-loving government members, who "could at the right time support the board's application in the Duma."[36] Treskin asked Prince Svyatopolk-Mirsky to act as the authoritative "musical lobbyist," and wrote to him. "Perhaps, Your Highness, you may find it possible as an honored member of the Imperial Music Society and as the founder and first chairman of the Vilna board to reiterate before the State Duma the good that our division brings in terms of the propagation of musical arts in our region. . . ."[37]

Jascha began his third year at the music school on September 2, 1908, and around this time he joined the classes of Konstantin Galkovsky (Galkauskas) (1875–1963) for the basics of theory, harmony, and solfège. Galkovsky had graduated from St. Petersburg Conservatory in spring of 1908 after studying with Nikolai Rimsky-Korsakov, Alexander Glazunov, and Anatoly Lyadov, and on returning to his native Vilnius, he received an invitation from Treskin to teach at the school. The young teacher quickly joined the musical life of the city; in 1909 he helped found the city's first permanent symphony orchestra and conducted, composed, and taught there throughout his life. In 1947 he was awarded the title of professor of the Vilnius Conservatory, and in 1955 the title of People's Artist of the Lithuanian SSR. In his memoirs Galkovsky wrote: "Jascha Heifetz was two heads higher than all my students in the theory, harmony, and solfège classes."[38]

Jascha performed in public only once during the first half of the year at the first student recital evening, held on November 2, 1908. "The large audience, having overfilled the entire school building, eagerly encouraged the performing youngsters," wrote Galkovsky in the *Severo-zapadny golos*. "The public, it seems, was deeply moved by the first four items on the program."[39] Jascha performed one of these four items, and Galkovsky dedicated a separate section to this part of the recital: "The very promising bright eight-year-old violin virtuoso Heifetz, student of Mr. Malkin, pleasantly astonished all listeners." According to the concert program, Jascha performed his first Sarasate piece, the *Faust Fantasy*, a performance that came just weeks after the death of the great Spaniard.[40]

Also performing at the November 2 concert was Evel Zamsteichman, a cello and bass student in Enders's class whose early life resembled Jascha's, albeit with a less successful outcome. In January 1909, two months after the student recital, Zamsteichman departed for the St. Petersburg Conservatory. The Kaunas newspapers showed particular interest in the young musician. His father came from the Kaunas *meshchanstvo*, and as a consequence, it was precisely in this city that Evel gave his two very successful concerts. One journalist wrote:

> His father is a watchmaker from Vilnius. In January he took his son to the St. Petersburg Conservatory where he was auditioned by Professor Verzhbilovich ("talent, 5 +"). He was accepted into the conservatory with the following affidavit: "We certify herewith that the eleven-year-old son of David Zamsteichman, Evel, possesses an extraordinary gift for cello playing and deserves conscientious attention and material support. For its part, the Conservatory will afford him free tuition. [Attested to by] Professor of the St. Petersburg Conservatory A. Verzhbilovich. Inspector S. Gabel. 17 January 1909." The artist of the Imperial Russian Opera, A. M. Davydov, and the pianist I. A. Vengerova have both played a part in the boy's destiny by underwriting his financial security. The Jurgenson Music Store has offered him free sheet music.[41]

Despite Evel's exceptional talent and the generous support offered to him, things did not proceed smoothly. According to the boy's personal student record from the conservatory, he was actually thirteen years old, not eleven as reported in the newspaper review. Evel's father submitted his entrance application on January 17, 1909, but failed to prepare all the necessary documents.[42] Evel's record contains a note from the conservatory register dated September 27, 1909, and he received his residency permit at the end of October for a period of two months, but it was never renewed. From that point on, the name Evel Zamsteichman no longer appears in any of the conservatory documents. Evel had four younger siblings, and his father, burdened with a large family, apparently could not overcome the obstacles connected with educating his talented son in the distant capital city. Talent alone might not assure one of a continuing education at the conservatory level; these same obstacles would soon concern the Heifetz family.

As if following Zamsteichman's lead, Jascha also performed in Kaunas at the end of the 1908–1909 school year. Located fifty miles from Vilnius along the river Neris (or Viliya), Kaunas was a small city with a population of 80,000. Jascha's concert took place in the six-hundred-seat City Theater, the largest in Kaunas, and as newspapers described, the purpose of the concert was to raise money for B. Yu. Milner, a lyric bass-baritone student of the St. Petersburg Conservatory in order to "give the young singer the possibility to continue his musical education."[43] Jascha performed alongside Milner himself and the singer Sofia Medem. Although initially scheduled for April 25, the concert actually took place on May 2: "Today in the City Theatre—Concert of B. Yu. Milner . . . Ms. Medem is well known to the Kovno public. The eight-year-old violinist, as they say, is a phenomenal talent, and a student of the famous Vilna violinist Malkin."[44] By all accounts, the concert was a huge success. Milner and Medem both performed opera arias, and as noted enthusiastically by the press, Jascha performed a difficult program worthy of any adult concert violinist:

> The young violinist Heifetz has created a furor. He is only eight years old, a child barely visible from the ground, having only just learned to speak, yet he walks bravely onto the stage to play the Mendelssohn Concerto and the Sarasate Faust Fantasy. And how he plays! His bow stroke is brave, his little bow is correctly positioned, and his performance is so musical as to be pleasant to listen to. The public was delighted with the talented boy and they threw up their hands in wonder—where did such a phenomenon come from? But it is unnecessary for such a child to be forced to play two difficult pieces in one concert. Already with the Mendelssohn it was clear that here was an extraordinary being on stage, yet they also forced him to strain his little fingers around the violin "tricks" of the Sarasate.[45]

Unbeknownst to the reviewer, Jascha had learned the "tricks" of the Sarasate half a year earlier and only recently began studying the Mendelssohn Concerto. This concerto, which Auer described as belonging to "the grand repertory," would feature throughout Heifetz's career.[46] The Kaunas review testifies that May 2, 1909 was the first time Jascha played in that city.

This corrects a widely held belief that Heifetz performed the Mendelssohn Concerto in Kaunas in 1907. As an indication of the general confusion, Heifetz himself said: "at the age of six, I played the Mendelssohn concerto in Kovno."[47]

On the night of the actual concerto performance, the public flooded the City Theater, and the organizers turned many away. As the Kaunas press reported, "all performers were much applauded, and they were not stingy with their encores."[48] The same review made a direct plea to Ruvin: "In general we recommend to Papa Heifetz to present his son to the public less and to teach him more. Then his name will become famous." Regardless of this admonition, Ruvin was delighted with the trip, and he and Jascha departed for home in a hurry.

The concert in Kaunas might be loosely described as Jascha's first "tour," but it was not his first performance outside of the music school. That spring, the press reported on an exhibition in Vilnius between April 1 and 23, "Art in the Life of Children," held in the former building of the State Bank in Vilnius.[49] Modeled on a similar event in St. Petersburg, the exhibition was the first of its kind in Vilnius. It occupied the entire second floor and contained art works by children from various countries. The exhibition included drawings by English and American children, along with other handiwork, books, and educational toys.[50] The event also included lectures on teaching the arts to children, and various ensembles performed concerts. On April 18 and 19 the music school orchestra performed a Grieg symphony, and a student recital evening took place on April 20.

Although there is no conclusive evidence that Jascha participated in this student recital, a reference does appear in a later article in Vilnius: "In all six years have passed since the talented seven-year-old violinist boy performed in Vilna for the first time before the public at the exhibit 'Art in the Life of Children.'"[51] When Jascha was seven—in 1908—there was no such exhibit in Vilnius, so it appears the writer misremembered the boy's age. Another children's exposition did take place during August and September of 1908, but newspaper reports do not mention the participation of students from the music school.[52] It is difficult to imagine the music school leaving out its star pupil for the student recital held on April 20, 1909, one of the culminating events of that year's exposition.

Jascha prepared a substantial new work for his upcoming graduation ceremony—the Wieniawski Concerto no. 2. Jascha and the other students graduating from the piano, violin, and singing classes performed for the public on May 29, at 8 p.m., in the school's main hall. For the occasion a committee was appointed under Treskin's directorship, and in attendance were the vice-chair of the Vilnius IRMO board, L. Nenarokomova, and the deputy from the Ministry of Internal Affairs, E. Goppe.[53] Just two students graduated from Malkin's violin class at that time: Isay Varon, performing the Bruch Concerto in G Minor, and Jascha. On the Russian school grading scale of 1 to 5, Jascha received the highest mark of 5 for his performance.[54]

The annual convocation took place in the school hall two days later, on May 31, at 1 p.m., during which eight-year-old Jascha received his first degree certificate from Treskin. The document bore the director's signature: "Director of the music school of the Vilnius Division of the Imperial Russian Music Society. May 31 1909, no. 191, City of Vilna." The main body of the certificate states: "This certificate is given to Joseph Ruvimovich Heifetz, born 20 January 1901, that in the month of May of this year at the graduation examination, he was declared to have graduated the full course of violin playing with the set program of the Mus. Sch. IRMO and at his last exam received the grade of five (5)."[55] The official proceedings ended with a reading of the school's annual report:

> In the course of the 1908/09 year, 162 people were trained at the school, of those, 121 in the fortepiano class, 18 in the voice class, 14 in violin, 4 in cello, 4 in wind instruments. Twenty students studied for free.... To encourage the students' musical development, they were permitted to attend for free the concerts organized by the Vilna division of the IRMO. Graduating from the full course with first degree certificates: in the piano class: Aleksandra Vladimirovna Stashevskaya, Lyubov Samuilovna Feinstein, Yanina Konradovna Shishkovskaya; in the violin class of faculty teacher I. D. Malkin: eight-year-old Joseph Ruvimovich Heifetz.[56]

A concert followed the convocation, during which three graduates from Treskin's class performed piano concertos by Moscheles, Mendelssohn, and Weber.[57] The program also included Luisa Barbier, a graduate of Karmilov's singing class who had appeared in every student recital. Of the violinists, only Jascha performed: "The morceau friand [tidbit] at the convocation was the Wieniawski D-minor Concerto. This phenomenal boy, with further systematic development of his enormous gifts, will with time occupy an honored place among famous virtuosos."[58] Jascha and his parents were delighted. The boy had another reason to be happy. For the first time, before the name Heifetz in the printed program stood the respectful "Mr." rather than just "Student." The title had a proud ring to it, especially for an eight-year-old: Mr. Heifetz, graduate of the School of the Imperial Russian Music Society.

From August 1909 onward, as previously mentioned, the school changed its address, moving, together with the IRMO board, into building number 4, on the corner of Skapo (then Skopovka) and the Palace Square. In September 1994, following the efforts of the violinist's eldest son Robert Heifetz, along with the Society of Lithuanian Jews, and the Vilnius State Jewish Museum, an inscribed memorial plaque designed by the architect Vytautas Zaranka was placed on this building. The inscription in both Lithuanian and English declares that between 1905 and 1909, Jascha Heifetz attended the music school located in the building. "A short time later," writes Genrikh Agranovsky of the Vilnius State Jewish Museum, "the building was passed on to the Vilnius arch-episcopate, and placed under capital renovation. The plaque was taken off and at the end of the renovation it was not put back in its former position."[59] The bishop apparently did not share the vision of those who erected the memorial; he believed that "there is no justification for attaching a memorial plaque dedicated to the violinist Jascha Heifetz onto a building belonging to the Church."[60] Fortunately, subsequent research into local history revealed the true location of the music school during Jascha's time as a student, and so in 2001, to celebrate the great violinist's centenary, the memorial plaque was placed in its rightful location on the building at 28 Vilenskaya Street, now 25 Vilniaus Street.

Just after the graduation exams, Vilnius newspapers reported a sharp deterioration in the weather, with heavy rain and strong winds. A dangerous typhus epidemic broke out in Vilnius at the end of April, leading to the overcrowding of the local medical facilities; by autumn, cholera had appeared in the city and its surrounding areas. In the midst of this dire situation, the Heifetzes continued their preparations for the move to St. Petersburg and the conservatory. They received papers from the birth register on May 6 and obtained the necessary health certificate from the Jewish hospital the following day.[61] In August, the Heifetzes traveled to Polotsk, where Ruvin received his passport.[62] Every visit to the Polotsk relatives brought great joy for the entire family. Jascha and his sisters received countless hugs and presents, and in return the boy played for his grandfather Ilya, for Uncle Aron and Aunt Malka, and for their six children: Fanny, Emma, Asya, Isaak, Paulina, and Elya. With the exception of six-year-old Paulina and two-year-old Elya, the other children were all significantly older than their cousin Jascha—Emma was fourteen and Fanny fifteen. Jascha developed the closest relationships with his older cousins; just a few years later he began to correspond with Fanny, and he kept photographs of his older cousins in his albums. Such close ties did not develop with the children of Jascha's other Polotsk uncle, Morduch-Dov, but Ruvin maintained contact with Morduch-Dov and his family.

From Polotsk the Heifetzes headed to the small town of Švenčionys (Sventsyany) located about fifty miles from Vilnius. The purpose of this trip remains unclear, and it is known only through postcards preserved in the Heifetz archive. One of these postcards carries a reproduction of a painting by Benedetto Luti called "Shepherd," and the inscription on the back reads: "To naughty little Jascha—M. Levina. 22 August 1909. Sventsyany."[63] Another postcard addressed "To Dear Jascha" includes a painting by the Russian artist Nikolai Ge and the following caption: "Emperor Peter I interrogates Tsarevich Aleksei Petrovich at Peterhof. Tsar Peter is angry and the Tsarevich very sad." These were not the first color postcards Jascha received. His first arrived in the spring of the previous year, sent by his uncle Samuil in Warsaw. It carried a picture of Beethoven on the front, and in Samuil's hand on the back read "Dear Josifka! This picture belongs to you as a musical person. Try to be as great as Beethoven."[64] Local music lovers in Švenčionys expressed a fervent desire to arrange a public concert for Jascha during these August days, but for some reason it never happened. Nevertheless, on leaving Švenčionys, the Heifetzes promised that sooner or later Jascha would perform in the small town.

On their return to Vilnius, the expense of a trip to St. Petersburg continued to preoccupy the Heifetzes. How would they get there, and how would they pay for it? Although an adult first-class ticket to St. Petersburg including all the extra fees cost as much as 29 rubles and 50 kopecks, a third-class ticket could cost fewer than 9 rubles. In practice, traveling with a small child in the third-class carriage was not ideal. As a compromise, a second-class ticket cost 19 rubles and 10 kopecks, and since Jascha fell under the category of "children between five and ten years of age," his ticket would cost just a quarter of the full price. Jascha and his father needed 23 rubles and 90 kopecks for two one-way tickets to St. Petersburg. Other expenses included new clothes appropriate for the capital and money to take on the long trip. They would also need to rent an apartment and feed themselves, and they had to leave enough for Anna, Pauline, and Elza back in Vilnius. However much they tried, the Heifetzes could not make it to St. Petersburg in time for the September admissions exams at the conservatory, and so they decided to delay the trip until the second set of exams in January. These extra few months gave the Heifetzes time to prepare and raise funds; a large responsibility fell on Jascha himself to earn money from paid performances. Since the Heifetzes had little experience in such organizational and logistical matters, it is likely the musical powers of Vilnius aided in the development of strategies for the upcoming concert campaign. The Heifetzes could hardly have dealt with the immense obstacles before them without the support of Malkin, Treskin, members of the IRMO, and other benefactors now unknown.

The fundraising "campaign" began on September 19, 1909, in a concert at the Vilnius City Club. Alongside Jascha, other performers included a Mrs. Feigelson, Malkin and his wife, the cellist and teacher at the music school, Mikhail Weinbren, and the tenor Mr. L. A. Halperin. A large audience came to see the evening performance, enticed by announcements printed in the local *Vilensky kurier* and *Severo-zapadny golos*. Jascha performed the Mendelssohn Concerto and the Sarasate *Faust Fantasy*, and the press reacted favorably. "What is there to say about the eight-year-old boy who performed in the concert in the Hall of the City Club? His success would be envied by many famous violinists," wrote the reviewer for the *Vilensky kurier*, who continued:

I saw him for the first time but cannot yet call him "the violinist" Heifetz. He is still too young for his playing to make a finished impression. However, one involuntarily wants to say, this boy is a genius.... Look at his little face. Very beautiful, open, with big expressive eyes that constantly gaze not at the audience, but into some far off distance, as if to say: "I am indeed extraordinary!" And as a musician, Heifetz is already extraordinary. His rendition of the [Sarasate] variations on "Faust" and the Mendelssohn Concerto testify to the rare, inborn ability of the future, indubitably great artist. Even if at times not everything in his playing is polished, even if at times it seems insufficiently inspired, still the sounds invoked by that miniature violinist from his tiny instrument amaze and captivate. His technique is truly astonishing. As we heard, the boy is being sent to St. Petersburg for the continuation of his musical education. It is impossible not to wish him success....[65]

The second fundraising concert took place the following day in the Hall of the Trade-Manufacturing Social Assembly (Merchants' Club). Jascha performed the Mendelssohn Concerto again. Other performers included Ms. Valentinova (mezzo-soprano), Ms. Svyadoshch (coloratura soprano), and again Halperin. Once more, the press wrote glowingly about the event:

> On 20 September in the Hall of the Merchants' Club, a concert was held for the Vilnius wunderkind, eight-year-old violinist J. Heifetz, who graduated this year from the music school and is now being sent off to the St. Petersburg Conservatory. The little artist captivated the audience with his astonishing (for his age) delivery of the extremely demanding first Mendelssohn Concerto.[66]

Jascha's third fundraising performance took place a month later on October 21, this time in the City Hall, the largest concert space in Vilnius. The evening was held for the benefit of disadvantaged students in the gymnasium of E. Nezdyurova and N. Reismiller. Performers included the violinist Mr. Dyshkevich, the cellist Mr. Tkhorzh, the pianist Mr. Sedzimir, and the harmonium player Mr. Ditkevich. The event was widely publicized: the *Severo-zapadny golos* printed two advertisements, and the *Vilensky kurier* ran announcements four days in a row, from October 18 to 21. The concert was followed by dancing and games.

On October 28, 1909, Professor Auer gave a much-anticipated concert in Vilnius. Afterward, the press reported that "Mr. Auer was brought a luxurious laurel wreath, it seems, from one of his former students."[67] There is little doubt that the former student was Malkin, and Jascha likely stood nearby watching with fascination. A wave of famous musicians arrived in Vilnius during November, including the pianist Josef Hofmann and the violinists Jan Kubelík and Bronislaw Huberman.

At the end of the year, a fire destroyed the enormous Zalkind store on the corner of Bolshaya and Rudnitskaya streets. The fire burned uncontrollably for three days; flames illuminated the whole city center, and clouds of smoke penetrated surrounding windows and shutters. The store and a number of neighboring buildings burned to the ground, leaving a scene of devastation. On December 26, just a few days after the fire, Jascha gave his next fundraising performance in the already familiar Hall of the Trade-Manufacturing Social Assembly, where he was joined by other performers.[68]

There is no record of how much Jascha earned from each of his fundraising concerts, but his and his father's passage to St. Petersburg was finally assured when the Vilnius Jewish Society granted them a princely sum of three hundred rubles. With this grant and the money raised from the concerts, the trip at last became a reality. Suitcases were gathered and Anna washed and packed clothing for her husband and son. One can imagine the mix of worry, pride, and excitement as Anna and her daughters prepared to say goodbye.

Just before Ruvin and Jascha departed, Malkin handed them a letter of recommendation addressed to Maksimilian Steinberg:

18 January 1910
Dear Maksimilian Oseevich!
I recommend this tiny-but-great violinist to you. Only you are in the position to appreciate the immense giftedness which Heaven has given to this miracle-child. I beg you, dear and beloved Maximilian Oseevich, to take him under your wing; I beg you, although I know that my request is superfluous. I am confident that you will love him with all the strength of your noble artistic soul.
I wish you all the best and remain sincerely affectionate and deeply respectful to you,

I. D. Malkin
Give my heartfelt greetings to your family[69]

Malkin counted on the help of his former student, the twenty-seven-year-old Steinberg, who already carried a certain authority within the capital's musical circles, having received a professorship in the theory of composition immediately upon his graduation from the conservatory. Steinberg's connection to his native Vilnius remained strong, and local newspapers followed his career with interest.[70]

The Heifetzes probably carried other such recommendation letters with them on their journey, and Malkin most likely spoke to Auer about Jascha's upcoming trip during the professor's recent visit to Vilnius. Malkin did everything in his power to assist his star student, and contact between Jascha and Malkin continued until the Heifetzes eventually left Russia. Heifetz described his relationship with Malkin in an interview entitled: "Heifetz welcomes one of his Teachers," printed after Malkin arrived in New York in the 1920s:

> I feel that I owe it to Prof. Malkin to correct the general idea that my father and Prof. Auer directed all my studies. The fact is, my father began to teach me when I was three and continued to guide me long afterward, but when I was five he placed me in the music school in Vilna where I remained for three years under Prof. Malkin's careful instruction. It was during that time that I made my first public appearances.[71]

Jascha and his father left Vilnius on January 18 or 19, arriving in St. Petersburg on January 20. From the window of the train Jascha and Ruvin waved as they began their journey of nearly twenty hours across more than 430 miles. Jascha left many beloved people behind, including his sisters, his grandfather, Uncle Isaac and Aunt Sonia, little cousin Anyuta, Malkin, and, of course, his dear mother. Saying goodbye to her son brought tears to Anna's eyes, but she consoled herself with the knowledge that Jascha was preparing for a bright and successful future. The train passed through the forests of Polotsk and forged onward through the sweeping, boundless snowy plains. Jascha was on his way to the city that would make him a truly great musician.

CHAPTER FOUR

1910: St. Petersburg Conservatory and Nalbandian

BY 1910, RUSSIA BOASTED TWO conservatories, one in St. Petersburg, then the capital, and one in Moscow. The St. Petersburg Conservatory was founded in 1862 by Anton Rubinstein and was the first and oldest Russian center of academic musical education. Notable graduates included Tchaikovsky, Lyadov, Fyodor Stravinsky (the composer Igor's father), Ivan Yershov, Vasily Safonov, and Anna Yesipova. A number of significant pedagogical schools developed at the conservatory, including the violin school of Leopold Auer, Anna Yesipova's piano school, and Aleksandr Verzhbilovich's cello school. In June 1908, a year and a half before the Heifetzes arrived in St. Petersburg, the conservatory's influential head of composition, Nikolai Rimsky-Korsakov, passed away. The memory of the composer lived on at the institution, however, and it is said that Rimsky-Korsakov's coat hook remained vacant for many years.

From December 1905 onward, the post of conservatory director was occupied by a former student of Rimsky-Korsakov, Alexander Glazunov (1865–1936). The conservatory generally kept a distance from social and political issues, but the 1905 Russian Revolution led to a struggle for autonomy from the main board of the IRMO. This new autonomy crystallized in the unanimous vote for Glazunov; earlier, directors had been appointed by the leadership of the IRMO. In 1909, the conservatory's artistic council voted to give Glazunov a second term and conferred upon him the title of Distinguished Professor. Glazunov's reign at the conservatory lasted more than twenty years.

The conservatory moved several times during its half-century history. It began in the small private home of Demidov on the river Moika, moved to a government building at the fifth corner of Zagorodny Prospekt, and from 1869 was located in the building of the Ministry of Internal Affairs on Teatralnaya Street (now Architect Rossi Street). Finally, in 1896 it moved to its own space on Teatralnaya Square where it remains to this day. Reconstructed by the architect Vladimir Nikolya, the grey four-story building stands directly opposite the famous Mariinsky Theater.

As long as a student had strong musical abilities and could pay between 200 and 250 rubles per year (300 for auditors), it was not difficult to enroll in the conservatory. Throughout the institution's history, the offspring of wealthy parents attended the conservatory without needing to take exams or participate in public recitals, and without receiving a certificate or diploma. By contrast, it was much more difficult to receive a partial or full scholarship, and students in this category never numbered more than a quarter of the total student population. The conservatory determined each student's status upon entry, and after six months it would decide on the exact size of the stipend (after only a month for bass and wind instruments). Essentially, the greater a student's success, the larger the subsidy he or she would receive; subsidies varied between 100 and 200 rubles. This money went toward tuition costs, so students receiving a 100-ruble stipend, for example, still paid between 50 and 100 rubles to cover the total fee. Over the course of the conservatory's existence, Russian music lovers donated large sums of money for the purpose of providing scholarships. Of the 1,762 students enrolled at the conservatory in the 1909–1910 academic year, 150 received stipends.[1]

The conservatory education was split into two stages—the preparatory division, known as the lower course (the equivalent of a middle and high school education today), and the upper course (today's college conservatory-level education). The IRMO conservatory charter did not impose age restrictions and in relation to admissions simply stated: "People of both sexes and all classes and conditions are accepted into the conservatory."[2] The St. Petersburg Conservatory's own rules (at least on paper) restricted the lower course to students ten years and older, and the upper course to those no younger than sixteen and no older than twenty-five.[3] The total period of time spent in the conservatory was also not strictly limited; officially, the lower course covered six years of training and the upper course lasted four years, but some students stayed far longer. In terms of general entry requirements to the conservatory, the charter stated that "the knowledge necessary for entrance to the conservatory is defined by courses of men's and women's progymnasia or of institutions equal to them."[4] This seemingly strict requirement carried the proviso that "for persons possessed of gifts for the development of real artistic talents . . . this level of knowledge may be somewhat lowered." Despite the many rules and regulations, the conservatory strove both to maintain the numbers of students paying the highest fees and to facilitate the development of genuinely talented students, who were allowed somewhat outside the boundaries of regulations. Jascha passed through his conservatory education violating countless rules, which the conservatory administration worked tirelessly to circumvent.

Ruvin likely heard all about the conservatory and its rules from Malkin back in Vilnius; thus as Jascha and his father arrived in St. Petersburg under the glass arches of Warsaw Station, they were probably aware that many obstacles awaited them. Newspapers reported that the winter of 1909–1910 was unusually warm in St. Petersburg; with the temperature slightly above freezing in the second half of January, thawing snow would have created a low-hanging, foggy haze across the city. At first sight, the city both impressed and overwhelmed Jascha and his father. In contrast to the familiar quiet streets back in Vilnius, St. Petersburg was a huge city filled with wide, geometrically ordered streets stretching far out of sight, including the impressive Nevsky Prospekt. Horse-drawn carriages rushed past with castanet-like clatter over the cobblestone streets, trams rang their bells incessantly, automobile horns honked, and traders called out from every street corner.

According to family recollections, Jascha and his father were greeted at the station by a member of the Olefsky family, but it is unknown whether it was Aron Olefsky himself, their Vilnius neighbor and friend who happened to be in St. Petersburg, or relatives who lived in the city. Nevertheless, the Heifetzes were fortunate to be greeted upon their arrival, to have somewhere to leave their luggage and settle in, and to have someone to ask for advice. Coincidentally, their arrival in St. Petersburg on January 20 fell on Jascha's ninth birthday. After arriving, the Heifetzes went directly to Auer's apartment. Auer answered the doorbell, but refused them entry and sent them to see Ioannes Nalbandian, assistant professor at the conservatory. Jascha and his father tried to contain their disappointment as they made their way to Auer's former student and assistant, whom they remembered from his performance in Vilnius and through Malkin's stories.

Prospective conservatory students could enlist the support of a professor prior to the admissions exam, and entrance papers were often accompanied by notes that might read, "I agree to accept such and such a student into my class." Although nothing was guaranteed, the exam commission tended to look favorably on such intercessions. After hearing Jascha play, Nalbandian wrote a particularly persuasive note on his calling card: "20 January 1910. I accept Heifetz as a non-paying student into my class. His talent is immense, astonishing, pitch and memory absolute. I. Nalbandian."[5]

A few days later, Jascha and his father appeared at the conservatory office to complete various documents, including an entrance application drawn up by the conservatory affairs manager, Dmitry Dzhiorguli, and the assistant to the inspector, Jan Tamm. Ruvin added his own signature at the end:

> 23 January 1910
> To the General Director of the St. Petersburg Conservatory
> From the Polotsk *Meshchanin* Ruvin Heifetz
>
> Request
>
> Wishing to enroll my son Joseph, born 20 January 1901, for spec[ialized]
> training in violin playing, I most humbly request you accept him as
> a stud[ent] in the conservatory; herewith I enclose the phys[ician's]
> cert[ificate] and my passport, given by the elder of the *Meshchane* of Polotsk
> on 17 August 1909, no. 2787, for a term of 5 years. R. Heifetz.[6]

The application was filed in the conservatory admissions book on January 23, and the admissions exam took place that same day in director Glazunov's first-floor room, where the director's office is still located today.[7] Generations of conservatory graduates recall the experience of entering the large room, overflowing, as it always seemed to hopeful entrants, with a crowd of judgmental professors.[8] In Sergei Prokofiev's memoirs, he recalled that at the age of thirteen his own entrance exam "went fairly spectacularly." He entered the room, "bent under the weight of two folders, in which lay four operas, two sonatas, a symphony and a great many piano pieces.... The exam went on for a long time."[9] Jascha, who appears never to have experienced performance anxiety, also passed his exam successfully. On the exam paper, under the column entitled "General musical abilities," Glazunov wrote, "pitch is amazing (perfect). Musical memory wonderful."[10] Under the column, "Opinion of the examiner on specialized subject," Glazunov wrote, "Remarkable talent." Finally, under "Conditions of admission," the note "VK" indicated that Jascha would enter the upper course, into Nalbandian's class.

It appears Glazunov knew of the Heifetz family's difficult financial situation. Although applicants usually paid a fee for the entrance exam, Glazunov made a note on Jascha's exam paper: "freed from payment for the exam by the Director." Nevertheless, partial payment was still required for Jascha's studies. In the 1909–1910 student log, in the column "ranks and payment," the Roman numeral VII beside Jascha's name indicated that although violin lessons would be free, he would be part of the category of students paying 100 rubles for general subjects such as solfège and music theory.[11]

Also on that day, Jascha received a document from the office allowing him to obtain a residency permit:

Imperial Russian Music Society
St. Petersburg Conservatory
23 January 1910 no. 6192

This certificate, which is signed and sealed, is given to the conservatory student Joseph Heifetz, of the Jew[ish] f[aith], in accordance with paragraph 57 of the conservatory charter, for free residency in rented apartments for the period through the 1st of June 1910.[12]

With this short document, nine-year-old Jascha earned the right to live in the capital of the Russian Empire. His father, however, did not yet have the same permission.

On the request submitted to the conservatory Ruvin noted their St. Petersburg address as Ofitserskaya (Officer) Street. This long street, surrounded by the neighborhood of Malaya Kolomna, stretches from Voznesensky Prospekt in the city center and reaches Teatralnaya Square, the home of both the conservatory and the Mariinsky Theater. At the start of the twentieth century, the street passed by a meat market and the Lithuanian Castle, which functioned as a jail. In contrast to the thriving area around the famous Nevsky Prospekt, Kolomna area residents lived much more modestly. Owing to the proximity of the conservatory and the Mariinsky Theater, Ofitserskaya Street became home to many musicians and music stores, including a bow workshop, various instrument stores, and a store that sold sheet music. In many ways, "Officer" Street could have been called "Musician" Street.

The Heifetzes resided in a building beyond the Kryukov Canal, just a five-minute walk from the conservatory, where they remained from January to April 1910. Little is known about Jascha's first dwelling in St. Petersburg. Those renting apartments from landlords often sublet rooms for extra income; the Heifetz family's financial situation at the time probably forced Ruvin to rent such a room in a shared apartment. Renting an apartment to themselves would have cost anywhere between several hundred to over five thousand rubles per year—an unimaginable sum for the Heifetzes.

The occupants of these sublet rooms were far from being the proletarian poor; the neighbors of Makar Devushkin, the hero of Dostoevsky's novel *Poor Folk*, set in the nineteenth century, were, as the author described, "respectable, educated, and even bookish people. In particular they include a tchinovnik (one of the literary staff in some government department), who is so well read that he can expound Homer or any other author—in fact, *anything*, such a man of talent is he! Also, there are a couple of officers (for ever playing cards), a midshipman, and an English tutor."[13] The housing situation had changed little by the end of the nineteenth century, when Dmitry Shostakovich, father of the composer, studied at the St. Petersburg University. Always searching for a cheaper or more hospitable dwelling, Shostakovich frequently moved between rented rooms near the university, sometimes staying no longer than a few weeks in one place. Students unable to afford an actual room could rent just a corner—hence the term "corner dwellers."

Jascha and Ruvin faced similar housing choices when they arrived in St. Petersburg at the beginning of the twentieth century. Buildings and shacks arose wherever space allowed, even in courtyards, leaving little space between buildings. For this reason, apartments with street-facing windows were more desirable and more expensive. The Heifetzes settled into a cheaper courtyard-facing apartment—apt. 49, 37 Ofitserskaya Street. Inhabitants of today's apt. 49 describe many changes since the early twentieth century, and archival documents support this account.[14] As of 1870, the building belonged to a noble family named Serebryakov, and a tax document describes it as a two-story residential wing covering an area of forty-eight-squared *sazhens*, situated on the left boundary of the court-yard.[15] It is described as smoothly plastered; under an iron roof; with two black, stone staircases. The five apartments in this building shared seven ovens, four kitchen hearths, two sinks, and two toilets—an expressive dash under the bathrooms column indicated the absence of this particular luxury. Apartment 49 consisted of six rooms and was located on the second floor. The entire wing was demolished during citywide renovations in the 1970s. All that remains of it today is a barely visible outline on the yellow plaster exterior wall—a shadow of Jascha's first St. Petersburg residence.

Positioned in the courtyard where the building once stood, one can still see the spire of the Mariinsky Theater and beyond that the conservatory. The Russian Family Garden, located on the other side of the building, once belonged to the merchant Demidov, and local residents called it the "Demidron." A theater erected in the gardens passed through many different owners, including the famous actress Vera Komissarzhevskaya; by 1910 Anatoly Levant headed the enterprise. Although known officially as the

"New Dramatic Theater," locals called it the "Andreevsky" after the famous writer Leonid Andreev, the theater's director. Unlike other theaters in the city, this one attracted mainly students.

During these early days in St. Petersburg, Ruvin faced the all-consuming problem of acquiring a residency permit. He knew that breaking the rules, especially as a Jew, would result in swift action by the authorities. Ruvin's brother Aron had himself experienced deportation from the city; Aron's name appears in the files of the St. Petersburg Police Detective Department for the period of January 1–15, 1891.[16] In that short, two-week period, hundreds of people were deported, including a large peasant family named Sinitsa; Johann and Leonard Oswald from Württemburg who were deported "for depraved behavior"; and a large number of families with Jewish names. Deportation was carried out in a humiliating and cruel manner: deportees were forced to wear shackles and travel in a convoy.

From 1887, a majority of higher education institutions in the Russian Empire became subject to a decree of the Ministry of National Education, which established rules for admitting Jews: within the Pale of Settlement, Jews could make up only ten percent of newly admitted students; outside of the Pale but still within Russia, only five percent; and, in the two capitals combined, only three percent. Moreover, many institutions of higher education were completely closed to Jews, including the Institute of Communications and the Electronic Technology Institute in St. Petersburg, the Moscow Agricultural Institute, the Imperial Theatrical Schools in Moscow and St. Petersburg, and the Military-Medical Academy in St. Petersburg. The St. Petersburg Conservatory was one of a few institutions not bound by restrictions on Jewish matriculation, but strict laws still interfered with the conservatory's ability to accept talented children from the Pale, since their parents were often denied residency permits.

The conservatory kept scrupulous records. The student book tallied the number of students of each religion by first letter of last names. Under the letter R, for example, were listed twenty-three Orthodox, six Lutheran, two Catholic, and thirty Jewish students. Under the Russian letter "X," for Heifetz, were listed two Orthodox, one Mennonite, and seven Jewish students.[17] This list served no practical purpose for the conservatory itself, but was used by the town governor to surveil the observance of residency rules (mostly by Jews, of course). An example of the hardships faced by students is the case of the mother of the violinist Efrem Zimbalist, who on arriving in St. Petersburg with her twelve-year-old son, was only permitted to remain for one week.[18] Similar situations were common, despite the efforts of the conservatory to assist its Jewish students.

Ruvin collected his passport from the conservatory office on January 28. It appears no effort was spared by the conservatory management in trying to secure a residency permit for Ruvin. In general, Jews were allowed to remain in the capital for six weeks, with the possibility of a two-month extension. The letter below, signed by both Glazunov and Nikolai Sokolov, secretary of the Artistic Council, is an application for the granting of these extra two months:

Imperial Russian Music Society
St. Petersburg Division
Conservatory
20 February 1910 no. 6528

Certificate

This document is given to the Polotsk *meshchanin* Ruvim HEIFETZ for presentation to HIS EXCELLENCY the Town Governor, in witness of the fact that his son Joseph, 9 years of age, at the trials for classes in violin performance, displayed surprising and exceptional musical abilities, and fully complete musical maturity, in consequence of which, despite his young age, he was admitted to the UPPER course.

Director of the Conservatory A. Glazunov
Secretary of the Artistic Council Professor N. Sokolov[19]

As director, Glazunov worked tirelessly on behalf of his students. Although he helped anyone who asked, regardless of nationality or religion, it was his Jewish students who needed the most support. As a result of his effectiveness, Glazunov became known (behind his back at least) as the "Jewish tsar"—a respectful nickname taken from a play by Grand Duke Konstantin Konstantinovich that was performed in 1913 with music by Glazunov. One of the director's former students who graduated in 1915, Anushavan Ter-Gevondian, recalled that:

... in the conservatory cafeteria, which was located on the first floor under the the Maly Hall, every student could have a tasty and satisfying meal for just 11 kopecks. We knew that the cafeteria could not feed us so well for that kind of money, but no one knew that half of the cafeteria's deficit was covered by Glazunov's personal resources. . . . Seeing a student in the winter on the street without a coat, he sent the porter out to Aleksandrovsky Market to buy a coat, and so on and so forth. Advanced students who could not pay for their studies could be sure that they would not be excluded from the conservatory because the director would not allow this and would pay from his own pocket.[20]

The letter on behalf of the Heifetzes signed by Glazunov and Sokolov was accepted by the authorities and Ruvin received the extension for his stay. The letter was, however, not the full extent of Glazunov's support. The director soon realized that the 100-ruble tuition payment required of the Heifetzes at the start of the year was an unbearable burden, and Glazunov wrote in his record book: "Regarding Nalbandian's student Heifetz [unintelligible] either lower or cancel payment for lessons by September 1."[21] The barely legible lines of the note differ markedly from Glazunov's usually neat handwriting; it seems the note was written on a day when Glazunov suffered from an attack of the so-called "Russian Sickness." It was no secret in the conservatory that Glazunov had an ongoing alcohol addiction. His colleagues would say among themselves: "Glazunov is *sick* again." Even in such a condition, however, Glazunov was moved to help the Heifetz family.

Concern over Ruvin's residency status temporarily shifted the focus away from the most vexing issue for Jascha—that he was assigned to study not with Auer, but with Nalbandian. Auer had previously taught young students—Efrem Zimbalist, Mischa Elman, Cecilia Hansen, and Myron Polyakin—all who came to him between eleven and thirteen years of age. At just nine, Jascha was still considered too young. A year and a half later, when Jascha made his first public performances in St. Petersburg, newspapers noted that "at first Auer was not at all astonished by the talent of Heifetz. He said that it was the first time he had seen such a developed left hand, but in terms of tone and musicality, the boy did not show anything remarkable."[22] Reviewers believed this was the reason Auer sent Jascha to Nalbandian. They predicted that future biographers would never forget that Heifetz had studied with Nalbandian, and that "Auer did not at first value the talent of this famous little boy."[23] In reality, history has almost forgotten Auer's initial reluctance to work with Heifetz and the subsequent time spent with Nalbandian. One thing is certain: with the determined pace of Jascha's development, the year and a half in Nalbandian's class was far from insignificant.

Nalbandian was born in 1872 in Simferopol in the Crimea into a relatively poor Armenian family. His original name was Ovanes Arakelovich, but he went by Ioannes Romanovich in the conservatory. Furthermore, in correspondence with him, Auer used the even more russified name Ivan Romanovich, and often just wrote "Dear Nal!" Nalbandian began the violin at the age of nine and by eleven started to perform in the south of Russia.[24] He entered the St. Petersburg Conservatory in 1886, and studied with Auer between 1888 and 1894. He graduated with a Free Artist's diploma and the title of laureate, and that same summer, was invited to perform as a soloist in concerts at Pavlovsk Station. During the fall of 1894, Auer arranged for Nalbandian to move with state sponsorship to Berlin, where he continued his studies with the great Joseph Joachim. "I heard Nalbandian's playing," wrote Joachim, "and found that he possessed the most superior qualities of a violin virtuoso, boding a wonderful future for him."[25] The famous Pablo de Sarasate wrote: "I had the great pleasure of hearing the outstanding student of Leopold Auer, Mr. Nalbandian, possessing the remarkable talent of a violin virtuoso."[26] Nalbandian toured many Russian cities, giving frequent charity concerts to benefit impoverished Armenians, and performed once or twice a year in St. Petersburg, usually in the conservatory's Maly Hall. Auer invited Nalbandian to work as his main assistant at the conservatory from 1895 onward, and as a result, Nalbandian taught almost all of Auer's most outstanding students—Kathleen Parlow, Joseph Achron, Hansen, Elman, Zimbalist, and, in 1910, Heifetz.

At this time, Nalbandian lived on the bank of the river Moika in building number 66, which on one side faced the Mariinsky Palace. Teachers at the conservatory often worked in their homes with their students. Thirty-eight-year-old Nalbandian was then unmarried and lived with his mother, Anna. Nalbandian's brother Anton, a bank clerk, also lived in the apartment. Nalbandian married Anna Gabrieliants in 1912, and all of them, including his mother and brother, moved to a more spacious apartment in building number 40 on Ofitserskaya Street, just across from where the Heifetzes began their St. Petersburg life.

Lessons with Nalbandian followed the next logical step in Jascha's training. The boy's technique, as if naturally programmed to the "Auer" method, seemed to require just one thing—the mastery of as much repertoire as possible. Nalbandian knew how to inspire his students. Years later, Heifetz said of his first St. Petersburg teacher: "He tries to bring out the best in a student by leaving him to his own individuality and intellectuality. He does not interfere with expression of the self."[27] It seems Jascha learned life-long lessons during this time with Nalbandian: "Practice and more practice is the rule at the Conservatory. You cannot learn to play the violin from a correspondence course."[28]

Jascha's lessons with his new teacher continued for three months, after which he played in the public exam for Nalbandian's class held on the morning of April 24. He performed before a panel of string teachers that included Auer, Verzhbilovich, Emily Gerbek, Vasily Zhdanov, Ivan Zeifert, Sergei Korguev, Aleksei Kolakovsky, Emmanuel Kreuger, Nalbandian, and Nikolai Tcherepnin.[29] Of the thirty-eight students in Nalbandian's class at that time, twenty-five came from the upper course. Ten other Nalbandian students were tested on April 24, and they varied greatly in age, from thirteen-year-old Aleksandr Gillersberg to twenty-seven-year-old Yakov Magaziner. At just nine, Jascha was by far the youngest to play, and although no record of the exam repertoire remains, the responses of each member of the panel provide fascinating reading. Although Glazunov and Nalbandian differed in their responses to other students in the exam, when it came to Jascha, they agreed fully: Nalbandian declared, "Talent by the grace of God," and Glazunov, "Genius giftedness. 5 +."[30] There was no higher grade.

Despite Jascha's incredible early success at the conservatory, nothing more could be done to extend Ruvin's residency permit, so both Jascha and his father were forced to return to Vilnius. Since the school year was not yet over, Jascha received permission to leave from Nalbandian, who clearly understood the situation. Nalbandian wrote: "Mr. Inspector. There are no obstacles to be met with regards to leave for my student Heifetz on my part."

Nalbandian. 1910. April 24."[31] The conservatory inspector responsible for all educational matters at the time was Stanislav Gabel, a former bass singer and one of the conservatory's oldest teachers. Gabel worked as Glazunov's main assistant in running the school and had occupied the post since 1904. The inspector took Jascha's student record and noted that the boy would be on leave, "until September 10."[32]

Before the Heifetzes left, Nalbandian gave Jascha an inscribed photograph: "To my student Joseph Heifetz in memory and with the wish for further such students. I. Nalbandian. April 24, 1910."[33] The next day, Ruvin and Jascha bade farewell to Nalbandian, and Jascha received yet another inscribed photograph from his teacher: "To my dear glorious boy and talent-by-the-grace-of-God Joseph Heifetz, in remembrance from I. Nalbandian. April 25, 1910."[34] Heifetz saved these photographs until the end of his life.

Although at this time Nalbandian belonged to the upper echelons of the St. Petersburg intelligentsia, he came from more humble origins—his father kept a paint store in Simferopol and the family belonged to the merchant class.[35] Like many non-nobles who had achieved a high level of education, Nalbandian developed an outlook that was closely connected with humanistic and democratic principles. The ability to relate to others formed a central part of his character. As one of his students recalled, Nalbandian "was a large personality. Proud, independent, not capable of pandering to anyone or playing up to people—such behavior was entirely foreign to his nature. From there came his nobleness and direct approach to people. Along with that he was a benevolent person who cared about the youth."[36] Both Jascha and Ruvin learned much from their relationship with Nalbandian.

The Heifetzes had mixed feelings as they departed St. Petersburg. On one hand, Jascha had created a sensation in the conservatory, but on the other, without a residency permit for Ruvin, Jascha would have to forfeit his chance to study in the big city. It is unknown whether a solution was devised before they left St. Petersburg, but one thing gave them confidence—the unfailing support of the conservatory administration.

The two returned to a warm welcome in Vilnius. Jascha recounted everything to his mother, sisters, grandfather, uncle Isaac, aunt Sonia, cousin

Anyuta, and, of course, to Malkin. The young boy spoke vividly of the big new city, of his impressive new teacher, of the conservatory and its many students, and of the other people he met at the conservatory, including the scary hunchbacked music librarian, Mr. Fribus, whom the students nicknamed "The Diminished Fifth." After the excitement of his return home subsided, it was time for Jascha to begin working again; Nalbandian had given him a large program to prepare. Ruvin also began working once more in restaurant orchestras, café shows, and the orchestras in the Botanical Gardens and Bernardinsky Gardens. The family needed every kopeck they could find.

Two photographs from the summer of 1910 survive in the Heifetz archive, both with the note "Druskeniki."[37] Located about eighty miles from Vilnius, Druskeniki (Druskininkai in Lithuanian) was a popular holiday resort among St. Petersburg residents, offering baths, mineral springs, and mud-healing spas. Ruvin probably found performing work at the resort and took the family with him. During their time in Druskininkai, the Heifetzes stayed on Zelyonaya Street in the house of Ivan Sezenevsky; Jascha received a postcard at this address from Marusya Malkina, the daughter of his former teacher: "Dear Jaschenka! I was very glad to get your letter. Thank God that you are healthy and spending the time well. My exam went neither well nor badly. We often go to the Vileika . . . and went to gather strawberries. Oh, my back hurts terribly from bending for every berry."[38]

At the end of August, the Heifetz family returned to Vilnius, where Grandfather Israel awaited them. Jascha's aunt Sonia and cousin Anyuta were on a trip to Polotsk and sent a postcard dated September 22 congratulating the family on the Jewish New Year. On one side was a picture of Mozart and Beethoven, and on the other a message: "Greetings to you, dear ones! Congratulations on the New Year. I send my sincere greetings. I wish you blessings and peace, happiness, health, many years. I hope that Jascha will also get my congratulations, we wish him success from the bottom of our hearts. Everyone be healthy. Kiss Polinka and Elzinka. Greetings to all. Sonia Sharfstein."[39] Ruvin and Jascha had left Vilnius before the postcard arrived, since as stated on the leave certificate, they were needed back at the conservatory by September 10.

Jascha started the new academic year in category IX, "those studying for free in specialized classes and freed from additional payment."[40] His transfer to this new category probably occurred at the end of the spring semester—Glazunov kept his promise to ease the financial burden on the Heifetzes. Nevertheless, the dilemma of Ruvin's residency permit remained. In his memoirs, Leopold Auer described the subsequent course of events:

> Some one hit upon the happy idea of suggesting that I admit Jascha's father, a violinist of forty, into my own class, and thus solve the problem. This I did, and as a result the law was obeyed while at the same time the Heifetz family was not separated, for it was not legally permissible for the wife and children of a Conservatoire pupil to be separated from their husband and father. However, since the students were without exception expected to attend the obligatory classes in solfeggio, piano, and harmony, and since Papa Heifetz most certainly did not attend any of them, and did not play at the examinations, I had to do battle continually with the management on his account. It was not until the advent of Glazounoff, my last director, who knew the true inwardness of the situation, that I had no further trouble in seeing that the boy remained in his parents' care....[41]

Auer's account is essentially accurate; Ruvin was accepted as a student into the conservatory, which, for the time being, resolved the residency problem. Uncertainty, however, surrounds the origin of the idea for Ruvin to enroll as a student. In an interview published in 1978, Heifetz added to the widely held belief that Auer was responsible for accepting Ruvin into his class, but this appears to be inaccurate.[42] Documents from the period reveal that the idea for Ruvin to enroll as a student originated not with Auer, but with Nalbandian, his colleague Professor Aleksei Kolakovsky (1856–1912), and from Glazunov himself.

The first document pertaining to these events is a report on Ruvin's musical abilities submitted to the directorate: "Having listened to Mr. Heifetz Sr., we find him completely prepared for the upper course. I agree to accept him to my class as a non-paying student. Nalbandian. 1910, October 4." This was also signed by Kolakovsky, who was also a former Auer student. Kolakovsky graduated from the conservatory with a silver medal in 1877, began concertizing, worked at the Bolshoi Theater in Moscow and in 1906 became a professor at the conservatory. He was considered one of the best Russian violinists of the period. The report on Ruvin's abilities also includes a note from the director: "May be accepted into the IX [category], with the condition to take exams in January in elem[entary] theory, solfège 1 and 2. A. Glazunov. No need to collect the fee for the exam."[43] A few days later, Ruvin submitted a formal application to the conservatory:

> To the Director of the St. Petersburg Conservatory
> From the Polotsk *meshchanin* Ruvin Heifetz
>
> Request
> Wishing to receive a full music education and choosing for spec[ialized] training violin performance, I most humbly request you accept me as a student in the Conservatory; herewith I enclose my passport.
>
> 7 October 1910
> Ruvin Heifetz[44]

With the formalities observed, Ruvin attended an exam before a panel that included Glazunov and Arthur Lemba, a recent graduate in his second year of teaching at the conservatory. According to the exam record, Ruvin had a good ear and a good musical memory, but had no knowledge of solfège or elementary music theory.[45] He received a grade of 4 for his violin playing and was accepted into the upper course with Nalbandian in the non-fee paying category, just like his son.

Shortly after the exam, Ruvin received the much-awaited certificate granting him permission to rent an apartment, and so he and Jascha presented their certificates at the Kolomenskaya Police Station number 1 on Ofitserskaya Street.[46] Their new address was written on the reverse of the documents: Bolshaya Masterskaya Street, building 11–55, apartment 39.[47] From this point forward, both Jascha and his father could reside in the city without fear of deportation, although they would have to reestablish their right to residency every six months. As long as the two Heifetzes remained conservatory students, the process would be only a formality: turn in the old documents to the conservatory and take the updated replacements to the police station. These stamped certificates saved in the conservatory records provide a comprehensive account of the Heifetz family's addresses throughout their entire time in St. Petersburg.

Ruvin and Jascha remained in their new home throughout the autumn and winter of 1910–1911. Bolshaya Masterskaya Street passed near the conservatory and their previous apartment on Ofitserskaya Street. They moved into the corner building number 11–55 (now number 9–55). The most notable building on Bolshaya Masterskaya Street was (and still is) the synagogue located on the opposite side of the street. This colorful building is adorned by stained glass windows and topped with a stone cupola decorated with rich, ornamental carvings. Built in 1893 and designed by the architect Ivan Shaposhnikov, the Grand Choral Synagogue seated 1,200 people and functioned as the center of worship for the city's Jewish community. A Jewish vocational school was located nearby, making this area a center for St. Petersburg's entire Jewish population.

The Heifetzes attended the synagogue, especially on major holidays, but their general level of religious observance was not high, even during their time in Vilnius. It was often necessary to break the Sabbath when Jascha needed to prepare for exams or play a concert. As for many who arrived in St. Petersburg from the Pale, the practice of Jewish law took on a diminished form and was frequently limited to the declaration of Jewish heritage in the ubiquitous "religion" column found on all official Russian documents. During their time in St. Petersburg, the Heifetzes slowly drifted away from religious traditions. Once in the United States, Heifetz called himself Russian and felt himself to be Russian as well as Jewish. His home in Beverly Hills, for example, included an entire "Russian Room," with a samovar, a balalaika, and decorative Russian scarves. The gradual path to a largely secular attitude represented an inescapable inner loss, but Jascha's parents understood that their dream of a great musical career for their son demanded that he eschew the traditional and the religious for a largely secular education and lifestyle.

At the start of the new school year, Nalbandian assigned Jascha new pieces, including the Paganini Concerto in D. Written in 1811, the concerto existed in two editions by the start of the twentieth century, one by the Hungarian violinist and pedagogue Carl Flesch and one by the German violinist August Wilhelmj. Flesch's edition remains closer to the original and includes all three movements plus an added cadenza. In comparison, Wilhelmj kept only the first movement, enriched the orchestral harmonies, and added his own cadenza. The Wilhelmj edition appeared more frequently around the start of the twentieth century, both as student repertoire and in concert.[48]

As Auer himself wrote, a successful performance of this virtuosic concerto requires more than just perfect technique.[49] Nalbandian felt comfortable giving such a difficult piece to ten-year-old Jascha, who performed it in a concert of upper course students on November 5, 1910.[50] This performance previously escaped the notice of Heifetz researchers, who believed that Jascha first played the Paganini Concerto in 1915.[51] As an adult Heifetz never recorded the Paganini Concerto and played relatively little by this composer, but during the 1910s he played the concerto at least ten times.

Jascha's performance of the Paganini Concerto took place in the Maly Hall, with the accompaniment of Emanuel Bay (1891–1967), another conservatory student. There were no regular staff accompanists in the conservatory at the time, so talented piano students found themselves in constant demand. Although these piano students accompanied other musicians as part of their own ensemble study, they sometimes received a fee paid by the teachers. Pianist Nadezhda Golubovskaya studied in the conservatory during these years and recalled, "I did this kind of work for Iretskaya [a vocal teacher]. Twice a week I attended for two or three hours, during which they sang songs they had already learned."[52] According to Golubovskaya, teachers and instrumentalists often fought over the best piano students: "I was always glad when, meeting in the corridor, grabbing me by the shoulders, Auer would 'abduct' me to his classroom, where interesting acquaintances with violin literature awaited us—the concertos of Beethoven, Brahms, Spohr, Paganini, Bruch."[53] During the student concerts of 1910, other piano students who performed similar duties included Aleksandr Borovsky, Boris Zakharov, and Sergei Prokofiev.

Between 1909 and 1911, Emanuel Bay featured no fewer than fifteen times as an accompanist. A newspaper reviewer later noted his "beautiful touch, musicality and special ability as a talented accompanist."[54] Born on January 7, 1891 (OS), Bay was ten years older than Jascha and came from the lowest class.[55] His father Shlioma Bay was a peasant from the Kaunas region and lived in Łódź during the 1900s. In 1908, Bay graduated from the N. V. Muravlyov Commercial School in Warsaw and in doing so received a certificate awarding him the right to "honored citizenship"—a privileged class in the Russian Empire. Bay entered the St. Petersburg Conservatory the same year and graduated in 1913 with the Free Artist's diploma. He began performing as a concert pianist and in 1915 returned to the conservatory to study organ; he did so for only a year during which he was away frequently on long concert tours. Bay concertized after the 1917 revolutions, and in early 1918 he performed the Liszt Piano Concerto no. 1 with the State Orchestra conducted by Albert Coates. Bay accompanied the famous dancer Isadora Duncan during her residence in Moscow in the early 1920s and he emigrated to the United States shortly thereafter.[56]

At the conservatory, Jascha looked up to Bay, both literally and figuratively. They performed and recorded together many times after meeting again in the United States, although at this point the relationship was reversed, since by then Heifetz was already a star. Bay figured largely in Heifetz's adult career; between 1932 and 1954, the two musicians performed together many times and made over one hundred recordings. Thus, the student concert on November 5, 1910, was significant for a number of reasons: it was Jascha's first public concert at the conservatory, his first performance of Paganini, and his first concert with his future professional accompanist.

Two days later news came of the death of the famous author Leo Tolstoy, a long-time critic of the government and religious establishment. With that, the country entered a period of mourning. Government authorities responded by banning public demonstrations and vigils, and it was decreed that all concerts, performances, and shows were to continue without disruption in spite of the great author's passing. Attempts to cancel events resulted in a visit from a government official who forced organizers to sign a pledge stating that there would be no cancellations, and the police department ordered surveillance of all entertainment venues to ensure events proceeded as planned. Despite the best efforts of the police and authorities, many shows and concerts on the day of Tolstoy's death and burial were canceled, most under false pretense—"canceled owing to illness of the artists." A poster for the New Dramatic Theater, located next to the first Heifetz home on Ofitserskaya Street read, "November 9, on the day of committing the body of L. N. Tolstoy to the earth, the show is canceled." In a courageous act of civil disobedience, the conductor Serge

Koussevitzky included Chopin's Funeral March at the start of a symphony concert in the Hall of the Assembly of the Nobility. As a result, he was later forced to answer to the authorities.

A month later, on December 10, 1910, yet another event brought grief to the people of St. Petersburg. A major leader in the St. Petersburg Jewish community, Baron David Günzburg, died at the age of fifty-four following a prolonged illness. Günzburg was a polyglot, a writer, an orientalist, a philanthropist, and patron of the arts; most importantly, he was responsible for securing the necessary permissions to build the synagogue in St. Petersburg. Funeral delegations arrived from across Russia, and thousands came to pay their respects, including Dmitry Stasov, with whom Günzburg had worked as an orientalist, and the Town Governor General-Major Daniil Drachevsky, with whom the Baron had worked as a community activist, championing the interests and needs of the St. Petersburg Jewish community.

Between the deaths of Tolstoy and Günzburg, the arrival of the famous Austrian-born violinist Fritz Kreisler (1875–1962) brought welcome relief to the city. Kreisler's unique and individual style influenced almost every violinist of the twentieth century, including Heifetz. The first meeting between the two would take place only in the spring of 1912, but already in 1910 Kreisler was quickly becoming one of Jascha's idols. Opportunities to hear Kreisler were plentiful; from 1910 onward, Kreisler toured St. Petersburg and Moscow every season with solo recitals and also played in Koussevitzky's symphony concerts.

Jascha was proud that with the recalculation of dates to the New Style Gregorian calendar, he shared a birthday with Kreisler—February 2, and he was equally proud that the names Fritz Kreisler and Jascha Heifetz both contained thirteen letters. Coincidentally, both Kreisler and Heifetz lived a similar number of years—Kreisler eighty-seven, and Heifetz eighty-six. Kreisler began the violin at the age of three and entered the Vienna Conservatory at seven. He graduated with a gold medal and began studying at the Paris Conservatory before embarking on a tour of America at the age of thirteen. After years of study, Kreisler remained uncertain about his own future and was tempted by other professions. He ultimately decided on music, and performances in Berlin (1899) and America (1900) marked the start of his world fame.

Kreisler came to Russia first in 1893 and then in 1900 to perform in Moscow, but these performances received little attention in the press. His 1910 tour included both Moscow and St. Petersburg; the St. Petersburg part of the tour included three concerts in the Hall of the Assembly of the Nobility. Kreisler appeared on November 24, 1910, in a symphony concert conducted by Koussevitzky, performing the Beethoven and Conus concertos. The press reacted positively: "A first-rate artist appeared before the public . . . I will say even more: first of the first. He has not only an all-conquering technique, but both enormous musical talent and an unusual temperament, firing up the public."[57] The Russian press began to understand the subjective and improvisatory interpretations that constituted Kreisler's originality: "Such a performance amounts to a free arrangement, a performance 'transcription' of these works. Do not look for much from the composer in these performances. It is not a Bach sonata, but a sonata by Kreisler-Bach, not a Beethoven concert, but a concerto by Kreisler-Beethoven."[58]

Although Jascha idolized Kreisler, he did not blindly reproduce the style of the older master. Kreisler's primary influence on Heifetz's career revealed itself in the programming of short recital pieces. Kreisler's recital structure surprised many musicians in St. Petersburg at the time. His programs usually included one or two serious works followed by numerous short pieces more often found as encores. Kreisler's devotion to the miniature piece divided his audiences; some complained of a lack of substance. Nevertheless, Kreisler strove to communicate with an intimate and personal voice not limited by academic musical forms. This reflected the wider ideals of Russia's Silver Age—the period of rich artistic and aesthetic advances during the early twentieth century. For Jascha, the performance style and repertoire of the Austrian violinist became an early lesson in the aesthetic principles of the time.

Kreisler performed solo recitals in St. Petersburg that autumn on December 3 and 7, both in the Hall of the Assembly of the Nobility. Kreisler played many works of composers from the seventeenth and eighteenth

centuries, including Pugnani's Praeludium and Allegro, Martini's An-
dantino, Couperin's *Chanson Louis XIII* and Pavane, Porpora's Menuet,
Francoeur's Sicilienne and Rigaudon, and Tartini's Variations on a Theme
by Corelli. The press reacted positively: "In Kreisler's performance, such
simplicity, but yet they are so elegant and smooth; all of this grey antiquity
is resurrected and brought back to life."[59] These "baroque" miniatures soon
became integral to the repertoire of almost every Russian violinist, including Jascha, whose early concert programs looked almost identical to those
of Kreisler. All was not as it seemed, however, and in 1935 Kreisler finally
admitted to the world that the "baroque" pieces he had championed for
many years were not transcriptions of old violin works. They were his own
original compositions.[60] Attempting to explain one of the biggest hoaxes in
the history of music, Kreisler described how as a young man he had wished
to widen and diversify the violin repertoire with his own pieces, but feared
his audiences would be overly critical of a young violinist performing his
own works. Kreisler kept his secret from the entire music world for more
than three decades, and only a very few close friends knew of the hoax
beforehand—Efrem Zimbalist, Albert Spalding, and Jascha Heifetz.

Jascha's next performance came on December 9, 1910, during a conservatory music recital. The concert program contained an abundance of
factual errors.[61] Not for the first time, Jascha's surname was given as "Heifitz," and Jascha supposedly began with "Nocturne by Chopin-Scarlatti."
As composers from the turn of the seventeenth and eighteenth centuries, neither Alessandro nor Domenico Scarlatti could have transcribed a
piece written in the nineteenth century. The correct work, "Nocturne by
Chopin-Sarasate," is a transcription of Chopin's Nocturne in E-flat, op. 9,
no. 2. During his career, Heifetz played a number of Chopin nocturnes in
transcriptions by Wilhelmj, Auer, and by himself, and his first contact with
Chopin's music came at this student concert in 1910. This particular performance remained in the memory of those present, and eight decades later,
the pianist Aleksandra Bushen wrote: "However many years have passed,
I still cannot forget how this little boy performed at the student evening
[recital]. With such authentic inspiration and unique poeticism he unveiled
the inaccessible elegance and musical beauty of the Chopin Nocturne!"[62]

Over the coming few years, as Jascha's two sisters started to learn the piano, he became very familiar with the works of Chopin.

The second piece Jascha played that evening is described vaguely in the program as "Etude Paganini-Auer." Paganini wrote twenty-four caprices, but Auer made only one arrangement, of the famous twenty-fourth. This thrilling virtuosic arrangement by Auer appeared in Jascha's programs throughout his childhood in Russia. It featured at his Carnegie Hall debut as the final piece, and he continued to play it well into adulthood.

In December, various conservatory professors gave concerts in the Maly Hall. Auer performed three Brahms sonatas and three Beethoven sonatas, including the famous "Kreutzer," on his Stradivarius. Nalbandian's performance was accompanied by Emanuel Bay. Such concerts attracted large audiences and provided the students, including Jascha, with vivid examples to emulate.

CHAPTER FIVE

First Performances in St. Petersburg

JUDGING BY THE ABSENCE of a certificate of leave, without which conservatory students were unable to leave the capital, Ruvin and Jascha must have remained in St. Petersburg for the rest of December and into 1911. The cost of a return trip to Vilnius was likely prohibitive; thus, for the first time, Jascha spent the New Year's holiday far from his family and friends, but they did not forget about him. Marusya Malkina wrote, "Dear darling Jaschenka! I congratulate you on the New Year and wish you all the best."[1] Each new semester, however, brought another round of bureaucratic hurdles. On January 2, for instance, Jascha and Ruvin received their residency permit from the conservatory for the period up to June 1, 1911, and had to present their documents at the police station in order to receive a stamp for their apartment on Bolshaya Masterskaya Street.[2] On January 20, Jascha turned ten, and for the second time in his young life, spent his birthday away from home and extended family.

All the same, a number of significant events in Jascha's life took place during the first half of 1911. In April he gave his first solo concert in St. Petersburg and prior to that, he performed twice for groups of important people. According to an account based on talks with Jascha's parents, the boy played in St. Petersburg "for the Italian Consul in the presence of high-ranking persons, and also in the Court Orchestra."[3] The Court Orchestra was an impressive ensemble, and at various times it had been conducted by famous individuals such as Richard Strauss and Arthur Nikisch. The ensemble existed primarily to provide music for the Imperial Court, and events were arranged to please the members of the Tsar's family. Tiny Jascha with his golden hair and cherub-like appearance surely delighted all those in attendance. Generally, court concerts would take place either at Anichkov Palace or at another court building at 9 Yekaterininsky Canal, near the Church of the Savior on the Spilled Blood. In return for their performances, young prodigies generally received valuable gifts, such as gold pocket watches. It is uncertain whether Jascha received such a watch at this particular event, but it is known that as a child he had an impressive watch and was deeply upset when it was lost.

The only indication of a date for the appearance with the Court Orchestra is a handwritten note, "before April 17, 1911." A performance at the Italian Embassy, the evidence suggests, took place during the second half of March 1911, a period of celebration in Italy connected with the fiftieth anniversary of the declaration of Rome as the new capital. The Italian Embassy was located on Bolshaya Morskaya Street in a luxurious building constructed in the 1840s by the architect Auguste de Montferrand. The audience for Jascha's performance probably included various Russian and Italian diplomats. In a description of a similar private event where Jascha was asked to perform, Aleksandra Brushtein wrote:

> The ball started late as usual—the first guests began to assemble around midnight. The concert for guests, with the participation of N. N. Figner, A. M. Davydov, and other stars, began around one in the morning. The hostess, a beautiful young woman in Parisian evening dress, led a small boy in a sailor suit to the middle of the hall. Curly headed like a Raphael cherub, he sleepily rubbed his eyes with his fist—children of his age at that hour should have been fast asleep—with the other hand held his violin to himself. "Now gentlemen, Jaschenka will play for us!" the hostess announced merrily, "And then Jaschenka will have tea and cake!" This she said directly to the little boy.[4]

At the end of February 1911, Nalbandian left St. Petersburg for a few weeks on a tour of cities in the Poznansk and Reinsk provinces. He per-

formed works by Vitali, Cui, and Tchaikovsky, as well as his own compositions, and was accompanied by the pianist Samuil Maykapar and his wife,
the singer Nina Ormeli. On his return, lessons recommenced for Jascha,
who was busy preparing for his St. Petersburg recital debut scheduled for
April. Throughout this period, Ruvin and Jascha continued to correspond
with family and friends in Vilnius, describing their life in detail. Jascha
received a postcard from Marusya Malkina on March 22; one side had a
bust of Anton Rubinstein and on the other was a message: "Your success
makes me very happy, and even more so, that we will see each other soon. I
have already been sitting at home for several weeks, although I am already
better, but I am still not allowed to go out. I wish you the very best and
remain your deeply affectionate Marusya."[5]

A poster announcing Jascha's debut was approved by the censor:
"Maly Hall of the Conservatory. Afternoon Concert on April 17, 1911, of
the 10-year-old violinist Joseph Heifetz. Accompanied by E. Bay. Beginning at 2.30 in the afternoon. Tickets in Schroeder's store (Nevsky 52)."[6]
A few days before the debut, on April 15, the newspaper *Rech* printed a
poster with the upcoming program. The debut included some of Jascha's
favorite repertoire—the Mendelssohn Concerto, which he performed for
the first time in Kaunas in 1909, and the Andante and Finale from the
Wieniawski Concerto no. 2, which he had played for his graduation from
the music school in Vilnius. Other pieces included the Paganini Caprice
no. 24 and a new work, the demanding *Introduction and Rondo Capriccioso*
by Saint-Saëns.

The debut concert caused a sensation. Almost every newspaper in St.
Petersburg printed a response, from the financial bulletins to the sports
and theater papers. The exception was *Novoe vremya*, which, as a rule, ig-
nored Jewish artists. The *Peterburgskaya gazeta* critic Nikolai Bernstein
wrote: "From the very first bars of the Mendelssohn Concerto, one felt that
before the public stood without doubt a future star, who with continuing
development will once again glorify Russian art and our high musical tradition."[7] Grigory Timofeev continued the lofty tone in *Rech*:

> The poetic strength of talent already runs in a bright flowing stream. With
> such expressive character and with such remarkable passion the little vir-

tuoso played the finale, Allegro molto vivace, of the Mendelssohn Concerto, in its real tempo, observing all nuances of slowing down or speeding up, piano and forte, correct phrasing, without the slightest defect in rhythm and intonation. The boy's tone is quite full and not shallow, and his musicality is simply astonishing.[8]

The reviewers praised Jascha's performance but many found his instrument to be of inferior quality: "One must be surprised that the boy can to such an extent manage the instrument, as if in jest overcoming difficulties! . . . The boy's violin is not valuable, but he has such a tender tone that the defects of the instrument are not very noticeable."[9] Another critic wrote that "the whole program, regardless of the despairingly bad violin, was performed wonderfully by the talented child . . . his success is enormous and fully deserved."[10]

Newspapers noted that "it is necessary to speak a good word of Heifetz's teacher, Professor Nalbandian, polishing the talent that has fallen into his hands,"[11] and a reviewer for the *Obozrenie teatrov* newspaper, having heard Jascha in Vilnius two years earlier, observed that "his lessons with his new teacher, Professor Mr. Nalbandian, continue with much success and at a great pace."[12] Another positive outcome was reported by the *Peterburgskaya gazeta*: "In the conservatory circles they said that Auer not only changed his first opinion, but is even getting ready to take the young virtuoso into his own hands, or, more accurately, into his class."[13]

The weekly *Russkaya muzykalnaya gazeta* printed a review of Jascha's concert a week later. The author of this review was Viktor Valter (1865–1935), who became a close friend and advocate for the Heifetzes. Valter reviewed each and every performance Jascha gave in St. Petersburg. As a professional violinist trained in the Auer School, and as one of St. Petersburg's leading music critics, Valter's opinion is particularly noteworthy:

> On Sunday, April 17, the little Heifetz, a boy with the face of a Raphael angel, gave his first concert, which cannot be called anything other than a miracle. From a technical perspective, the boy's playing presented the height of perfection. He played pieces of the utmost difficulty (XXIV Capriccio of Paganini-Auer) with such lightness, fineness and clearness, which is possible only for first-class violinists. But even more notable were the warmth of expression and noble simplicity in the cantilena (Andante from the Mendelssohn Concerto)! It seemed that before us was not a real creature,

but an ethereal angel, a vision! . . . God grant that wise teaching manages to preserve this wonderful gift for the world.[14]

Conservatory records provide more insight into Valter's life. According to the certificate from the local rabbinate, Valter was born on February 10, 1865 (os), in Taganrog, and his father was a dentist. He graduated from the Physics and Mathematics department of Kharkov (Kharkiv) University in 1886, and in 1887, at age twenty-two, entered Auer's class at the conservatory. It was unusual for a student to begin classes at that age, and in 1889 Auer wrote the following about Valter: "Very good, he could have gone far had he not been of such an age; he is an exemplary student."[15] Although Valter did not become an international star violinist, after graduating in 1890, he worked for thirty years as soloist and concertmaster of the Mariinsky Theater Orchestra and as the first violinist in a quartet. As a chamber musician, Valter was highly respected in St. Petersburg musical circles and sometimes played at the home of Rimsky-Korsakov. In addition to performing, Valter wrote about music and published two books in 1912— one about the Beethoven string quartets and one about Richard Wagner. He also wrote violin method books and various opera handbooks. Valter worked as a music critic for various St. Petersburg newspapers from 1897 onward. In 1926, he recalled fondly the time he first met Jascha:

> I saw Jascha Heifetz for the first time in the winter of 1909/10 when his parents brought him to me to listen to his playing. On that day I was captivated forever by the boy. His playing in a technical sense was already then (he was nine years old) ideally perfect. But what astonished even more was the nobility in the emotional side of his playing. How could a nine-year-old boy have the ability to express feelings (Mendelssohn Concerto, Chopin Nocturne) which cannot be known at that age?[16]

Certain facts in Valter's 1926 recollections, however, are incorrect; the dates and repertoire contradict what is already known about Jascha's early studies in St. Petersburg. Back in 1911, Valter accurately reported that he "heard this boy for the first time at his concert on the 17th of April [1911]."[17] Valter quickly became a mentor to Jascha and an advisor to the rest of the Heifetz family; he helped the Heifetzes make important connections in the music world. Jascha developed a genuine attachment to Valter and felt a deep sense of gratitude for his support and friendship. Valter wrote about Jascha in his memoirs:

> The most surprising thing in the behavior of the child was his simplicity, naturalness and calmness. In a year the child was surrounded by admiration on all sides, but one could never sense any interest toward such delights in him; the question "are people looking at me or not" never occupied him. . . . Who could have taught the boy to behave that way? His father, a violinist in a small restaurant orchestra, and his mother—a beautiful woman whom Jascha resembled—were simple Jews, not having any concept of the "regal manner" before the public, which the boy Heifetz displayed (later) on stage.[18]

Shortly after Jascha's successful St. Petersburg debut, Ruvin sent a card, in Yiddish, to his older brother Morduch-Dov in Polotsk. The cover of the card carried a photograph of Jascha. The father's overwhelming pride in his young son permeates the entire message:

> My dear brother Mordechai-Dov, wife, and children, live in joy and happiness for many long years. Amen.
>
> Dear ones, excuse me for not immediately answering, because I was busy with my little son's brilliant concert. What I should tell you, dears, is that all of the St. Petersburg press wrote about Jasinka's present solo concert. All editors and reviewers are writing about Jasinka in all the Petersburg newspapers. I do not have the power to describe to you the furor which he has created among the Petersburg public. No artist in the world has ever had such a welcome as Jasinka, and the hall just thundered from the cries of the audience: "bravo" and "encore," and they could not get enough of his divine playing. In short, all the professors and public admit that he is unique in the whole world. Not just in Russia but in the whole world. They compare him with Mendelssohn, Mozart and Rubinstein. If you had only heard them, Jasinka [will have] many long years! Some even cried hearing his wonderful playing, and I also had tears pouring down. So it is, dears . . . you have a nephew. He is really beautiful, in a word. Heifetz, let him live for us for many years yet. All the professors sat as if enchanted by his playing. I still want to send you the reviews of the concert. . . . I will write to you about everything in detail. Jasinka greets you and all of yours. . . . How are you all doing in health? How is Tsirele? What is Yosif doing? We send greetings to them and to you all. . . . Well, how do you like your nephew? They are inviting him to London for 4 concerts. But I don't know if we will go, since we don't want to go so far with a child. . . . the exam is the 28th, and we will

leave right away [illegible]. I don't have a job for the summer. They are writing a biography of Jasinka in the journals "Solntse Rossii" and in "Niva." Write and, for the sake of your health, be as healthy as we are. All wishes to you from me. Your R. H.[19]

Morduch-Dov was connected throughout his life to Polotsk. According to his grandson Ilya Heifetz in Riga, Morduch-Dov had three children: Zalman (Solomon), whose descendants now live in Riga, and two daughters, the older of whom married the Yosif mentioned in Ruvin's letter, but died after bearing four children. Following her death, Yosif married Morduch-Dov's younger daughter Feyga, and she raised her older sister's children. Feyga and Yosif had a daughter of their own—Etya. Grandchildren from this branch of Morduch-Dov's family include Ruvim, a navy officer who served in the general headquarters, Roza, a doctor who lived and worked in Frunze (now part of Bishkek, in Kyrgyzstan), Simcha, the assistant director of an aviation factory in Bashkiria (now Bashkortostan), and Malka and Etya, who both lived in Omsk. Ruvin maintained regular contact with this side of his family, but their family archive was destroyed by fire in 1941 during the German occupation. The April 1911 postcard survived only because it was returned to Ruvin and is now saved in the Library of Congress. Letters in Yiddish from Ruvin to his Moscow relatives also survive, providing a fascinating view of a father astonished by the success of his son.

The annual exams for Nalbandian's class took place in the Maly Hall between April 18 and 28; Jascha played on the final day. The results appear in the enormous conservatory record book entitled: "Record of the Examination Committee Chairman."[20] Reactions to Jascha's performance attest to his continuing success. Glazunov wrote: "5 ++. Beyond competition." Nalbandian gave an even stronger response: "Talent by the grace of God, phenomenal success. I refuse to give a grade. I. Nalbandian." Next in the student list came Ruvin Heifetz, but since he did not take any exams, there were no grades or comments for him.

A few weeks after the exam, on May 13, Jascha performed his first St. Petersburg concert with orchestra in the concert hall at Pavlovsk Station, one of the city's most impressive venues. Summer music in St. Petersburg centered on Pavlovsk Station, which hosted a wide variety of music. By 1911, concerts at Pavlovsk Station were already in their seventy-fourth season. From its creation in 1838, the venue grew from just a restaurant with background music into a prominent musical center. Although concerts took place across the city, those at Pavlovsk Station traditionally commanded the most attention. Many famous names graced the Pavlovsk Station stage: from 1856–1866, Johann Strauss conducted the summer orchestra; in 1882 Eugene Ysaÿe performed the Mendelssohn Concerto; Nalbandian played in the orchestra during the 1890s; Auer performed there from the beginning of the twentieth century; the famous opera singers Fyodor Chaliapin and Leonid Sobinov sang there; and Glazunov frequently conducted the orchestra.

The Pavlovsk Station Symphony Orchestra, created by the Moscow Society for the Mutual Aid of Orchestral Musicians, consisted of seventy performers under the baton of Alexander Aslanov (Aslanian) (1874–1960). Aslanov conducted the summer symphonic seasons at Pavlovsk Station from 1910 until 1916. Between 1912 and 1913, Prokofiev performed the premieres of his first two piano concertos under the direction of Aslanov. In 1919 Aslanov departed for the United States, where he worked as a teacher and a conductor for productions by Russian choreographer and dancer Mikhail Fokin. In 1924 Aslanov published his recollections of meeting the young Heifetz in 1911:

> . . . I directed the symphony orchestra in Pavlovsk. Somehow one early morning a gentleman came to see me, introducing himself as the violinist Heifetz from Vilna. He had just arrived in St. Petersburg and asked me to listen to his son, a violinist, and if possible, to arrange a performance for him with the orchestra in one of the concerts. Then I turned my attention to the child who had come with his father, in appearance about nine or ten years old, and was immediately astonished at his marvelous beauty: red-cheeked, with light-blond curls to his shoulders and the hugest dark blue-gray eyes with long lashes. Usually these child prodigies give the impression of some kind of puny starvelings, but here was a child radiating health and cheerfulness.
>
> I asked him to play for me. After his father helped him tune his violin, the sounds of the Mendelssohn Concerto poured out. After a few bars, in which Jascha showed his tone, perfectly exceptional in its beauty, I stopped playing

the accompaniment, convinced that before me was a vast talent, talent still not fully polished, raw, but already shining with all the colors of authentic giftedness.

We settled on the day of the rehearsal and concert and payment for . . . twenty five rubles! The father of little Jascha was in ecstasy: finally his Jascha, the object of his love and pride, would perform in St. Petersburg in a big concert, with a big orchestra.[21]

The meeting between Aslanov and Ruvin was most likely arranged by a third party—perhaps Nalbandian or Valter—since it was unlikely that Ruvin simply arrived at the home of the conductor. In any case, Aslanov set about preparing for the concert. He invited many important musicians, including Glazunov, and alerted all the city newspapers to the special upcoming performance. Aslanov described how at the rehearsal the orchestra applauded enthusiastically, while the other violinists were left gaping, especially after the finale of the Mendelssohn Concerto, which Jascha took at a furious tempo. After the rehearsal, Jascha drank tea and Valter treated him to numerous pastries.

Programs from the Pavlovsk Station concerts are preserved in the library of the St. Petersburg Philharmonic. Each one bears a handwritten note about the day's weather and the soloist's fee. The note on the program for Jascha's concert on May 13, 1911, reads: "Dry. Very warm. Heifetz—50 rubles." Aslanov misremembered the actual fee, but even fifty rubles did not compare favorably with the money received by other established musicians; an average soloist at Pavlovsk Station received four times that figure, and fees for the biggest names stretched to many hundreds of rubles. Preserved alongside the printed program is a special advertising page with biographical information and a portrait of Jascha. Aslanov wrote that, "on the day of the concert, there was an unbelievable throng," and although general entry was free, there were 676 numbered seats, "separated by a railing from the unnumbered section." Tickets for the single concert ranged from between 10 and 25 kopecks, while season subscriptions cost between 15 and 25 rubles.

On May 13, all the numbered and unnumbered seats were full, and in addition to the Mendelssohn Concerto, Jascha played as an encore David Popper's challenging cello piece *La Fileuse,* arranged for violin by Auer. The event was a huge success with the St. Petersburg press:

At the end of the second half a little boy came out onto the stage, scrambled up onto the conductor's platform, and everyone laughed—some enthusiastically and others just good-naturedly. Someone even called out "You ended up in the wrong place, little boy!" He very much wanted to perform the Mendelssohn Concerto, but this wish was criticized, since people thought the famous concerto was not for 10-year-old children! There were, of course, also those in attendance who had seen Heifetz's recent concert, and knew what kind of talent they were about to witness. . . . In any case, before us was a rich talent, in the good hands of Mr. Nalbandian. He immediately humbled the Pavlovsk audience, almost with one bar. And of course, when he had calmed the whirlwind of the Mendelssohn Finale Presto, then the Pavlovsk adults came right up to the boy and examined him. Perhaps some carried out anthropometric measurements on him? . . . I congratulate the boy . . . on his complete victory.[22]

Reports of Jascha's success soon reached Vilnius, where the proud *Severo-zapadny golos* printed: "the young violinist from Vilna, J. Heifetz, after graduating from the local music school and entering the St. Petersburg Conservatory, performed the other day in Pavlovsk before a large audience and inspired a resounding ovation with his performance of the Mendelssohn Concerto."[23] In the St. Petersburg press, Valter compared Jascha with some of the greats: "I can with confidence say that Heifetz shows himself to be a phenomenon of that same category to which belong Anton Rubinstein and Franz Liszt, that is, to the category of geniuses."[24] In 1923, Valter cited this same review in his published response to a concert of the then seventeen-year-old Dmitry Shostakovich, sensing in the young composer the same "joyful and calm confidence of genius."[25] Valter was one of the first to predict a bright future for Heifetz—he was also probably the first to describe Shostakovich as a genius. The paths of Heifetz and Shostakovich first intersected during the early 1920s, when Valter arranged for the world-famous violinist to send financial aid to young Shostakovich in cold and deprived Petrograd. Heifetz and Shostakovich later met in 1934 when Heifetz visited the Soviet Union.

The noteworthy events of the spring of 1911 continued in May, when Jascha made his first gramophone records. An announcement appeared on June 25 in the St. Petersburg magazine *Grammofonny mir*:

The representative of a new foreign company, which sells its gramophone records under the "Zvukopis" label, recently managed to record the famous bass S. Shumov . . . and thirteen-year-old singer Katyusha Sorokina. . . . Also recorded was the remarkably successful young violinist Jascha Heifetz, a portrait of whom we include in this edition.[26]

Jascha's records appear in the Zvukopis catalog as numbers 215 to 220 and include a variety of short pieces: François Schubert's *The Bee,* Kreisler's *Caprice Viennois,* Dvořák's *Humoresque,* Auer's Romance, and Drdla's *Souvenir* and *Serenade.*[27] François Schubert (1808–1878), known as "the Dresden Schubert" to avoid confusion with the famous Franz Schubert, published his short *moto perpetuo* piece, *The Bee,* in 1856. The work was popular at the start of the twentieth century and still appears in student repertoire today. The Czech composer and violinist František Drdla (1869–1944) wrote his miniature pieces based on popular folk songs and enjoyed wide recognition and success during his lifetime. Of all the works Jascha recorded in 1911, only the Dvořák *Humoresque* remained in his repertoire later in life.

The Zvukopis record company opened its St. Petersburg factory and main offices in April 1911.[28] The owners initially planned to name the company Svetopis, but by the middle of May, the final name of the company was determined. *Grammofonny mir* published the following announcement: "Urgent telegram! Coming Soon—new Russian two-sided discs of original 'Zvukopis' recordings will appear for sale. The factory and main office for 'Zvukopis' gramophone discs—St. Petersburg, Voznesensky Pr[ospekt], 18. Representative S. A. Zhitlovsky."[29] Many other record companies appeared in Russia at this time, including Pathé Records, Syrena, Orpheon, and Metropol-Records, but the most important was the English company Gramophone, which had opened its factory in Riga around 1902. Gramophone advertised hundreds of recordings during this period, including those by violinists including Fritz Kreisler, Joseph Szigeti, Willy Burmester, and Mischa Elman.

Despite the strong competition, Jascha's Zvukopis recordings sold well. Nevertheless, very few examples of the recordings survive today. Preserved in the Russian State Archive of Recorded Documents in Moscow is a two-sided Zvukopis record with Jascha's recording of *Caprice Viennois* (no. 216) on one side and a recording of Wieniawski's *Obertas* performed by the now unknown violinist V. I. Zeilinger (no. 234 in the catalog) on the other.[30]

The Zvukopis disks are significant not only because they were Heifetz's first recordings; for the first time in print, the name Joseph was replaced with Jascha. The complete label reads: "Performed by: Jascha Heifetz, 10-year-old violinist-virtuoso."[31] The idea might have come from Zhitlovsky, noticing that other successful child prodigies went by the diminutive forms of their names—*Mischa* Elman, *Katyusha* Sorokina, *Sasha* Dubyansky.[32] The diminutive form emphasized the youth of the performer and helped to draw the public's attention (and sell records). Posters still referred to "Joseph" Heifetz for the next few concerts, but before long, the name Jascha appeared on all programs, posters, and reviews, and the name Joseph was soon forgotten. Shortly thereafter, yet another Auer student followed this same strategy; Anton Seidel became Toscha Seidel.

At home, Heifetz was called Jascha, and family and friends used other similar diminutives for him. Since Jascha is traditionally the diminutive form associated with the name Jacob (Yakov), rather than Joseph (Yosif), some references to the name Jacob also appear in print, particularly in early concert reviews and correspondence. It remains unclear why Jascha's parents called him by the diminutive of Yakov and not that of Yosif. In later years, unlike Elman and Seidel, Heifetz distanced himself from his first name, preferring to go by "Mr. Heifetz," "Mr. H," or just "Heifetz." Only a very few close friends were allowed to call him Jascha.

Summer vacation loomed, and with it a chance to see family and friends back in Vilnius. One person in particular who missed Jascha was Marusya Malkina. She sent a heartfelt postcard to St. Petersburg:

My dear darling Jaschenka!
  Why don't you write to me? Are you angry at me? What is this? Have I somehow not pleased you? Or do you just not want to talk to me? Since the time that you left for St. Petersburg, you have completely changed! You don't want to have anything to do with me. I wait and wait for a letter, and can't wait anymore.... [33]

CHAPTER SIX

Summer 1911: Concerts in Pavlovsk and Odessa

THE HEIFETZES SPENT THEIR SUMMER vacation at a dacha in Antakalnis, one of the twenty-six suburbs of Vilnius and a popular area during the summer. A local guidebook from the period described it as follows: "Heading along the bank of the Viliya to the Church of St. Peter and Paul, one can stop in the suburb of Antokol which stretches along the Viliya for almost three *versts*. Scattered hills to the right of the church are covered with beautiful green pine forests. Not far from there is the Sapezhinsky Garden and Palace . . ."[1] The Heifetz family stayed at 9 Petropavlovsk Lane, in a house belonging to a man named Pyotr Guryanov.

The Heifetzes were joined by their young cousin Anyuta Sharfstein-Koch during their summer retreat. Some eight decades later in a phone conversation, Sharfstein-Kochremembered fondly her time with the Heifetz siblings in the hills outside Vilnius. Elza showed her the chickens laying eggs and Pauline took her up to Jascha's room in the house: "He was busy at the table with all these dead butterflies. . . . I said to him, 'Where did you get all those butterflies?' And he said he'll show me. And he went out and he was running with the net after the butterflies. Can you visualize it? Running after butterflies with a net!" Butterfly catching became a widespread and fashionable hobby during the beginning of the century, and one could often find children and adults alike running through the countryside with nets chasing the colorful insects.

"And we went upstairs," Sharfstein-Koch recalled, "and [Jascha] showed me he had a board—a cork board with pins and he took the butterflies and he was sticking them with pins. Then he said when they dry up, he puts them in a special box—a glass box, which you then hang up on the wall. And that was a regular thing. He had a couple of boxes with various bugs and butterflies. It amused me for a while." Sharfstein-Koch then added, "I was born in the city, so anything happening in the country was interesting to me (the chicken interested me more than the poor butterflies)."[2] Butterfly catching gave Jascha an early connection with the world around him, stimulating a life-long appreciation for nature and the outdoors.

Around this time, another phenomenon capturing the imagination of the public—not least that of a little boy—was aviation. The Wright brothers were becoming famous around the world for their winged creations, and the Frenchman Louis Blériot had made the channel crossing between France and England. In Russia, aviators such as Gakkel, Grigorovich, Slesarev, and Steglau were also developing original aircraft. Fame surrounded the brave men who risked their lives to pilot these new flying contraptions. One popular Russian aviator named Sergei Utochkin held flight demonstrations in various Russian cities. Utochkin was an all-around athlete: a swimmer, fencer, wrestler, and boxer. Between May and June 1911, Utochkin showcased flights in the Baltic region, and he also appeared in Vilnius at the Hippodrome of the Racing Society in Antakalnis-Pospeshki, close to the Heifetz family's summer residence. Local newspapers followed the events closely, and in Vilnius Utochkin completed his eighty-seventh and eighty-eighth flights—a record number at the time. For a generation of youth of Russia, including young Jascha, Utochkin became an idol.

Meanwhile, Ruvin continued to take care of logistical matters related to Jascha's career. Following the invitation to Jascha from London, which Ruvin turned down on account of the distance, another arrived in June, from the management of the Odessa Exhibit (Odessa Factory-Plant, Industrial-Artistic and Agricultural Exhibit). The Odessa Exhibit took place in 1910 and 1911, and was run by the local branch of the Imperial Russian Technical Society and the Imperial Agricultural Society of the South of Russia, and it included outdoor symphonic concerts. Unsure of how to respond to the Odessa invitation, Ruvin turned to Viktor Valter for advice:

> Vilna, 16 June 1911
>> Dear Honorable Viktor Grigoryevich!
>> On June 14th I received a letter from Odessa, which I am sending to you. I am very grateful to you for your efforts on behalf of my son and I am turning to you with the request to advise me how to answer Mr. W. Israel, or would you be so kind as to write to him yourself, for it is impossible to go there for so small an honorarium, but at the same time, in my opinion, it is important to give a couple of concerts in Odessa at the time of the exhibit. On June 30 of this year, Jascha is playing at Pavlovsk for 100 rub. plus 50 rub. travel allowance, and considering it is a benefit concert for the orchestra, I cannot refuse them. He will play the Glazunov Concerto and moreover, the composer himself will be the accompanist. I beg you, respected Viktor Grigoryevich, forgive me for the trouble, but I do not have anyone to turn to for real advice and, knowing you as the best sort of person, who up to now has done much for us, I dare to disturb you and I hope you will not leave my request unattended. Sincere greetings to your wife and children, and also greetings to you from my wife and children. With respect, yours truly, R. Heifetz.
>
> Our address: Vilna, Antokol, Petropavlovsk Lane, no. 9 dacha of P. Guryanov, for R. H.[3]

Mikhail Wolf-Israel (1870–1934), mentioned in the letter, was a violinist, conductor, teacher, and former Auer student at the St. Petersburg Conservatory. From 1892, Wolf-Israel worked as assistant concertmaster of the Mariinsky Theater Orchestra, sitting next to Viktor Valter. In the summer of 1911, Wolf-Israel accepted an extra job as the symphony orchestra conductor at the Odessa Exhibit. After receiving Ruvin's letter, Valter did write to Wolf-Israel and also sent Ruvin advice on the payment issues.

The other side of the page from Ruvin's correspondence contains a letter written to Valter from Jascha, his handwriting carefully following the pencil-ruled lines. This short charming letter is the earliest existing example of Jascha's writing, and judging by the content, Jascha probably received some help from his parents:

Much Respected Viktor Grigoryevich!

Forgive me for not writing to you till now. We live at the dacha not far from Vilna. From Vilna you have to go in a cab or horse-drawn buggy. We have a very nice dacha. I am on vacation now, and only practicing violin and piano a little bit. I am now studying the Tchaikovsky Concerto and the Handel Sonata. I thank God that I am healthy and feel very good. How are you, dear Viktor Grigoryevich? How is your health? How is everyone by you? Heartfelt greetings to all of yours, and also to Tsarskoye, if you will write there. Kisses to you all.

Joseph Heifetz[4]

As the letters from the Heifetzes reveal, Jascha spent June working on three new pieces—the Tchaikovsky Concerto, a Handel Sonata, and the Glazunov Concerto, in preparation for a concert at the end of the month. Jascha performed the Tchaikovsky and Handel works in the following spring, and it is likely he played those works in his autumn audition for Auer.

On June 26, an announcement appeared in the Vilnius press: "A concert of the young virtuoso Joseph Heifetz (violin) and Gustav Katz (cello) will take place in the near future at the Druskeniki Concert Hall."[5] Jascha had visited there the previous summer, but for whatever reason, it appears this concert never took place—no further information or reviews appeared in print, and in any case, by the end of June the Heifetzes were back in St. Petersburg preparing for Jascha's concert in Pavlovsk Station.

On June 30, the day of the benefit concert featuring Jascha, the concert organizers were forced to postpone the event because of the burial of Grand Duchess Alexandra Yosifovna, the great-aunt of Nicholas II; all entertainment was forbidden during the period of state mourning. A sheet of paper found between the programs in the archive reads: "30 June. Damp. Cool. There was no music."[6] The rescheduled performance took place on July 2, and since Glazunov was unable to attend, Jascha did not perform the composer's concerto. In addition to the first movement of the Mendelssohn Concerto, the program included Aslanov and his orchestra, as well as the ballerina Olga Preobrazhenskaya and famous dramatic artists from St. Petersburg. According to reports, the weather that day was rainy. In later years, Anna Heifetz would frequently boast that the weather was never bad on the days of her son's performances, but of course this belief was the result of motherly pride rather than actual weather patterns.

The critics at Pavlovsk Station were impressed by the young violinist, but not enthralled overall with the event. The reviewer for *Rech*, Vyacheslav Karatygin, described the "pitiful, but fairly usual picture of summer benefits." Karatygin frequently questioned the presentation of child performers, and, for now at least, saw Jascha as more of an attraction than a serious artist. "It was yet again curious," Karatygin wrote, "to wonder at the virtuosity and confidence with which the young wunderkind Mr. Heifetz plays the most difficult things in the violin literature."[7]

The opportunity to perform at Pavlovsk Station was a great honor and privilege for any musician, especially one as young as Jascha, and the venue became deeply woven into the St. Petersburg period of his life. In his postcard collection, Jascha collected many scenes from Pavlovsk Park. The image of Pavlovsk Station and its beautiful surroundings encapsulated the poetic fabric of the Silver Age in Russia, and it became the subject of a poem, "Concert at the Railway Station," by the famous Russian poet of the era Osip Mandelstam: "... and again the violin-laden air is sundered ... and fused together by the whistles of trains."[8]

Jascha continued his vacation back in Vilnius with his family. The nearby botanical gardens screened films during this time, and Vilnius residents flocked to witness this exciting new entertainment. This period saw the rise of Max Linder, the highly influential pioneer of silent film, whose comedies included *Max and his Dog, Max Takes Tonics,* and *Max Hypnotized.* Linder's comedies attracted large audiences of all ages, and it is possible that this was Jascha's first experience with film. Cinematography remained an important theme throughout Heifetz's life. When he grew a little older, he often acted out costumed scenes with his sisters that featured dramatic poses in the style of the silent era. After arriving in the United States, he purchased an early film camera and filmed many of the costumed scenes with his sisters.[9] Heifetz had numerous friends and acquaintances in the movie world, including Charlie Chaplin, and his first wife Florence Vidor was a former silent movie star. Heifetz also appeared as himself in a number of films, including *They Shall Have Music* (1938) and *Carnegie Hall* (1947).

In early July, Ruvin wrote again to Valter, who had also left St. Petersburg and was staying with his family in Shebekino, in the Kursk province:

Vilna, 13 July 1911
Deeply Respected Viktor Grigoryevich!
We received the letter which you sent about Mr. Wolf-Israel's letter, but we have not written to you since then because we were waiting for an answer from Odessa. I wrote to Mr. Wolf-Israel immediately, as soon as I received your answer, and proposed to him the conditions as you advised, but I have not received any answer, and therefore did not write to you, and the letter, which you received (from Vilna), is not from us. We, thank God, are healthy. Jascha sends his heartfelt regards, as do my wife and the girls. We can in no way thank you enough for being so interested in us. Sincere regards to all of yours. Jascha is now playing the Tchaikovsky Concerto and also Eron-grois and many other good things, and he performs all these concertos rather well. Good health to you all.
Respectfully yours, R. Heifetz.[10]

The long-awaited Wolf-Israel letter from Odessa arrived the next day, and Ruvin wrote back to Valter:

Deeply Respected Viktor Grigoryevich!
Just today I received a letter from Odessa. They agreed to our terms and ask us to come for two concerts for a hundred rub. and for the journey there and back a hundred rub., so 300 rub. in all, and with the condition that if the boy is a success, then they have the right to keep him for another one or two concerts with the same pay, and they've asked that we come to Odessa right away. The last condition I do not like especially, but I do not know what to do. All the same, I think we should go.
Respectfully yours, R. Heifetz[11]

Jascha added his own greeting to Valter at the bottom of the page: "I send my heartfelt regards to you, respected Viktor Grigoryevich and all of your family. I am doing well, I walk and swim and practice a little. How are you all doing? I wish you the very best, with all my soul. Lovingly yours, J. Heifetz."

A few days later they began the seven-hundred-mile journey to Odessa. This was Jascha's first extended train trip, and for the first time both Ruvin and Anna accompanied him, leaving Pauline and Elza in Vilnius with the Sharfsteins. The monotony of the long journey was broken up by numerous stops and transfers, during which snacks and drinks were usually available on the platforms. Three days into the journey, views of the majestic Black Sea heralded the train's imminent arrival. Odessa was the capital of the Kherson province, and in terms of population, ranked as the fourth largest city in the Russian Empire after St. Petersburg, Moscow, and Warsaw (then part of the Russian Empire). By the start of the century, Odessa was a colorful and diverse city, known for its multitude of luxurious buildings, its granite- and limestone-paved streets, and its ever-expanding port.

Jascha and his parents stayed at the Hotel Passage, one of twenty first-class hotels in Odessa, located in the city center on the boulevard section of Preobrazhenskaya Street, one of Odessa's most beautiful areas. The neighborhood around the hotel included the New Russian University, the extensive City Gardens, the Cathedral and Cathedral Square, and a monument to Prince Vorontsov. Concert life in Odessa mirrored that of other provincial Russian cities. Events included a preponderance of chamber music evenings, as well as regular visits by famous artists from St. Petersburg and Moscow and from abroad. Unlike many other provincial cities in the Russian Empire, Odessa boasted a popular series of affordable symphony concerts.

The Odessa Exhibit stretched along Mikhailovskaya Square in the Moldavanki neighborhood, and concerts took place in the outdoor summer theater that had a covered stage and could hold an audience numbering in the thousands. The orchestra included musicians from the City Orchestra, which usually performed in the City Gardens, under the direction of Wolf-Israel. Most of the ten summer concerts staged before the Heifetzes arrived in Odessa featured Wolf-Israel as conductor, but he attracted some negative criticism: "The Exhibit concerts this season are lacking almost any interest," wrote the Odessa correspondent for the *Russkaya muzykalnaya gazeta*. "The main reason for this is Mr. M. A. Wolf-Israel, apparently completely by chance ending up behind the conductor's stand, for his complete incompetence was revealed from the very first concerts."[12] The conductor was rebuked for his lack of interpretative understanding, his sloppy attention to detail, and for posturing seen as unworthy of any serious musician. Yosif Pribik, already in his second decade working at the Odessa Opera Theater, took turns with Wolf-Israel to direct the orchestra. Unlike the exhibit concerts conducted by Wolf-Israel, those under Pribik received praise from both the public and the critics, particularly for the performances of new music, including the Saint-Saëns Symphony no. 3 as well as works by Elgar and Stanford. In addition to Wolf-Israel and Pribik, other touring conductors directed the orchestra, among them were Zinovy Kogan, Eugene Plotnikov, Ariy Pazovsky, and Nikolai Malko.

Advertisements for Jascha's concert appeared in the local press on July 19 and 21: "The Exhibit Committee has invited for today's symphony concert two celebrities: the famous Moscow conductor E. E. Plotnikov, and a rising star—ten-year-old violinist-virtuoso J. Heifetz.... Why not come to the Exhibit?"[13] The conductor Plotnikov figured prominently in Russian musical life. In the 1900s he directed the ballet orchestra for the Bolshoi Theater and from 1911 headed the Zimin Moscow Opera Theater Orchestra. In 1918 Plotnikov left Russia, and in 1922 he settled in the United States. He conducted performances of Russian operas with Fyodor Chaliapin in New York and in 1934 became the conductor of the New York Symphony Orchestra.

In addition to the performance of the Mendelssohn Concerto with Jascha, Plotnikov and his orchestra played various works by Tchaikovsky. According to the press, the conductor displayed "great erudition, rare composure, wonderful interpretation of the music, great and noble temperament."[14] Both Jascha and Plotnikov received praise for the performance of the Mendelssohn Concerto:

> The soloist for the evening was little violinist Heifetz, about whom so many miraculous things were written in St. Petersburg. He sharply differs from all other precociously maturing talents, from children, who reason like adults. Heifetz plays like a child, like a phenomenal, surprising child. He is, they say, ten years old, and in his playing there is something pure, simple, light, not knowing life and the world. He plays the Mendelssohn Concerto, difficult even for adults, and these difficulties are not noticeable. He performs it with unusual, almost naïve artistic simplicity, and this moves one almost to tears.... It is just a shame that many small details of the performance are lost on the open stage.[15]

Local newspapers wrote about Jascha and his concert. After announcing July 29 as a children's holiday, with costumes and a parade, a local newspaper related the following charming story:

The prominent violinist Heifetz is after all still a child, and nothing childish is alien to him. One episode with him during the time of his first concert set all the exhibit organizers laughing. "I need a ticket to the children's holiday," he told Mr. Van Der Schkroof, a member of the "entertainment" commission. "They will just let you in," was the answer. "I need it, or they might not let me in," insisted the violinist, to whom that evening a crowd of several thousand would give a standing ovation.[16]

Plotnikov and Jascha performed only one concert together; the conductor received a telegram from Moscow summoning him for other rehearsals. Jascha's second concert scheduled for July 26 took place under Wolf-Israel's direction and featured works Jascha knew well: the Wieniawski Concerto no. 2, Paganini Caprice no. 24, and Saint-Saëns *Introduction and Rondo Capriccioso*. "Yesterday's second concert by J. R. Heifetz attracted a mass audience to the Exhibit—around 5,000 people," reported the *Odesskie novosti*. "All the places under cover and also the enormous space around the covered stage were overflowing with people. Heifetz's performance of the Paganini Caprice and the Saint-Saëns evoked enthusiastic applause not only from among the audience, but from members of the orchestra directed by M. A. Wolf-Israel. When J. Heifetz left the stage, accompanied by his parents, the audience gave him a standing ovation."[17]

Local newspapers vied with each other in their coverage of Jascha's "artistic career." They focused on the boy's studies at the conservatory and mentioned that his teachers considered a grade of 5 to be insufficient for his achievements. The *Odesskie novosti* reported:

Soon Joseph Heifetz and his parents will leave for Vilna, where they will stay at their dacha until September, and then they will return to St. Petersburg. The parents do not intend to exploit their amazing son's talent. They refused eight concerts offered to him in London and also declined all offers from many southern provincial cities. Even the offer from Odessa they accepted only after receiving advice from the music critic, Professor Valter: "It would do no harm for the people of Odessa to become acquainted with Joseph Heifetz."[18]

Jascha's contract stipulated that in the event of a successful performance in Odessa, further concerts could be added, and an open slot did appear in the schedule:

The Exhibit committee held telegraph negotiations concerning the participation of the famous soloist Arthur Rubinstein, but yesterday the committee received an answer from A. Rubinstein that he is unable to come to Odessa at this time. In light of this, and taking into account the enormous interest of the Odessa public in the young violinist-virtuoso J. Heifetz, the committee has proposed that the young artist take part in a concert on July 28.

The Heifetzes agreed, and Jascha played in Odessa for the third time, now under the direction of Wolf-Israel, who once again received negative press: "If only everything had been cleaner, more well-studied and prepared, and if only one could have had the impression that one was attending a concert rather than a rehearsal." As an accompanist, Wolf-Israel evoked further irritation: "Mr. Wolf-Israel apparently has little experience with accompanying. His accompaniment holds the performer in constant tension. And misunderstandings in the second part of the Wieniawski, when J. Heifetz played, and in the second part of the Mendelssohn, when Mr. Bretanitsky played, were even more surprising, because Mr. Wolf-Israel is himself a good violinist and knows these pieces by heart!"[19] The public, however, seemed willing to forgive the faults of the conductor, focusing on the "child with the face of a cherub and soul of an artist." As the press reported, the "symphony concert by the young violinist Joseph Heifetz attracted an enormous mass audience to the Exhibit grounds—around 8,000 people."[20]

Jascha performed in Odessa for the fourth and final time on July 31 in a benefit concert held for Wolf-Israel. As was traditional for such concerts, many performers participated, including musicians from St. Petersburg, such as the pianist Esfir Chernetskaya-Geshelina and the soloist of the Imperial Russian Opera, Yelena Katulskaya. Both Wolf-Israel and Pribik conducted the orchestra. Accompanied by the pianist A. Nemirovsky, Jascha performed the Paganini Caprice no. 24 and a Chopin Nocturne. The event concluded with a performance of the *Symphonic Duet for Two Violins* by Jean-Delphin Alard. Jascha probably learned the final piece specifically for this event; he played the first violin part and Wolf-Israel the second. The press reacted with delight: "Sunday's festivities at M. A. Wolf-Israel's benefit concert was very successful. The public numbered over 10,000 people. The beneficiary (Wolf-Israel) was presented with a silver laurel wreath and many flowers. Admirers also brought the young violinist-virtuoso J. Heifetz a wreath, a large portrait of him in an elegant frame, a basket of flowers and a box of candy."[21] A reviewer for the *Odesskie novosti* wrote:

> I likely will never forget the remarkable impression made by Heifetz's playing. The crowd thronged the space before the stage, the spaces under the awning, the additional seats continuing endlessly, and the chairs. Everyone froze; the spirit of the genius captivated the crowd, which had just a minute before been bustling and indifferent. All that is painful, that we sometimes cannot part with, all that often troubles, frightens us, that persistently torments us—vanished somewhere. Such serene impressions as given by this little boy are possible only in the blissful dreams of childhood.[22]

Without doubt, the trip to Odessa proved a huge success, and newspapers as far away as Warsaw, Vilnius, and St. Petersburg all reported on the growing excitement surrounding the young violinist. The reports recounted the events and also discussed the boy's earnings from his concert, for whatever he received was significantly less than the committee made from the huge audiences he attracted. The *Solntse Rossii* reported on how Jascha had nearly interrupted a concert, a comical incident highlighting the boy's youthfulness: "[Jascha] went onto the stage and out of the blue began to beat on a drum while the orchestra was still playing."[23]

The Yiddish-language Odessa newspaper *Gut-morgn* wrote about Jascha's grandfathers and their love of singing, especially in the synagogue, and reported that Jascha "is now studying general subjects and Yiddish, prays every day, reads a great deal and has a very fine library. In quiet moments he likes to devote himself to Jewish folk songs."[24] Evidently, the newspaper interviewed Ruvin, and in response to the question, "How does Jascha feel when he performs in front of the public?" Ruvin answered, "Quite good. He's already used to it. And the more people there are, the better he feels."[25]

The performances in Odessa left an impression not only on the young violinist, but also on the history and folklore of the city itself. Heifetz appears in Isaac Babel's 1931 story "Awakening," in which the author presents little Jascha Heifetz as a musical miracle in whose image Odessa parents struggled to mold their own children, putting them in "a factory that churned out child prodigies, a factory of Jewish dwarfs in lace collars and patent leather shoes."[26] Babel's autobiographical story depicts the author resisting the expectation from his father that he, too, would become a musician. The young Babel dreamed of other more literary pursuits, but was forced to practice: "Sounds scraped out of my violin like iron filings. These sounds cut even into my own heart, but my father would not give up.... The child prodigies brought wealth to their parents. My father was prepared to resign himself to a life of poverty, but he needed fame."[27] Babel describes how his father bumped into Jascha's "Uncle Mendelson" who told him that the boy was paid eight hundred rubles per concert. Babel's father exclaimed to his family: "So go ahead and add up how much that comes to at fifteen concerts a month!"[28]

Babel's story takes many liberties with facts and chronology. For example, among the child prodigies of Odessa, he included Ossip Gabrilowitsch, who was actually from St. Petersburg, and Efrem Zimbalist, who was born in Rostov-on-Don. The reference to an uncle in Odessa named Mendelson is simply fictional. Ultimately, the story serves less as a factual report on the period than as an insight into the general atmosphere of Odessa life, of which the name Heifetz became an integral part.

During the early part of the century, Odessa was home to the prominent violin teacher Pyotr Stolyarsky (1871–1944), who, like Auer, produced a number of world-famous violinists, including David Oistrakh, Boris Goldstein, and Nathan Milstein. Milstein later also studied with Auer. Oistrakh was only three years old at the time of Jascha's performances in the city, but the young Milstein was in attendance and later wrote about his recollections:

One fine day (this must have been in 1911; I was still seven years old), Mama announced, "We're going to a concert today. The wunderkind Jascha Heifetz is playing." ...
Jascha Heifetz's concert was at the old Turkish fortress, in the open air. I remember the ornate Moslem arches and the embrasures for the cannons. It was summer and very hot. People sat at tables, eating and drinking. There were lamps on the tables. Flies swarmed all around, fighting for a spot on the lamps. A captivating sight. The flies were so numerous that even without buzzing they made noise!"[29]

Although Milstein remembered relatively little of the actual event, certain aspects stood out:

> Little Heifetz came out. I think he played concertos by Mendelssohn and Paganini; I can't swear to my accuracy. In fact, I have no memories of Jascha's playing, and I'm not about to make them up now. To be honest, I paid more attention to the flies than to the performance. But I do remember how Jascha looked: a real angel! A curly haired blond in a sailor suit, short pants, and knee socks. He was so beautiful! . . . Mama and Papa, like the rest of the audience, were delighted by little Jascha's playing.[30]

Unaware of the trouble he would cause future generations of young violinists in Odessa and elsewhere, Jascha enjoyed his time off from the Odessa Exhibit exploring the city and its sights with his parents. As an adult, Heifetz always enjoyed the experience of visiting a new place where he routinely took photographs, experienced local cuisines, and purchased postcards and souvenirs. Heifetz's own film footage from the 1920s and 1930s provides a perfect record of the sightseeing he did during his tours. This footage includes, among a vast array of sights, the Taj Mahal, the Australian Outback, Niagara Falls, and the Egyptian Pyramids.

Just as in Vilnius, the sound of aircraft motors hovered above Odessa, and the famed aviator Sergei Utochkin, an Odessa native, drew large crowds to his aerial demonstrations. During these summer months, however, Utochkin suffered a terrible accident. On a flight from St. Petersburg to Moscow his propeller broke and he crashed. Odessa newspapers reported the horrific details of the incident; Utochkin broke numerous bones and began coughing up blood. His plane, which had taken two months and ten thousand rubles to build, was destroyed, and supporters started a campaign to raise money for a replacement. Utochkin's injuries, however, forced him to abandon flying, and four years later, forgotten by the public, Utochkin died of serious pulmonary disease related to his accident.

Jascha's fascination with flight remained in spite of Utochkin's demise; at home, Jascha enjoyed piloting airplanes constructed out of chairs and other furniture. He would wear big sunglasses, and his passengers usually included his sisters or cousins. In 1920 he was flown from Los Angeles to a recital in San Diego on a plane belonging to Charlie Chaplin's brother.[31] Also during that period, Heifetz flew several times on a small aircraft between Croydon (near London) and Paris. With air travel in its infancy, such trips were far from routine and required a certain measure of courage on the part of the passengers.

It was during his time in Odessa that Jascha first began to enjoy the art of photography, as well—a passion that remained with him throughout his life. Many of Heifetz's photograph albums now reside in the Jascha Heifetz Collection at the Library of Congress, and the earliest examples date from his trip to Odessa in 1911. Jascha provided captions to many of the photographs; one scribbled line from 1911 describes an image Jascha took from his hotel window, and other captions identify some of the people the Heifetzes met during their visit.[32] Photographs taken of Jascha himself during the Odessa trip show the boy wearing his traditional sailor suit.[33] This outfit might have been made by Jascha's mother, since Anyuta Sharfstein-Koch recalled that Anna Heifetz was a gifted seamstress, and for many years she made shirts and suits for her son.

One of the photographs Jascha took in Odessa shows a man captioned as "I. R. Brodovsky."[34] Isidor Brodovsky (b. 1875) worked as a publicist for the *Odesskie novosti* newspaper and lived at 10 Deribasovskaya Street, not far from the Heifetz family's hotel.[35] The photograph was taken at a meeting with Brodovsky relating to the publication of a special portrait of Jascha in the *Odesskie novosti* on August 3. On July 29, one of their free days, Jascha and his father visited the newspaper office. Brodovsky took a liking to Jascha and helped the boy print a few words on paper: "J. Heifetz visited the printers of the 'Odessk. Izv.' 29. VII 1911." Brodovsky also gave Jascha a number of picture postcards with views of Odessa and inscribed the reverse sides: "To the golden-curled, lively, cheerful and intelligent Joseph Heifetz from Isidor Brodovsky. Odessa, 28 July 1911"; "Beloved, Dear Jascha Heifetz! Don't forget that in Odessa you have a good and devoted friend (at the *Odesskie novosti* office), Isidor Brodovsky, who will always answer your letters and with pleasure is at your and your wonderful parents' service."[36] On August 1, the friendly *Odesskie novosti* announced that the Heifetzes had left for home.

After a few days back at their summer retreat in Vilnius, the family departed for yet another performance. This one was much closer, in the little town of Švenčionys (Sventsyany), about fifty miles northeast of Vilnius near the St. Petersburg-Warsaw highway, which the Heifetzes knew from a previous trip. As a local newspaper explained: "Ten-year-old Heifetz, here to give a concert in Sventsyany, kept his word, given two years ago. ... And the Sventsyany residents remembered this promise—a promise remembered and kept ... Heifetz refused many profitable engagements and came to give concerts in the Sventsyany Social Assembly in order to keep his word."[37] This time, Jascha shared the concert with other musicians: "6 August 1911. Big concert by remarkable child virtuosos: violinist Joseph Heifetz and cellist Gustav Katz, with the gracious participation of pianist Yelena Moiseevna Kovarskaya. A ball will be held after the concert. A portion of the proceeds will go to the construction fund for the new building of the Men's Classical Gymnasium which is to open in Sventsyany."[38]

Gustav Katz, a fourteen-year-old cello student from the Leipzig Conservatory, performed pieces by Chopin, Klengel, and Popper. Jascha played the Mendelssohn Concerto and the Paganini Caprice no. 24: "Wild delight captivated the listeners when this phenomenal boy first left the stage, then reappeared on it. One wanted to listen to him, listen endlessly. ... But with a lyre in his hands made of fresh flowers that was brought up to him, to the general sorrow he for the last time left the stage."[39] Newspapers in Vilnius also wrote about the concert: "The talented child, after creating a storm of delight in St. Petersburg, Odessa, and other musical centers, was received especially warmly in Sventsyany. The enthusiasm of the audience was very strong. Long unceasing applause followed after each piece. The performer received many flowers and a great deal of candy."[40]

Back in Vilnius, Ruvin finally had chance to send a thank you letter to Valter:

> Vilna, 14 August 1911
> Deeply Respected Viktor Grigoryevich!
> Forgive me for the long silence. We kept meaning to write to you from Odessa, but never managed to. The time went by so quickly. We are all obliged to you for our trip to Odessa, though. We have no words to express to you our gratitude. Jascha was tremendously successful. He performed there four times. I would write about it in detail, but knowing that you are interested in Jascha, I'm completely certain that you have already read and heard about everything... [41]

Sure enough, stories about Jascha appeared in newspapers as far away as Warsaw and even New York. In Warsaw, the Yiddish-language *Der Fraynd* wrote:

> The audience greets him with stormy applause. He thanks them with a graceful bow and remains standing on a chair, resolute and proud, ready for his divine service—that is, to play. A nod from the conductor, and the service begins. The audience is amazed and enchanted. All eyes are directed toward one point, where two big blue eyes sparkle, immersed in the boundless sea of melody that pours forth from Joseph's magic violin.[42]

In New York, the Yiddish-language *Forverts* printed a sensational headline: "Another boy violinist whose name resounds all around Russia. Major critics compare him with Franz Liszt and Anton Rubinstein. *Forverts* correspondent A. Litvin visits the 10-year-old Joseph Heifetz at his father's home":

> When I came to see his father, an ordinary Jewish musician, he first of all took a notebook out of the desk drawer and gave it to me to read. Pasted into the notebook were all the reviews and critiques of his son published by Russian and Yiddish newspapers. I opened the first page—it was a review by Viktor Valter, the greatest contemporary Russian music critic.[43]

Litvin's article continues with excerpts from the clippings in Ruvin's notebook. A number of these early notebooks, filled with clippings and newspaper reports collected by Jascha's parents, now reside in the Library of Congress. Heifetz saw these notebooks only years later, since his parents thought it necessary to keep the ceaseless praise away from their son. Litvin made note of the home atmosphere at that same point in 1911: "... around the child it is quiet, peaceful, homey. Without any theories, with only a healthy, natural feeling of parental love to keep from him the loud admiration, flattery and idle curiosity seekers."

During Litvin's visit to the house, Jascha was playing outside with friends. In order not to interrupt the games, Litvin returned to the house a second time to speak to the young prodigy: "At home there was only the servant and aunt [probably Sonia Sharfstein]. The grandfather finished his lesson on the Torah with [Jascha], and the boy started to occupy himself with a box of gifts, which constantly arrive for him from all countries. I had Turkish and Finnish silver coins with me, and so I gave them to him."

Litvin's gift might have contributed to Heifetz's life-long passion for coin and stamp collecting. The violinist amassed one of the largest collections of music-themed stamps in the world and eventually donated it to the National Postal Museum in Washington, D.C. As a child, Jascha collected many items and made use of a large padlocked tin box which he kept hidden from his sisters. During one of his tours, however, Pauline and Elza, unable to resist the urge to discover the contents, broke into the box. They found nothing more than a collection of used bottle corks. On Jascha's return home, the sight of the desecrated box left him very upset, and some relatives recalled that from then on the box always traveled with him.

Maybe this "betrayal" contributed to the closed personality Heifetz developed later in life as he increasingly distanced himself from reporters and journalists. Back in 1911, however, Jascha reacted warmly to the reporter Litvin's visit: "When I offered [Jascha] a ride on my bike, this future Liszt, like any ordinary child of his age, kept asking about all the features of my bike." Jascha dreamed of having his own bike, but the family could not afford such a luxury. Despite the payments Jascha had received from his performances in Pavlovsk, Odessa, and Švenčionys, the family decided it was necessary to make another visit to Odessa before the end of the summer. This was a chance to capitalize on the wave of the boy's enormous success.

During this visit to Odessa, Jascha participated in two concerts, the first a benefit scheduled for August 30. What Jascha played is not known, but a report states that "in the absence of an orchestra," several "small concert pieces" were performed. The reviewer spent little time evaluating what and how Jascha played, preferring to focus on the issue of child performers:

> If, generally speaking, for the correct development of talent, from the didactic point of view, it is not necessary for children to appear onstage, in a given case, exceptions are maybe possible, because no others play the way little Heifetz does.... And he himself in time will probably not play like that. It would be fitting for him to be shown in big musical centers.... Amidst that worry, unusual interest and even arguments, which Heifetz's concerts evoked in Odessa one thing is certain: in the giftedness of this boy there is some kind of internal strength . . . [44]

The young cellist Gdal Saleski also participated in the concert, along with singers and soloists from the Odessa Opera Troupe, but the focus fell upon the young violinist: "The attention of the whole audience, naturally, was concentrated on the young violinist J. R. Heifetz. At the end of the concert the whole mass of listeners poured to the exit from the stage, so that the police had to carry the young performer out in their arms."[45]

The episode with the police was also recounted in a book published by Saleski in the 1940s. Saleski was born in Kiev in 1888 into the Ignatovsk *meshchanin* class, and attended the Leipzig Conservatory between 1909 and 1911.[46] His description of the Odessa concert in 1911 appears in *Famous Musicians of Jewish Origin,* an updated version of his 1927 book, *Famous Musicians of a Wandering Race.* Despite a few inaccuracies, the description provides great insight:

> After my graduation from the Leipzig Conservatory, I received an offer to become solo 'cellist of the Symphony Orchestra in Odessa, Russia, at the World Exposition [the exhibit did not actually have "World" status] during the summer of 1911. It was there that I heard Jascha Heifetz for the first time.
>
> He was only nine [ten] then. His first appearance attracted an audience of 5,000 persons, his second, 14,000, and his third and final, 28,000 [newspapers reported the number as 10,000]. After his last recital the audience was so impressed by his playing, that each person was eager to see and touch this chosen one of the gods. The people refused to leave the grounds. Little Jascha, with his parents and two younger sisters [this is the only reference to Pauline and Elza being in Odessa], could not leave by the stage door, for all exits and windows were blocked by a raving and milling crowd. The family was nearly suffocated from fright and lack of air. I happened to see some policemen in the distance and beckoned frantically to them to come to our rescue, and with their help managed to get the family through the streets. Suddenly I heard Jascha's mother scream, "Bozhe moy! (My God!) My child! Where is my Jascha?" I seized Jascha and hid him under my coat, breaking through the surging mass. Just then someone saw me with the boy in my arms, overwhelmed me, and exposed poor Jascha to view. We became separated from the other members of the family, and had to search for them until late into the night. In the meantime the parents, who had to force their way through a side exit, almost collapsed from anxiety over Jascha's fate, until they learned that he was safe with me.[47]

The Heifetzes were introduced to Saleski during their first trip to Odessa in July 1911. At that time Jascha gave the young cellist a photograph of himself with the inscription: "With fond remembrances to the wonderful cellist Mr. Saleski from Joseph Heifetz. 27.VII.1911. Odessa."[48] Shortly after this episode in Odessa, Saleski traveled to St. Petersburg to enter the conservatory, and he settled close to the Heifetzes.

Jascha's next performance at the Odessa Exhibit came on September 1. A day earlier, as local newspapers announced, the Heifetzes attended an open rehearsal of *Aida* at the City Theater, and among the large audience the Heifetzes met the famous American bass Adamo Didur, a soloist at the Metropolitan Opera.[49]

Held for the benefit of those working at the Odessa Exhibit, the September 1 concert included Saleski, the singer Dolinskaya, and of course, Jascha. "Heifetz was born under a lucky star," one reporter wrote, "both for himself and for others. He himself does not know how he plays, this little magician. . . . He of course brings his good fortune for the benefit of the Exhibit workers. It doesn't cost him anything to bring good fortune. It runs after him by itself."[50] At this farewell appearance, Jascha played the Mendelssohn Concerto with an accompanist named Aron Simtsis, and a new work for him—the Glazunov Concerto, a piece he had studied earlier in the year in preparation for the concert at Pavlovsk Station that never happened. Local newspapers emphasized with pride that Jascha's first performance of the Glazunov Concerto took place in Odessa.[51]

After Jascha's final performance in Odessa, the Heifetzes departed for home. Around this time, a newspaper in Odessa printed an article about Jascha and the ethics of presenting young performers in public.[52] One of the conductors of the Exhibit Orchestra, Ariy Pazovsky, supported the inclusion of child performers. Another Exhibit conductor, Yosif Pribik, expressed a more restrained position, declaring that a child with special gifts should be treated with more care. Local music teachers held a broadly negative opinion concerning child performances, and Vitold Malishevsky, director of the music school in Odessa, declared: "Unfortunately I did not hear Heifetz and cannot judge the character and completeness of his talent. In any case my principal opinion is that any performances of child prodigies bring them enormous harm." Jascha's playing impressed Dmitry

Klimov, a teacher at the Odessa music school, but Klimov cautioned: "First of all he needs to study, study, and study. Not go on tour, perform on stage, and study at the same time—it is physically impossible and impermissible."

As if defying the opinions of the Odessa music teachers, and despite the start of the academic year on September 10, newspapers announced that Jascha would perform in Kiev on September 11 and 13: "Impresario Mr. Tovbin will pay Mr. Heifetz 500 rubles for each concert."[53] Despite the advance publicity, no further evidence of these two concerts appears in any Kiev newspaper. The events were perhaps canceled due to the serious events unfolding in Kiev during the days leading up to the concerts. On August 29, Tsar Nicholas II and his family arrived in Kiev for the unveiling of a monument to Alexander II. The Tsar and other important dignitaries, including Prime Minister of Russia Pyotr Stolypin, all attended a gala performance on September 1 at the Kiev Opera House. During the second intermission of the performance, an assassin named Dmitry Bogrov shot Stolypin, who later died. Bogrov was captured, and his death sentence was carried out on September 9. Since it was stated that Jascha would perform in Kiev during these very same days, it seems likely that the family decided to stay away owing to the tense atmosphere and harsh extra security measures. In any case, the conservatory and Professor Auer awaited Jascha.

CHAPTER SEVEN

Fall 1911: In the Class of Professor Auer

PROFESSOR LEOPOLD AUER, born on June 7, 1845 (NS), was already sixty-six years old when Jascha entered his class in 1911. His father was a painter from the small Hungarian town of Veszprém near Lake Balaton. In his 1923 biography, *My Long Life in Music*, published in New York, Auer wrote about his journey from difficult beginnings in the backwaters of the Austrian Empire to a successful musical career in the upper circles of the Russian Empire. The only major Russian work on Auer's life is a 1962 monograph by Lev Raaben.[1] Owing to the absence of documents pertaining to Auer's career in the archives of the conservatory and the Russian Music Society (RMO), Raaben relied on personal correspondence, conservatory reports, and other indirect sources. There was a reason for the absence of documents: the files of professors still in Russia after the 1917 revolutions were kept, but those belonging to Auer and others who departed, such as Nikolai Malko and Vladimir Drozdov, were discarded.

Considering the shortage of official material on Auer's life, an unpublished document about Auer discovered in one of Heifetz's scrapbooks holds significant historical value.[2] The document is Auer's official Russian work record, and it is unclear how Heifetz acquired it. Perhaps Auer gave it to him as a gift, or maybe Heifetz received it after Auer's death. In any case, it is clear from the accompanying envelope that the documents were originally sent from the Petrograd Conservatory to Auer's address in New York City. The package is dated October 11, 1923, and the document includes a stamp and the signature of the Petrograd Conservatory business manager. Another stamp from the Petrograd regional council states that there was no objection regarding the removal of the document from Russia. This suggests Auer made the request himself from New York. The impressive document dates from the year Auer arrived in Russia on the invitation of the RMO, 1868, and continues chronologically, according to the Julian Calendar (Old Style):

September 1, 1868
Appointed Adjunct Professor of Violin at the St. Petersburg Conservatory.

November 1, 1872
By order of the Minister of the Imperial Court, No. 3299, dated October 3, 1873, assigned to the administration of the Directorate of Imperial Theaters, as Artist-Violinist, with an annual salary of 1300 rubles.

March 20, 1874
The Minister of the Imperial Court most humbly declares that His Majesty, the Most Gracious Emperor, has deigned to bestow upon the violinist Auer the title of His Majesty's Soloist.

March 2, 1879
By decree of the Artistic Council of the St. Petersburg Conservatory, affirmed by the Most Worthy Chairman of the Imperial Russian Music Society, promoted to Adjunct Professor First Degree.

January 1, 1882
Most graciously appointed Cavalier of the Order of St. Anne, Third Degree, for exceptionally devoted service to the St. Petersburg Conservatory.

January 28, 1883
With the approval of the Minister of Internal Affairs, administered the oath of Russian citizenship in the presence of the Chief of Police of St. Petersburg.

January 1, 1888
For exceptionally devoted service to the St. Petersburg Conservatory, most graciously appointed Cavalier of the Order of St. Stanislav, Second Degree.

January 1, 1892
For exceptionally devoted service to the St. Petersburg Conservatory, Auer is most graciously appointed Cavalier of the Order of St. Anne, Second Degree.

February 1, 1895
For exceptionally devoted service to the St. Petersburg Conservatory, appointed Cavalier of the Order of St. Equal-of-the-Apostles Prince Vladimir, Fourth Degree.

June 19, 1896
By decision of the Governing Senate, June 8, 1895, admitted into the Hereditary Nobility with the right to be entered into the Genealogical Book of the Russian Nobility, Part Three, Certificate No. 2705 from the Department of Heraldry.

April 6, 1903
By order of the President of His Majesty's Chancellery, on the sixth day of April, 1903, most graciously granted the rank of State Councillor.

April 2, 1906
By order of the President of His Majesty's Chancellery, on the second day of April, 1906, most graciously granted the rank of Acting State Councillor.

April 7, 1908
By order of the Minister of Internal Affairs, on the petition of the Most Worthy Vice-Chairman of the Imperial Russian Music Society, confirmed by his Royal Highness to the honorary rank of Professor Emeritus.

December 18, 1909
For exceptionally devoted service to the SPB Conservatory, most graciously appointed to the Order of St. Equal-of-the-Apostles Prince Vladimir, Third Degree.

December 16, 1912
For exceptionally devoted service to the SPB Conservatory, most graciously appointed as Cavalier of the Order of St. Stanislav, First Degree.

According to his work record, by the time of his departure from Russia, Auer's annual salary at the St. Petersburg Conservatory reached 4,600 rubles. In addition to this, he received income from performances in Russia and abroad, from the string quartet of the St. Petersburg division of the (Imperial) Russian Music Society, which he led for forty years, and as a conductor, promoting the symphonic works of Russian composers. Auer also published editions and transcriptions which entered the repertoires of many violinists at the end of the nineteenth century and start of the twentieth century.

Auer was a successful pedagogue, performer, and editor, and his contemporaries struggled to place him in a single category. One wrote, for instance, the following:

> However great his service as a teacher was, he also stands alone as an artist-virtuoso; his brilliant technique, his charming tone rich with nuances, his intelligent and inspired performances, place him at the head of all the outstanding soloists of Europe. His performance of chamber music is not inferior—it is with style, and is noble, reminiscent of the playing of Joachim. Those who had the chance to hear the quartets he and the famous cellist Davydov performed in 1890 and also the Beethoven sonatas, cannot fail to agree with the opinion that it is hard to decide in which area of his work this remarkable artist succeeds the most.[3]

Auer is now known primarily as a pedagogue, as the head of the illustrious St. Petersburg school of violin playing. By the start of the 1910s, the professor had accumulated more than forty years of teaching experience. He taught hundreds of students, many of whom became prominent concert performers and influential teachers at the St. Petersburg Conservatory, including Pyotr Krasnokutsky, Aleksei Kolakovsky, Nikolai Galkin, Sergei Korguev, Emmanuel Kreuger, and of course Nalbandian. Graduates of the Auer class taught in almost every music school and conservatory in Russia, and these graduates in turn sent their own best students to Auer. By the start of the 1900s, Auer's first generation of star pupils included Joseph Achron, Efrem Zimbalist, and Mischa Elman. The professor's reputation continued to grow with the success a few years later of other students, including Mishel Piastro, Myron Polyakin, Cecilia Hansen, Richard Burgin, Kathleen Parlow, and Thelma Given. The final few additions to Auer's list of stars at the beginning of the 1910s included Jascha Heifetz and Toscha Seidel.

Observers from outside Russia believed the Auer school owed its success in part to the natural talent entering the St. Petersburg Conservatory. The pedagogue Carl Flesch wrote: "At the Berlin Hochschule, for instance, of forty students sitting for the entrance examination, about four are above average, whereas in Petersburg the proportion is 90–95 per cent."[4] Many of the most talented students in St. Petersburg were Jewish, and there was a reason for this. State anti-Semitism severely limited the career options for Jews, and music was one of a small number of open paths to a successful and respected professional life in the Russian Empire. Ultimately, the St. Petersburg Conservatory became home to both a deeply successful and influential violin professor and a continuous flow of gifted violin students.

Auer remained remarkably active even in his sixties. One of his contemporaries, the famous Russian-Jewish author Rachel Hin-Goldovskaya (1863–1928), left a vivid description of the professor: "He has beautiful, black, enormous eyes that look as though they have oil poured on them. This veil disappears only when he plays great pieces . . . Beethoven, Bach. Then sparks of fire flash in them . . ." She continued: "He himself was a great musician, an astonishing violinist, a very 'refined' person on European stages and in all society circles . . ." Auer associated with many important political and musical figures, but as Hin-Goldovskaya points out, "for all his outward refinement, in all his manners one can always feel the plebeian—a man of the people, intelligent, agile, witty, rather coarse, and kind."[5]

Auer's immediate family included six people: the professor himself, his wife Nadezhda, and their four daughters, Zoya, Nadezhda, Natalya, and Maria.[6] "At home," writes Hin-Goldovskaya, a friend of Auer's wife, "Auer was a dear, affectionate, attentive husband, a kind though strict father, seeing to it that the girls knew 'order.'"[7] This story relates to an earlier period in the life of the professor, since he and his wife separated around 1900, and by 1911 their four daughters lived independently.

During the years Jascha studied with Auer, the professor lived in a four-bedroom apartment in building number 53–26 on the corner of Ofitserskaya Street and Angliisky Prospekt. Just a fifteen-minute walk from the conservatory, the large building housed many musicians, including Rimsky-Korsakov, Maksimilian Steinberg, and Ivan Yershov. The building has since become a communal apartment. On entering the apartment all these years later, one is struck by the peeling paint and the partitions that now divide the once-spacious rooms into numerous smaller nooks. The present inhabitants had heard rumors about a famous gentleman living there before the revolution, but were unaware that it was the famous professor. Only two rooms remain in their original state, one thought to have been the professor's office. This room also includes an enormous window looking out into the quiet internal courtyard. In the 1990s, one resident explained how there had been a metal safe in the wall but that it was removed, and years earlier he had dismantled and disposed of a dark green malachite fireplace. The former splendor of the apartment is hard to imagine after decades of communal living.

The Heifetzes decided to move closer to Auer. A residency document dated September 23, 1911, provides the new address: 40 Angliisky Prospekt.[8] Proximity to Auer appears to have been the only virtue of this residence. The large red-brick building belonged to an infamous property owner who witnessed the collapse of two of his buildings during construction; those buildings that were eventually completed were shabby and remain in disrepair today. Not surprisingly, the Heifetzes soon needed to move, and by October 11 resided in building number 20, apartment 17, on Voznesensky Prospekt.[9] This new residence was a little farther from both the conservatory and from Auer, but it was next door to the building of the Zvukopis recording company, where earlier that year Jascha had made his first gramophone recording.

After their arrival back in St. Petersburg, one of the Heifetz family's first trips was to the home of Viktor Valter, whose entire family took great interest in Jascha's musical development. Valter lived in a large impressive building number 22–24 Nikolaevskaya Street, which was adjoined to the Old Believer Church of St. Nicholas the Wonderworker. Valter's apartment (number 16) was situated away from the bustle of the street in the second internal courtyard, where he lived with his wife, Yekaterina

(Kitty); daughter, Tosya; and sons Vladimir and Aleksandr (Shura). A card from this period signed by Jascha is probably addressed to Valter's youngest son. It reads: "Shura! Come visit if you can, today—when you're free. You promised me, and you haven't come. I'm waiting for you today. Yours, Joseph Heifetz."[10] The friendship between the Heifetzes and the Valters became very solid. On September 20, Valter wrote in his diary: "Today Jascha Heifetz and his father came to visit us, he looks very well: cheerful and rosy-cheeked. He became occupied with Tosya's Kodak. Kitty asked him: what would you prefer to be, a violinist or a photographer? Jascha unhesitatingly answered, 'a photographer.'"[11]

Lessons at the conservatory had already begun by this time. Much is known about classes with Auer. The author Raaben draws on stories from musicians including Yuly Eidlin, Lyubov Sigal, and Mikhail Bikhter, and a two-volume commemorative book published in the 1980s about the Leningrad Conservatory contains the recollections of composers Anushavan Ter-Gevondian, Heino Eller, Jāzeps Vītols, and pianists Nadezhda Golubovskaya, Aleksandra Bushen, and Samary Savshinsky. The Auer student Semyon Bretanitsky wrote about lessons with the professor in the journal *Sovetskaya muzyka* and in a special edition of the *New York Times Magazine* published in April 1925 for Auer's eightieth birthday, which contains the memories of Thelma Given, Max Rosen, Joseph Achron, Efrem Zimbalist, Paul Stassevich, and of course, Heifetz.

Auer students gathered on Wednesdays and Saturdays for violin lessons, and although Auer did not require every student to play at every lesson, he "categorically insisted on punctual attendance to his class, and he sent reminder postcards to those who had missed classes."[12] Auer insisted on order and discipline both at home and at the conservatory, and he instilled this into his students. The professor never arrived late for a lesson; students gathered early in order to mark their attendance in a notebook resting on the piano, and they then played in the same order as they signed in the book. On Auer's arrival in the conservatory building, news flowed quickly to the upper floors and students used a system of signals to pass on information about Auer's general mood. The professor refused to use the elevator, which was reserved for staff, and instead marched up the stairs. According to Savshinsky,

The arrival and exit of A. Yesipova and L. Auer were particularly ceremonial events. They went surrounded by an entourage. Yesipova was accompanied by O. Kalantarova, V. Drozdov, I. Vengerova and a group of students. Auer was surrounded by professors Nalbandian, S. Korguev, E. Kreuger, and M. Gamovetskaya. They walked slowly and majestically; students, running up to look at the famous professors, respectfully yielded the way to them.[13]

If Auer appeared in a bad mood, the students tried to avoid him. "And at 2:35 precisely—Zimbalist often set his watch correctly by the master's entrance—Professor Auer walked briskly into the death-like silence of his classroom, closed the big double doors and began the lesson."[14]

The pianist Golubovskaya often accompanied Auer's students:

Auer's class was an interesting spectacle. His students sat all around along the walls, not daring to stir. The venerable professor's disposition was very stern. Only those who had learned the assigned work well were allowed to play, after playing it earlier for their classmates and finding out from them Auer's fingerings and instructions. By this they not only preserved the professor's work, but also received lessons that were much more artistically rich, not drawing away Auer's attention with the trivialities of such preparatory work. Of course, what drove them was not a wise awareness of the advisability of doing this, but simply a fear of provoking the anger of their teacher and disgracing themselves in front of their comrades.[15]

Semyon Bretanitsky studied with Auer from 1911 and recalled the following:

Technical exercises were not played in class, but were consistently demanded as part of independent homework. With great skill [Auer] would select artistic material that was [in terms of technique] equal with the etudes [of Kreutzer], Dont and Rode, and this would serve as a test of growth. By the way, there were sometimes unexpected direct exercise tests. But even scales were performed with accompaniment: Auer would sometimes accompany the student on the piano, and sometimes on the violin. On other days Nadya Golubovskaya, the student of Lyapunov, would provide the accompaniment.[16]

According to reports from various contemporaries, Auer had only average talent for the piano, but his remarkable musicianship enriched his playing substantially.[17] Paul Stassevich, who studied with Auer from 1909 to 1917, recalled the following:

Up and down the room the master strode, stopping a bit, beard bristling, head cocked on one side, eyes bright and searching, his hands clasped behind him. He smiled, he walked to the windows, he suddenly circled the class like a wary cat, sometimes ducking under the violinist's bowing arm and peering into his face while he was playing—and always the eternal cigarette in his mouth, smoking, smoking, smoking. The floor was covered with ashes.[18]

The talented pianist Mikhail Bikhter wrote about Auer in his memoirs:

Leopold Semyonovich had a fiery nature. He hated dull playing, giving it the scornful nickname "unterkleid" [underwear] . . . In most cases he walked around the class, approvingly shouting, nodding his beautiful, although almost completely bare head, opening his big, round, expressive eyes, flaring the nostrils of his eagle-like nose. And when Achron, or Zimbalist, or Polyakin played—all aflame, all in movement—he shouted in an ecstatic outburst.[19]

Heifetz also spoke passionately and at length about his beloved teacher:

Prof. Auer was a wonderful and incomparable teacher. I do not believe that there is any teacher in the world who could possibly approach him. Don't ask me how he did it, for I would not know how to tell you, for he is completely different with each student. Perhaps that is one reason that he was such a great teacher. I think that I was with Prof. Auer about six years. I had both class lessons and private lessons from him, though toward the end, my lessons were not very regular. I never played exercises or technical works of any kind for the professor, but outside of the big things—the Concertos and Sonatas, and the shorter featured pieces which he would let me prepare, I often chose what I wanted.

. . . The Professor's pupils were supposed to have been sufficiently advanced in technic that they only had to depend upon the Professor for his wonderful lessons in interpretation. Yet, there were all sorts of technical finesses which he always had up his sleeve; any number of fine, subtle points in playing, as well as in interpretation, which he would disclose to his students as it became necessary. What was very important was that the more interest and ability the pupil showed, the more the Professor gave of himself. He was a very great teacher![20]

Years later, Heifetz remembered in detail how he first learned to play staccato bowing in the cadenza of the first movement of Wieniawski Concerto no. 1, and he recalled how the students strove to discover the "secrets" of Auer's teaching:

In Prof. Auer's class, there were usually between twenty-five and thirty students. While we each gained individually from the Professor's criticisms and corrections, it was interesting to hear the others who played before your turn came. Then, we would get all kinds of hints from what Prof. Auer told them. I know I always enjoyed listening to Poliakin, a very talented violinist, and Cecile Hansen, who attended the classes at the same time I did. The Professor was a stern, strict, and very exacting teacher, but at the same time, he was very sympathetic. If our playing was not just what it should be, he always had a fund of kindly humor upon which to draw. He would anticipate our stock excuses and say: "Well, I suppose you have just had your bow rehaired!" Or, "These new strings are very trying" or "It's the weather that's against you again, is it not?" Or something like that.[21]

For the special edition of the *New York Times Magazine* celebrating Auer's eightieth birthday, Heifetz described a particularly memorable classroom incident:

We were very much afraid of him then. He hated mediocrity and stupidity. I remember one poor creature trying to play a concerto. Professor Auer, eyes riveted on the victim's face, sat some distance away astride a small chair. A sour note floated from the nervous young artist's bow. Auer scowled and bumped his chair a bit closer. The unfortunate, hypnotized by Auer's flashing eyes, played more wretchedly. The fatal chair thumped closer. Suddenly Auer's hand shot out and struck his pupil's elbow. A broken bow flew in the air, a violin crashed to the floor. Yes, Professor Auer broke a good many bows and violins in those days, but he always repented afterward and bought better ones for his adoring pupils.[22]

Many musicians recall Auer's quick-tempered disposition; Golubovskaya wrote:

One day, taking music out of a student's hand (of course, everyone was supposed to play by memory), he said—in the beginning quietly and distinctly: 'I told you not to buy this edition!' Then he repeated this phrase louder and higher, and so on six times. With the last ferocious cry the music scattered all over the floor, and there was no lesson. However, he brightened up when people played with talent. I remember how affectionately he looked at the little Heifetz—he and I played the Kreutzer Sonata together when he was eleven years old.[23]

Jascha probably knew little of Auer's anger. In 1925, Heifetz remarked, "half an hour with Auer is always to me a great emotional and intellectual

stimulus. He has a remarkable mind, a remarkable wit, a remarkable nervous system, a remarkable magnetism. You see—everything about him
is remarkable."[24] Auer had such an all-encompassing ability to teach that
neither Heifetz nor any other student could articulate exactly how he im-
parted his knowledge. Often, his students reported, he seemed to correct
a student's playing with merely a look, a movement of the eyebrows, or just
a wave of the hand. Paul Stassevich recalled the comments of an American
student who, after taking some lessons with Auer, complained that "he
doesn't do anything." Two weeks later, the American said in a puzzled tone:
"He doesn't do anything, but I certainly play better than I ever did before."[25]

Auer required a high level of discipline from his students—good behavior, but also clean clothes and polished shoes. The professor's desire
for "punctuality" occasionally pushed the boundaries of rationality; Auer
would stand at the entrance to his apartment with his watch in hand, opening the door only if the invited student rang the bell at exactly the appointed time. If the bell rang a minute early or two minutes late, the door
remained closed. On his own teaching methods, Auer wrote: "I have never
tried to mould my pupils to any narrow aesthetic theories of my own, but
only to teach them the broad general principles of taste out of which individual style develops. As regards interpretation I have always encouraged
them to find *themselves*. I have always allowed them all freedom except
when they have tried to sin against the aesthetic principles of art."[26] In the
late 1950s, when Heifetz taught at the University of California, Los Angeles,
and then the University of Southern California, he drew extensively on
Auer's pedagogical approaches. Heifetz even used the same cadenza from
the Wieniawski Concerto no. 1 to teach his students the method for playing staccato. Like Auer, Heifetz insisted on a high level of discipline and
punctuality, always keeping an eye on his watch, never hesitating to turn
students away if they arrived even a minute late.

Auer expected his students to play at a high level at all times. According
to the cellist Aleksandr Shtrimer, quartet classes with Auer proved highly
beneficial:

> The lessons took place once a week, on Tuesdays from nine to twelve.
> Students gathered in the green room and Auer arrived ten minutes before
> the beginning of class. There were no fewer than 6–8 cellists. They brought

music from the library, and Auer assigned parts, deciding who would play first violin, who second, and who the viola (all his students were supposed to be able to play the viola). We would worry a lot, because often we had to play quartets we did not know, and Auer demanded professional performance standards from the very first time. Simply sight-reading from the page did not satisfy him. He demanded insightfulness of performance and understanding of stylistic particularities. He often doubled the group of students, in that way involving larger groups of participants. If the quartet played well, Auer would be satisfied and would schedule a performance at a students' evening after one lesson. At that next lesson, after having determinedly worked all week, we would show him our work. It would sometimes happen that he would yell and even ask to stop the class if someone broke the rules of quartet playing. Most of all he hated vulgar, forced sound. When he liked our playing, then he shared his memories of performances of that or another quartet by great artists, and sometimes he would tell about the composers and so on. He almost always attended our student concerts. In terms of performance, he never limited our initiative. He only demanded expressive, clean playing, the observance of style, and penetration into the substance of the music.[27]

Bretanitsky recalled that Auer often moved students around during chamber music classes so that they learned both the violin parts and the viola part, thereby ensuring a deeper understanding of the principles of ensemble playing.

Along with his violin and quartet classes, Jascha studied elementary theory and solfège with Mikhail Klimov (1881–1937). Klimov was primarily a choral conductor. He graduated from the Moscow Synodal School in 1900 and began working as a conductor and teacher in the Tambov Women's School and then sang in the St. Petersburg court. He studied at the St. Petersburg Conservatory from 1904 to 1908, specializing in compositional theory with Rimsky-Korsakov and conducting with Tcherepnin. Klimov soon became a senior instructor at the conservatory where he taught theoretical subjects, and he also ran the Opera Studio. Klimov maintained a constant interest in theoretical disciplines, and shortly before Jascha entered his class, Klimov published a book on counterpoint, canon, and fugue. Jascha's absolute pitch and remarkable musical memory positioned him in the top of Klimov's class.

Jascha's father accompanied his son to lessons at the conservatory, partly because Auer needed to create the impression that Ruvin also took regular lessons. Ruvin continued to belong to category IX, "those study-ing for free in specialized classes and freed from additional payment." By this time, Jascha became a category III student, meaning that he studied for free and received a stipend. He was awarded the 100-ruble Kondratyev Stipend which also freed the recipient from any other payments.[28] This particular award began in 1873 when Staff Captain Mikhail Kondratyev donated 15,000 rubles to the conservatory; half was to be used for student stipends and the other half for the support of Russian composers. Among the earliest conservatory students to receive this stipend was Pyotr Lody, who became a famous singer and soloist at the Mariinsky Theater, as well as Vasily Zolotarev, who in 1902 won a symphony writing competition and later became a famous teacher and composer.

With the success of Jascha's summer concerts, the financial situa-tion for the Heifetzes had improved somewhat, and, as one newspaper explained, Ruvin now had "the possibility to no longer play in cafes, but to wholly dedicate himself to his son's upbringing."[29] The gramophone record Jascha made earlier that year also brought in a reasonable profit. In October 1911, a reviewer for the journal *Grammofonny mir* reported on the first results of the Zvukopis company:

> To tell the truth, I did not expect that the company would see the light of day—before this the first steps of its beginnings were timid. . . . Yes, to enter the market in our days with a new brand—this is a sure way to end up with grey hair on your head and a Torricellian vacuum in your pocket! S. A. Zhit-lovsky was not afraid of this pleasant prospect and put out for sale the first release of his "Zvukopis" records with an original Russian label and, thank God, without a German title! The repertoire is still limited, but there are al-ready "hits" and above all—the records of ten-year-old violinist Jascha Hei-fetz. What a dear, talented boy! So much feeling, and in technical places—brilliant vigor, rising in places to the level of full virtuosity! In terms of the recording—the records are very successful, even more than the others. . . . Good job, Zhitlovsky! For now the new St. Petersburg manufacturers "pre-pare themselves"—he "prepared himself" relatively early and went out on the market with a really great trump card.[30]

In September, following the assassination of the Prime Minister of Russia, Pyotr Stolypin, the shrewd Zhitlovsky had released a record entitled "On the Death of Stolypin," which contained a reading of poetry accompanied by music on one side, and a funeral march on the other—a memorial sung by the choir of the church of the Ministry of Internal Affairs under the direction of Aleksandr Arkhangelsky. This record sold as successfully as Jascha's records. Other releases around this time included recordings of Gypsy romances by Katyusha Sorokina, and a reading of poetry by Princess Ksenya Vyazemskaya. In January 1912, Jascha's name appeared again in the advertisements of the Zvukopis company. The firm re-released some of Jascha's recordings on two records with new catalog numbers, one containing Schubert's *The Bee* (no. 2001) and Dvořák's *Humoresque* (no. 2002), and the other, with Drdla's *Serenade* and *Souvenir* (nos. 2003 and 2004). Sometime later, the same recordings were released by the St. Petersburg firm Russian Joint-Stock Company of Gramophones (RAOG), a firm that first appeared in the Russian market in early 1912. It is possible these re-releases were pirated, since they do not appear in RAOG's catalogs, but it is also possible that they were released at the time when Zvukopis, RAOG, and many other St. Petersburg firms joined under the Association of United Manufacturers. In such a case, the RAOG label on Jascha's record dates from no earlier than 1914.[31] It is unknown whether Jascha continued to receive royalties for re-releases.

In addition to being featured on the pages of the journal *Grammofonny mir* during the autumn of 1911, Jascha appeared in an extended article about child virtuosos published in *Solntse Rossii,* a popular St. Petersburg newspaper.[32] The article contained information about the ten most famous young performers of the era. Most of these prodigies failed to fulfill their early promise. Who now remembers the name of Eleonora Damskaya,[33] then a thirteen-year-old harpist, or the young pianists Raya Livshitz and Ana Lazerson? Andre (Andryusha) Prang, for example, who entered Nalbandian's class in 1911, became famous in 1915 as the youngest recipient of the Mikhailovsky Palace Prize when he graduated at just fourteen. Following successful performances in Prague and Antwerp, Prang received an invitation to perform in Paris, but he did not have a long and successful career. The first name in the article was the exceptional young pianist Aleksandr Dubyansky (1900–1920), a student of Yesipova and Felix Blumenfeld, who was known as a serious interpreter of Scriabin's music and who influenced the pianistic style of Vladimir Sofronitsky. Dubyansky's career was cut tragically short when he committed suicide.

Of the ten child prodigies presented in the *Solntse Rossii* article, two succeeded in fulfilling their early potential—Myron Polyakin and Jascha Heifetz. The two boys shared biographical details: both were taught initially by their fathers and both earned a living by performing. Unlike Jascha, who remained firmly under the care of his parents, Polyakin's mother died when her son was just seven and Myron spent most of his remaining childhood living with distant relatives. Both violinists left Russia on tour during the revolution and then remained abroad—Polyakin for several years, Heifetz for the rest of his life. Polyakin became a professor at the Moscow Conservatory but died in his prime at the age of just forty-six. As students of the same professor, Heifetz and Polyakin were often compared, and their differences were said to reflect Auer's genius for harnessing individual talents without stifling individuality. At the time the *Solntse Rossii* article was published, Polyakin was starting his fourth year with Auer, and Jascha was just beginning. As a result, Jascha is still named in the article as a student of Nalbandian and is shown in a photograph posing proudly with his first conservatory professor.

The autumn of 1911 also witnessed the first ever Leopold Auer Violin Competition, open to all former Auer students no more than two years past graduation. The thousand-ruble prize was supposed to come from the interest deriving from the competition fund, which was founded in 1908, but by the time of the competition it had still not generated enough. To compensate, several former students made donations, including Mischa Elman, who by that time was concertizing internationally. The special competition took place on October 21, 1911, under the chairmanship of Glazunov, who was joined by well-known musicians including Aleksei Kolakovsky, Emmanuel Kreuger, Nalbandian, Ilya Brik, Vasily Bezekirsky, Viktor Valter, Serge Koussevitzky, and others. The four competitors were Solomon Lazerson, Yosif Lesman, Myron Lednik, and Mishel Piastro. The prize was awarded unanimously to twenty-year-old Piastro, who had graduated from the conservatory the previous year with a gold medal. For the Auer Competition he played the Adagio and Fugue from Bach Sonata in C for solo violin, the Brahms Concerto, and several other pieces including Auer's own *Tarantella*. This was probably where Jascha first heard the Brahms Concerto. For Auer, the most important pieces in the violin literature included the concertos of Mendelssohn, Beethoven, and Brahms. Of this triad, the Mendelssohn had been central to Jascha's repertoire since his time in Vilnius. The concertos of Brahms and Beethoven, however, would only feature permanently after his arrival in the United States, even though the boy did perform the Beethoven twice, in 1913 and 1917.

During Jascha's first half-year with Auer, he learned many new pieces, including the Bach-Wilhelmj Aria (on the G string) from the Suite in D for string orchestra. Auer considered this one of the best violin arrangements and gave it to his students because its "interpretation, first of all, demands control of a fine singing tone on the violinist's part."[34] Jascha also played *La Ronde des Lutins* by Antonio Bazzini, a piece Auer considered not just an effective concert piece, but also useful for technical development.[35]

Working on the Tchaikovsky Concerto with Auer, a piece Jascha had started in the summer under the watchful gaze of his father, proved stimulating for both student and teacher. Auer often shared personal recollections with his students, telling them the history of the concerto and how Tchaikovsky once planned to dedicate it to him. He never concealed the fact that at first he did not fully appreciate the work. While acknowledging the lyrical beauty of the music, he nonetheless complained that certain passages were unplayable. Auer, in fact, had promised Tchaikovsky he would edit those passages, but after two years had passed with no changes, Tchaikovsky became disillusioned and withdrew the dedication. On this matter, Auer wrote: "Quite frankly admitting that I was to blame, I thought him perfectly within his rights."[36] Over the coming decades, Auer became one of the concerto's most zealous promoters, publishing his own edition of the work in 1899, about which he wrote the following:

My own revision appeared in Russia more than twenty-five years ago and, quite recently, in a new edition here in New York, and has been played in that form by all my older pupils on both sides of the Atlantic. I often played it in Europe, as I had revised it, and thus—after a sufficiently protracted delay, for which I trust Tchaikovsky's manes will forgive me—I have kept the word I gave the great Russian composer long years before.[37]

Jascha also worked on Sarasate's *Zigeunerweisen*. Although this piece had never before been featured on a printed program, according to a newspaper report, Jascha had played it two years earlier as an encore when he was just eight (probably during his pre-conservatory Vilnius concerts in 1909). Concerning that performance, the reviewer for the *Vilensky kurier* wrote:

> Look, what a little kid, sawing away at the violin! And certainly, to tell the truth, Jaschenka sawed away pretty well. . . . And then when they were clapping for him, he played the stormy "Zigeunerweisen" by Sarasate. In this piece there is an unexpected twist—a plaintive melody, from which comes the crying and wailing of children abandoned by the road, stretching out their hands for a piece of bread. Heifetz pulled on my soul, playing those bars. I looked at him. He clung to the violin (this is rare for him), and hid his eyes. Could he have been crying?[38]

As an emigrant from Austria-Hungary, Auer held a strong passion for the *Zigeunerweisen* and felt that the Spaniard Sarasate had a unique ability to express the style and character of Hungarian music: "Without exception all that Sarasate has written calls for a perfected bow and finger technique, good taste and elegance in phrasing, and keen sensibility for proper tone-color and tempo on the part of the player if the effects which lie hidden in the music are to be adequately exploited."[39] This evocative work became an important performance vehicle for Heifetz throughout his career, and his recordings of the piece are widely considered among the most successful ever made.

At the end of December, Ruvin and Jascha returned home to Vilnius. At home, the family began to plan for Anna and the girls to join Jascha and his father in St. Petersburg. For some time Pauline had been taking piano lessons, and the family now discussed the possibility of her entering the conservatory. Ruvin began to prepare the necessary documents for his daughter and, on December 28, received Pauline's birth record as signed by Rabbi Itsko Rubinstein.

On December 29, Jascha performed at an evening benefit concert in the Hall of the Vilnius Railroad Society intended to aid the Society of Jewish Children's Colonies. Participants in the fundraiser included the soloist

Zakharova from the Imperial Opera Troupe, the storyteller and mimic Lersky, and the singer Dobrin. According to the *Severo-zapadny golos*, "the hero of the evening was Jascha Heifetz, that wonderful child, who became extraordinarily successful in his absence from Vilna. It was no longer a 'wunderkind' performing, whose mastery at his age was astonishing, but a fully formed, artistic, first-class celebrity."[40] According to the *Vilensky kurier*, "those who have not heard his playing will not believe that a ten-year-old boy has not only improbably good technique, which gives him the ability to play such things as 'Zigeunerweisen' by Sarasate, but also bright individuality, and his own understanding of the piece."[41] The charitable event was a success.

Before the Heifetzes departed for St. Petersburg, a photograph was taken of the whole family: Ruvin, Anna, Jascha, Pauline, Elza, and cousin Anyuta.[42] Also in the group is Hyman Gerber, a musician and close family friend. The Heifetzes received Pauline's health certificate from the Jewish hospital on December 30 and departed for St. Petersburg almost immediately.[43]

On January 2, the entire Heifetz family received their residency permit from the conservatory, and as usual, the permit lasted for six months (until June 1) and bore the same address as before: Voznesensky Prospekt, building 20, apartment 17.[44] The entire family lived in this small apartment for the remainder of 1912. During the Soviet period, Voznesensky Prospekt became Mayorov Prospekt, and by the end of the 1990s, after years of standing empty and boarded up, the building was completely rebuilt—the courtyard buildings were demolished and the internal plans of the main building were changed. Essentially, only the façade of the previous building was left behind, and all evidence of early twentieth-century life disappeared.

Anna, Pauline, and Elza began to familiarizing themselves with their new home and surroundings, and on January 4, Ruvin submitted the request for Pauline's conservatory admission:

> To the Director of the St. Petersburg Conservatory
> From the Polotsk *meshchanin* Ruvin Eliev Heifetz

Request

Wishing to place my daughter Pesya (Polya) Heifetz, born June 23, 1903, into the St. Petersburg Conservatory for classes in piano playing, I most humbly request you accept her as a student for the second half of the 1911/1912 school year. Herewith I attach: the birth certificate from the Vilna Rabbi from December 28, 1911 for no. 4486 and the doctor's certificate.

January 4, 1912, Mr. Ruvin Heifetz

My address: Voznesensky pr., 20, apt. 17.[45]

Pauline was registered in the book of admissions applications and like her older brother, she was exempt from the five-ruble fee for her entrance exam, which was set for January 5. Pauline also received a note of recommendation: "I accept Heifetz, Pesya into my class as a non-paying student. Prof. Drozdov."[46]

Two of the most experienced piano teachers in the conservatory were present at Pauline's entrance exam, Nikolai Dubasov (1869–1935) and Nikolai Lavrov (1861–1927). Earlier in his career, Dubasov performed frequently and in 1890 won the piano prize in the Anton Rubinstein Competition. A hand injury forced him to end his performing career, and in 1893 he joined the faculty of the St. Petersburg Conservatory, where he remained until the end of his life. Dubasov taught many talented pianists, including Isidor Achron, another of Jascha's accompanists in the United States. Lavrov, the other professor at the exam, was a notable figure in the Belyaevsky circle of the 1880s, alongside Rimsky-Korsakov, Glazunov, Lyadov, and Tcherepnin. He premiered Rimsky-Korsakov's Piano Concerto. Lavrov received the rank of professor in 1899, but between 1915 and 1921 he worked as inspector and deputy director of the conservatory. Pauline's exam sheet reads: "Pitch—absolute, musical memory—excellent, she did not display any knowledge of elementary theory and solfège."[47] For her specialized subject, piano playing, Pauline received a grade of 4.5—"shows great ability." She was accepted into the lower course in category IX, and piano lessons with Drozdov would be free.

Professor Vladimir Drozdov (1882–1960) had studied with Yesipova, became a senior piano instructor in 1908, and then a professor in 1914. He was also the teacher of Emanuel Bay, Jascha's accompanist. Along with Maria Barinova, Leonid Nikolaev, and Samuil Maykapar, Drozdov belonged to the younger generation of conservatory piano instructors of the pre-revolutionary times. He resisted joining the Soviet pedagogical school, and at the end of 1921, Drozdov followed the wave of emigration to the West. From 1923, Drozdov lived mostly in the United States, where he performed and taught. Pauline also met with her former teacher in the United States.

Not counting the quasi-student Ruvin, there were now two conservatory students in the family. Ruvin accompanied Jascha and Pauline to and from their classes and supervised their homework. Anushavan Ter-Gevondian recalled:

> Little Jascha Heifetz, the student of Auer, came to all his classes accompanied by his father. During lessons in scholarly subjects, father and son sometimes occupied their own desk. Jascha's father would actively participate in the classes: he wrote down homework assignments from the board, helped Jascha neatly arrange his books and music, and made sure that "Jascha's thoughts didn't wander." One day, when after the lessons in one of the general-education subjects father and son were leaving the class, I heard Jascha ask his father, "Papa, did you understand everything?"[48]

There is probably some truth to this recollection—Ruvin did accompany his children to lessons and was constantly helping and supervising them. The conservatory offered scholarly subjects in many areas, including Russian language, mathematics, geography, writing, German, French, natural history, history, and physics. Ter-Gevondian's story, however, was probably not based on actual memories, but more on stories, since there is no actual record of Jascha ever attending any of the scholarly subject classes at the conservatory. To be sure, there are other famous names listed in the scholarly subjects records, including Prokofiev (with a string of 5s), Piastro (consistent 4s), and Zimbalist (who struggled for 3s in Russian and physics). In reality, these classes were not compulsory. It was necessary only that by the time of earning a diploma from the conservatory, students master general education subjects or present certification showing they had received a general secondary education elsewhere.

It is unlikely Jascha fulfilled the requirements to pass the necessary scholarly subject classes at the conservatory. According to Valter, who was so closely connected to the Heifetz family, the Heifetzes invited someone to their home to teach Jascha general subjects, a man named Zinovy Kisel-gof.[49] Kiselgof and Ruvin Heifetz shared much in common. Both came from the Vitebsk province, and Kiselgof's birthplace of Velizh was located near Ruvin's hometown, Polotsk. Both of their fathers had worked as teachers in Jewish boys' schools. As a child, Kiselgof spoke no Russian until he started Jewish primary school. He had absolute pitch and was a talented accordion and shepherd's pipe player. At the age of eleven he began violin lessons with Meir Berson, to whom his parents paid one and a half rubles a month. Following his graduation, Kiselgof began tutoring, and at the age of sixteen, with the money he made, he moved to Vilnius. Kiselgof graduated from the Pedagogical Institute in 1898 and left Vilnius long before the Heifetzes arrived. In 1906 following several years of work in Vitebsk in the *Talmud Torah* and local primary school, Kiselgof moved to St. Petersburg to fill a position at the Jewish Industrial School. Kiselgof continued his studies in St. Petersburg and audited classes at Lesgaft High School. In the 1910s, during his period of involvement with the Heifetzes, Kiselgof studied in the physics-mathematics department of St. Petersburg University.

During the 1910s, Kiselgof became one of the most active figures in the St. Petersburg Jewish community and was known widely as an ethnographer and collector of Jewish musical folklore. He had no formal musical education, but in 1908, Kiselgof and a group of young Jewish composers, who were then still students at the conservatory, organized the Society for Jewish Folk Music, aiming to collect and study Jewish folklore and to establish a school of professional Jewish composers. As a founder and leader of the society, Kiselgof worked with many Jewish leaders, including Lazar Saminsky, Mikhail Gnesin, Solomon Rosovsky, and Pavel Lvov. All of the composers were students of Rimsky-Korsakov, who actively encouraged his Jewish students to write in their own style. The composers graduated after Rimsky-Korsakov's death in 1908 and continued to follow his precepts. Jewish folk songs and melodies collected and recorded by Kiselgof served as the foundation for arrangements and editions by Saminsky, Gnesin, Rosovsky, Zhitomirsky, and other members of the Society for Jewish Folk Music. These works appeared in popular annual concerts, which became something of a tradition in St. Petersburg. It is through these musicians that Kiselgof became closely connected to the conservatory, which is likely where he met Jascha. In the coming years, through his connection to Kiselgof, Jascha would be featured in concerts for the Society for Jewish Folk Music.

Jascha worked on a number of subjects with Kiselgof, including Russian, penmanship, and arithmetic. Concerning Jascha's work with Kiselgof, Valter wrote, "it was for me a constant pleasure to look over the boy's studies and read over his written work."[50] Kiselgof was a talented and passionate teacher who was well liked by children and trusted by parents. Kiselgof lived with his wife, Guta, on Fontanka, in building 154. The school where Kiselgof taught was close to the Heifetzes' apartment, and he came often to teach Jascha. During breaks between lessons he would tell many interesting stories and sing Jewish songs to the family. Cousin Anyuta Sharfstein-Koch recalled being present during one of Kiselgof's visits and remembered his stories as interesting and sometimes a little frightening. Over time, Kiselgof became a close and trusted friend to the Heifetzes.

CHAPTER EIGHT

The Beginning of 1912

THE NEW YEAR BROUGHT VARIOUS interruptions to Jascha's violin lessons. In January, Auer left St. Petersburg to visit Kiev and Odessa to assist in the conversion of the two Imperial Russian Music Society schools into conservatories. Journalists in Odessa interviewed Auer a number of times, questioning him about the music schools, and also asking incessantly about his student Jascha Heifetz, whose past summer concerts in the city had so astonished the local public. Auer spoke passionately of Jascha's potential:

> He is a most genius boy out of whom I do not doubt will come a great artist of world fame. You ask, will his performances onstage negatively affect his talent? It seems to me that Heifetz's talent is so great that his public performances barely affect his abilities. On the contrary, sporadic performances will only be of good use for him.... Clearly, constant travel could harm the boy's future, but at the present time the boy, who performs fairly rarely onstage, is doing very well in his general studies, and is quite successful.[1]

In St. Petersburg, Jascha received an invitation to perform at a benefit concert on January 14, 1912, for the Society for the Aid of Impoverished Jews Working in Commerce and Petty Trade. This charity was based in Nikolaev (Mykolaiv), a trading port near Odessa. Jascha and Ruvin took advantage of their teacher's absence and left for Nikolaev. Advertisements for the concert appeared in local newspapers, and they described the event as a "Musical-vocal concert with dancing." The event would take place in the city's assembly building, the largest concert hall in the city, "with the participation of young violinist-virtuoso Jascha Heifetz (he is Joseph) and with the gracious participation of A. S. Dobrovain-Vansova (soprano)."[2] The inclusion of the name Joseph in parentheses suggests the concert organizers wished to capitalize on Jascha's success in nearby Odessa during the summer of 1911, where advertisements and posters referred to Joseph Heifetz.

Jascha thrilled his audience and critics who wrote that "he showed so much poetry, power, inspiration and creativity in his performance of all three movements of the Mendelssohn Concerto!"[3] Jascha also played the Paganini Caprice no. 24, the Chopin-Sarasate Nocturne in E, Dvořák's *Humoresque,* and as an encore, Bazzini's *La Ronde des Lutins.*[4] Accompanying Jascha in Nikolaev was Emanuel Bay, who received leave permission from the conservatory from January 11–17.[5] Reviewers described Bay as a great ensemble musician, and his growing public profile can be seen through his appearance in local advertisements: "Mr. Bay from St. Petersburg plays the accompaniment on a Schroeder piano."[6] The charity concert organizers spared no expense and were justly rewarded.

> The success was remarkable and fully deserved. We will not be mistaken if we say that the appearance of Jascha Heifetz on the concert stage will diminish the glory of more than one ordinary virtuoso. In conclusion we consider it necessary to say that the public of Nikolaev is extremely grateful to the leadership of the Society for the Aid of Impoverished Jews Working in Commerce, which, not hesitating a significant expenditure, brought us great aesthetic pleasure by their invitation of Jascha Heifetz.[7]

By Jascha's eleventh birthday on January 20, the Heifetzes were back in St. Petersburg. There was little time to rest, however, since just a week later they departed for yet another concert, this time in Poland. On January 28 they arrived in Łódź, where Jascha performed with the Warsaw Philharmonic Orchestra, conducted by Zdzisław Birnbaum. Unrestrained admiration filled newspaper reports in Polish, German, and Yiddish publications.

He is a marvel—with his big blue eyes and rosy cheeks, and with his golden curls, which become even more charming when he shakes his head while playing. It is impossible to imagine him any way other than as a little angel, appearing to us from heaven. From the first phrase of the Mendelssohn Concerto Heifetz immediately showed his artistic talent. Bach's Air on the G string was masterfully performed. He has a strong tone, even though he plays on a three-quarter sized violin, which costs 40 rubles. Playing the Popper Spinning Song, he showed his wonderfully developed technique; it seems to me that difficulties just do not exist for Heifetz.[8]

Jascha played the Bach-Wilhelmj Aria and *Melodie Orientale* by Cui for the first time, and was accompanied by the local pianist Vass. According to the reviews, the orchestra played inconsistently, and the conductor appeared nervous during Jascha's concerto, which as a result suffered from tempo problems. Nevertheless, the audience applauded loudly after the boy finished, and a crowd of admirers awaited him on the street after the performance.

The Heifetzes traveled to Warsaw after the concert in Łódź. Despite the city's modest provincial status in the hierarchy of cities in the Russian Empire, the Poles in particular still considered Warsaw the capital of the Kingdom of Poland. In many ways the city felt somewhat European, largely owing to its proximity to the western border of the Russian Empire. Even after a century under Russian rule, Warsaw managed to preserve its distinct character. As in the West, the streets of Warsaw bustled with street cafes and stores plying all sorts of trade.

The Warsaw Philharmonic performed in a building built in 1901 at the center of the city. This building, unlike any in Russia, was designed specifically to house the orchestra, which was also founded in 1901. The venue contained two halls and quickly became a cultural center. The smaller hall, with a capacity of five hundred, was used primarily for chamber music, and the larger hall, with a capacity of two thousand, housed large symphony concerts. It was in the larger hall that Jascha performed his first two Warsaw concerts.

The first of Jascha's two concerts took place on February 3 (NS February 16) with a similar program to that in Łódź, playing the Mendelssohn Concerto with the Warsaw Philharmonic Orchestra under the direction of

Birnbaum. Since its founding in 1901, the orchestra had employed conductors such as Zygmunt Noskowski, Emil Młynarski, and Grzegorz Fitelberg, all familiar names in Russian musical life. Noskowski was one of the first Polish symphonic composers and conducted his own works in Moscow. As a former violin student of Auer and composition student of Lyadov, Młynarski worked for many years in the St. Petersburg music scene. Fitelberg, a violinist and conductor, often toured Russia and later began working permanently in Moscow and St. Petersburg. Jascha would perform with Fitelberg in 1917 just before departing for the United States.

Thirty-year-old Zdzisław Birnbaum had only recently taken the position of conductor of the Warsaw Philharmonic at the time of Jascha's performances. Born in Warsaw in 1880, Birnbaum studied the violin and began conducting the Warsaw Philharmonic in 1911 at the age of thirty-one; he died in 1921 in Berlin at the young age of forty.[9] Overall, the Warsaw press reacted positively to Birnbaum's interpretations. Although he received some criticism for the first concert with Jascha in Łódź, the Warsaw performance on February 3 proved more successful. Jascha played the Mendelssohn Concerto again as well as several short pieces with piano, including, for the first time, a Wieniawski Caprice.[10]

The Warsaw press reacted favorably to Jascha's concert, and reports appeared in *Słowo, Nowa gazeta,* and *Kurjer poranny.* The Yiddish paper *Der Fraynd* described how the concert "exceeded all expectations," and reprinted a review by the music critic of the authoritative Polish paper *Kurjer Warszawski:* "As a music critic for around thirty years, I have written about hundreds of child prodigies, but none of them can compare with Heifetz. . . . The strength of tone and the deep seriousness of the Bach Aria evoked enthusiasm from the listeners. . . . The little ten-year-old, deeply sensitive Heifetz, is a rare virtuoso."[11] Another fascinating report appeared in the Yiddish paper *Haynt:*

> The public could not sit still and surged toward the stage after each piece in order to look more closely at this marvel and called the young virtuoso back to the stage. Little Heifetz in his sailor suit did not need much persuading. He came out onto the edge of the stage, wiped the sweat off his brow with a handkerchief and simultaneously brushing his beautiful, girlish blond hair

down over his forehead, bowed so innocently and so adorably in his young child way that the enthusiasm of the audience became even greater.[12]

Local Russian-language newspapers hardly noticed Jascha's first concert in the city; only the *Varshavskoe slovo* printed a few lines about the performance. This was not surprising considering the regular stream of visiting virtuosos into Warsaw. On January 29, shortly before Jascha's appearance, the Belgian Eugene Ysaÿe played in the city. Along with Joachim and Sarasate, Ysaÿe was one of the greatest living violinists and for three decades had maintained artistic ties with Russian musicians including Anton Rubinstein, Rachmaninoff, and Siloti. For his Warsaw concert, Ysaÿe was joined by the Russian singer Maria Wieniawska-Muromtseva, who was well known at the time, but is largely forgotten today.[13] The accompanist for the concert with Ysaÿe was the St. Petersburg pianist Mikhail Bikhter. As the *Varshavsky dnevnik* described, "Ysaÿe, returning to boisterous applause, forced the dazed pianist to come out with him, and with this emphasized [the pianist's] exceptional mastery."[14] Jascha would later meet Bikhter in St. Petersburg and would play with him several times.

Two other famous violinists, Jacques Thibaud and Fritz Kreisler, appeared with the Warsaw Philharmonic during the start of 1912. Even in the company of such famous names, Jascha made headlines in Warsaw, especially after his second performance on February 10 (NS February 23), which was again with Birnbaum and the Warsaw Philharmonic. For this concert Jascha performed two movements of the Tchaikovsky Concerto with a cadenza by Auer, the first time he had performed this concerto in public. Jascha also played a few pieces with piano, including the Saint-Saëns *Introduction and Rondo Capriccioso* and a few Kreisler selections as encores. The accompanist was Gisela Springer.

The day after the concert, the press erupted with excitement over Jascha's performance. Reviews appeared in at least eight Polish newspapers in both Warsaw and Łódź, and also in the local Jewish and Russian press. According to the *Varshavsky dnevnik*, "in the philharmonic hall there was literally not even room for an apple to fall, and not only were all seats sold out, but all the aisles were packed with a thick crowd."[15] It was no surprise that the audience "demanded endless encores from him," and it was noted that Jascha owed much to Auer, "that highly talented teacher, who has already turned out many violin virtuosos."[16]

In addition to the overwhelming praise, the Warsaw papers expressed concern for Jascha's well-being: "I can't help but feel some worry for this lovely fair-haired boy, worry that exhausting concerts and unnerving ovations could damage his health."[17] The harshest observation came from the *Varshavskoe slovo:* "He is being terribly exploited. The boy is almost constantly playing concerts with no break. This, of course, only proves the extremely low level of development of the people who are in charge of his fate."[18] Throughout Jascha's childhood, his parents read the comments directed at them in the Russian and European press, and although opinions often varied, the accusation of exploitation in the *Varshavskoe slovo* stands apart for its spitefulness. The author of the review was the music reviewer for the *Varshavskoe slovo,* Korobkov, listed as a voice teacher in the "All of Musical-Theatrical Russia" directory. Many of those opposed to children concertizing were teachers, whose opinions usually stemmed from genuine concern for the young performers. In need of a source of income, however, the Heifetzes relied on the boy's performances for survival, although during this period Jascha never performed more than once a week. Not surprisingly, the article from the *Varshavskoe slovo* is missing from the Heifetz scrapbooks.

For Ruvin, the trip to Warsaw gave him the chance to see his brothers Samuil and Natan. Samuil graduated in 1904 from the department of medicine at Warsaw University; he worked as a dentist and lived as a bachelor on Nowolipki Street. By all accounts, Samuil was a kind and affectionate uncle who cared deeply for Ruvin's children and regularly sent them letters and colorful postcards with pictures of composers and landscapes. Natan was the youngest of the brothers, and by 1912 he had lived in Warsaw for a number of years. Aged twenty-nine, Natan was as bald as his older brother Ruvin, and both sported mustaches. Natan had entered the Warsaw Conservatory in 1896 as a thirteen-year-old and worked as a teacher after graduation.

According to a personal employment record that Natan completed during the Soviet years, he graduated from the Warsaw Conservatory on June 15, 1903, in piano and choral singing. The document also indicates that

Natan's original diploma was lost. Owing to political sensitivities, getting a replacement document from Warsaw to the Soviet Union during the 1920s and 1930s was extremely complicated, so Natan made do with personal references. Oddly, however, a notarized copy of the diploma from 1909 is preserved to this day in the family archives of the Moscow Heifetzes. No one knows why Natan hid his diploma for many decades, but this was perhaps an attempt to understate his Jewish heritage or to hide the relatively poor marks he received for piano playing:

> Diploma no. 154. Pedagogical Council of the Warsaw Musical Institute certifies that student Shevel Itsko (who is Nison Itsko), by the second name of Elyevich, Heifetz, has completed the course of studies in the Institute and passed his exam in cornet and history of music with a mark of Excellent, choral singing with a mark of Good, and piano playing and counterpoint with a mark of Satisfactory, and therefore on the basis of the 16th article of the Royally established Statute of the Warsaw Musical Institute, has attained the right to teach in private lessons and to receive the accompanying responsibilities in state institutions. 15 June 1903.[19]

After graduating, Natan taught in the gymnasiums and in national and commercial schools of Warsaw. The diploma cited above indicates that in 1908 Natan presented the document to the Inspectorate of the Schools of the City of Warsaw, and at the time Ruvin and Jascha arrived in Warsaw, Natan was teaching at the Froebel Institute.

It was around this time that Natan decided to get married and did so to eighteen-year-old Fanny Heifetz, his niece—the daughter of his older brother Aron. Born in Polotsk in 1894, Fanny worked and studied from the age of fourteen, and although little else is known about her early years, she graduated from Moscow University in 1925.[20] At first, Fanny's parents found their daughter's marriage to such a close relative objectionable, but Fanny's deep love for Natan eventually won them over. A surviving photograph from this period shows Natan and Fanny standing together happily. Having finally convinced Fanny's parents to support the marriage, the family explained to Jascha who Fanny would be after the marriage, that by birth she was his cousin, but by marrying Jascha's uncle Natan, she would become Jascha's aunt. A fascinating glimpse into the situation can be found in a postcard Jascha wrote to Fanny during this period:

To Mr. Aron Heifetz

Polotsk Vitebsk Province
(on butcher's row) his own home
Personally for Fanny
Dear Fanichka!
Thank you for your letter. You see, I'm not making you wait as long as you
did me. In this letter you wrote a lot of nonsense to me, but all the important
things to Mama. Where is your promise from Dubbeln? Where did it go?
And Fanny, this is very bad on your part, you promised to write all the secrets, about Nison [Natan] and how it ended up for you, but it turns out you
wrote this to Mama. Fanechka, I beg you, don't upset me, write about everything. Tell me if you'll give my letter to anyone else to read. Really write this
time. Greetings to all. All of us greet you. Mama, Polya and everyone will
write to you.
Your loving cousin Jascha Heifetz
P.S. Again Fanichka, write about Uncle Nison and how everything turned
out, including serious things. Jascha.[21]

Ruvin and Jascha left Warsaw and returned to St. Petersburg in the
middle of February. With Anna and the two girls also now living in the
apartment on Voznesensky Prospekt, it really felt like home. Jascha began
intense daily practice and Auer started to prepare the boy for two important tests—a solo concert in the Maly Hall at the conservatory and a trip
to Berlin.

Auer made no secret of his desire for Jascha to perform outside Russia.
Warsaw newspapers wrote in February that the professor was extremely
impressed by the young student and "now plans to show him in a concert
tour of the major European musical centers."[22] In April, Auer began planning for this tour and sent a letter to his longtime acquaintance Hermann
Fernow, the manager of the well-known and successful Berlin agency Concert-Direction Hermann Wolff:

St. Petersburg, April 2, 1912
Dear Mr. Fernow:
I shall send you next month my latest pupil with the request that you
arrange for his Berlin public debut. His name is Jascha Heifetz and he is
only eleven years old, but I assure you that this little boy is already a great
violinist. I marvel at his genius, and I expect him to become world-famous
and make a great career. In all my fifty years of violin teaching I have never

known such precocity (*Fruehzeitige Entwicklung*) and as you well know, I have had many great talents, especially since Mischa Elman's sensational Berlin debut in 1904. Mischa, too, was a wonder, but he was thirteen years old at that time, and two years make a vast difference.

Jascha cannot arrive in Berlin before the middle of May, and I know that that is too late for a public concert, but I hope that you can arrange for him a special private press matinee as you did for Mischa Elman eight years ago, and with the encomiums of the critics you will have material with which to build up Jascha's reputation and prepare the way for his public debut next fall.

Please let me know at your earliest convenience in regard to this matter. With friendly greetings,
L. Auer[23]

Jascha's violin lessons proceeded intensely throughout March. In preparation for the April 8 solo concert, with the exception of the Tchaikovsky Concerto, Auer gave Jascha an almost entirely new program. One of these pieces was Bach's musically and technically demanding Chaconne for solo violin—a work Auer himself believed to be one of the most challenging pieces in the violin repertoire. Auer wrote about the Chaconne in his book *Violin Master Works and their Interpretation,* devoting attention to specific difficulties in the piece:

1. There is the matter of memory. Ordinarily, when playing with piano or orchestra accompaniment, the solo artist has a musical support which helps him over many little memnotic [sic] weaknesses; in the case of the "Ciaconna" the very slightest lapse of memory would at once stand out and distract from the effect of the whole performance.

2. Another vital problem is that of making the strings stay in tune in a crowded hall.[24]

Jascha's remarkable musical memory allowed him to approach the Chaconne confidently. Furthermore, he always followed Auer's advice not to play the Chaconne at the start of a concert. As Auer explained, "I always advise my pupils *never* to play the 'Ciaconna' at the *beginning* of a recital or concert, but to introduce it in the *middle* of the programme, so that it will be possible for the violin—or rather the strings—to adapt themselves to the temperature of the hall in question."[25]

Alongside the Chaconne, Jascha also prepared other pieces, including the Schubert *Ave Maria* and various miniatures by his idol Fritz Kreisler, including *La Chasse* and *Schön Rosmarin*. Auer gave his students pieces suited to their individual characters: "I have always developed the repertory of my pupils on broad lines of general appreciation and individual preference. The best of all schools, the best of all types, the music best adapted to the character and powers of the individual—this makes up the repertory of the true artist violinist."[26]

In the Heifetz household no distinction was made between weekdays, weekends, and holidays, and the daily practice routine continued unfailingly. Nevertheless, two events in April could not escape the attention of Jascha and his family. The first was the sinking of the Titanic on April 2 (NS April 15). Newspapers and children's magazines published photographs and reports on the tragedy, and headlines such as "Echoes of the Perishing Titanic" appeared everywhere. The second major event occurred on April 4 in St. Petersburg—a total solar eclipse. Many schools suspended classes so that students could watch the event, and by noon crowds of people had gathered on the streets.

Jascha's performance took place a few days later, on the afternoon of April 8 in the conservatory's Maly Hall. Drawing from recent publicity, advertisements for this concert referred to the little violinist as "Jascha"; the name Joseph never appeared again. Accompanied by Emanuel Bay, Jascha played a program that included the best of what he had studied with Auer during the year: all three movements of the Tchaikovsky Concerto, the Bach Chaconne, the Schubert *Ave Maria*, Kreisler miniatures, the Auer arrangement of Chopin's Nocturne in E Minor, and Wieniawski's *Souvenir de Moscow*. Since it was Jascha's second solo appearance in St. Petersburg, the press and public already knew what to expect; nevertheless, the success was astounding and almost every St. Petersburg newspaper responded.

The *Peterburgsky listok* struggled to explain how an eleven-year-old boy could "feel or understand . . . the religiosity [of Bach],"[27] and the *Vechernee vremya* went as far as to state that "those present witnessed a miracle."[28] The *Peterburgskaya gazeta* continued the theme of divine inspiration, explaining that Jascha "plays as only those specially chosen play—freely, instinctively guessing the greatness of the music he performs."[29] That same review also touched on a theme continued throughout Heifetz's career, his restricted stage mannerisms: "On the serious but so very comely face of his could not be perceived any traces of what one might call an automatic artistic reflex; his inner world is not reflected in his deep eyes, but his violin wails with hot tears and conveys in such a genuine manner that which is experienced in moments of genuine suffering and prayerful ecstasy." The boy's reserved stage mannerisms even led the *Sankt-Peterburgskie vedomosti* to question whether the boy enjoyed being on stage. The paper concluded, however, that "there is no doubt music lovers have fallen in love with him and that they follow his evolution like stockbrokers the valuation of especially valuable bonds."[30]

Two German-language newspapers in St. Petersburg also printed reviews of Jascha's concert. The *St. Petersburger Herold* reported that "there were of course calls for Jascha's teachers, the Professors Auer and Nalbandian, but they—very wrongly—avoided the thanks of the audience."[31] The review continued: "We can expect from Professor Auer that he will guard and nurture the jewel which has been entrusted to him according to the best of human common sense. When the genius has grown wings and conquers the world in full swing, humanity will offer thanks to his guardians which they will not then be able to avoid."

Of all the many responses to Jascha's performance, one of particular significance is that of the respected conductor of the Mariinsky Theater, Nikolai Malko (1883–1961), whose review appeared in two St. Petersburg newspapers, *Rech* and *Sovremennoe slovo*. A former student of Rimsky-Korsakov and Tcherepnin, Malko later played a significant role in the establishment of a Soviet school of conducting and became the first serious advocate of Shostakovich's symphonic works in both Soviet Russia and abroad. Malko was also a successful music critic, and his review of Jascha's concert is both balanced and nuanced:

> . . . Heifetz's age is just a curious detail, playing no role in his performance. This is the playing of a fully mature artist, gifted as a genius, a giftedness not only in one aspect of musical ability, but reflected in the entire nature of the amazing boy. His appearance is endlessly pleasing, and his behavior shows rare modesty and sincerity. There is no effort or striving to give something

which is not there, and so Heifetz's playing in its classical simplicity creates an unusually convincing impression: this is how truly elevated art functions. One had to see what happened with the audience of this concert. We have never had the chance to see a more electrified mood, stronger enthusiasm, and along with this excited, agitated crowd—a charming boy on the stage, calm and clear.

The program of the concert was great both in volume and in significance: the Tchaikovsky Concerto, the Bach Chaconne, and a whole array of small pieces. Marvelous tone, perfect technique, astonishing diversity of bowing, unusual internal feeling of rhythm—all this was present in Heifetz, the main thing being that expressiveness which no words can describe. Specialists went into raptures over the performance of the Bach Chaconne. To hold listeners spellbound by this piece over the course of fifteen minutes—that is the height of artistic ability. Every piece in Heifetz's performance had its own style: the Schubert-Wilhelmj "Ave Maria" was prayerful, "La Chasse" of Kreisler (a piece of baffling difficulty) had a bravura style, the Chopin-Auer Nocturne was poetic. Kreisler's "Schön Rosmarin," played with completely exceptional mastery, evoked an explosion of delight. Even the trivial Wieniawski piece "Souvenir de Moscow" did not spoil the wonderful impression of the concert. Fortunately, Heifetz does not perform often, and his family clearly looks after the genius child with care. Let us wish him from our hearts the necessary conditions for the full development of genius.[32]

Viktor Valter responded to Jascha's concert in the *Russkaya muzykalnaya gazeta,* ending with the words: "Yes, to see and hear this child is true happiness, and those people will be blessed who come to the aid of the parents of this child, to preserve his health and give him a proper upbringing."[33] Reviewers also mentioned that "Heifetz's guardians forbade any gifts," and that "Auer kissed him, as Liszt had the little Anton Rubinstein."[34]

The second half of April witnessed a rare occurrence—Jascha became ill. News of this reached as far as Vilnius, and on April 29 Marusya Malkina wrote to Jascha: "Dear Jaschenka! I'm extremely upset at the rumors I've heard about your illness. What's wrong with you? I hope the rumors are exaggerated and that you won't wait to heal my aching heart with the joyous and hoped for news about you. Honor and Glory to you, incomparable virtuoso!"[35]

The rumors were indeed exaggerated, since on April 28, the day before Marusya sent her postcard, Jascha sat and passed his elementary theory and first solfège class exams for the 1911–1912 academic year. Of the sixteen students sitting the exam, eleven-year-old Jascha received the highest results: "elementary theory, 5; first course solfège, 5; average result, 5."[36] A week later, Jascha took the exam for the more advanced second solfège course: "Grade, 5; result: completed."[37] No doubt Jascha made his theory teacher Mikhail Klimov proud; out of the twenty-two students taking the second solfège class, only one other student received the highest grade. Although Jascha completed a number of theory exams, he did not take a violin performance exam at this time.[38] Considering the recent success of Jascha's solo concert in St. Petersburg, Auer felt it unnecessary to burden the boy with yet another performance, especially since a more serious test awaited him—his Berlin debut.[39]

Above. The Heifetz Family in Polotsk, 1899. *Seated left to right:* Malka with Asya in her arms, Aron with Emma in his arms, Ilya with Fanny, and Morduch-Dov. *Standing left to right:* Natan (?), Ruvin, and Samuil. *Courtesy of Leonid Heifetz and Ilya Lamov.*

Left. Ilya Heifetz, early 1890s. *Courtesy of Albina Starkova-Heifetz.*

ПОЛОЦКЪ. Видъ съ Краснаго Моста на Городъ.

Polotsk, ca. 1900. From the Russian National Library.

Wedding Invitation, Ruvin Heifetz and Anna Sharfstein.
Courtesy of the Maltese Collection (Nemirovsky Archive).

Ruvin and Anna Heifetz, ca. 1900. *Courtesy of the Maltese Collection (Nemirovsky Archive).*

ВИЛЬНА
Стеклянная улица
WILNO
Ulica Szklana

Steklyannaya St., Vilnius, ca. 1900. From the Russian National Library.

ЧАСТЬ I-а.—О РОДИВШИХСЯ.

חלק ריאשון פן נולרים

Above. Birth register, Jascha Heifetz. *Courtesy of the State Historical Archive of Lithuania.*

Left. Jascha Heifetz in Vilnius, ca. 1905–1906. *Courtesy of Anne Chotzinoff and Lisa Chotzinoff Grossman.*

Left: Heifetz family in Vilnius, late 1905 to early 1906. *Courtesy of Anne Chotzinoff and Lisa Chotzinoff Grossman.*

Below: Jascha Heifetz and Ilya Malkin, Vilnius, ca. 1906–1907. *Courtesy of the Maltese Collection (Nemirovsky Archive).*

Left. Jascha Heifetz in Vilnius, ca. 1906–1907. *Courtesy of the Library of Congress, Prints & Photographs Division, LC-DIG-ggbain-30215 (Bain News Service).*

Below. Jascha Heifetz and (probably) Gustav Katz, ca. 1907–1908. *Courtesy of Albina Starkova-Heifetz.*

The location of the music school of the Imperial Russian Music Society during Jascha's years of study, and the modern memorial plaque in Vilnius.

Internal corridor, St. Petersburg Conservatory, early 1910s. *Courtesy of the Manuscript Office of the Russian Institute for the History of the Arts.*

St. Petersburg Conservatory, early twentieth century. *Courtesy of the Manuscript Office of the Russian Institute for the History of the Arts.*

Ioannes Nalbandian and Alexander Glazunov, early 1910s. *Courtesy of the Manuscript Office of the Russian Institute for the History of the Arts.*

Jascha Heifetz and Ioannes Nalbandian, 1911. *Courtesy of the Central State Archive of Film, Photo, and Audio Documents, St. Petersburg.*

Jascha Heifetz, Druskininkai, 1910. *Courtesy of the Heifetz family. From the Jascha Heifetz Collection at the Library of Congress.*

Maly Hall of the St. Petersburg Conservatory, early 1910s. *Courtesy of the Manuscript Office of the Russian Institute for the History of the Arts.*

Heifetz concert poster, Maly Hall, St. Petersburg Conservatory, April 17, 1911.
*Courtesy of the Heifetz Family. From the Jascha Heifetz Collection at the
Library of Congress.*

Fritz Kreisler, 1912–1913. *Courtesy of
the Manuscript Office of the Russian
Institute for the History of the Arts.*

Viktor Valter, early 1910s. *Courtesy of the Manuscript Office of the Russian Institute for the History of the Arts.*

Цѣна **5** коп.

Павловскій вокзалъ.

ПРОГРАММА.

Въ пятницу, 13-го Мая, 1911 года

подъ упр. **А. П. Асланова** и **М. О. Цирельштейна.**

1 отдѣленіе.

Вагнеръ
1. Маршъ изъ оп. „Тангейзеръ".
2. Вступленіе къ оп. „Лоэнгринъ".
3. Увертюра „Ріенци".

2 отдѣленіе.

Вагнеръ
1. Увертюра къ оп. „Тангейзеръ".
2. Вступленіе къ III д. оп. „Лоэнгринъ".
3. Полетъ Валкирій, антр. къ III д. муз. др. „Валкирія".

4. **Мендельсонъ.** Концертъ, E-moll, для скрипки съ оркестромъ.

    a) Allegro molto apassionato
    b) Andante
    c) Allegro non troppo. Allegro molto vivace.

Исп. на скрипкѣ **I. Хейфецъ.**

3 отдѣленіе.

1. **Мейерберъ.** Танецъ съ факелами.

2. **Гретри.** Тамбуринъ.

3. **Штраусъ.** Вальсъ „O, Schöner Mai".

ЧОПО-ЛИТ. Б. АВИДОНЪ, НЕВСКІЙ 17

Heifetz concert program, Pavlovsk Station, May 13, 1911. *Courtesy of the Manuscript Office of the Russian Institute for the History of the Arts.*

Label from the first gramophone recording of Jascha Heifetz, Zvukopis, May 1911.

Antakalnis (Antokol), Vilnius, ca. 1900. *Courtesy of the Russian National Library.*

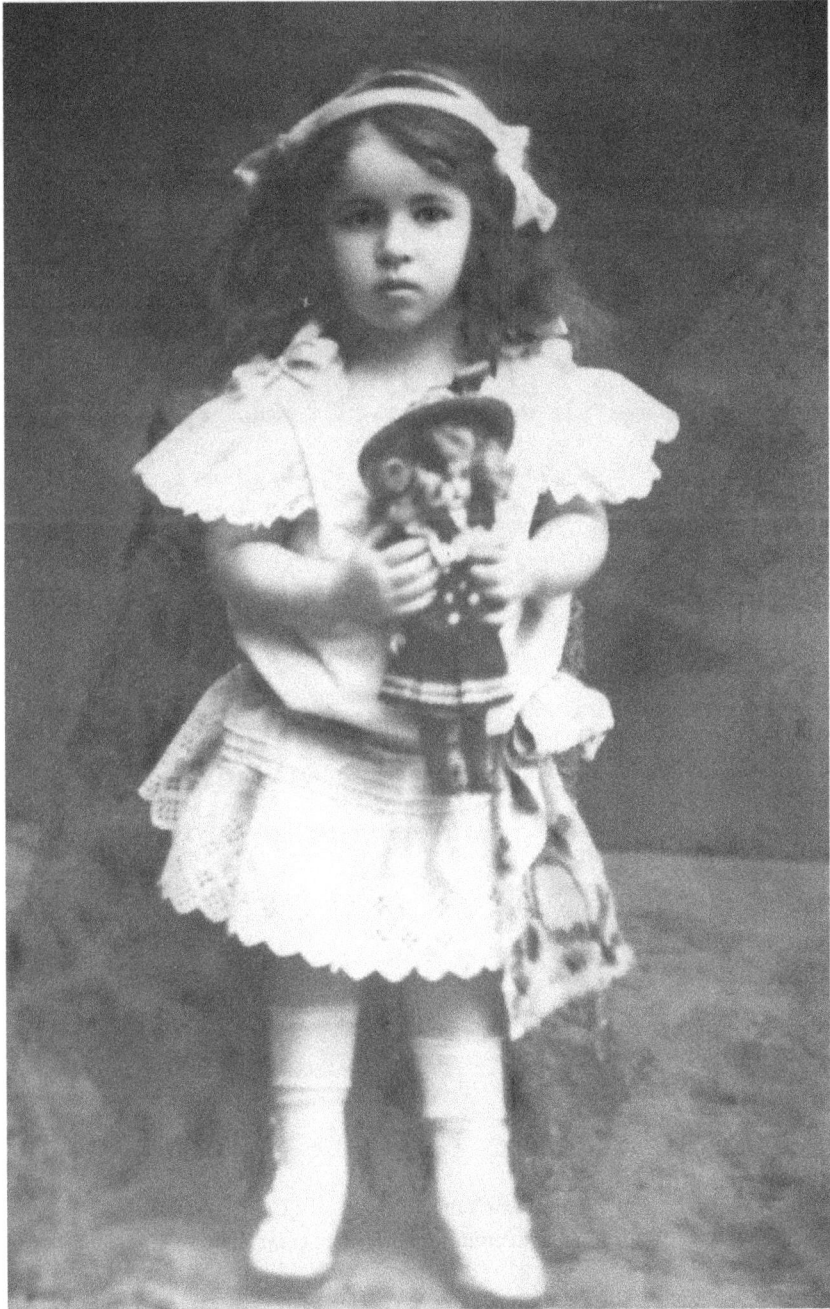

Anna (Anyuta) Sharfstein-Koch, Vilnius, 1911. *Courtesy of Anna Sharfstein-Koch.*

Многоуважаемый
Викторъ Григорьевичъ!

Простите, что я Вамъ до сихъ поръ не писалъ. Мы живемъ на дачѣ недалеко отъ Вильны. Изъ Вильны надо ѣхать извозчикомъ или конкой. У насъ очень хорошая дача. Я теперь отдыхаю, но только немного занимаюсь на скрипкѣ и на роялѣ. Я теперь учу концертъ Чайковскаго, Генделя Соната. Я слава Богу здоровъ и чувствую себя очень хорошо. Какъ Вы дорогой Викторъ Григорьевичъ поживаете? Какъ ваше здоровье? Какъ у Васъ всѣ поживаютъ? Сердечный поклонъ всѣмъ Вашимъ, а также поклонъ отъ меня въ Царское село буду писать. Цѣлую Васъ всѣхъ.
Іосифъ Хейфецъ

Letter from Jascha Heifetz to Viktor Valter, June 16, 1911. *Courtesy of the Manuscript Office of the Russian Institute for the History of the Arts.*

Jascha and Anna Heifetz, Hotel Passage, Odessa, July 1911. *Courtesy of the Heifetz Family. From the Jascha Heifetz Collection at the Library of Congress.*

Jascha Heifetz during his tour to Odessa, July 1911. *Courtesy of Albina Starkova-Heifetz.*

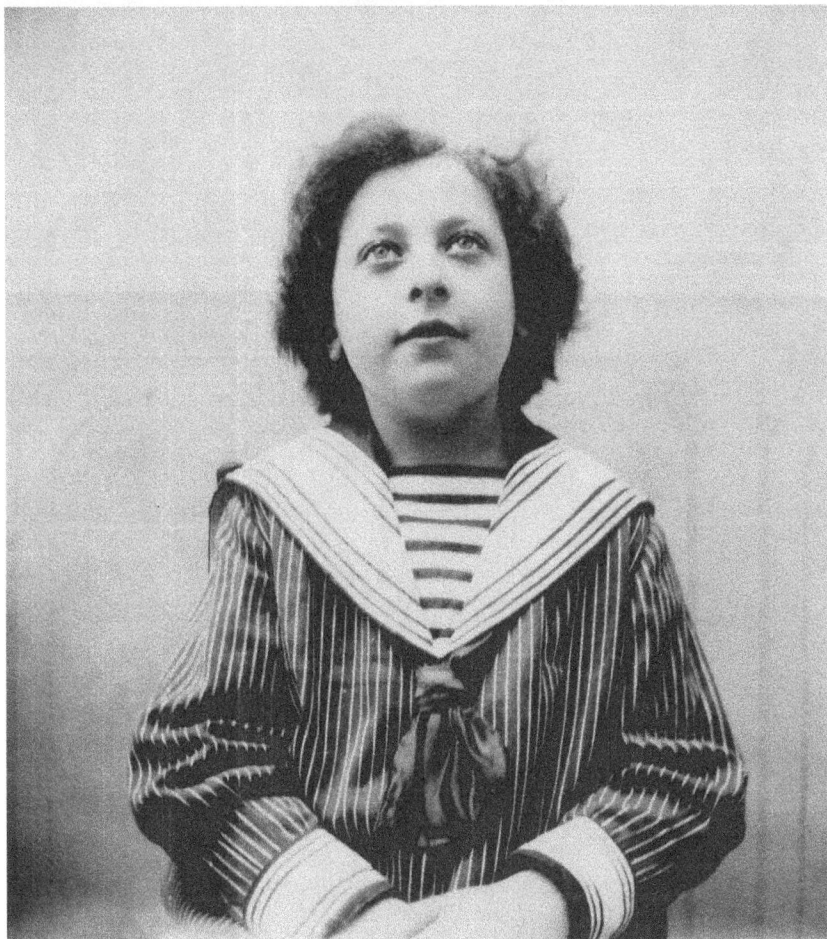

Jascha Heifetz during his tour to Odessa, July 1911. *Courtesy of the Heifetz Family. From the Jascha Heifetz Collection at the Library of Congress.*

Jascha Heifetz and Hyman Gerber, late 1911. *Courtesy of Anne Chotzinoff and Lisa Chotzinoff Grossman.*

Zinovy Kiselgof, early 1910s. *Courtesy of the Heifetz Family.*
From the Jascha Heifetz Collection at the Library of Congress.

Above. Musical Evening at the Berlin home of Arthur Abell, May 20, 1912. From the *Musical Courier.*

Left. Leopold Auer. *Courtesy of the Manuscript Office of the Russian Institute for the History of the Arts.*

CONCERT-DIRECTION HERMANN WOLFF, BERLIN W. 35.

Theatersaal der Königl. Hochschule für Musik

Fasanenstrasse 1, Portal V.

Freitag den 24. Mai 1912, abends 8 Uhr

EINZIGES CONCERT

des 11 jährigen Violinisten

Jascha Heifetz

Am Klavier: Josef Schwartz.

PROGRAMM.

1. **Mendelssohn:** Violin-Concert (E-moll), op. 64.
   Allegro molto appassionato.
   Andante.
   Allegro molto vivace.

2. a) **Chopin:** Nocturne 9, No. 2.
   b) **Haydn-Auer:** Vivace.
   c) **Haendel-Hubay:** Larghetto.
   d) **Kreisler:** Caprice Viennois.

3. **Henri Wieniawski:** Souvenir de Moscou.

Concertflügel: BECHSTEIN.

Während der Vorträge bleiben die Saaltüren geschlossen.

Heifetz concert program, Königliche Hochschule für Musik, Berlin, May 24, 1912. *Courtesy of the Heifetz Family. From the Jascha Heifetz Collection at the Library of Congress.*

Above: The Heifetz and the Schwarz
families. *Courtesy of Patricia Schwarz.*

Right: Waldemar Liachowsky, 1909.
Courtesy of Rudolph and Henry Lea.

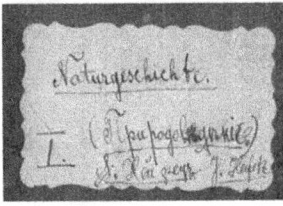

Above: Notebook with plants
collected by Jascha Heifetz.
*Courtesy of the Maltese Collection
(Nemirovsky Archive).*

Right: Arthur Nikisch. *Courtesy of
the Manuscript Office of the Russian
Institute for the History of the Arts.*

Gratis.

CONCERT-DIRECTION HERMANN WOLFF, BERLIN W.

Montag den 28. Oktober 1912, Abends 7½ Uhr pünktlich

II. Philharmonisches Concert
Dirigent: Arthur Nikisch
Solist: Jascha Heifetz (Violine)

❧

PROGRAMM

1. Vyšehrad, Symphonische Dichtung . . . F. Smetana

2. Concert für die Violine mit Orchester,
   D-dur, op. 35 . . . . Tschaïkowsky
   Allegro moderato. — Canzonetta, Andante. —
   Allegro vivacissimo.

3. Ouverture zu einem Gascognischen Ritter-
   spiel, für grosses Orchester (zum 1. Male) R. Mandl

4. Symphonie A-dur, No. 4 (italienische),
   op. 90 . . . . F. Mendelssohn
   Allegro vivace. — Andante con moto. — Con
   moto moderato — Saltarello (Presto).

🙢

III. Philharmonisches Concert: Montag, 11. Novemb. 1912
Dirigent: Arthur Nikisch
Solist: Carl Friedberg (Klavier)

PROGRAMM. Schumann: Ouverture zu der Oper «Genoveva», op. 81. —
Brahms: Klavier-Concert B-dur. — Braunfels: Carnevals-Ouverture zu
«Prinzessin Brambilla», für grosses Orchester, op. 22, No. 8 (zum ersten
Male). — Beethoven: Symphonie No. 7, A-dur.

Während der Musik bleiben die Saaltüren geschlossen.
Zwischen No. 3 und 4 Pause von 10 Minuten

Verlassen des Saales nach Beginn des II. Teiles des Concerts kann — um
ungen während der Symphonie usw. zu vermeiden — nur durch die rück-
wärtige Tür (bei den Stehplätzen) bewerkstelligt werden.

Die Foyers in der oberen Etage sind dem geehrten Publikum geöffnet.

Programmbücher à 30 Pfennige.

Heifetz concert program, Berlin Philharmonic and Arthur Nikisch,
October 28, 1912. *Courtesy of the Heifetz Family. From the Jascha Heifetz
Collection at the Library of Congress.*

Natan and Fanny Heifetz. *Courtesy of Leonid Heifetz and Ilya Lamov.*

On the tennis court, Loschwitz, 1913. *Front from right to left:* Max Rosen, Jascha Heifetz, and Eddy Brown. *Courtesy of the Heifetz Family. From the Jascha Heifetz Collection at the Library of Congress.*

Loschwitz, near Dresden. *Courtesy of the Manuscript Office of the Russian Institute for the History of the Arts.*

Jascha Heifetz inscription to Leopold Auer, summer 1913.
Courtesy of the St. Petersburg Conservatory.

Heifetz family, 1913. *From left to right:* Natan, Jascha, Fanny, Anna, Elza, Ruvin, and Pauline. *Courtesy of the Maltese Collection (Nemirovsky Archive).*

Jascha Heifetz and his sisters Pauline (*left*) and Elza (*right*).
Courtesy of Albina Starkova-Heifetz.

Hall of the Assembly of the Nobility in St. Petersburg. *Courtesy of the Manuscript Office of the Russian Institute for the History of the Arts.*

19 13

Залъ Дворянскаго Собранія

Въ Пятницу, 22-го Ноября,

КОНЦЕРТЪ

13-ти лѣтняго СКРИПАЧА

Яши ХЕЙФЕЦЪ.

Heifetz concert program, Hall of the Assembly of the Nobility, November 22, 1913.
Courtesy of the Manuscript Office of the Russian Institute for the History of the Arts.

ИМПЕРАТОРСКОЕ Русское Музыкальное Общество

С.-Петербургское Отдѣленіе.

ТЕАТРЪ С.-ПЕТЕРБУРГСКОЙ КОНСЕРВАТОРІИ.

Въ Субботу, 18-го Января 1914 года,

П Е Р В Ы Й

Симфоническій Концертъ,

(Не состоявшійся 19-го Октября 1913 г.).

Симфоническій оркестръ, состоящій при СПБ. Отдѣленіи

И. Р. М. О. подъ управленіемъ

А. К. ГЛАЗУНОВА

при участіи

Я. ХЕЙФЕЦА (скрипка).

У рояля М. Т. ДУЛОВЪ.

Рояль фабрики К. М. ШРЕДЕРЪ.

Начало въ 8½ часовъ вечера.

Государственный
Научно-иследов. Институт
театра и музыки
В. типографии 1 апреля
Инвент. № 14872

Above: Heifetz concert program, Bolshoi Hall, St. Petersburg Conservatory, with Alexander Glazunov, January 18, 1914. *Courtesy of the Manuscript Office of the Russian Institute for the History of the Arts.*

Facing: Willy Ferrero, 1913. *Courtesy of the Manuscript Office of the Russian Institute for the History of the Arts.*

Glazunov and Heifetz, caricature by A. Arnshtam, *Den,* January 1914.

CHAPTER NINE

1912: First Trip to Germany

PRIOR TO THE OUTBREAK of World War I, Berlin was one of the most important cities in the world, politically, industrially, and in terms of its standard of living. The city underwent significant development after it became the capital of the German Empire in 1871, and further growth continued from 1888 with the ascension of Wilhelm II to the throne. As industry increased, the city grew, and by the start of the 1910s, the population of Berlin and its suburbs reached over three-and-a-half million, making it Europe's third largest city.

Led by its universities and institutions such as the Royal Academy of Sciences, Berlin also became one of the premier academic centers of Western Europe. The city gained a reputation for its culture, which was showcased in its numerous museums, galleries, and educational and entertainment establishments. Aside from those run by the state, Berlin boasted twenty-five private theaters, including the *Deutsches Theater* headed by the world-famous director Max Reinhardt. Berlin musical life thrived, and institutions such as the Stern Conservatory had an international reputation for providing a high level of music education. In addition to its fondness for lighter genres, the Berlin public was passionate about serious music. Among the several concert halls and orchestras in Berlin, attention focused on the Royal Capella and the Berlin Philharmonic Orchestra, which offered evening concerts twice a week, often with the participation of international stars. The high-profile concerts of the Berlin Philharmonic usually took place in the Philharmonic Hall and were conducted, at this time, by Arthur Nikisch, who also led the Leipzig Gewandhaus Orchestra. In addition to the Berlin Philharmonic performances, symphonic and chamber music events took place in many other concert venues throughout Berlin, including the Beethoven-Saal, the Bechstein-Saal, the Hall of the Vocal Academy, and two halls in the Königliche Hochschule für Musik.

Professor Auer had visited and performed in Berlin a number of times during his long career, and he set about helping Jascha prepare for his Berlin debut. Auer's own teacher, the great violinist Joseph Joachim, had lived in Berlin during the second half of his life until his death in 1907. In 1868, Joachim founded a school of instrumental music in the Akademie der Künste, which in 1872 became the Königliche Hochschule für Musik. For many years, Joachim performed concerts with his famous Joachim String Quartet and contributed much to the musical life of the city. Believing strongly in the abilities of his former teacher, Auer often sent his own students to Joachim for further study. In 1894 Auer sent Nalbandian to study with Joachim, and a decade later sent Elman to Berlin to perform his debut. Elman's successful appearance on October 14, 1904, set in motion the young violinist's worldwide career, upstaging the then-ascendant prodigy Franz von Vecsey, a student of Hubay and Joachim. Elman's Berlin success in 1904 was followed by a London debut in 1905 and one in New York in 1908. These events secured Auer's position in the ranks of the greatest pedagogues of the era.

Elman's appearance in Berlin had been facilitated by Hermann Fernow, who was at the time director of the Concert-Direction Hermann Wolff. The Wolff agency was founded in 1881 by Hermann Wolff (1845–1902), a German impresario and founder and editor of a host of Berlin musical periodicals such as *Neue Berliner Musikzeitung* and *Musikwelt*. After Wolff died, the leadership of his agency passed to his widow, Louise Wolff, and to Hermann Fernow, who had been Wolff's closest associate; the agency name remained the same.

The concert promotion business in Berlin was ruthless, and agencies competed to attract the biggest names and consequently the biggest profits. In a conversation with Maksimilian Steinberg, composer Julia Weissberg shared her impressions of the Berlin music scene in 1910: "It is certainly very difficult to break through here, and only by living here can you see just how much foulness is a part of the entire concert staging business—the Konzertdirektion [Concert-Direction Hermann Wolff] and so on."[1] Success depended on Louise Wolff, and Berlin musical life was made in the salon of this powerful woman. Fernow, on the other hand, conducted the logistical side of the agency's business.

Auer and Fernow had kept up friendly relations ever since Elman's debut in 1904. Auer found a dependable business partner in Fernow, and thus in the spring of 1912 he turned to the concert promoter to arrange Jascha's trip to Berlin. Fernow did not disappoint. He organized an appearance for Jascha on May 19 (os May 6) at the Bechstein-Saal. The solfège exams at the St. Petersburg Conservatory took place between May 2 and 4 (os), giving Jascha and his father just a few days to travel to Berlin for the concert. The thousand-mile railroad journey from St. Petersburg to Berlin took approximately thirty hours, which included time for changing wheels at the crossover between the wide Russian railroad tracks and the narrower European ones. In Verzhbolov, Russian customs officers boarded the train, and in Eidkunen, their German counterparts also passed through the cabins, checking for goods such as tobacco, cigars, and tea, which were all taxed at the border.

Russians heading to Berlin usually arrived at the centrally located Berlin Friedrichstrasse Station. Owing to its proximity to many hotels and its connections to other main stations, arriving visitors could avoid dealing with the local cabs and their confusing meters. Although it is unknown in which hotel the Heifetzes resided during this visit, on their return to Berlin later that year they stayed at Hotel Sanssouci, a large, first-class establishment at 37 Linkstrasse, close to where Jascha would perform—the Bechstein-Saal at 42 Linkstrasse.

Fernow advertised Jascha's concert through his own private channels. Since the event was aimed primarily at professional musicians and the press, newspaper advertisements were unnecessary. One flyer for the concert read: "A new wunderkind has appeared, who makes one's head spin. And of course, this is a Jewish boy from Russia!"[2] Fernow's preparations proved successful, and on May 19 all five hundred seats of the Bechstein-Saal were filled. Joined for the first time by the accompanist Otto Bake, Jascha performed a familiar program, including the Tchaikovsky Concerto, the Bach Chaconne, Schubert *Ave Maria*, Kreisler *Schön Rosmarin*, the Auer arrangement of the Chopin Nocturne in E Minor, Paganini Caprice no. 24, and Popper *La Fileuse*. Jascha played well, and later that day Ruvin sent a telegram to Valter recounting the responses of the reporters gathered in the lobby of the Bechstein-Saal after the performance: "The press claims never to have seen anything like this before. A great number of invitations. Heifetz."[3]

The next day, May 20 (OS May 7), Jascha attended a musical evening at the home of the noted music critic Arthur Abell, the director of the Berlin branch of the New York journal *Musical Courier*. Fernow arranged the evening to honor two young violinists, Jascha Heifetz and László Ipolyi. Ipolyi was a talented student of the famous Italian violinist and teacher Arrigo Serato, at that time a professor at the Königliche Hochschule für Musik in Berlin. Fernow gave an account of the evening to Auer in a letter:

> Dear Professor Auer:
> The Abell reception for Jascha Heifetz came off at his home this afternoon and it exceeded my fondest expectations. He had some twenty violinists assembled in his room, eight of whom were famous soloists, and you should have seen the amazement on their faces when that little tot was playing Mendelssohn's Concerto accompanied by Marcel van Gool; and when Fritz Kreisler sat down at the piano and accompanied Jascha in his Schoen Rosemarin [*sic*] pandemonium broke loose in the room. Jascha's father said to me, "Jascha's cup of joy is now full and running over. He will never in all his life forget this day." Immediately after the playing I questioned each one of those famous violinists and this is what they said:
> "Never in all my life have I witnessed such precocity; the technical perfection with which Jascha played the Mendelssohn Concerto reminds me forcefully of Sarasate. FRITZ KREISLER."
> "Little Jascha takes my breath away—he has just given us older violinists an uncanny exhibition of violin mastery, I am proud of my little countryman. ALEXANDER PETSCHNIKOFF."

"Jascha's playing of Mendelssohn will forever live in my memory as an extraordinary feat of virtuosity. CARL FLESCH."

"The consummate ease with which little Jascha encompassed the difficult passages reminds me forcibly of my old friend Henri Wieniawski; no difficulty, however great, could force that great Pole to change his posture or draw an extra breath. HUGO HEERMANN."[4]

In addition to Abell and his wife, as well as Fernow, many notable musicians attended the musical event. These included former Joachim students Gustav Hollaender, now director of the Stern Conservatory, his colleague Theodore Spiering, and Willy Hess, who had performed as soloist with the Boston Symphony Orchestra and now worked at the Königliche Hochschule für Musik in Berlin. Among the most respected guests were Fritz Kreisler and his wife Harriet and Ipolyi's teacher Arrigo Serato. Representing Russian musicians was Michael Press, a graduate of the Moscow Conservatory, who often toured abroad and who, since 1906, lived in Berlin where he performed in the Trio Russe with his cellist brother Joseph and his pianist wife Vera Maurina. Alexander Petschnikoff, mentioned in Fernow's letter, and his wife, were also present at the evening. Like Press, Petschnikoff trained at the Moscow Conservatory, graduated in 1901, and then studied with Joachim before embarking on a successful performing career in Europe. Joachim's name held great meaning for many of the guests, as it did for Auer, who conveyed to Jascha a reverence for his great teacher. Other notable names gathered at the Abell home included the violinist and pedagogue Carl Flesch, concertmaster of the Berlin Philharmonic Julius Thornberg, American pianist Eleanor Spencer, the pianist Marcel van Gool, the music critic of the Berlin newspaper *Lokal Anzeiger,* Paul Ertel, and the director of the Berlin Women's Orchestra, Elisabeth Kuyper.

Finding themselves surrounded by such an array of world-class musicians was thrilling for both Jascha and his father. To thank the host, Jascha gave Abell a signed photograph with the inscription: "In fond remembrance, to Arthur Abell from J. Heifetz. 1912. Berlin."[5] A photograph of all the assembled musicians appeared twice on the pages of *Musical Courier,* the first time in 1912, with the inscription: "Remarkable Group of Violinists. Photographed on May 20 at the Berlin Home of The Musical Courier."[6] The accompanying text reads:

Ipolyi played the Paganini Concerto and a Veracini sonata, and Heifetz, whom Leopold Auer declares to be the greatest genius that ever studied with him, played the Mendelssohn Concerto and a number of smaller pieces. Marcel van Gool accompanied the concertos and Fritz Kreisler all the other numbers, including several of his own compositions played by Heifetz. The sight of these two children playing before such a group of famous violinists was impressive and inspiring.

In 1952, the photograph appeared again on the pages of *Musical Courier* in Arthur Abell's article "When Heifetz, Aged 11, Stormed Musical Berlin,"[7] Also in 1952, Abell gave Heifetz the original photograph with an inscription: "To my valued friend Jascha Heifetz, as a souvenir of the reception I gave for him at my home in Berlin on May 20, 1912. When he amazed the celebrated violinists seen in this group with his playing. Arthur M. Abell. June 23, 1952."[8]

Heifetz's own recollection of the evening appeared in Louis Lochner's biography of Fritz Kreisler:

> I met Kreisler for the first time in 1912 in Berlin. There was a gathering of critics and musicians at the home of a man named Abell. I simply worshiped Kreisler, and when, somewhat later, I gave a recital in Bechstein Hall, Berlin, I tried to imitate my idol. During the gathering at the Abell home someone suggested that "the young man from Russia play a number or two." I was willing enough, but what about an accompanist? What about the piano score? Fritz Kreisler kindly jumped into the breach and played my accompaniments from memory. I chose the Mendelssohn Concerto and Kreisler's own *Schön Rosmarin* for that informal but portentous introduction to the musical world of Berlin.[9]

This event also surfaces in an account by the violinist Benno Rabinof, a close friend of Heifetz in the American years of his life. Rabinof's story is problematic; his list of attendees inaccurately included the violinists Bronislaw Huberman, Juan Manén, and Jan Kubelík. Rabinof also relates that after Kreisler accompanied Jascha in the Mendelssohn Concerto, he turned to the group of violinists and said: "Well, gentlemen, we can now all break our violins across our knees."[10] This charming line occurs throughout Heifetz folklore, often in different forms. Although there is no conclusive evidence that Kreisler called on his colleagues to break their instruments, it certainly makes for a good story.

The first reviews of Jascha's concert at the Bechstein-Saal appeared the following day, and Fernow wrote about them in a letter to Auer:

Dear Professor Auer:
The way the Berlin papers this morning responded to those encomiums of the celebrated violinists left nothing to be desired. Knowing the public as I do, I am now confident that all musical Berlin is agog to hear this little Russian violin marvel.
Hurriedly,
Hermann Fernow[11]

Newspapers from across the entire political spectrum applauded Jascha's performance, including the liberal *Berliner Tageblatt*[12] and the *Vossische Zeitung,* which was popular in business circles and among the old Berlin bourgeoisie:

A new wunderkind appeared on the stage of the Bechstein Hall, Jakob Heifetz by name. The boy displayed his gifts on the violin and is one of the strongest talents among those who mature early which one has encountered in the last few years. The aspect which is so reassuring in relation to this latest apparition is the total absence of technical drill. He performed difficult pieces; but he performed them effortlessly, with the aware bowing of an adult; with the delicacy and the alertness of a true music soul. If he is allowed to continue growing in peace, he will flourish to become a very precious artist.[13]

In addition, the national-liberal *Volks-Zeitung* and the openly anti-Semitic *Staatsbürger-Zeitung* both published rave reviews of the boy's performance. The *Volks-Zeitung* described Jascha as hailing "from the land of the wunderkinder, Russia. . . ."[14] and the *Staatsbürger-Zeitung* added that "little Heifetz is a veritable miracle of nature and of art."[15]

Jascha's talent caused such a stir that a second Berlin concert was organized, something neither Auer nor Fernow had planned. By the end of May, musical life in the concert halls of Berlin usually gave way to the gardens and parks, where outdoor performances by popular military concert bands and the like attracted large audiences. Nevertheless, a concert for Jascha was planned on one of the most impressive stages in Berlin, the 1,600-seat Theater Hall of the Königliche Hochschule für Musik. On May 22, just two days after the evening at Abell's home, morning editions of *Vossische Zei-*

tung and *Berlin Lokal-Anzeiger* printed announcements for Jascha's second concert, set for May 24.

The days between performances gave the Heifetzes a chance to see the impressive city and visit some of its many sights, but all focus remained on the upcoming event. Not surprisingly, tickets for the May 24 concert quickly sold out. The program included the Mendelssohn Concerto and Wieniawski *Souvenir de Moscow*. The program also offered new works for Jascha, including Handel's Larghetto from the Sonata in E (Hubay edition) which appeared frequently in later programs, the Haydn-Auer Vivace, and Fauré *Lullaby*. Also, for the first time, Jascha performed *Caprice Viennois* by his adored Fritz Kreisler. Piano accompaniment was provided by Joseph (Yosif) Schwarz, a talented pianist of Russian origin who became friendly with the Heifetzes and who gave Jascha piano lessons two years later. Schwarz's six-year-old son Boris also studied the violin. After emigrating to the United States years later, Boris Schwarz became a famous musicologist, authoring a number of books, including *Great Masters of the Violin*.[16] The Schwarzes and Heifetzes became especially close at the start of World War I. Jascha signed a photograph for his accompanist: "To the respected Yosif Filippovich in memory of our joint playing in Berlin from Jascha Heifetz."[17]

The May 24 performance was successful; Fernow wrote to Auer the next day:

> Dear Professor Auer:
> Jascha scored a sensational success last night. The hall was completely sold out and the public was wild with enthusiasm. I would not have believed it possible to arrange such a successful debut at this late season, nor indeed would it have been but for the invaluable assistance of Abell. I am now determined to have Jascha appear as soloist with the Berlin Philharmonic Orchestra under Arthur Nikisch, notwithstanding his tender age.
> Yours fraternally,
> Hermann Fernow[18]

The German newspapers praised the boy for his excellent performance. The *Berliner Tageblatt* remarked, "Here we are probably facing the greatest violin talent that the modern age has produced."[19] The *Berliner Lokal-Anzeiger* wrote:

The little fellow who faces the world as a healthy, childlike and modest chap, increases the roll call of musical wunderkinder by a new, exceedingly remarkable specimen. In his program, he included classical and modern items, and he played everything with the same stunning technical perfection, with the same beautiful and pure tone, and the same faultless intonation. But by no means in a monotonous way. On the contrary, his playing, enlivened by an admirable rhythmic energy, bears witness to feeling and intelligence and acquires its own flavor by sudden flaring of temperament.[20]

Specialist music publications also joined in the praise. Hugo Rasch in *Allgemeine Musik-Zeitung* stated:

What this eleven-year-old, rosy-cheeked and chub-faced, uncomplicated boy achieves on his instrument is more than the achievement of a wunderkind, which in itself would suffice to raise astonishment. You can feel the disciplined training by his teacher (unless I am mistaken, Prof. Auer). And yet this young head already has something specifically his own to give us. And the way in which he already manages to feel the styles of the most different composers; the way he followed his Handel with the Caprice Viennois by Kreisler! . . . If there were a league table of wunderkinder of this age, then Jascha Heifetz would already have to be ranked behind Mischa Elman and before Franz von Vecsey. We can only hope that this phenomenally gifted boy will not fall victim to commercial ambitions. Then, maybe, we can hope for great things from him.[21]

The authoritative Berlin journal *Die Musik* emphasized:

Looking at purely technical aspects, this wunderkind-like boy has been trained in a manner that leaves him hardly anything still to aspire to. Finger and bowing technique are that of a mature virtuoso and enable him to play the last movement of the Mendelssohn Concerto at a speed one rarely hears. But fortunately, out of the abilities of this boy peep not only excellent tuition, but also true talent. May a merciful fate protect him from un-artistic exploitation, may it be granted to him that he may develop his strong talent in a calm manner, in the service of art.[22]

News of Jascha's success traveled westward as far as the United States and eastward all the way back home to Russia. In New York, *Musical Courier* printed Arthur Abell's report: "Jascha Heifetz, a tiny eleven-year-old violinist, is the sensation of the day in Berlin. . . . Berlin is so surfeited with music and has heard so many wonderful prodigies that one would not have thought it possible for a new one to come and make such a profound impression as this little tot has made."[23] In Moscow, the *Putevodny ogon- yok* wrote that Jascha brought "stern music experts to ecstasy. By heritage Jascha Heifetz is a Jew, a Russian citizen; he was trained with the famous musician-virtuoso Auer, who early on noticed in him remarkable abilities …"[24] Since Jascha had yet to perform in Moscow, the critic based his report on the opinions of others. For now at least, Jascha had conquered Berlin and was sure to return.

Jascha received a warm welcome back home in St. Petersburg; his mentors, Auer and Valter, congratulated the boy on his successful foreign debut. On Jascha's behalf, Auer immediately began to plan a contract with Concert-Direction Hermann Wolff for a tour of European cities that coming fall.

With great hopes for later that year, the Heifetzes began to organize their summer vacation. A conservatory leave certificate from May 29 reads: "for all cities of the Russian Empire for the period from this date forward through the tenth of September 1912."[25] The choice of destination was the Latvian coast, one of the most beautiful resort areas of the Russian Empire's northwest region and only a 200-mile journey by railroad from St. Petersburg. Riga, Latvia's capital, was an impressive city with narrow-winding streets, green gardens, and leafy alleys. To the west was Jūrmala, a resort town on the Baltic Sea. Sand dunes stretched along the coast, and the pine forests were filled with hundreds of small summer cottages that hosted over ten thousand vacationers every summer.

A printed stamp on the reverse of the leave certificate reads: "Seen in the office of the police master of bathing places near Riga. June 18, 1912."[26] It is likely the Heifetzes settled in the specific resort settlement of Dubulti (then Dubbeln), since that name appears in family correspondence from this period, and a surviving photograph with an inscription in Jascha's hand reads: "Dubbeln. Taken in the woods at the request of Pa."[27] The resort had much to offer, including wide and spacious beaches with the famous white quartz sand of the Latvian coast and the warm water of the Gulf of Riga. The place was a veritable paradise for children; nearby forests were home to a multitude of butterflies and bugs, and strawberries grew everywhere.

Given the idyllic summer scene, one wonders at Heifetz's later discomfort with his childhood. As an adult, why did he speak so reluctantly of his earliest years? Why did he reveal so few details? One possible explanation relates to the constant necessity to practice, a necessity that inevitably restricted the usual joys of childhood. Bitterness surrounding Heifetz's childhood might also be linked to early cracks that emerged in his parents' marriage; after all, Ruvin and Anna eventually separated, a decision that was likely years in the making. Jascha's parents had opposing personalities. Ruvin was garrulous, fussy, and foppish, with a strong desire to fit in with elevated company. At the same time, he was a warm and loving man who cared deeply about his family and sacrificed much for them. On the other side of the marriage, Anna Heifetz showed a sober decisiveness and circumspection in dealing with the outside world, and over the coming years, especially after the Heifetzes arrived in the United States, she came to dominate family decision-making. Ultimately, she was a dedicated and loving mother who felt a great need to protect her children. Jascha cared deeply for both his parents, but this could not suffice to relieve the friction that gradually built between Anna and Ruvin.

All of this likely clouded Heifetz's adult memories of childhood, but there was still much to be enjoyed in his formative years, including his butterfly collection and a Leica camera that he treasured. Another of Jascha's favorite childhood pastimes involved collecting and arranging plants for his herbarium. Two of his personal notebooks filled with pressed plants and flowers survive to this day. Until recently, these notebooks were preserved but forgotten in the home of Heifetz's Moscow relatives. Remarkably, after nine decades, the dried plants have retained both their form and color, and beautiful inscriptions in German and Russian appear next to each specimen.

Jascha continued to practice during his time at the resort, and in July and August he performed two concerts with the Riga Symphony Orchestra, which appeared in Dubulti during the summer season. The Finnish conductor Georg Schnéevoigt (1872–1947) directed the concerts and continued to do so for the following decade and a half. Schnéevoigt began his career as a cellist and appeared as principal cellist and soloist with the Helsinki Philharmonic Orchestra, but his real success came with conducting.

Jascha's first concert with the Riga Symphony Orchestra took place on July 26 and was held as a fundraiser. According to reports, a storm arrived the day of the concert, but, as the local newspaper *Rizhskaya mysl* wrote, "thunder and rain did not stop supporters of the orchestra, who overfilled the park. The large gathering of people was drawn not only by the grandeur of the fundraising concert, but also by the child prodigy Jascha Heifetz."[28] Jascha played the first movement of the Tchaikovsky Concerto with orchestra and three pieces with the pianist Jugel-Janson: the Paganini Caprice no. 24, Bach Aria, and Tchaikovsky *Melodie,* the third piece from the violin and piano cycle *Souvenir d'un lieu cher.*

For his second performance on August 4, Jascha played the Mendelssohn Concerto with orchestra, a Largo by Handel, and the Wieniawski *Capriccio-Valse* with piano accompaniment. Newspapers in Riga responded enthusiastically to both of Jascha's performances as captured in the words of the *Rizhsky vestnik:* "A remarkable tone, wonderful technique and sense of rhythm, unusual expressiveness!"[29] Enthusiastic reviews also appeared in German-language newspapers, including the *Rigaer Tageblatt,* the *Rigaschen Zeitung,* and the *Rigasche Rundschau.*[30]

The final summer weeks passed without any additional concert performances, permitting Jascha a well-earned rest. Meanwhile, negotiations with Concert-Direction Hermann Wolff were completed. The contract between the Heifetzes and the concert agency stipulated a two-month tour around the cities of Germany with the first performance scheduled for September 29 (NS October 12). Preparations for the trip then began in earnest.[31]

CHAPTER TEN

1912: A German Tour

UPON THEIR RETURN from the Latvian coast, the Heifetz family moved from their apartment on Voznesensky Prospekt to building 8–10 Bolshaya Masterskaya Street, a tall corner building facing Torgovaya Street. This was a familiar place for Jascha since it was just across the street from where he had lived with his father two years earlier. The building was new, and some final work on the inside continued for almost a year after the Heifetzes arrived. In one direction the building looked onto the dome of the synagogue, and in the other, beyond the Kryukov Canal, one could see the back of the Mariinsky Theater and also the conservatory, which was just a five-minute stroll along Torgovaya Street. That year, an amusement park with roller coasters, a Ferris wheel, swings, and other attractions opened in the nearby Demidov Gardens on Ofitserskaya Street, but Jascha had little free time for the many temptations. Leading up to important performances, Auer paid special attention to his students and made every effort to help them perfect their concert programs.

In the time remaining before his return to Germany, Jascha needed to prepare enough music for fifteen performances. This included works he knew already, such as concertos by Mendelssohn, Wieniawski, and Tchaikovsky, but also many new pieces. Over a period of just twenty days in

September, with Auer's guidance, Jascha prepared concertos by Bruch and Conus, the Ernst Variations on an Irish Theme, and more than ten other pieces, including the Bach Sicilienne, the Mozart-Auer Gavotte (from the opera *Idomeneo*), Cui's *Berceuse,* and Tchaikovsky's *Sérénade mélancolique.* Auer encouraged Jascha to learn some German and gave the Heifetzes introductory letters to his German friends and colleagues, along with plenty of advice on what to expect. It was around this time that Auer himself was also preparing for a chamber concert tour. In October, chamber concerts with Wanda Bogutska-Stein were scheduled in several Central Russian cities, including Saratov, where on October 21, a celebratory concert was scheduled for the opening of its conservatory, the first in the Russian provinces.

In planning their own trip, the Heifetzes decided that both of Jascha's parents would accompany him. Ruvin's conservatory certificate states: "Accompanied by wife Chaya Israelevna, 38 years old."[1] Another note confirms Ruvin's absence from conservatory lessons, "until February 13." Just as they made the final preparations to leave, Pauline was taken ill, and so Jascha and his parents departed in subdued spirits. Jascha's uncle Samuil wrote to Pauline from Warsaw sometime later:

> Dear, sweet Polyusha!
>   How are you my dear? Your papa wrote to us from Berlin to say that on the day they left, you got sick! I can't imagine how terrible it was for them to leave you like that. Polyusha! I'm asking you, my dear, to let me know how you're doing and if you're still going to the conservatory. Who takes you to the conservatory? Ask the servant to buy some postcards so you can write back. I'll be writing to Elza, also.[2]

While Pauline stayed home with the governess in the apartment on Bolshaya Masterskaya Street, Elza, on the other hand, was sent to Pavlovsk to stay with a friend of Zinovy Kiselgof. Before leaving, Jascha's parents promised Elza they would bring back for her a beautiful Dresden doll with eyes that could open and close.

Once in Berlin, Jascha and his father eagerly showed Anna the sights of the city. They stayed in the Hotel Sanssouci on Linkstrasse, close to both the Bechstein-Saal, and the home of the Berlin Philharmonic. From here, they could walk to the famous Unter den Linden and the bustling shopping area on Friedrichstrasse, and the nearby metro stop at Potsdam Station made the whole of Berlin accessible.

A day before Jascha's first concert, the *Berliner Lokal-Anzeiger* printed a concert notice reminding readers of the great reaction that followed Jascha's May visit to Berlin.[3] The notice was filled with inaccuracies: Jascha was described as twelve when he was still only eleven, as a "miracle-violinist from Odessa," and as a student of "Jozef Auer." The notice also mistakenly reported that prior to his journey to Berlin, Jascha had only ever performed two concerts in Odessa and in Warsaw. Despite the many factual errors, the notice was extremely positive in tone.

Concert-Direction Hermann Wolff released a publicity booklet with a portrait of Jascha on the cover and the caption: "One of the most sensational artistic successes of the last thirty years!" A plea followed on the second page: "We earnestly beg you to read the following reports!" The booklet's fifteen pages contained twelve reviews from Jascha's visit to Berlin in May. Alongside the advertising, the Wolff agency announced the pre-sale of subscriptions to four concerts in Jascha's present tour. The agency rented the thousand-seat Beethoven-Saal, one of the largest halls in Berlin, and Fernow convinced the influential Louise Wolff that all the tickets would be sold. The first concert was held on October 12 (os September 29), and as expected, the hall was completely packed.

The most substantial work in Jascha's program was the Bruch Concerto no. 1. It was fitting that Jascha first performed this piece in Berlin, since the composer at that point still lived and worked in the city. Seventy-four-year-old Max Bruch was approaching the end of his post as vice-president of the Royal Academy of Arts, which he occupied after Joachim's death. Jascha's performance of Bruch's concerto left the public and press raving. Otto Lessmann, a reviewer for the respected *Allgemeine Musik-Zeitung,* wrote in delight that he did not expect anything like it.[4] Lessmann believed the only person with whom one could compare Jascha was the famous violin virtuoso Henri Marteau, who by 1912 was a respected professor of the Königliche Hochschule für Musik in Berlin. As a young boy of twelve, Marteau had performed the same Bruch concerto in Vienna in 1887, and it was this event that connected the two violinists. Despite these early similarities, the lives of Heifetz and Marteau differed significantly. Although Heifetz rose from poverty to the heights of fame and material success, Marteau, on the other hand, grew up in prosperity and comfort and struggled to support himself by the end of his life.

Berlin music critic Paul Ertel, whom Jascha had met at Abell's home, reported that Heifetz was at his best in the Saint-Saëns *Introduction and Rondo Capriccioso*. Astonished by the violin playing, Ertel addressed the young talent in his review with the word "Glückauf! [Best of luck!]."[5] Similarly enthusiastic reports of the concert appeared in other Berlin papers such as *National-Zeitung* and *Norddeutsche allgemeine Zeitung*, which announced with great admiration that in putting all the skeptics to shame, the little violinist from Russia had "conquered the whole world."[6] The French-language *Journal d'Allemagne* in its October 13 edition included a portrait of Jascha with the simple caption: "Jascha Heifetz, wunderkind."

The press also noted the excellent ensemble playing between Jascha and his pianist Waldemar Liachowsky (1874–1958). Liachowsky was born in Stolptsy, Belarus, but moved to Berlin when he was still a young child. He was largely self-taught, but took some lessons with Artur Schnabel, among others. In 1907, Liachowsky became secretary and accompanist to Mischa Elman and traveled with him to the United States, where he accompanied Elman at his Carnegie Hall debut. Elman recommended Liachowsky as a highly educated and capable person with excellent manners.[7] After graduating from Berlin University, Liachowsky gained a reputation for himself as an excellent accompanist and chamber musician thanks to his musicality and brilliant technique. Liachowsky remained Jascha's accompanist for the entire two-month tour around Germany. He became close to the Heifetzes, and their artistic ties and friendship flourished for many years.

After reading the first press reviews, Ruvin sent a telegram to Valter in St. Petersburg. The telegram was stamped on October 1 (NS October 14): "Jascha a remarkable success. The public is raving. Nikisch enthusiastic. A letter follows. Heifetz."[8] The press continued to write about the "young genius" all week, and an especially large number of reviews appeared on October 18. The *Berliner Tageblatt, Der Reichsanzeiger, Vossische Zeitung,* and *Volks-Zeitung* all discussed the beauty and power of the sound resonating from Jascha's three-quarter-size violin.

Naturally, the public eagerly anticipated Jascha's second concert in the Beethoven-Saal on October 23. The program included the Wieniawski Concerto no. 2, a piece Jascha first played four years earlier. The Berlin audience was stunned by the concerto performance and also raved about the performances of Bazzini's *La Ronde des Lutins* and Tchaikovsky's *Sérénade mélancolique*. Above all, the crowning piece of the whole evening was the Bach Chaconne, with which Jascha totally enthralled his audience; once again, ecstatic reviews appeared in the Berlin press over the course of many days.

As related in Ruvin's telegram to Valter, the famous conductor Arthur Nikisch was impressed by Jascha's first performance, and this eventually led to a great opportunity for the young violinist. Nikisch not only maintained close ties with the circle of Russian musicians to which Auer belonged, but he also came from the same ethnically diverse region of Hungary as Auer. Among his ancestors were not only Hungarians, but also Slavs and even Romanies (Gypsies). He was known widely as a conductor of Wagner, Bruckner, and Tchaikovsky, and it was he who successfully championed the Tchaikovsky Fifth Symphony following the composer's unsuccessful premiere of that work. Nikisch's love for Tchaikovsky's symphonies brought him to Russia, where he gave concerts every season from 1895 to World War I.

In Berlin, Nikisch's concerts were the most popular and prestigious of the entire symphonic season. One can therefore imagine the excitement when Nikisch invited Jascha to participate in the Berlin Philharmonic's upcoming symphony concert on October 28. The event should have featured the famous cellist Pablo Casals under Nikisch's direction, but a sudden illness prevented Casals from fulfilling the commitment. This gave Jascha the opportunity to perform the Tchaikovsky Concerto with Nikisch and the famed Berlin Philharmonic. Although Jascha had performed the first movement of the concerto in his May debut before the Berlin press and in April in the Maly Hall at the St. Petersburg Conservatory, both of these performances were with piano accompaniment only. In Warsaw that February, Jascha had played the Tchaikovsky Concerto with orchestra, but again, not in full. That Jascha would play the entire concerto with orchestra for the first time in Berlin made Nikisch's invitation all the more extraordinary.

On the morning of October 27 in the Philharmonic Hall, Jascha participated in an open rehearsal, which was advertised in the leading Berlin newspapers.[9] The popular Berlin Philharmonic frequently opened its rehearsals to the public, and those who could not attend the actual concert packed the hall for these events, for which admission was less expensive. The hall quickly filled up the morning of Jascha's open rehearsal, and many were turned away. The rehearsal went brilliantly, and during the ensuing applause, orchestra members nodded and tapped their bows on their stands in approval of Jascha's performance. Afterward, the Wolff agency organized a brunch for participants of the open rehearsal, a tradition started by the agency's founder. Usually, the most prominent people at these brunches were the conductor and soloist, thus at the head of the table, next to Louise Wolff and Hermann Fernow, sat Arthur Nikisch and the young Jascha Heifetz.

The next day, crowds flocked to the Berlin Philharmonic's concert. They were attracted both by the illustrious conductor and by the program, which also included Smetana's *Vyšehrad* and Mendelssohn's *Italian* Symphony. It is easy to imagine the contrast between the two figures standing before the orchestra—the fifty-eight-year-old Nikisch, and the nearly-twelve-year-old Jascha. The performance was a success. *Die Musik* wrote:

> Owing to the illness of cellist Pablo Casals, the program for Nikisch's second concert had to be changed. Instead of Casals, the little Heifetz, the new wonder, arrived with his violin and played the Tchaikovsky Violin Concerto. Although it was not even a full-size instrument, the tone sounded remarkably warm and full. Really, one must listen with unrestrained amazement to the playing of this precocious boy for whom there are hardly any technical difficulties.[10]

The *Berliner Tageblatt* highlighted "the accuracy of his technique and the unerring purity of his intonation . . ."[11] and the *Berliner Zeitung am Mittag* noticed that since Jascha first played in Berlin, he "has developed very impressively. . . . In the cantilena passages he produces a sweet, soft, sensuous tone."[12] The *Märkische Volks-Zeitung* also fell under the boy's spell: "How wonderful, how perfect both inwardly and outwardly! From where does the soul flow into this child, possessing of such brilliance that made the hearts of those considerably older than he beat faster?"[13]

There were, however, some dissenting voices amidst the adulation. A few Berlin newspapers expressed discomfort at the participation of such a young performer in what was considered a very prestigious Philharmonic concert. A reviewer for the *Berliner Lokal-Anzeiger* wrote: "In my opinion, the parading of a wunderkind is not consistent with the noble level of these performances. There is certainly no shortage of traveling artists in Berlin who could have appropriately filled the gap."[14] The reviewer for the *Berliner Börsen-Courier* wrote about the element of sensation: "The fact that the public gave the young soloist such an overtly dazzling reception hardly needs mentioning. The 'great masses' will never be able to resist the charm of the sensational and will always pay tribute to it."[15] The reviewer for *Berliner Allgemeine Zeitung* believed that Jascha still had some way to go: "I have not missed the opportunity in the past to point out the unusual talent of this boy, but I cannot be silent about the fact that he does not yet come into consideration where serious music-making is concerned."[16] Notably, none of the critical Berlin reviews were published in Russia.

One of the more measured reviews in the Berlin press came from Otto Lessmann, who had previously written about Jascha several times. He felt that to force a little boy to perform with an orchestra in the large Philharmonic Hall was not ideal, since the size of the hall did not do him any favors: "His tone, which in smaller halls sounds remarkably large and expressive, sometimes dies away to inaudibility in larger spaces."[17] According to Lessmann, under such conditions, the audience was unable to fully appreciate the depth of Jascha's playing, which, he believed, resided in the quality of his sound.

A particularly pointed rebuke to the concert organizers came from the pages of Berlin's respected *Vossische Zeitung*: "There is no place for a wunderkind in a prestigious Philharmonic concert."[18] To be sure, however, the critic reacted more than kindly to Jascha himself, noting that the young violinist performed the Tchaikovsky Concerto faultlessly, and his "style of performance displayed an unusually intellectual talent." This reviewer from *Vossische Zeitung* was the first to identify the element of intellectualism in eleven-year-old Jascha's playing, an element that came to distinguish his performance style.

The Berlin phase of the tour was complete, and at long last, the Heifetzes received replies to the letters they had sent to Russia. A postcard addressed to Jascha with an image of Beethoven at the piano arrived from Hyman Gerber. Gerber had moved from Vilnius to Kiev, and since then had corresponded regularly with the Heifetz family, sending greetings from his wife Rose, and personal greetings to Jascha from his daughters Klara and Nyusya. On this occasion, Gerber wrote:

> My wonderful Jaschenka!
> Thank you for the note. I'm incredibly glad at your success and wish you always and everywhere to be everyone's favorite and that your muse and energy will be inexhaustible. Let your lucky star guard you forever![19]

Around that time, Jascha also received a postcard written jointly by two youngsters. One of them was his sister Pauline, who wrote simply: "Dear Jaschenka, I'm sending a big kiss. Polya. Write!!" The other correspondent, a young girl named Mina, belonged to Jascha's close group of friends and acquaintances and was also close friends with Pauline. Mina was born Minnie Louise Roubleff, in June 1896, in Hackney, England.[20] Her father Adolf was a *meshchanin* from Tomsk and worked in England as a "translator of languages."[21] Mina enrolled as a piano student at the St. Petersburg Conservatory in January 1910, the same time as Jascha. Before that, her father co-owned the agrochemical factory "A. Rublyov and Co." in Theodosia, where Mina regularly traveled on vacation. Mina started her piano studies with Leonid Nikolaev in the lower course, paying fees of two hundred rubles and receiving the Anton Rubinstein stipend. She moved to the upper course in May 1912 and received high praise from Glazunov.[22] Mina lived in the same building as the Heifetzes, on the corner of Bolshaya Masterskaya and Torgovaya Streets. As neighbors, then, Mina and Pauline sent Jascha's postcard together. On the shared postcard Mina wrote:

> Dear Jascha,
> Today I finally found out that I've been let off paying and so I'm very happy about that. Yes, I also met Nalbandian today—I really don't like him, he's really crude. Guests are coming today and tomorrow. Now I have to

do my harmony study so I can write only a little to you. Greetings to your mama and papa. Kisses, Mina.[23]

Judging from this and subsequent letters, Mina was quite sharp-tongued and impulsive, and it is unlikely Jascha shared Mina's dislike for Nalbandian. One month later, Jascha wrote back to Pauline from abroad. He spoke his mind, complaining about Mina's influence on his younger sister. The correspondence was postmarked in Berlin on November 25, 1912:

Dear Polinka!
I got your letters. Shame on you, writing things like that. Do you understand? You probably learned them from Mina, right? She's such a fool, what she said to you. You ought to write me by yourself, without anybody else's help. What you wrote sounds as if it's been dictated. You're never going to learn to write correctly and well. Just pretend you're talking to me, understand? Oh, you Polka-mazurka, you're not going to pay any attention to me anyway, are you? So how are you, Polinka? How're you feeling? We'll be seeing each other before long. If Elinka is in Petersburg, Polinka, I'll write a few words to her, if you don't mind. (Dear Elinka! How are you? Thanks for your little letters. We'll be seeing each other soon, and I'm going to give you a lot of nice things. Stay well. Your brother Jascha.) I'm not done writing you, Polinka. I'm not angry with you, although I ought to be. Stay well. Your loving brother Jascha.[24]

Jascha and his parents spent the next three weeks on tour with Liachowsky. Following the appearances in Berlin, Jascha performed twice in Königsburg, and then on November 5 (os October 23) he gave his first concert in Prague at the Stadthalle. The next day Jascha played a concert in Dresden at the Vereinshaus, where a large poster incorrectly labeled him as the "Miracle Violinist from Odessa." On November 8, he performed once again in Prague. This time, the singer Lorle Meissner joined Jascha in a performance given for the benefit of German schools in the city. On November 14 Jascha appeared in Brandenburg and played in Hohenzollern Park. Throughout these performances, Jascha rotated through concertos by Bruch, Tchaikovsky, and Wieniawski, along with pieces such as the Schubert *Ave Maria*, Kreisler *Schön Rosmarin*, the Chopin Nocturne, Popper's *La Fileuse*, Saint-Saëns's *Introduction and Rondo Capriccioso*, Cui's *Melodie Orientale*, and the Paganini Caprice no. 24.

Typically, Jascha and his parents stayed in each city just one or two days. Their schedule in Prague, for example, saw them arrive on the day of the November 8 concert and depart the following day by train. The time spent on trains gave Jascha the opportunity to write postcards to family and friends, even if the motion of the wagon turned the boy's handwriting into more of a scrawl:

> Dear Polinka! How come you haven't written to us? I'm writing from the train, my hand is shaking lots, and I can hardly write. Well next time I'll write more to you. I'm [here the train slowed or stopped and the handwriting became normal again] sending you a scene from Prague. It's a city in Austria-Hungary. Keep it safe. I'll also send one from Dresden.[25]

On November 4, between the Königsburg concert and the first Prague concert, the Heifetzes stopped in Grünewald at the home of Julius Block (1858–1934), a patron of the arts and owner of an Edison recording machine. The main purpose of the visit was to make recordings of Jascha's violin playing. Enthralled by the possibilities of the phonograph from as early as the 1890s, Block invited many famous musicians to record in his home, including Sergei Taneyev, Anton Arensky, Anna Yesipova, and a young Josef Hofmann. Remarkably, Block's collection also included voice recordings of Tchaikovsky and Tolstoy. Block moved to Germany in 1899 where he continued to add to his collection of home recordings. Among those who came to perform for Block and his Edison machine were Egon Petri and Elena Gerhardt, who sang while Arthur Nikisch accompanied her at the piano. As a rising musical star, it was only natural that Jascha also took his turn to record. Thus, over six cylinders, Block recorded four pieces played by Jascha, including Cui's *Melodie Orientale,* the Mozart Gavotte, Kreisler's *Schön Rosmarin,* and Popper's *La Fileuse.* All four pieces came from the current touring repertoire.[26]

Jascha's recordings with Liachowsky are now barely discernible through the persistent noise and crackling of the phonograph recordings. At the start of each cylinder a woman announces in German the name of the piece to be played, the name of the performer, and the place and time of the recording. Block often invited guests to the recording sessions; applause and exclamations of delight ring out after each piece. Two years later, another Auer student named Eddy Brown made recordings in the same place. For many years, Block kept these cylinders in Berlin as part of his large collection, but after World War II they were taken to the Soviet Union and placed into the Phonogram Archive of the Institute of Russian Literature (Pushkin House) in St. Petersburg (then, Leningrad).[27]

A friendship developed between Jascha and Block and it lasted well into the American period of Heifetz's life. In a letter from the composer Paul Juon to Heifetz, dated July 27, 1931, Juon refers to Block as "our mutual friend."[28] The acquaintance between Heifetz and Juon probably began during these years, since Juon also made recordings for Block. Paul Juon was the older brother of Konstantin Juon, a famous artist of the World of Art (*Mir iskusstva*) movement who studied at the Moscow Conservatory during the early part of the 1890s. In Moscow, he studied composition with Sergei Taneyev and Anton Arensky, and violin with Jan Hřímalý. Juon then graduated from the Königliche Hochschule für Musik in Berlin, where from 1906 onward he taught a composition class. The connection between Juon and Heifetz continued. Years later in the United States, Heifetz recorded Juon's pieces and included them in his concert programs.

Jascha performed in Hamburg during the second half of November 1912. On November 19, he appeared in the Curiohaus and on November 30, he played in the Musikhalle. After the first of the two concerts, local newspapers wrote that, "among violinists, naturally the sensation of the month was little Jascha Heifetz, who in his first concert was enthusiastically celebrated and caught the attention of even those usually unsympathetic to the culture of wunderkinder."[29] After the second of the Hamburg performances, at which Jascha played the Mendelssohn Concerto, the Hamburg reviewer of *Allgemeine Musik-Zeitung* declared categorically that "Jascha Heifetz aroused in all violinists performing here the strongest sense of competition. The brilliant boy caused a great sensation."[30]

On November 21, between the two Hamburg performances, Jascha played his third subscription concert in Berlin, this time at the Blüthner-Saal. He played the Mendelssohn Concerto. The reviewer in *Germania* posed the following question: "What else can be said about artistic achievements of the highest order which unite a finely honed and faultless technique with an astonishingly intellectual maturity for a person of this age?" The reviewer continued: "In this boy everything is so surprisingly, so fortunately united, that every human being who understands art cannot help but open his heart to this favorite of the muses."[31]

On the day Jascha gave his third subscription concert in Berlin, Arthur Nikisch was already in Russia, where he conducted *Eugene Onegin* at the Bolshoi Theater in Moscow and then Beethoven symphonies in St. Petersburg in a Siloti concert (the prominent pianist and conductor Alexander Siloti founded an orchestra under his name in 1903). Nikisch undoubtedly shared the story of Jascha's Berlin success with many of the St. Petersburg musicians, not least with Jascha's teacher Auer.

Back in Berlin, Jascha received a startling postcard from Mina Roubleff in St. Petersburg. The picture was of four human skulls with empty eye sockets staring at a pile of assorted objects, including a fool's cap, a book, a crown, and a globe.[32] The caption asks: "Who was the fool, who the wise man, beggar, or king?" The postcard was sent on November 5 and contains an excited message to Jascha. There is no explanation for Mina's comments, but she felt able to write openly to Jascha, even if we do not know his response:

> Berlin
> Hotel Sanssouci, Linkstrasse.
> Für Jascha Heifetz
> (To Germany)
>
> Dear Jaschenka!
> I'm in such a mood right now I could even hang myself. I have to go to the conservatory now, but I so want to lie down and fall asleep and not feel anything at all! Do you like my postcard? I like it very much. Kisses, write.
> Mina
> A big kiss

Jascha's final Berlin subscription concert did not happen as planned. Newspapers announced that "Heifetz's fourth concert in Blüthner-Saal, set for December 4th, is canceled. Tickets bought in advance may be returned to the sales outlets."[33] The announcement gave no explanation for the cancellation, but added that Jascha "will appear for the last time in Berlin in a charity concert on December 13, tickets for which can be obtained from the same sales outlets." The reason for the cancellation can be found in an invitation that the Heifetzes received from Uncle Aron: "Dear Sir! We would consider it a pleasure to see you among our guests at the wedding of our daughter Fanny to Naum [Natan] Ilyich Heifetz, which will take place on the 21st of November of this year in the city of Warsaw. The service is at 5 p.m. Respectfully, A. I. Heifetz and wife. Address for telegrams: Warsaw, Nowolipki Street, 36."[34] The date of the wedding referred to the old style calendar; on the new style calendar the date was December 4—the exact day of the canceled performance in Berlin. That day also happened to be a state holiday for the Orthodox Christian feast of the Presentation of the Virgin Mary to the Temple, and by the Jewish calendar, this day was the 24th of the month of Kislev—the eve of Hanukkah.

Since Jewish tradition dictated that the bride should set the wedding date close to the actual event, the Heifetzes probably did not know the date of the wedding when they signed the tour contract with the Wolff agency during the summer. The invitation forced Jascha and his parents to decide between the obligations of the contract and their family traditions; on this occasion, the wedding proved to be of greater importance. Fernow convinced Louise Wolff to compromise on the situation and took charge of canceling the concert. Meanwhile, loaded down with gifts, the Heifetzes departed for Warsaw.

The concurrence of the wedding and Hanukkah meant the celebrations would be even greater. Of course, Jascha and his parents were among the most anticipated guests at the wedding, and there was no shortage of violin playing. Natan the groom played, along with his brother; his father-in-law, Aron; and, of course, Ruvin. It is not known whether Samuil also played the violin, but he was no doubt among those present, since it was his address on the wedding invitation. Jascha probably played the folk dances that he first heard in Vilnius and more recently in St. Petersburg with Kiselgof, as well as a few concert pieces for his proud family.

Natan and Fanny were happy together; Natan idolized his young wife. Their difficult life together was warmed by Natan's adoration, which over time, Fanny began to take for granted, preoccupying herself almost entirely with scholarly work. In 1945, under accusations of "anti-Soviet agitation," Fanny was imprisoned in the torture chambers of the Gulag. From there, in May 1946, she wrote to her husband Natan:

> Why did I live only for work? Why did I give myself up to work to the point
> of oblivion, forgetting about everything in the world . . . why did I devote
> only fragments of my time to you—why, why? . . . Now I am in my old age, I
> have seen that I drank from an empty cup instead of drawing from a living,
> flowing spring. What a terrible, bitter conclusion. . . . Will I see you again,
> my dear? What bitter irony—now all of my strivings, all of my thoughts, all
> of my wishes are concentrated on you. . . . I so want to believe that we will
> still be together again![35]

Fanny castigated herself, but Natan remained content to love and serve her;
his happiness lay in her very existence. Sadly, the couple was never again
united. Natan died in 1950, just three years short of Fanny's liberation.

A few days after the wedding celebration, Jascha and his parents began
the final stage of the tour. On December 7, Jascha appeared at his second
and final concert in Dresden at the Vereinshaus. He performed the Mendelssohn Concerto and works by Handel, Bach, Kreisler, and Wieniawski.
A local newspaper wrote about the unusually strong effect of the young
violinist's playing on the audience, and the reviewer described a wrenching
feeling, as though witnessing a miracle or the manifestation of some other-
wordly source in the music. The reviewer observed that the behavior and
appearance of the boy is so natural and fresh that he looks unlike the usual
"trained wunderkind. . . . you quickly forget about the totally uncanny
power which speaks from him, and you are uplifted by the sounds, as if
by a beautiful miracle, which he conjures up with his little hands from the
three-quarter-size violin."[36]

Two days later, on December 9, Jascha played his third concert in the
Hamburg Musikhalle. The Heifetzes arrived in the city the night before the
performance and stayed until the morning of December 10. In Germany,
Hamburg was considered the second most important city after Berlin, and
Hamburg citizens were proud of their rich history. Located on both banks
of the Elbe, Hamburg was not only Germany's main seaport, but one of
the leading ports of the world. The Heifetzes visited Hamburg three times
during the course of Jascha's German tour and stayed at the Hotel Reichshof at 35/36 Kirchenallee, adjacent to the City Theater. The impressive
hotel contained three hundred rooms and salons, fifty rooms with private
bathrooms, porcelain sinks with hot and cold water, telephones in every
room, a hair salon, and a car garage.[37]

A page of the Hotel Reichshof's headed notepaper survives in the Heifetz Collection at the Library of Congress. There was little to keep Jascha occupied after a concert and before leaving for the next train, and it appears the notepaper proved too tempting. Down the left side of the page, the young boy practiced his own signature again and again, taking great care over the individual letters: "Jascha . . . Heifetz . . . Heifetz . . ." The perfection of one's own signature captivates many youngsters; it remains a ritual of growing up and forms a graphic embodiment of one's own self. Down the other side of the page, Jascha wrote in German, "Hamburg, den 10 Dezember 1912" and began to copy the hotel bill for the Heifetz family's stay at the Reichshof. Jascha's transcription of the December 8 evening bill reads: "Ein Glas Tee und Glas Milch. 2 Kuchen."

The Heifetzes arrived back in Berlin, and in place of the canceled concert, Jascha appeared in the Marmor-Saal of the Zoological Garden. By the entrance hung a huge advertising board: "Charity celebration-ball for the benefit of the Jollos Foundation, on Friday, December 13, at 8:30 in the evening: last performance of 12-year-old violin virtuoso Jascha Heifetz."[38] That evening, on the bank alongside the Lichtenstein Bridge, crowds flocked to the venue, not so much out of support for the charity, but out of a desire to hear the "sensation of the season." The evening proceeded on a grand scale. A program printed in Russian suggests many Russians attended this concert. Other entertainment listed on the program included dancing and a raffle with impressive prizes such as a gramophone and a piano. Jascha's repertoire for the evening included Sarasate's *Zigeunerweisen*, Dvořák's *Humoresque*, Wieniawski's *Souvenir de Moscow*, and a new piece for the young violinist, the Tartini-Kreisler Variations on a Theme by Corelli. Jascha had alternated throughout his tour between the concertos of Mendelssohn, Tchaikovsky, and Bruch, but at this final concert he played the Conus Concerto.

With that, Jascha's tour came to an end after almost exactly two months, and after no fewer than fifteen concerts. The tour had lasted from October 12 through December 13 (os September 29 through November 30), and had passed through six cities in Germany and Austria-Hungary, namely Berlin, Brandenburg, Dresden, Hamburg, Königsburg, and Prague. As set out in their contract, Jascha and his parents received a guaranteed payment for each concert, which meant a set amount for each performance, regardless of how much money the organizers collected. All of the concerts sold out, so the Wolff agency made a large profit. In St. Petersburg, Viktor Valter wrote bitterly about this situation in *Solntse Rossii*, directing his criticism at both German and Russian concert promoters:

> Despite the sensational success, the majority of the money that the public so eagerly throws at the feet of the young artist, and on which his father, mother and two little sisters live, undoubtedly ends up in the pockets of the impresarios. Can our art patrons really not (or do they just not want to) arrange it such that little Jascha, this boy with blue eyes and blond curls, with the face of an angel, would be able to feed his family, while the impresarios would receive their revenue from adult artists?![39]

After Jascha's final concert in Berlin, the Heifetzes departed laden with gifts and souvenirs. On the way to St. Petersburg they stopped in Warsaw, where on December 14 (os) Jascha performed with the Warsaw Philharmonic Orchestra under the direction of Zdzisław Birnbaum, with whom Jascha had already appeared earlier that year. The Heifetzes stayed with Fanny and Natan and visited Uncle Samuil.

Jascha and his parents arrived in St. Petersburg at the very end of December.[40] The whole family was united once more. Jascha gave his sisters the pile of "nice things" he had promised, including postcards, stamps, coloring pencils, and beautiful picture books, and he gave Elza the precious Dresden doll. Mina Roubleff traveled to Theodosia to stay with her father for the holidays and sent Jascha a postcard. On one side of the postcard was a view of the Theodosia resort "Suuk-Su," and on the other side was a slightly smudged message: "I'm sending you my best wishes for the new year. I hope you'll change your character for the better. You know, people have been complaining to me about you! But it's nothing, I'm just kidding!"[41] After Jascha read the postcard, he no longer wanted it, and re-addressed it "To Dear Polka from Jascha." Perhaps his feelings were hurt, but most likely he just wanted to give the postcard to his sister. Pauline also received her own postcard from Mina with the caption "Alupka. Ai-Petri in Winter." Mina wrote on the back: "Greetings for the new year, I hope that you and I will be as good friends as last year."

While the Heifetzes were on tour, a number of interesting and important events occurred in St. Petersburg. The conservatory held celebrations between December 16 and 19 to mark its fiftieth anniversary. The celebrations took place in the conservatory's Bolshoi Hall which had been renovated but not quite completed. Five of Auer's students performed in the celebratory concerts, including Myron Polyakin and Cecilia Hansen. The conservatory also commissioned a series of photographs that show the concert halls, classrooms, library, kitchen, and the famous conservatory corridors; the teaching faculty also posed for photographs with their students.[42] In the Auer class photograph, the professor is surrounded by familiar faces, including the mischievous-looking Toscha Seidel, who entered the class just a few months before Jascha and who later became his close friend.

Pianist Josef Hofmann also began giving concerts while the Heifetzes were away from St. Petersburg. On his international tours starting in 1895, the famous student of Anton Rubinstein often stopped in Russia and his appearances always caused great excitement. Osip Mandelstam recalled the atmosphere at these performances in his autobiographical *Noise of Time,* describing how these concerts would have a siege-like atmosphere about them:

> Gendarmes on prancing horses, lending to the atmosphere of the square the mood of a civil disturbance, made clicking noises with their tongues and shouted as they guarded the main entry with a chain. . . . Through the triple chains the Petersburger made his way like a feverish little trout to the marble ice-hole of the vestibule, whence he disappeared into the luminous frosty building, bedraped with silk and velvet. The orchestra seats and the places behind those were filled in the customary order, but the spacious balconies to which the side entrances gave access were filled in bunches, like baskets with clusters of humanity.[43]

During his previous trip to St. Petersburg two years earlier, Hofmann gave twelve solo concerts, and a similar number was set for the current visit. The tour began on October 30 and was supposed to end by the middle of January, but owing to overwhelming public interest, Hofmann stayed until the end of April, giving nearly twenty concerts. Once Jascha and his parents returned to St. Petersburg, it is likely they heard Hofmann perform at least once during his tour. Samuel Chotzinoff, the future husband of Pauline Heifetz, wrote in his memoirs that "the Heifetzes revered Hofmann," and that

> Mrs. Heifetz recalled that when Hofmann announced a series of twelve recitals in Petrograd back in 1912, she had sent her maid, Dunyasha, to stand all night in a queue that stretched for blocks to buy the coveted tickets. Both Pauline and Jascha attended these concerts and had never forgotten them. Pauline even confessed that she had always been secretly in love with Hofmann.[44]

According to the Moscow Heifetzes, Jascha owned a portrait of Hofmann by Leonid Pasternak, father of Boris Pasternak, author of *Dr. Zhivago*.

There was much about Hofmann that impressed Jascha, including his external restraint, his calm and serious behavior onstage, and his intellectualism. On stage, Hofmann followed a strict performance plan that he devised away from the piano during hours of examining the music scores. This rigid intellectualism was present not only in Hofmann's piano playing, but also in other spheres of his work, such as his passion for engineering and inventing. Legend has it that his father once chained him to a balcony railing in order to keep him from digging endlessly in car motors and the like. During his lifetime, Hofmann patented over sixty inventions, including a windshield wiper that was apparently inspired by the motion of a metronome. Jascha looked up to Hofmann for many reasons, and before long, Jascha would also command the same level of admiration from a worldwide public.

CHAPTER ELEVEN

The Beginning of 1913

A NUMBER OF EXCITING musical experiences for the residents of St. Petersburg ushered in the New Year, starting on January 7 with a performance by the violinist Jan Kubelík at the Hall of the Assembly of the Nobility. Despite the audience's enthusiastic response, the critics reacted with restraint to Kubelík's playing, noting a lack of inspiration only partially masked by his confidence and impressive technique. For Jascha, Kubelík's performance presented the chance to hear the Ernst *Concerto pathétique* in F-sharp Minor, a piece he had begun to study with Auer in preparation for a spring performance. Later in January, the violinist Henri Marteau arrived from Berlin to perform the Beethoven Concerto, a piece Jascha had yet to learn, but one that would become integral to his adult repertoire. On January 23, Fritz Kreisler performed the Elgar Concerto at the Hall of the Assembly of the Nobility under the direction of Serge Koussevitzky. Although Jascha performed Elgar's miniature piece *La Capricieuse* in Russia, he did not perform the composer's beautiful and demanding concerto until after he left for the United States. Following the symphony concert with Koussevitzky, Kreisler gave three successful recitals in the same venue on January 29, February 5, and February 7, all accompanied by Rudolph Merwolf, who in the near future would also accompany Jascha.

The January 23 program featured excerpts from Stravinsky's ballet *Petrushka,* along with the Elgar Concerto, performed by Koussevitzky and the orchestra. The Paris productions of Stravinsky's *Firebird* (1910) and *Petrushka* (1911) by Sergei Diaghilev's "Ballets Russes" brought Stravinsky fame across all of Europe. Stravinsky's music left the St. Petersburg audience spellbound with its bold harmonies and polyphonic fabric. Stravinsky's innovative musical language evoked only disgust in some, while others saw in it artistic perfection. Auer was more attuned to the classical style, but to his credit, he did not inculcate any fear of the new and unusual in his students, and as an adult, Heifetz did play some of Stravinsky's music.

Toward the end of January another exciting musical event occurred—composer Richard Strauss's first visit to St. Petersburg. On January 24 and 25, Strauss conducted two concerts of his own music with the Court Orchestra at the Hall of the Assembly of the Nobility. The concerts comprised excerpts from several operas, including *Salome,* and the best of Strauss's symphonic poems, including *Don Juan, Till Eulenspiegel, A Hero's Life, Death and Transfiguration,* and *Symphonia Domestica.* These concerts evoked stormy controversy and became a prelude to Strauss's *Elektra,* which Vsevolod Meyerhold produced at the Mariinsky Theater. The premiere of *Elektra* on February 18 divided the St. Petersburg musical world into those who admired Strauss's operatic innovations and those who furiously opposed them.

On February 4, Marusya Malkina sent Jascha a card from Vilnius, writing about their friendship and also about the musical progress of a relative:

> I know you're in beautiful, busy, St. Petersburg, and you're drowning with new friends and experiences, but even so Jaschenka, aren't we still friends? I know I'm not equal to you on the violin, but is that why you don't want to write to me?! L. S. Auer was here recently. He heard Biba and liked her playing. Jaschenka, I'm waiting for your letter.[1]

Did Jascha respond to Marusya's message? Probably not immediately, since as indicated by a conservatory leave certificate, between February 5 and 13 he was already in Riga at the Hotel Commercial.[2] After the recent summer vacation on the Latvian coast, this trip gave Jascha the chance to see the city in the wintertime. The Heifetzes had maintained a warm relationship with the Finnish conductor Georg Schnéevoigt, who invited them back to Riga. Schnéevoigt visited St. Petersburg frequently to direct symphony concerts at the Hall of the Assembly of the Nobility and opera productions for the recently founded Theater of Musical Drama. Since the Theater of Musical Drama held its performances in the conservatory's Bolshoi Hall, Schnéevoigt and the Heifetzes often came into contact. Jascha was invited to perform with the Riga Symphony Orchestra on February 7, and once again he played the Mendelssohn Concerto. Jascha also played Dvořák's *Humoresque,* Cui's *Berceuse,* and Wieniawski's *Souvenir de Moscow* with pianist Oskar Springfeld. According to one local paper, "at this age there cannot be such strong tone and finely developed, emotional phrasing, but Jascha Heifetz has achieved everything that a young virtuoso can: ideal intonation doing credit to his musical ear and wonderful speed and purity of playing, also in his harmonics, which are uncommonly beautiful and soft."[3] Another wrote, "In his playing there is no effort to give what is not there, and therefore with such simplicity his playing makes an unusually convincing impression."[4]

Before leaving Riga, the Heifetzes met with several friends, including former Auer student Mishel Piastro. Born in 1891, Piastro had accomplished much by 1913. He graduated from the St. Petersburg Conservatory with a gold medal; received first prize in the Auer Competition; toured successfully in Kiev, Kharkov, and Odessa; and was now soloist with the Riga Symphony Orchestra. Shortly after his arrival home, Jascha received a postcard from Piastro with an image of the Riga City Theater:

> Dear Jaschenka! I promised your papa I'd send reviews from the papers that you weren't able to find here, but unfortunately they haven't materialized. Jascha, if you're not too lazy, write me a couple words about yourself and also about which of Auer's students are graduating from the conservatory this year. Kisses. Your Misha. Krepostnaya Street, Building 24, apt. 9.[5]

A few days after returning to St. Petersburg, Jascha, Auer, and a group of students from the conservatory attended a concert at the Maly Hall by the American violinist and composer Albert Spalding. Much of Spalding's program was familiar to Jascha, including the Handel Sonata in A, Mozart

Rondo in G, pieces by Kreisler, the Franck Sonata, and Hungarian Dances by Brahms. Spalding also played the Max Reger Sonata for Solo Violin in A Minor, a piece Jascha had also heard Nalbandian perform.

Born in Chicago in 1888, Albert Spalding later traveled to Europe where he studied at the Bologna Conservatory. His debut in Paris as a teenager was followed by a New York debut in 1908 with the New York Symphony Orchestra. From then on, he toured the United States and Europe. Following Spalding's appearance in St. Petersburg, the well-known music critic Grigory Timofeev wrote: "Amidst an abundance of concerts and the performances of so many stars, the concert of violinist A. Spalding passed almost without the public's notice . . . there is nothing surprising in this: A. Spalding is a foreigner, an American, who still has no name and did not advertise himself. Nevertheless, his concert showed that he is worthy of great attention."[6] This was not Spalding's first appearance in St. Petersburg; he had also appeared in January 1910. During the 1913–1914 concert season, Spalding performed twice more in the city, each time with growing success. On December 14, 1913, he played a Bach concerto for violin and orchestra in Siloti's sixth subscription concert and appeared once more in January 1914.

Spalding described his visits to St. Petersburg in his memoirs, which were published in the early 1940s. Of most interest are his interactions with Auer and his students: "The old friends were there to greet me, and I found some new ones. Leopold Auer, the violinistic autocrat of all the Russias, was an unexpected ally. He proved to be kindness itself, coming to all my concerts and bringing with him many of his pupils. Had I been one of his students he could not have shown more interest or enthusiasm."[7]

At Auer's home Spalding met Glazunov, and at a reception given by Andrei Diederichs, the co-owner of the Diederichs Frères instrument factory, Spalding met a "new star in the field of conductors," Serge Koussevitzky, with whom he developed close personal and artistic ties. At the Mariinsky Theater, Spalding saw the opera *Boris Godunov* by Mussorgsky and Rimsky-Korsakov's *The Maid of Pskov* with Chaliapin, both of which made an enormous impression on the young American violinist. Spalding continued his tale:

One day Auer asked me to come to a class lesson. He had several extremely gifted students; one, in particular, he was anxious to have me hear. I remembered that some weeks earlier Kreisler had been full of praise for a small boy he had heard there. Was it the same one, I wondered?

When we arrived at the Conservatory the following afternoon, Ben and I were shown into the large, low-ceilinged classroom. Small chairs flanked the walls. The grand piano stood like an ebony island in the centre of the room. The students, instruments in hand, silently waited for a summons to play. Some were accompanied by parents who masked, as best they could, any suggestion of jealous rivalry. On my arrival they all rose and stood until Auer's welcome ended, and we were shown to our chairs.

A small boy stood up to play. He had only recently graduated to a full-sized violin, and it made him look even smaller than he was. One of Fra Angelico's seraphs seemed to have stepped from his background of goldleaf, disguised himself in modern dress, and exchanged a trumpet for a fiddle. He played the Ernst concerto. It is not one of my favourites; its unsubstantial themes might have had a naïve charm if treated simply, but faithful to the tradition of the day they were a continuous scenic railway of coasting thirds and ascending octaves, the work being designed to amaze rather than to please. Needless to say, its technical difficulties tax the most seasoned veteran. What a cruel test, I thought, for a child!

But I quickly found that there was no need for apprehension. The first flourish of fingered octaves was attached with a kind of nonchalant aplomb; the tone was firm, flowing, and edgeless, the intonation of fleckless purity. A kind of inner grace made itself felt in the shaping of the phrase. I completely forgot the tawdriness of the piece in the elegance and distinction of its delivery. I had never heard such perfect technique from a child.

Jascha, they called him—Jascha Heifetz.

While the boy was playing, Auer strode nervously about the room, glancing at me now and then to appraise my reactions. His dark, restless eyes danced with delight as the wonder boy threaded his effortless way through the tortuous technical problems. He expected nothing less than paralyzed astonishment from me—nor was he disappointed. He would turn away with a helpless shrug of his shoulders, as if to say: "Was there ever anything like it?" Other talented students performed later, but they were eclipsed by this miniature wizard in his early teens.[8]

The person named in the beginning of the story as Ben is André Benoist, Spalding's accompanist. Benoist later became Heifetz's accompanist during his first years in the United States and wrote about his experiences accompanying many famous instrumentalists. His unpublished manuscript was printed in 1978 in the United States under the title *The Accompanist . . . and friends.* The book includes a photograph of Leopold Auer with the inscription: "L. Auer. St. Petersburg, 2/3. 1913."[9] As the caption below the photograph explains, "when Benoist visited Auer in St. Petersburg in 1913, he was given this photograph, suitably autographed, as a souvenir. It was during this visit that he and Spalding first heard Jascha Heifetz." Benoist's recollections provide another account of the trip to St. Petersburg:

> At all our concerts we began to notice the presence of an elderly, distinguished-looking gentleman, generally surrounded by youths of both sexes. We could not quite make out who he was, until after our last recital the gentleman came backstage with his entire little brood. He was short, with eyes that shone like live coals, a short beard, and incessant, furious gesticulations. He walked truculently up to Mr. Spalding, and at first I was afraid he meant him harm. But not at all. It was his way of being enthusiastic. He exclaimed, "I am Leopold Auer. This is my class. I bring them here for all your concerts. It is a better lesson than I can give them." With that, he introduced a few: Thelma Given, Alexander Bloch, Toscha Seidel, Jascha Heifetz, etc. Then he asked whether we would be interested in coming to the Imperial Conservatory the next day to hear some of his more promising pupils. Would we like to? Needless to say, we accepted the invitation with "alacrity and dispatch." The next day we arrived in due time at the frowning old building that housed the world-famed institution and were ushered to the sanctum of the great master. There we found the professor pacing up and down restlessly with the reverent faces of his students looking on. As Spalding entered the room, they rose in a body, bowing respectfully. "Just like home," thought I, "but in reverse!"
>
> The two pupils that stood out in our minds were Seidel and Heifetz. They were about twelve or thirteen years old. Toscha played with fervor and warmth and had the Elman habit of walking while he played, like a caged young lion. His tone was large and luminous. He was exciting. Then came young Jascha. His appearance made the contrast between the two boys startling. Whereas young Toscha, swarthy, fiery, energetic and self-confident, acted like a young bantam rooster, Jascha was fair and blue-eyed, with a mop of blonde, wavy hair that would have been the envy of a Hollywood glamour girl; besides, it owed nothing to the art of the beauty emporiums. His features were of the utmost beauty, in fact, the shape of his mouth would have better suited the aforementioned Hollywood princess. In short, he looked like one of the angels descended from a painting by Raphael. This exquisite youth attacked the outrageous difficulties of the *Ernst F Sharp Mi-*

nor *Concerto* with such sureness that it left one stunned. Technical problems virtually did not exist for him. He just tossed off runs in thirds, sixths or tenths while counting flies on the ceiling. All this he did with an air of boredom and listlessness that sometimes became annoying. His facial expression never changed. Whether his violin sang like a thrush, or his fingers galloped through well-nigh insuperable difficulties, he remained "poker-faced." All he had done was incredibly beautiful, but the ease and indifference with which it had been done left one with a sense of futility. After it was over, we congratulated the lad, to which he replied with a grave little bow and went back to his seat in the class.

All the while, Professor Auer had been pacing up and down like one possessed. Now he came over to us and bluntly asked: "Now you've heard them. Which of these two would you advise me to send to America?" Here was a dilemma! What to advise the great man? Spalding and I looked at each other, and I could see by the twinkle in his eyes that he disagreed with the thought I had in mind. Of course, with the fiery restlessness of Mischa Elman having been such an overwhelming success, there was no doubt that his legitimate follower should be the little bantam Toscha, and I so expressed our opinion. The maestro shrugged his shoulders and in a half whisper said, "Well, we shall see!"

The future did, in fact, tell.[10]

Jascha began preparing for two important concerts that would take place during the coming months. Meanwhile, St. Petersburg celebrated the 300-year anniversary of the Romanov dynasty on February 21. At eight in the morning on the day of the celebration, a twenty-one-gun salute from the Peter and Paul Fortress alerted St. Petersburg citizens to the commencement of festivities. Church bells rang, religious services filled cathedrals, and at one in the afternoon, the royals left the Winter Palace for a prayer service in the Kazan Cathedral. That evening, a fireworks display sparkled above the Peter and Paul Fortress, half a million electric lights were used to illuminate the city, and Imperial theaters put on shows, including Glinka's *A Life for the Tsar* at the Mariinsky Theater. The conservatory also participated in the celebrations with a gala event attended by students and professors.

The fireworks, gala performances, and other celebrations saturated the city, but for the Heifetzes, the credo remained the same: weekday or holiday, work came first. Jascha's first performance in Moscow would take place at the start of March. Until now, the Moscow public had heard about

Jascha only through reports in the newspapers. Earlier in the year, the Moscow *Teatr* wrote:

> In recent years Russian concert performers have begun to command exceptional attention from European palaces. The violinist Elman (a pupil of the St. Petersburg Conservatory), was in particular favor at the London court during the life of King Edward VII, and continues to command the same attention, now, under King George V. The violinist Efrem Zimbalist (also a pupil of the St. Petersburg Conservatory), as is known, is receiving special attention at the palace of the aged Austrian monarch Franz Joseph. Now, as we have heard, the Berlin palace has become particularly interested by the young violinist Jascha Heifetz. . . . He has over the course of the past November given six concerts in Berlin, and moreover, extremely notable representatives of the royal court were present at his last two concerts. As a result, the young violinist is invited for two concerts at the Berlin Court.[11]

The most pressing aim was for Jascha to win over the Moscow public; his opportunity came on March 5 in the Bolshoi Hall of the Moscow Conservatory. The performance was held for the benefit of the Society for the Spread of Enlightenment Among Jews in Russia, whose organizer was David Shor (1867–1942), a well-known acquaintance of Zinovy Kiselgof, the famous pianist and head of the Moscow division of the Society for Jewish Folk Music. The program included the Mendelssohn Concerto, the Handel Larghetto, Bach's Aria, Bazzini's *La Ronde des Lutins,* a Chopin nocturne, and Wieniawski's *Souvenir de Moscow.* Among the many reviews published in the press, the review by Joel Engel, a leading Moscow critic of the time, stands out for its insight and poise:

> Jascha Heifetz, who performed in a concert on March 5 (in the conservatory's Bolshoi Hall) is one of the most charming wunderkinder I have ever seen on stage. This strong, chubby, towheaded creature of 12–13 years, with a kind of truly childlike lightness and tranquility, extracts from his child's ¾ size violin the brilliance of true violin technique, full of real tone, real accuracy, a polished performance.
>
> Heifetz studies with Auer at the St. Petersburg Conservatory, and as a child-student, creates the impression of a true miracle. Moreover, he looks so joyful and pleasant, that with a glance at this calm and sprightly person, somehow, the usual suspicions of overwork and exploitation related to wunderkinder disappear.
>
> With Heifetz, many purely virtuosic feats sound natural and brilliant, more than for other famous violinists. For example, his harmonics, not

laborious and anemic as often occurs, but strong, ringing and substantial, like the young artist himself; tenths, which demand a particular stretching of the fingers (the Paganini-Auer Capriccio), runs to high notes, and so on. Here one must mention also the head-spinning tempo chosen for the finale of the Mendelssohn Concerto. For Heifetz it seems this tempo was a little "over the top," but in any case the violinist managed it (which cannot be said of the accompanist). And almost nowhere was there even the smallest mistake, even if he hit a few snags. The purity of an ideal "pianola!"

If an artist even five or six years older played this way, it would still be possible, having given him his due, to repeat the rebuke of A. Rubinstein to one of his students: "You should be ashamed! So young—and you play so purely!" But who could possibly say that to this boy. . . . It is natural that the traces of individualistic "soul" are yet barely distinguishable in Heifetz's playing in contrast to the astonishingly inherited and developed "resonances" of the ear (musicality) and hands (technique). . . .

The true artist still sleeps in him, and this, maybe, is for the best. . . . We know wunderkinder who in this respect, it seemed, developed earlier but then did not reach higher . . . and, as adults, became mediocrities. . . . It is hard to say when this higher spirit of the "true" artist will awaken in Heifetz (and even if it will awaken) and how widely it will spread its wings—but, judging by that which this charming boy already does, one wishes to think that it will be something wonderful . . . [12]

After returning from Moscow, Jascha spent the rest of the month preparing for his March 27 performance at the Maly Hall in the St. Petersburg Conservatory. In the meantime, other Auer students performed solo concerts, including Cecilia Hansen on March 7 and Myron Polyakin on March 13. Following Polyakin's concert, the *Russkaya muzykalnaya gazeta* wrote that it was not just a student performance, but

one of the spring exhibitions of our famous Professor L. S. Auer, an exhibit of a remarkable talent in the artistic development of the great pedagogue-artist. Mr. Auer may show us not one, but three talents, each one different and trained differently. Polyakin, Hansen, Heifetz—these are like three living symphony compositions by L. Auer . . . and each one original in its own way, as it should be, because otherwise it would be like factory production, and not the work of a remarkable pedagogue. . . . Our famous pedagogue does not impinge upon the originality of talent, and therefore such amazing works come from his hands. Mr. Auer has made many such living symphonies over his many years of work, and they have long been heard in concerts around the world. Not in vain do students come to Auer from all over the globe to study. Clearly, he is a pedagogical authority to the world, the glory and pride of our conservatory.[13]

The article ended with a request that Auer's students should receive a chance to perform at the Hall of the Assembly of the Nobility, St. Petersburg's most prestigious concert venue, which was usually reserved for foreign stars. The tone of the request suggested that such an outcome was extremely unlikely; nevertheless, just a few months later, Jascha did perform on that famous stage.

For now, however, the smaller Maly Hall began to feel like home to Jascha, and on the day of his concert, a large and exacting audience of professional musicians, professors, and students filled the seats and the aisles. A solo performance for this audience was by no means an easy test. The *Sankt-Peterburgskie vedomosti* explained that the concert passed "with poor financial success, even though the hall was overflowing with all stripes of conservatory audience there to hear 'their own'—not surprising given the special discounts."[14] The reviewer expressed sympathy for Jascha, who was faced with such a knowledgeable and critical audience.

Newspapers noted that "Heifetz already has his own name, his own reputation,"[15] and they discussed the question of whether Jascha enjoyed being on stage, concluding that even if he did not, he was already used to it. The boy prepared well for the performance, and in addition to familiar pieces such as the Bruch Concerto no. 1 and the Bach Aria, he performed several new works, including the Giovanni Sgambati *Serenade,* the Wieniawski Polonaise in A, Paganini's Moto Perpetuo, and Kreisler Praeludium and Allegro in the style of Pugnani (at that time one of Kreisler's hoaxes yet to be revealed). For the first time Jascha also played the Ernst *Concerto pathétique.*

Accompanying Jascha for this recital was thirty-five-year-old Mikhail Dulov, an accompanist considered among the best in St. Petersburg. Dulov had started his conservatory training in the violin class of Pyotr Krasnokutsky but later transferred to a piano class. His instinctive ability for accompaniment led his contemporaries to talk of "the gift of Dulov's harmony"; he collaborated with many prominent violinists, with the cellist Verzhbilovich, and with vocalists such as Medea and Nikolai Figner and Fyodor Chaliapin. Auer greatly respected Dulov and tried to have him accompany his students for their most important performances. Jascha would play many times with Dulov.

The St. Petersburg press applauded Jascha's March 27 recital, comparing the boy with Mischa Elman, but the reviewer for the *Obozrenie teatrov* added that Elman's playing had exhibited signs of stress: "the overstrained nerves of the talented child could be felt. . . . [Elman was] left to this day half-literate and undeveloped, due to the exploitation and greed of his father."[16] With Jascha, however, there was "an element of culture growing in him, independent of anyone's influence."

Other reviewers compared Jascha to Fritz Kreisler, and in describing his youthful talents they invoked the memories of Mozart, Liszt, and Rubinstein. The authoritative music critic Karatygin, who approximately two years earlier had found little in Jascha aside from virtuosity, now responded differently:

> Close your eyes: you are hearing the playing of a mature, adult artist, playing the Bach Aria with remarkable emotionality. He who has put enormous feeling into his interpretation of the Prelude and Allegro of Pugnani, who has shown excellent development of technique in the Bruch Concerto, who revealed a remarkable performance gift in a whole host of difficult and varied pieces. . . . It is not hard to predict the future of the young artist. This will be a first-rate star.[17]

Practical issues relating to Jascha's continuing development became the focus of Viktor Valter's review:

> Compared with last year the boy has grown noticeably, and in the near future he will inevitably have to switch to a full-size violin, for now he still plays on a three-quarter-size violin. But on such a pitiful instrument Jascha creates an enormous, magnificent sound of marvelous beauty. Jascha's technique is simply fantastic . . . and I do not know a violinist who could play the Ernst Concerto in F Sharp Minor or the Paganini Perpetuum Mobile with such perfection and at such speed. At the end of the Ernst concerto the fingered octaves were simply blinding. But what astonishes even more in Jascha's performance is the spiritual side. The serious, meaningful tone in the Bruch Concerto, the mystical depth in the Bach Aria, the noble grace and power of expression in the Prelude and Allegro of Pugnani-Kreisler—these are all features of genius individuality, which cannot be learned. The boy was brought a bow as a present. But of course, he who brings Jascha a violin worthy of his talent will be happy, for to serve genius is the greatest happi-

ness. The mood in the completely full hall was rapturous and heightened, and the audience lingered long afterward in amazement sharing their reactions to the unusual event.[18]

The bow given to Jascha at the concert turned out to be one by Nicolaus Kittel (ca. 1806–1865), a famous German-born bow maker who lived most of his life in St. Petersburg and had his own instrument workshop for many years. Kittel worked as the supplier to the Imperial Court; St. Petersburg musicians considered it an honor to maintain links with him. Kittel's son Nikolai continued his father's work until his own death in Finland in 1893. By the middle of the nineteenth century, Kittel bows had an international reputation and were considered similar in standard to those of the French master, François Tourte. Many famous violinists preferred the so-called "Russian Tourte" to all others; Vieuxtemps, for example, owned six Kittel bows and used them exclusively. Kittel bows now often command tens of thousands of dollars at auction. Heifetz cherished his Kittel bow and in an interview in 1978 explained that the bow had been given to him many years earlier by Professor Auer.[19]

Around the middle of March 1913, plans for a tour to Odessa were being finalized with the Odessa entrepreneur G. S. Baltz, Commissioner of the Odessa Institute of Emperor Nicholas I. Baltz organized concerts, tours, and lectures, and tickets to these events were available to the public from the organization's office. The contract for Jascha's tour survives in the Library of Congress archive.[20] Dated March 16, 1913, the contract between "J. Heifetz" and "G. S. Baltz" outlines six main points in elaborate legalese. The first stipulated that Jascha would appear in two concerts between April 15 and 18, 1913, in Odessa. Secondly, the Heifetzes were obligated to provide their own accompanist and to furnish the organizers with printed advertising material. The next two points dealt with finances: Jascha would receive a total of 3,700 rubles for the two performances; half would be paid a week before the first concert, and the other half on the day of the second concert before the actual performance. Finally, the last two points dealt with logistical issues: the contract would be canceled in the case of unforeseen events such as war, epidemics, political upheaval, and so on, and if Jascha was not in Odessa by the morning of the first concert day, he was liable to pay G. S. Baltz a penalty of 2,000 rubles. For such a young performer, the contract was hugely impressive, the fees comparing favorably with those of many star performers from the period, including Kreisler and Nikisch.

Several parts of the contract were changed during negotiations. First, since Jascha was too young to enter into the agreement himself, the name J. Heifetz was changed to R. Heifetz, so that the contract would be in his father's name. Also, the number of concerts was reduced to just one, set for April 18. A wide-reaching advertising campaign began around the start of April, and an announcement appeared on the pages of the *Odesskie novosti* and *Odessky listok*: "Merchants' Exchange Hall. On Thursday, April 18, a concert will take place, the only one of the violinist Jascha Heifetz following his concert tour to Germany and Austria. Tickets from 1 r. 75 k. are available from the Central Theatrical Booking Office in the store of G. S. Baltz."[21] The *Odesskie novosti* recalled Jascha's successful tour to Odessa two years earlier and reprinted reviews from the German press. Despite all the preparations, on April 18, the day of the concert, newspapers announced: "Yesterday news was received that as a result of a cold, Jascha Heifetz could not come to Odessa, therefore his concert, planned for today, will take place in a few days."[22] In the days and weeks that followed, however, there was no evidence of the concert. The Heifetzes did not fulfill their part of the contract.

Coincidentally, on the day of the canceled performance, the *Odesskie novosti* published an extended interview with Fritz Kreisler, who was touring in Odessa. The famous violinist shared his general thoughts on performance, pointing out that mastery of violin technique should be used to pursue broader musical aims: "Only if the artist is able to create images does he then have the right to the name of artist." In answer to the question of which contemporary violinists he admired, Kreisler responded: "I would put Ysaÿe above all others. After that, I would place Auer and Brodsky very highly. Although they are elderly, by their playing one would never say that they were so old." Kreisler also admired Kubelík, but felt that he had begun performing too early, and so by the age of thirty had already become overworked and burned out. "Take Jascha Heifetz," added Kreisler. "He commands remarkable technique; he is also very talented by nature, almost genius. But he started to perform too early, and this could destroy him."[23]

The spring exam period arrived at the conservatory, but neither Jascha nor Cecilia Hansen performed in the public exam on May 1, since once again performances at the Maly Hall proved evidence enough of their achievements. Jascha did, however, participate in a smaller exam held on March 18 for a committee chaired by Sergei Korguev (the acting director, since Glazunov was sick). In the exam list under "Opinion of the instructor," Auer gave the boy a 5 and wrote: "outstanding talent."[24]

The Heifetzes also received good news from Pauline's exam. Following her performance in Professor Drozdov's public piano class exam on May 5, the teacher wrote the following about his student: "Resounding success over this year and a bit. Has studied for two years in all. Extreme signs of musicality. Can contemplate a future career."[25] As head of the examining commission, Glazunov added that "despite her young age, she has already developed a beautiful tone. Respectable technical preparation. Probably, something will come of it . . ."[26] With that, the school year was behind them, and the Heifetzes looked forward to the summer.

CHAPTER TWELVE

Summer–Fall 1913: Loschwitz

JASCHA HEIFETZ SPENT THE SUMMER of 1913 with Leopold Auer in Germany, for what was the first in a series of summer vacations spent with his professor. For many years, Auer had spent his summers in England, but in 1912 he began to vacation in Loschwitz, a charming suburb of Dresden. Auer wrote warmly of these vacations: "Loschwitz was a delightful village flanked by a green hill on the bank of the Elbe. On one side we had a view of Dresden, on the other we could look out toward the green mountains of the Saxon Alps."[1] Spread along both banks of the Elbe, Dresden was known as the "German Florence"; its world-famous gallery housed a collection of paintings by great Flemish and Italian artists. Tourists traveled great distances to visit the city. Other attractions included Zwinger Palace, Dresden Castle, and several museums. Located just two miles from Dresden, Loschwitz was one of many resorts located in the valley and was surrounded by deep picturesque gorges, green forests, and mountain streams.

Auer's visit transformed Loschwitz into an international colony of violin students just as it had London before 1912. Auer recalled that Loschwitz "had in a way become a kind of violin center, and every house harbored one or more young aspirants to the concert stage. During the summers of 1913 and 1914 some thirty or forty from every land were gathered there, among them Kathleen Parlow, Isolde Menges, and two prodigies, Jascha Heifetz and Toscha Seidel."[2]

Documents in the conservatory archives reveal the story of Seidel's admission into Auer's class. In August 1912, Tauba Seidel, originally from Brest, wrote from Odessa to the conservatory director requesting an entrance violin exam for her eleven-year-old son.[3] In addition to the formal request, Seidel added: "Professor L. Auer listened to my son in Dresden a month ago and gave me a letter in which he certifies that he can accept him into his class. I will personally bring the letter and deliver it to your office." Toscha and his mother had spent the summer of 1912 with Auer in Loschwitz. The fact that Seidel gives her son's age as eleven is startling, since the birth certificate attached to the application indicates that he was actually thirteen (born OS November 4, 1899, to the *meshchanin* of Brest-Litovsk, Shmuil Seidel, and his wife Tauba). Exaggerating the youthfulness of a child prodigy was clearly a common practice. After Toscha Seidel and Heifetz both arrived in the United States, commentators took pleasure in discussing which of the two Auer students was actually older.

Toscha's first year in St. Petersburg proved difficult. Auer recalled that "Mme. Seidel and her son were obliged to live more than fifteen miles from the capital, in Finland, and, until she could obtain permission to reside in St. Petersburg, the mother had to make the two wearisome journeys every week in order to bring her son to my class in the Conservatoire."[4] Despite these difficulties, Toscha quickly became one of Auer's top students, and for the second year in a row, Toscha was invited to spend the summer of 1913 with Auer in Loschwitz.[5]

In contrast to the Seidels, the five members of the Heifetz family were new to Loschwitz. Nevertheless, Jascha and his family quickly found an apartment to rent in the Neue-Rochwitz quarter at the edge of Loschwitz. The center of the little town consisted of two- and three-story, stone buildings spread around the base of a hill. The Heifetzes settled on Hauptstrasse, which consisted of small wooden houses set throughout the thick forest. Further details about the Loschwitz trip emerge in a letter Ruvin wrote to Valter:

14 July 1913
Neue-Rochwitz near Dresden
Hauptstrasse no. 8 for Heifetz

Deeply Respected Viktor Grigoryevich!

We received your letter to Professor Mr. Auer. We are very grateful that you are so supportive of us. We send our greetings to you and from the bottom of our hearts wish your children all the best. How is your health, dear Viktor Grigoryevich? How is everyone? We have settled in very well here. We don't live too far from the professor. We were lucky to find a good little three-room apartment with a kitchen and conveniences. My wife keeps house just like at home. We also have a servant here, and it costs us no more than in Russia, and some things here are actually cheaper; overall we are glad that we came. Auer was very happy at our arrival and has worked with Jascha three times already. During this time Jascha has managed to get through Bruch's Scottish Fantasy, Vitali's Chaconne, Paganini's "Palpiti" and also the Vieuxtemps 5th Concerto. This week Wolff is coming to us from Berlin to discuss concerts in Germany, and in three weeks the impresario Daniel Mayer will come from London. Recently we managed to get a German girl for the children, recommended by one of Mr. Auer's acquaintances. Jascha will write to you himself. Sincere greetings to you and yours.

Yours, R. Heifetz[6]

The negotiations with Louise Wolff mentioned by Ruvin were concluded successfully, and the Heifetzes signed a contract with her for autumn concerts in Berlin and Dresden. In contrast, the meeting with the impresario Daniel Meyer (not Mayer as Ruvin writes), whose agency advertised itself as the top agency in England, came to nothing.[7] As Ruvin promised, Jascha wrote a message to Valter:

Dear and respected Viktor Grigoryevich!

Forgive me for not writing for so long. I was just waiting for Papa to write. We live near Lyoschwitz [sic]. It's very beautiful by us, there is a lot of forest here where we pick many kinds of berries. Not far from us is a tennis court. I often play and have already learned to play pretty well, though I don't have time to play every day. A German lady comes to us and I'm studying some harmony. In Dresden there is a Russian library where we borrow books to read. I've already had four lessons with Professor Auer. Many of his students live in Lyoschwitz. They often come here to play tennis. So I am very happy and very glad that we came here. Polinka and Elinka are also having a good time and send their greetings to all of you. Yours affectionately, Jascha.[8]

Jascha saved some photographs from the trip in one of his scrapbooks, and labeled them with short inscriptions; one was inscribed: "My Lea," as the boy lovingly named his Leica camera.[9] Other images show Jascha on the tennis court with his classmates. Also present in photographs from this trip is a woman named Dorothea Grosse, the German governess mentioned in Ruvin's letter. Photographs reveal that the Heifetzes occasionally took the electric tram to Dresden, where they visited the library and walked around the park. Some of Jascha's inscriptions on the photographs reveal his growing interest in the art of photography. On one over-exposed image, Jascha wrote: "The plate was placed into the slide in a room that wasn't dark enough."

It was not all fun and games for the students in Loschwitz, however, and in addition to lessons with Auer, the youngsters spent hours practicing independently. A break to the routine came when Auer organized an afternoon musical celebration, something that became a tradition during these summer vacations. Auer explained: "This was always an exciting event in the life of the little colony. It was my custom to hire a small hall, admirably situated on a terrace which allowed a fine view of the Elbe. The program was always a serious one, and comprised no more than three or four numbers; the Bach Concerto in D Minor for two violins was usually played."[10] Further details about this musical event appear in a letter from Auer to the music critic Arthur Abell:

> Loschwitz bei Dresden, 17/7 1913
>> Dear Mr. Abell;
>> It has just come to my notice that you are back in Berlin; that's resulted in an idea!
>
> On Monday 21 July, here in the Hotel Loschwitzhöhe (right next to the cable car), I've got an afternoon party *with* (or rather) *for* my pupils and a very few friends from Dresden.—Would you provide me with the great pleasure of also coming, together with your wife? The musical menu consists of only two items, duets for 2 violins.—I can't have them perform "solos" because I have several outstanding soloists among my pupils.
>
> The double concerto by Bach (d minor) will be played by the boys
>> 1.) Heifetz
>> 2.) Seidel (also from Petersburg)

Serenade (2 violins) by Sinding
Miss Berson (St. Petersburg)
and
Rhoderick White (America).

Over and above that I would like to suggest lunch at my place at 1.00 and then together at 3–30 to Loschwitzhöhe. What do you say to that idea? It would be such a pleasant opportunity to meet up again!

Please kiss your wife's hand for me, and best wishes to you!
L. Auer[11]

The musical celebration went wonderfully and culminated with the Bach Concerto for Two Violins in D Minor. Auer years later wrote:

> I remember one occasion on which not only I but all the guests, who had come from Dresden and even from Berlin to do honor to the occasion, were deeply moved by the purity and unity of style, and the profound sincerity, to say nothing of the technical perfection, with which the two children in little blue sailor suits, Jascha Heifetz and Toscha Seidel, played that master work. The impression produced was so powerful that when the players had finished, and one of the guests from out-of-town stepped on the stage and, with tears in his eyes, expressed his gratitude for the wonderful artistic pleasure it had been his privilege to enjoy, he was only putting into words what was felt by everyone present, including myself.[12]

To commemorate these unforgettable days, Jascha presented Auer with an inscribed photograph: "To the one and only Professor Leopold Semyonovich von Auer from his deeply affectionate student. Jascha Heifetz. Loschwitz. Summer 1913."[13]

In early September, still in Loschwitz, the Heifetzes received a letter from the law firm Netcke und Dr. Löser representing the American concert agency Musical Celebrities and its manager R. E. Johnston.[14] The letter set out a contract for a tour of North America, to include fifteen concerts between November 10, 1913, and January 10, 1914. The agreement proposed the following conditions: a payment of five hundred dollars per concert; no more than two concerts per week; a break of no fewer than two days between concerts; concert length of no more than ninety minutes; performances only in first-rate concert halls; the first concert to be with orchestral accompaniment; the Heifetz family provided with first-class tickets on all modes of transportation and two-bedroom suites in first-class hotels; and a daily allowance of thirty-five dollars. Despite the generous terms, an insurmountable problem presented itself—performers in the United States and Canada needed to be at least fourteen years old, otherwise the Society for the Prevention of Cruelty to Children would oppose the tour. The contract with R. E. Johnston remained unsigned.

For the time being, the Heifetzes remained in Loschwitz, and on September 16 they received a greeting card from Liachowsky, informing them of his imminent return to Berlin from London. Friends and family sent greetings to the Heifetzes in Loschwitz for the Jewish New Year, which fell on October 2. The Heifetzes remained in Loschwitz until it was time for Jascha to begin his German tour with the Wolff agency. Further details appear in correspondence from Ruvin to Arthur Abell. Ruvin could not write in German, so the well-crafted letter was produced by Dorothea Grosse, who fulfilled the roles of both governess and secretary while the Heifetzes were in Germany:

> Rochwitz 17. 9. 13
> Dear Mr. Abell!
> We were very pleased to receive your kind invitation and would like to thank you for it most sincerely. Unfortunately, however, we will not be in a position to come to Berlin as early as the 28th of the month, as we still have a lot to do here in the lead-up to Jascha's concert. We will stay in Rochwitz till after Jascha's concert in Dresden on 2 October and will then travel to Berlin. There we will stay till around 15 October, and during that time, we will be very pleased to accept your kind invitation.
> With kind regards from all of us
> Your
> R. Heifetz[15]

Judging from Ruvin's letter, it appears that Jascha's Berlin concerts were supposed to begin after his performance in Dresden on October 2. Programs and printed advertisements, however, indicate that Jascha played a concert with Waldemar Liachowsky in Berlin on September 30 at the Königliche Hochschule für Musik. The program included many new or almost new works, including Beethoven Romance in G, the Mozart-Burmester Minuet, and the Glazunov Violin Concerto. Glazunov completed his concerto in 1904, for Auer, who premiered the work under the composer's direction in early 1905. A witness to Jascha's early work on the piece was the composer Yury Shaporin, who began his studies at the St. Petersburg Conservatory in 1912. In his memoirs, Shaporin wrote:

> So as to hear how Auer worked with Heifetz, I had to resort to cunning: I squeezed into the space between the two doors of Auer's classroom, scraped off a little paint from the glass of the inner door, and through this little peephole I observed how before the venerable professor stood a boy in short trousers playing the Glazunov Concerto. . . . Auer, then already quite an old man, sat in a deep chair and it appeared he was dozing. When Heifetz finished playing, he turned to his professor with the question,
> "Like that?"
> "I don't know, like that or not!"
> "Well then, how?"
> At that, Auer stood up, took the small violin from the boy's hands, and began playing with such brilliance and inspiration that I stood bewitched behind the door. After finishing his demonstration of the concerto, Auer said, "like that!"[16]

Jascha's Berlin program for September 30 also included the virtuosic Paganini Concerto in D. The Berlin critics reacted with fervor to Jascha's appearance, and positive reviews appeared in the major German publications.[17] On October 2, Jascha played his next concert, this time at the Dresden Vereinshaus. This concert was not part of the agreement with the Wolff agency; the printed program carried the name of the F. Reiss agency. This Dresden performance included some of the pieces Jascha played in Berlin. New to the program was the Schumann-Auer *Prophet Bird*, a piece he returned to frequently, and the Vitali Chaconne, which Jascha had just learned with Auer in Loschwitz. Over the next three years, Jascha performed the Vitali Chaconne no fewer than fifteen times.

The second Berlin concert took place on October 7 at the now-familiar Königliche Hochschule für Musik. The program differed entirely from the previous concert, featuring the Ernst *Concerto pathétique*, Paganini's Moto Perpetuo, Tchaikovsky's *Sérénade mélancolique*, and two short pieces Jascha had just learned by Swedish composer Tor Aulin, *Humoresque* and *Lullaby*. Jascha's third and final Berlin concert, on October 14, also included new works. In addition to the Auer Concert *Tarantella*, Jascha performed Lalo *Symphonie Espagnole*, a piece Auer considered one of the most original of the entire concert repertoire. In his book *Violin Master Works and their Interpretation,* Auer writes that "Lalo entered into the very soul of this elemental music and in every case revealed only its noblest essence without any external overelaboration."[18]

Among those present to hear Jascha perform in Berlin was Alexander Schmuller, a violinist who had studied with Auer at the St. Petersburg Conservatory between 1905 and 1906. Schmuller moved to Berlin in 1908 to teach at the Stern Conservatory and later moved to Amsterdam. As the Berlin correspondent for the *Den* newspaper in St. Petersburg, Schmuller wrote a review of Jascha's concert series. Although Schmuller calls himself "old," he was born in 1880 and so was only thirty-three at the time. Clearly, he wished to emphasize the musical experience that enabled him to comment on the talent of the young prodigy:

> Now, after attending several Heifetz concerts, I, an old and seasoned artist, stand dejected, weighed down by the incomprehensible miracle to which I was witness. I will not say that Heifetz is a phenomenon. When talk turns to the highest technical and spiritual maturity, and when you see the highest beauty and controlled artistic intensity of the twelve-year-old child's creative powers, one must speak not of a phenomenon but of a miracle. Without hesitation I name Heifetz the greatest artist of our time, and maybe also of all times and of all peoples. I consider "Jascha" to be this most perfected maestro, who would be better known as "Beauty," "Sun," "Genius." I saw tears in the hall, real ones, not theatrical tears, and even artists—the greatest masters—felt joy and fright at Heifetz's last concert, like children dreaming of a white, pure angel with wings on its shoulders. Listening to Heifetz, I remembered the words of Y. Halevi: "And when the Lord created his soul, he kissed it." These words relate perfectly to the little Heifetz, on whose brow this godly kiss burns with a bright, inextinguishable flame.[19]

A few days after Jascha's third and final Berlin concert, he found himself in the audience for the evening recital of Eugene Ysaÿe in the Hall of the Berlin Philharmonic. Jascha saved the original program from this concert, dated October 17, 1913, in his scrapbook.[20] Accompanied by the pianist Raoul Pugno, Ysaÿe performed the Mozart Sonata in D, the Franck Sonata, and Beethoven's *Kreutzer* Sonata. This was already the second time Jascha had heard Ysaÿe.

For the Heifetzes, the Ysaÿe recital concluded a more than four-month, highly productive stay in Germany. On the way home from Germany, the family stopped in Warsaw where Jascha gave a concert with Liachowsky. The performance included works Jascha played in Berlin. After the concert, Liachowsky departed for his home in Charlottenburg, from where he corresponded regularly with Jascha and his family. Before leaving Warsaw, the Heifetzes met with friends and family, including Uncle Natan and his wife Fanny, who was heavily pregnant at the time.[21]

The Heifetzes arrived in St. Petersburg in the first week of October (os), but there was little time to relax, especially for Jascha and Pauline, who were both required to return immediately to the conservatory. On October 9, the family received their residency certificate in the conservatory office, covering the period through January 29, 1914.[22] Soon after, the Heifetzes moved to the bank of the Yekaterininsky Canal, into apartment 35 in building 119, located by the Kharlamov Bridge on the corner of Yekateringofsky Prospekt. Not long after, Mina Roubleff moved to the same building, into apartment 56.

Life gradually settled into a normal rhythm for the Heifetzes. After saying goodbye to Dorothea Grosse in Germany, Jascha's parents found a new governess in St. Petersburg named Maria Borisovna. They also employed a woman named Zelma Diamant who tutored the children in German. Lessons in Russian, mathematics, history, and other general subjects were conducted by Zinovy Aronovich Kiselgof. The children affectionately nicknamed Kiselgof the "Green Aronovich," since the name Zinovy closely resembles the Russian word for the color green (*zelyony*). That summer, while the Heifetzes were in Loschwitz, Kiselgof had taken part in an ethnographic expedition led by S. An-sky (Shloyme Zanvi Rappoport) to a region now part of Western Ukraine. Kiselgof told the Heifetzes all about his trip, describing how he had traveled around the cities and towns of Volhynia recording Jewish songs and stories. The expedition returned with a multitude of valuable finds, including antique handwritten and printed books, religious artifacts, and many photographs. Kiselgof also returned with hundreds of wax disks with recordings of musical folklore; he sometimes sang the tunes or played them on the violin for the Heifetz children.

Jascha began working toward a concert he would give on November 22 in the most prestigious venue of St. Petersburg, the Hall of the Assembly of the Nobility. A performance there would place Jascha among the true artistic elite of the city. Throughout the remainder of October and into November, Auer worked tirelessly with the boy, preparing an impressive program that included the Vitali Chaconne, the Beethoven Romance in G, the Mozart Minuet, Tchaikovsky's *Melodie,* Wieniawski's Polonaise in A, Schumann's *Prophet Bird,* and the Ernst Variations on an Irish Theme. The accompanist was once again Mikhail Dulov.

The day before the concert, newspapers reported severe weather in the area: "Tonight and all day 22 November, floods were expected, which, according to the data of the Nikolaevskaya Observatory, could surpass even the flood of 1904."[23] By midday, water levels reached six-and-a-half feet higher than normal, and warning flares were fired from the Peter and Paul Fortress every fifteen minutes. The strong storm reached its peak around midday, tearing some barges from the wharf and sinking others carrying coal. The storm uprooted trees and tore roofs from houses. The weather calmed a little by evening, however, so Jascha's concert took place as planned.

Praise for the young violinist abounded. The *Peterburgskaya gazeta* wrote: "Jascha Heifetz does not disappoint the public. . . . Having migrated from the Maly Hall of the Conservatory to the Hall of the Assembly of the Nobility, he has in no way changed his artistic physiognomy, but has remained just as charming a boy and artist, astonishing for his years. His artistic maturity is stunning. . . . Jascha Heifetz is Auer's student, but it seems he is more of a student of Apollo himself."[24] The reviewer of the *Den* appreciated the absence of cheap sensationalism: "Yesterday's performance by Heifetz really had the character of a serious concert, and not a display: there was none of the scent of a circus or *café chantant.*"[25] The *Peterburgsky listok* agreed:

> this dear, sweet boy with light, intelligent, expressive eyes . . . carries in his child's soul the truth of God. . . . The entire program was full of such technical perfection, with such mature forethought, elegance and taste. In the difficult Ernst Variations, he impressed with harmonics so astonishing in their purity, transparency and lightness, that he enraptured the entire hall, which

warmly and loudly applauded the young violinist. The gifted Mr. Dulov, as always, accompanied magnificently.[26]

Amidst the chorus of praise were also several critical observations. For example, the reviewer for the *Teatr i zhizn* newspaper wrote that the short breaks between pieces did not allow listeners to sufficiently enjoy the program, which was organized to highlight contrasting works.[27] Viktor Valter wrote of another type of hurriedness:

> One must rebuke the young artist for poor use of fast tempos (the first movement of the Mendelssohn Concerto, the Mozart Minuet): true, the pulse of the boy genius beats faster than that of an adult artist, but I consider it necessary to make this rebuke so as to bring the attention of the boy and his instructors to the fact that the highest purpose of an artist's performance is the spiritual communication of the work, for which technique is only a means. With such special technical gifts he is threatened by the danger of being caught up in virtuosity.[28]

Valter concluded his review with further advice: "For the parents of this child, the most difficult period of upbringing and education (musical and general) of a genius is beginning. Let such radiant names in the musical world as Liszt and Anton Rubinstein serve them as a guiding star in such a difficult task."

Jascha's concert prompted the critic Karatygin, who had previously written about the boy, to ponder the "phenomenon of wunderkinder." In Heifetz, the critic saw a rare example of a musician who "despite his twelve years has an excellent five-year artistic past and who does not raise the smallest doubts about his 'geniusness.'" Karatygin concluded with a question: "Jascha Heifetz, like Willy Ferrero, is a wunderkind of wunderkinder. There are very few of them. But overall the number of wunderkinder has greatly increased in recent years. What does the future hold? . . . What are we facing—a game of nature or a new trend which in the future will fill concert stages with children?"[29]

Seven-year-old Willy Ferrero's name also filled the pages of the St. Petersburg press that fall. Ferrero and his parents arrived in St. Petersburg on October 25, 1913, and the *Peterburgsky listok* reported that "waiting to meet the young maestro at the station were representatives of the press and the musical world, along with a multitude of representatives of high society, all familiar with the boy genius from his concerts in Rome the previous year." An article from 1912 provides more detail: "the five-year-old boy Willy Ferrero attracted much attention to himself. . . . From the age of three years he displayed an unusual love for music and over the course of two years of study achieved such that he now successfully conducts entire orchestras, giving brilliant concerts in Milan, Paris, London and other cities."[30] Following Ferrero's arrival in Russia in 1913, performances were announced in St. Petersburg on November 3, 8, 19, and 24, along with two concerts in Moscow and a second cycle of concerts in St. Petersburg, on December 6, 8, 12, and 15.

The day before Ferrero's first performance, newspapers reported that he visited the Italian Embassy, where he gave an improvisational concert on the piano. Since the boy did not play the piano (or any other instrument), and could not even read music, one assumes the reporters meant that Ferrero conducted as a pianist played. Ferrero conducted his first rehearsal with the orchestra of Count Sheremetyev on October 31, and then an open rehearsal on November 2. The first concert took place the next day in the Hall of the Assembly of the Nobility; the program included Beethoven's Symphony no. 1, Berlioz's *Hungarian March*, "Anitra's Dance" from Grieg's *Peer Gynt,* and the overture to Wagner's *Die Meistersinger von Nürnberg.* The reviewer for the *Peterburgskaya gazeta* wrote that although "this program was of course not performed so well . . . what is important is the fact that an eight-year-old [*sic*]conducted, standing with his face to the public and not using any written music."[31] Both the public and the critics reacted with astonishment. Karatygin described how

> . . . a small frizzy-haired and thin-legged boy with a long lovely face . . . begins to move unconstrainedly in all directions. The applause continues unabated . . . I must admit that this whole entire concert atmosphere, saturated with an unhealthy thirst for sensation, is so unpleasant . . . my principal prejudices against wunderkind concerts reached their peak right before the first wave of Ferrero's baton. And then after the first wave—what a miracle! All my musical and philanthropic foibles vanished . . . the living imp, standing on the high pedestal in the middle of the stage and directing the Beethoven symphony overturned all my preconceptions . . . by the remarkable expressiveness of all his gestures, by his impeccability, the iron exactness of his

rhythm . . . you see that this little artist truly leads the orchestra. . . . the concert finished. I am already on the street and my former indignation toward the phenomenon of "wunderkinder" captures me with new strength . . . [32]

After his first concert in St. Petersburg, Ferrero fell ill with a cold and the second performance on November 8 was canceled. The boy's illness provoked stormy words in the press, starting with the conductor Siloti, who published an open letter on November 7: "I must appeal to the public, I must appeal with such a voice that all of St. Petersburg will hear me. Gentlemen! What are you doing? . . . I did not want to participate in murder. I did not go and will not go to a single Ferrero concert, and Nikisch also did not go this Sunday for the same reason." Siloti reminded his readers of the case of ten-year-old Josef Hofmann; although Siloti confuses various facts in his letter, the comparison with Josef Hofmann reinforced his argument. A tour of the United States by twelve-year-old Hofmann in 1887 was interrupted by a court decision. The New York patron Alfred Corning Clark then offered his family $50,000 to ensure that Hofmann continue his studies and resist the urge to perform concerts.[33] Many musicians in St. Petersburg supported Siloti's position. Nikolai Tcherepnin, for example, wrote that "Ferrero's public performances are criminal acts by his parents, supported and encouraged by the crowd. He burns like a candle from both ends . . ."[34]

Following Siloti's open letter, the St. Petersburg division of the Society for the Prevention of Cruelty to Children began an investigation led by its division manager Maksim Mandelstam. Working with Chiaramonte Bordonaro, the affairs attorney at the Italian Embassy, Mandelstam met with Ferrero's family and interviewed the boy twice. A meeting then took place, attended by Siloti, Glazunov, Tcherepnin, Auer, the conductor of Count Sheremetyev's orchestra (Aleksandr Khessin), psychiatrists (headed by Vladimir Bekhterev), the doctors caring for Ferrero during his illness, teachers, and jurists. The proceedings of the meeting were kept strictly confidential at the time. All the uproar ended with nothing, however, and Ferrero fulfilled his remaining engagements in November and December with a further two added to satisfy public demand.

Many people brought gifts for the young boy, including a canary in a cage. During the intermission of one performance, the conductor Khessin, who unlike other local musicians, was charmed by the young boy, gave him a train set and other gifts. It took some effort to tear the young musician away from his new toys and convince him to go onstage again. All the efforts of the Society for the Prevention of Cruelty to Children resulted in just one recommendation, sent to the impresario Vladimir Reznikov, which stated that Ferrero's concerts should take place only during the day. Although the society was highly influential in the United States—recall the unsigned contract between the Heifetzes and R. E. Johnston—it was essentially powerless in the Russian Empire.

Altogether, Ferrero's performances in St. Petersburg and Moscow lasted for three months, from the beginning of November 1913, to the end of January 1914. There were private concerts in addition to the original dates, including one in the Anichkov Palace, where Ferrero conducted the court orchestra in the presence of the Empress Maria Fyodorovna, who in return gave the boy a gold watch and chain decorated with the state crest. Ferrero also appeared before Grand Duchess Maria Pavlovna in the hall of the Court Orchestra.

On November 22, Ferrero's parents brought their son to hear Jascha's debut in the Hall of the Assembly of the Nobility. It is possible the two children had met previously, since newspapers had talked of a possible joint concert a week earlier. Nevertheless, the *Peterburgsky listok* eventually discounted the possibility of the two musicians appearing together.[35] The curious manner in which Ferrero arrived at Jascha's performance speaks of Willy's exploitative parents and the spectacle-craving nature of the public. According to the *Peterburgskaya gazeta,*

> Willy Ferrero entered the hall at the very moment when his contemporary had finished the second movement of the Mendelssohn Concerto and should have begun the performance of the finale. The public noticed the little conductor and started to applaud. It turned into something like a triumphal procession through the entire hall. He sat together with his parents in the front row. In light of the fact that the violinist could not continue because of the applause, a smaller part of the audience began to hiss at those applauding. Heifetz began to play, yet the public still stared at Ferrero. Only with his brilliant playing did the violinist manage finally to distract the attention of the hall from the interesting guest.[36]

The *Obozrenie teatrov* explained that "during the intermission the audience streamed to the place where the tiny conductor sat, and it was difficult to protect him from the pressure of the crowd. Despite such 'distracting' conditions (of course, Ferrero himself is not guilty, since he came only to greet his 'colleague'), Jascha Heifetz with all the strength of his talent continued to draw the attention of the audience on his playing, which quite literally bewitched them."[37]

Willy Ferrero became a successful but unremarkable conductor as an adult. In 1936 he returned to St. Petersburg (then Leningrad) and met again with Khessin, the conductor who had embraced the young boy in 1913. In his memoirs, Khessin wrote:

> I had held that feeling for many years and with impatience awaited a meeting with the adult Ferrero. After the symphony concert under his direction in the Bolshoi Hall of the conservatory, I stopped by the artists' room to greet him, and to remind him of his time in St. Petersburg. However, when I tried to give Ferrero a fatherly embrace (the same Ferrero who was once an adorable child charming not only for his amazing giftedness but also his directness and sincerity of character, finding in my home affection and love), I could not fail to experience bitter disappointment, sure that my remembrances of those days evoked in him for some reason unpleasant feelings, which he could not hide.[38]

Khessin continued, explaining that Ferrero declared that he did not remember Khessin or his family, nor the train set that had almost disrupted his concert. Ferrero said that he remembered almost nothing about his visit to St. Petersburg as a child, and Khessin noted that the conductor abruptly tried to change the subject. The adult Ferrero strove vehemently to forget his childhood. Heifetz also kept early memories hidden from the public, as if he were protecting himself from something uncomfortable.

CHAPTER THIRTEEN

Winter 1913–1914: Bar Mitzvah

DURING JASCHA'S PERIOD OF STUDY at the St. Petersburg Conservatory, he returned often to Vilnius to visit, but two years had passed since he last performed in his hometown. The previous appearance was in December 1911 at a charity concert, during which he performed only Sarasate's *Zigeunerweisen*. The music-loving residents of Vilnius were in luck when toward the end of November 1913, local newspapers published the following announcements: "Vilnius Symphony Orchestra. City Hall. 4 December 1913. Symphony Concert with the participation of world-famous violinist Jascha Heifetz. Conductor A. Wylezinski."[1]

The Heifetzes arrived in Vilnius on December 3 and that same day Jascha participated in a rehearsal with the Vilnius Symphony Orchestra. For the first time, the young boy was to perform the Beethoven Concerto, one of the greatest and most challenging works in the violin repertoire. This concerto featured prominently in Heifetz's career, and in his old age he remarked that "there is so much beautiful music. But the Mozart and Beethoven Concerti are special. They are the most difficult, too."[2] Coincidentally, just prior to Jascha's arrival in Vilnius, his conservatory classmate Cecilia Hansen had also performed the Beethoven Concerto there.

Cecilia-Antonia Hansen was born in Kamenskaya, into the Evangelical Lutheran faith, on February 4, 1897 (os).[3] Hansen's parents, collegiate assessor Genrikh and his wife Emilia, lived at 81 Yekaterininsky Canal with their two musical daughters, Cecilia and Elfrida. Cecilia began studying piano at the age of three and soon after started the violin, entering Auer's class in 1908 and preparing for a spring 1914 graduation.[4] She performed in Vilnius on November 23, 24, and 26, 1913, at City Hall and in the City Club with the Symphony Orchestra conducted by Konstantin Vout. Cecilia played concertos by Beethoven, Paganini, and Glazunov and performed violin chamber music together with her sister, Elfrida, who was also a conservatory student. By all accounts the performances were successful.

Jascha's upcoming Vilnius concert was advertised widely on posters and in newspapers: "Tomorrow, December 4, the genius Jascha Heifetz performs in concert with the Vilnius Symphony Orchestra. Needless to say, for Vilnius this concert is a significant event.... Thirteen-year-old [sic] Jascha is like Sarasate at the zenith of his fame. Of contemporary violinists there is no one who could be compared with Heifetz."[5] City Hall was filled to capacity on the day of the concert, and newspapers reported that many in the audience were attending their first concert and were unfamiliar with concert etiquette. As a result, the general noise from the audience swallowed up the finer nuances of the pieces accompanied by piano in the second half of the concert. Nevertheless, after each piece, the Vilnius audience applauded their native prodigy enthusiastically. At the end of the concert, Ivan Schumann, director of the Botanical Gardens, stepped onstage to give remarks. According to the *Stranitsy proshlogo*, "Despite his German surname—and such a musically famed one!—Schumann was a pure-blooded Russian (his real surname was Shumanenko), sociable, cheerful, with roguish cunning, with proven organizational capabilities and a strong grasp of business matters."[6] After a short but passionate speech praising Jascha, Schumann crowned the boy with an enormous laurel wreath with an inscribed banner: "To the highly talented Jascha from Ivan Antonovich Schumann. Vilna. 4. XII 1913"; Heifetz kept the banner throughout his life. After Jascha received the wreath, Ilya Malkin, his former violin instructor also received a large bouquet of flowers.

The Vilnius newspapers praised Jascha for his "enormous success" and noted that "despite the extremely high prices, the hall was overflowing."[7] The *Vechernyaya gazeta* wrote that "Thirteen-year-old J. Heifetz is already a first-rate star and a star shining with all the colors of the rainbow. . . . His musical development is proceeding wonderfully harmoniously."[8] A reviewer in the *Vilensky kurier* compared Jascha with Willy Ferrero: "Willy is made up wholly of raw elements . . . [on the other hand] Jascha Heifetz is far from a primary element and more like a real personality. That which he does is remarkable, but there is no mystery in it. This boy with the singing soul . . . is a special gift of nature . . ."[9]

One exception to the adulation was a review published in the *Vilensky vestnik* on December 6 (signed only as "M"):

> Sensational advertising passing all boundaries preceded the concert on December 4 of the unremarkable wunderkind Jascha Heifetz. Of course, aware that advertising often makes mountains out of molehills, we attended the concert expecting to find in Heifetz the most complete lack of giftedness. Of course, one cannot accuse Heifetz of ungiftedness—he certainly has ability, but to announce, as advertisers in the papers have shrieked, that he "already now plays better than all the violinists in the world," is absolutely ridiculous.[10]

In response to the question "what did we find in Heifetz?" the reviewer summarized: "That which one could expect from a twelve-year-old boy: a child's performance. There was nothing penetrating or genius. The boy played like a good student, and, I suppose, shows some promise for the future. This reservation is necessary in light of the destructive effect of the advertising surrounding him." Regarding Jascha's performance of the Beethoven Concerto, the reviewer stated that it "was performed . . . only adequately; his performance not only cannot be compared with the performance of Ysaÿe or Barcewicz, but not even with the performance of Ms. Hansen, who in this very same Beethoven violin concerto exhibited much grace and taste. With Heifetz this did not appear and several passages were in fact inaccurate."

The strength of the rebuke is remarkable, especially given how it differs from the general response of the public and the press; it seems the reviewer was incensed by the over-commercialization of Jascha's performance. This disastrous review did not go unnoticed by Malkin, who wrote almost immediately to Valter in St. Petersburg, enclosing a copy of the review:

Vilna, 7 December 1913.
Respected and Dear Viktor Grigoryevich!
On the 4th of December Jascha Heifetz gave a concert here; there are no words to express even a small percent of the delight created by his wonderful and incomparable playing. The hall was full to capacity, and I cannot remember such unanimous, spontaneous delight even in the past years during concerts of Sarasate. And this is not surprising. Such playing as Jascha Heifetz possesses has never been heard. From whichever aspect you approach it—technical, musical—it is unique and incomparable. Imagine then, dear Viktor Grigoryevich, what I must have felt reading the review that I am sending to you. I do not have the ability, living here, to start an argument with this fool: first of all, they either simply won't print what I write, or will print it with such distortions and comments that it will be pointless, and secondly, I will be considered biased, in light of the fact that Jaschenka was my former student.
Knowing that you write, I beg you in the name of truth and love for divine art to dismantle his "criticism" and give him a proper answer. I ask you sincerely to answer this letter with at least a few words. Dear Viktor Grigoryevich, I send you my sincere greetings.
Your old friend I. D. Malkin.
21 Sirotskaya Street, I. Malkin.[11]

The Heifetzes had left Vilnius by the time Malkin wrote to St. Petersburg. Meanwhile, Jascha wrote to his sister back in St. Petersburg: "Dear Polya! We got your letter. Mama will answer you. So, how are you? Are you studying? We're now sitting in the train carriage on our way to Kiev. Thank God we're all healthy. I got a laurel wreath from Schumann and a big box of chocolates. I'll write to Elza separately . . ."[12] True to his word, Jascha also wrote to Elza (in large letters): "Dear Elza! How are you? . . . Are you behaving for Maria Borisovna?"[13]

In Kiev, the Heifetzes stayed at the Hotel Palace on Bibikovsky Boulevard, and in their free time met with Hyman Gerber and his family. Jascha also sent postcards, including one to his uncle Samuil in Warsaw.[14] The trip to Kiev was motivated by two concerts to be staged under the auspices of the local agency Philharmonia. Kiev audiences were treated to many impressive concerts during the autumn of 1913: a sonata recital by Auer and Yesipova on October 15; a violin concert by Efrem Zimbalist on November 28; and, on December 8 and 11, concerts by the "world renowned twelve-year-old violinist Jascha Heifetz." Zimbalist, who was also an Auer student, graduated from the St. Petersburg Conservatory in 1907. Known by his St. Petersburg friends as "Frika," Zimbalist had lived in the United States for two years by the time of his Kiev concert, which constituted part of an extended Russian tour. Despite the difference in age, Heifetz and Zimbalist became close friends and remained in contact for many years in the United States.

At his first Kiev concert on December 8 in the Merchants' Club, Jascha performed the Tchaikovsky Concerto, Schubert's *Ave Maria,* Wieniawski's Polonaise in A, Cui's *Melodie Orientale,* Handel's Larghetto, and Paganini's Caprice no. 24. At his second concert on December 11, Jascha played the Mendelssohn Concerto, Vitali's Chaconne, Beethoven's Romance in G, Mozart's Minuet, a Chopin Nocturne, Kreisler's *Schön Rosmarin,* and Bazzini's *La Ronde des Lutins.* The concerts were a massive success. According to the *Kievskie novosti,* "at the time of the concert in the halls of the Merchants' Club, one witnessed rare excitement. The audience was very large, and an ecstatic welcome greeted the boy genius. The guard on duty had to call up a police detachment to guard Jascha Heifetz from the expressions of enthusiasm of his admirers . . ."[15]

Despite their shared enthusiasm for Jascha's performance, newspapers tried to distance themselves from the hysterical excitement of the public. The reviewer for the *Kievskaya mysl* wondered "how to convey an impression of this evening without falling into hypocrisy nor into excessive ecstasy?" The reviewer continued:

Unarguably, all the secrets of violin technique are known to this little virtuoso. . . . But besides the bow and fingers, we demand from an artist also a chronicle of his own soul. For every work of art is a living thing, fed by the blood of a wounded heart. Therefore much of what Jascha Heifetz played seemed to me only a divine masquerade, a terrible oath pronounced by childish lips. Nevertheless, the Handel Larghetto and partly the Schubert "Ave Maria" convinced me that before me was not only a miracle-violinist, but also a boy with the soul of a great artist. His bow spoke with such immaculate purity of the joys of life and of the sacrifice of suffering, that it was impossible to believe that the sounds came from a tiny heart, for whom the whole world and all the attachments in life are still limited to his mother's knees...[16]

The pianist for Jascha's concerts in Kiev was Isidor Achron (1892–1948). Isidor and his violinist brother Joseph (1886–1943) belonged to the musical committee of the Society for Jewish Folk Music in St. Petersburg; Zinovy Kiselgof introduced the Achrons and the Heifetzes. Joseph Achron had studied with Auer and made a name for himself in the early 1900s, giving concerts both in Russia and abroad as a violinist and also working as a composer. Joseph composed violin pieces based on Jewish folk melodies and often performed them at concerts of the Society for Jewish Folk Music. At these same concerts Joseph's piano compositions were performed by his brother Isidor.

The Achron brothers came from the border area between Poland and Lithuania. Their father Abram (Yudel) worked as a craftsman in the settlement of Łoździeje (now Lazdijai, Lithuania). In 1899, when the elder son Joseph was studying in St. Petersburg at the conservatory, the entire family received the right of residency in St. Petersburg, and they settled at 61 Nevsky Prospekt.[17] Isidor became a resident of St. Petersburg at the age of seven and in 1903 entered Aleksandr Miklashevsky's piano class at the conservatory. Isidor was a highly gifted pianist and a sensitive and responsive ensemble player. His musical character was influenced by the teaching of Professor Yesipova, in whose class he had studied for the previous five years. Yesipova played in a duo with Auer for many years, and she passed on to her students her innate understanding of ensemble playing. After the two Kiev performances in December 1913, "Achronchik," as he was known affectionately to the Heifetzes, became Jascha's permanent accompanist and in the following years would join him on a number of tours in Russia. The collegial relationship between the two continued in the United States, where Achron would accompany Heifetz for many years.

Following the Kiev performances, the Heifetzes headed back to Vilnius. By that time, Valter had honored Malkin's plea for him to write to the editorial offices of the *Vilensky vestnik* in response to the negative review of

Jascha's concert. Valter's letter appeared in the paper on December 15 and also in the *Vilensky kurier* on December 16:

> I was sent from Vilnius a copy of your paper from December 6 of this year, in which a review of Jascha Heifetz by your permanent music critic was printed. This review states condescendingly that Heifetz played "like a good student, and I suppose, shows some promise for the future." Of course, one cannot argue about taste, but for the sake of the readers of your paper who have not heard Heifetz, allow me to inform you that Heifetz had sensational success in St. Petersburg, Berlin, Hamburg and Dresden, that Auer, from whose hands have come Elman, Zimbalist and with whom Cecilia Hansen still studies, personally said to me that Heifetz is not a miracle-child, but a true miracle and that, most probably, Arthur Nikisch is of the same opinion of Heifetz if he invited Heifetz to play in a symphony concert in the "Gewandhaus" in Leipzig. Such an invitation to a thirteen-year-old violinist is an exception for which only Joachim was worthy in 1843 when Mendelssohn invited him, at twelve years of age, to play in the "Gewandhaus." For my part, I add that the kind of technique Heifetz has does not exist with any other violinist in the world, and of the artistic beauty of his playing I can only say that it completely corresponds to the beauty of his face when he plays. One would have to be blind and deaf in this case to argue with the positive verdict of the public.[18]

Jascha played the Mendelssohn Concerto with the Vilnius Symphony Orchestra and the conductor Konstantin Vout for his second concert in Vilnius on December 20. The second half of the concert included the Wieniawski *Faust Fantasy,* Schubert's *Ave Maria,* and Cui's *Melodie Orientale.* The public wrangling between Valter and the reviewer for the *Vilensky vestnik* known as "M" only increased the audience's sense of expectation. Perhaps as a result of Valter's correspondence "M" wrote more positively of Jascha after the second concert, while still cautioning against the negative effects of advertising:

> The second performance of thirteen-year-old violinist Heifetz on December 20 in the City Hall attracted an audience in even greater numbers than the previous concert: the public very warmly greeted and applauded the young virtuoso and several times demanded repeats. The boy artist performed the Wieniawski Fantasy on a theme from the opera "Faust" wonderfully: he was himself carried away and carried away the whole audience. In the performance of Mr. Heifetz there is something very valuable—sincerity. My only

fear is that the advertising around him will extinguish this most precious quality in an artist . . . [19]

Along with preparing for concert performances, Jascha and his parents filled their time in Vilnius with visits to friends and family, including Grandfather Israel, Aunt Sonia and Uncle Isaac Sharfstein, and their daughter Anyuta, who was already almost six. They also met with their neighbors the Olefskys. Maxim Olefsky by then was nearly fifteen and planned to enter the St. Petersburg Conservatory to study piano in the coming January. Jascha also visited the home of his former teacher Malkin and gave him an inscribed photograph: "To deeply respected Ilya Davidovich Malkin from his sincerely affectionate Jascha Heifetz. 21. XII 1913."[20] From Biba Malkina, of whose musical success Marusya had written to Jascha, Jascha received a signed portrait: "To the genius Jaschenka Heifetz as a sign of eternal love and devotion from B. Malkina. Vilna. 21-XII-913." Jascha saved this portrait in a scrapbook.[21]

The next concert took place in Vilnius on December 22 under the aegis of the St. Petersburg Society for Jewish Folk Music. Lev Tseitlin, an active member of the society and a member of its music committee, conducted the Vilnius Symphony Orchestra in a program of pieces by society members, including Joseph Achron, Lazar Saminsky, Solomon Rosovsky, Aleksandr Zhitomirsky, and Tseitlin himself. Through their friendship with Kiselgof, the Heifetzes became part of the artistic life of the society and knew many of the prominent members personally. The pieces performed in Vilnius were originally for voice or violin and piano, but on tour Tseitlin performed his own orchestral arrangements. Many of the works had been played ten days earlier in St. Petersburg at the Maly Hall in a concert dedicated to the fifth anniversary of the St. Petersburg Society for Jewish Folk Music. This event celebrated the development of the young Jewish school of composition from the simple harmonization of folk melodies to the creation of large-scale musical works. The composers were highly talented, and many, such as Saminsky and Rosovsky, had both conservatory and university educations. The society's composers shared a passion for joining the different layers of Jewish musical culture. By contrast many others within the Jewish intelligentsia insisted that it was hardly appropriate for educated people who had broken loose from the Pale to turn back toward old traditions.

The efforts of the Society for Jewish Folk Music were representative of a larger movement during this period—growing numbers of people were becoming interested in ethnomusicology as part of a wider trend toward greater national consciousness and a stronger assertion of social and cultural identity. From impressionism to modernism, the entire artistic atmosphere of the Silver Age in Russia was permeated with a thirst for the past. In the music world, this was expressed with a turn toward ethnic folk music. Important artistic developments from this period included the fairytale motifs of the World of Art movement, the Russian *balagan* style of theater, the provocative theater of Vsevolod Meyerhold, Stravinsky's *Petrushka* and *Rite of Spring,* and the work of the influential balalaika player Vasily Andreev. Jewish composers during this period contributed to the general artistic atmosphere through works such as Mikhail Gnesin's cycle of songs entitled "Tale of the Redheaded Motele" and his trio "To the Memory of Our Lost Children." *Hebrew Melody,* written by Joseph Achron in 1913, with its ancient melody sung in a modern harmonic voice, would become an important part of Heifetz's repertoire both in Russia and later in the United States; he even included it in his 1917 Carnegie Hall debut.

In Vilnius, however, all was not well for the Heifetzes. Jascha became sick with a serious cold, so they returned to St. Petersburg as soon as possible. Joining the Heifetzes for this journey was Ruvin's friend Aron Olefsky, who planned to enroll his son Maxim in the conservatory piano class. Olefsky submitted his son's application on December 28 and designated the Heifetz address as his home in St. Petersburg.[22] Entrance exams for piano were set for the first ten days of January, so Olefsky hastily returned to Vilnius to fetch his son.

Back in St. Petersburg, Jascha still felt sick, so his parents reluctantly refused an invitation to visit Pavlovsk. The invitation had come from the family who had looked after Elza during Jascha's tour the previous autumn. Olga Trofimovna replied: "It's certainly quite a shame that you could not come to stay with us, but the opportunity has not gone—there will be another time. We hope that your sickness is not dangerous and that on

Sunday we'll find you healthy. Not all of us will be coming to see you, either Manya and I or Sonia and I."[23]

As on previous occasions, news of Jascha's illness spread quickly. Kiselgof wrote all the way from the Kherson province: "Your health worries me greatly. . . . Write to me without fail about how you feel. I hope that everything is well and that you have already recovered from your cold. Greetings to Mama, Papa, Polya and Elza. Make me happy, write me a few words."[24] From Warsaw, Uncle Samuil wrote: "I beg you: If you feel healthy, then write to me and to us a few words. I ask you, dear, to write a letter and include a list of books you have, including textbooks. You hear me? . . . If you want to put on 'Tifilim' [tefillin] then I will send them to you. Many kisses from afar, Samuil."[25] Uncle Samuil's request for a list of books might seem curious, but it related to the boy's upcoming birthday. The list would help Samuil choose something appropriate as a gift, since this was not just any birthday. It would be Jascha's Bar Mitzvah.

For Jewish boys, the Bar Mitzvah is celebrated at the age of thirteen and represents entrance into adulthood. As part of the Bar Mitzvah, the tefillin (mentioned by Samuil) are placed on the boy for the first time. The tefillin consist of two small black boxes attached to black bands, one of which is tied to the left arm in a particular way, and the other, around the head. The small boxes contain tiny printed parchment pages with the commandments of the Torah. Tefillin are a necessary part of the morning prayer. The ritual of putting on the tefillin usually occurs during a celebration at home, attended by relatives and close friends. Unfortunately, Uncle Samuil could not be present for Jascha's important day, but he wrote a letter to Jascha shortly after: "How are you, dear Jascha? What did it feel like to have your Bar Mitzvah? It wasn't fated for me to come to this solemn (for us Jews) celebration. But I so wanted to be there! Do you remember when I wrote to you about my arrival? Then without meaning to, the expression came from me—'If Providence does not disturb my trip'—as if my soul somehow foresaw something . . ."[26]

Among the guests who did gather for Jascha's Bar Mitzvah were Aron Olefsky and his son Maxim, who had been staying with the Heifetzes for a few weeks. Maxim had successfully passed his conservatory entrance exam and was enrolled in Yesipova's piano class. As a Bar Mitzvah gift, Maxim gave his friend a beautiful photograph album with the inscription: "With fond memories to my dear friend Jaschenka on the day of his entrance to Judaism, with the sincere wish to be and to remain such. Your friend, Monya Olefsky." Jascha also received another photograph album, this one with a beautiful red velvet cover with a metallic inlay and an inscription: "In remembrance to Jascha from the Sinelnikovs. 1914."[27] Many significant events in the history of Russian theater relate to the efforts of Nikolai Sinelnikov (1855–1939), who was an operetta actor, director, and entrepreneur. It was in Sinelnikov's troupe that Vera Komissarzhevskaya debuted in Novocherkassk in 1893, and the first performance of Chekhov's *Uncle Vanya* took place under Sinelnikov's initiative in 1897. By the 1910s, after forty years in the business, Sinelnikov was known as an authoritative figure in Russian theatrical life.

The most important guest at the Bar Mitzvah was Israel Sharfstein, Jascha's grandfather, who brought with him a multitude of gifts and a card from Uncle Isaac in Vilnius. A card also arrived from Jascha's cousin Anyuta in Vilnius, who had turned six that January. Since she could not yet write, her mother Sonia wrote the postcard: "I congratulate you, Jaschinka, on your birthday and wish you good health, happiness and long life. Thank you for the greetings sent to me. We will also have a celebration on Sunday, except there will be many fewer guests. Just grandfather, but even he's left us. Well, I wish for you to spend your day happily, and also your Bar Mitzvah. . . . Thank you to Polya and Elya for their greetings. Yours, Anyuta Sharfstein."[28] This postcard helps to date Jascha's celebration to the Sunday closest to his birthday, January 19, since by the next Sunday, January 26, the Heifetzes were already away from St. Petersburg.

Many of those absent sent Jascha greetings for his special day. Natan and Fanny in Warsaw were unable to attend, since their daughter Lyusya had just been born. Fanny's sister Emma sent congratulations from Daugavpils. In the 1920s Emma worked in the Foreign Trade Board in Paris, Rome, and Venice. At the time of her letter to Jascha, Emma was eighteen and in her seventh year at the A. Savitsky Gymnasium. She wrote: "What to wish you, Jaschuta? I have no words to express all that I wish you with my whole heart. Absolutely all the best! May God grant you much happiness, to be a good person and a good Jew . . ."[29] Congratulations also arrived from Ruvin's relatives in Polotsk and from Dorothea Grosse in Dresden. They all wished Jascha well, and some affectionately scolded him for not writing more often. Along those lines, Waldemar Liachowsky wrote from Charlottenburg: "Even though you are a little lazy one, I'm still sending you my most heartfelt wishes for your birthday. . . ."

The list of those who attended Jascha's celebration or sent him their congratulations on January 19 was long: Zinovy Kiselgof, Emanuel Bay, Gdal Saleski, Viktor Valter, the family of Olga Trofimovna from Pavlovsk, Mina Roubleff, and Pauline's friend Vera. There was another reason to celebrate: the previous day, Jascha had performed the Glazunov Concerto in Bolshoi Hall at the conservatory with an orchestra conducted by the composer himself. The concert had been planned for October 19, 1913, with Leopold Godowsky playing the Glazunov Piano Concerto under the composer's direction, but following a misunderstanding between Godowsky and the IRMO directorship, the concert had been postponed to January 18, 1914, and the piano concerto was replaced by the violin concerto. Legend has it that Jascha would not play unless he received a bicycle, and that Glazunov gave him one. Apparently, Jascha's mother told Glazunov: "Well tomorrow my little son *might* get sick. . . ." It is quite possible that this rumor was started by someone jealous of the young prodigy. All that is known for sure is that Jascha did receive a bicycle around this time, possibly from Glazunov; Jascha and Kiselgof would ride together around Pavlovsk Park that spring.

Jascha had performed the Glazunov Concerto with piano accompaniment in Odessa, Berlin, Dresden, and Warsaw, but never before with an orchestra, nor with the composer himself conducting. Russian newspapers responded with delight: "The Violin Concerto was wonderful and was played with artistic maturity by Jascha Heifetz. What a charming and highly gifted child!"[30] A caricature in the St. Petersburg newspaper *Den* on January 21 underlined the difference in size between the large conductor and small violinist. For Jascha, his Bar Mitzvah, which took place the next day, was no less important than the concert with Glazunov; it represented his mature embrace of the Jewish faith.

One is left to wonder what religion really meant to Heifetz. Jewish faith and culture permeated Jascha's early family life, but his adult career led him ever further from those traditions. To be sure, Heifetz did not actively move away from Judaism, but through the pursuit of his talent left behind the environment of his ancestors. Nevertheless, Heifetz always observed Yom Kippur and Rosh Hashanah and remembered the prayers he learned in childhood. For Heifetz, as for many of his contemporaries, religion was replaced by culture, and music largely took the place of prayer. The issue of faith appeared to dwindle over the years, and as a great artist, he seemed to believe that human life would continue through music and culture.

For his birthday, Jascha received a poem from Mark Rivesman (1868–1924), a translator, author of children's plays and stories on biblical subjects, a teacher, and an associate of Kiselgof's in the Society for Jewish Folk Music.[31] Rivesman produced the Yiddish translation of texts of vocal works in Kiselgof's compilation "Songs for Jewish School and Family," and in the post-revolution years he worked on a translation of Rubinstein's opera *Maccabee*. In 1919 Rivesman participated in the creation of the first Jewish chamber theater in Russia. Not long before his death, Rivesman assisted the composer Moses (Mikhail) Milner in compiling a libretto for Milner's opera *The Heavens Aflame*—the first Yiddish opera in Russia, performed in Petrograd in 1923. Rivesman's poem for Jascha approached the issue of anti-Semitism in Russia and the general difficulties facing Jews; it hints at the potential for Jascha's divine gift to inspire change:

> And he descended to our earth,
> And he dedicated to it his gift,
> And people, hearing this song,
> Came to know the delights of the highest magic . . .
>
> Not in vain are Abraham's children
> Proud of their Joseph,
> Through the long flow of nations and centuries
> He will make their road easier.
>
> So sing, Joseph, glorious and youthful!
> Perhaps Pharaoh will understand
> The meaning of your sobbing strings
> And will lighten our heavy burden . . .

Awaken with your magic bow
The cold stone, like Orpheus;
But, hearkening to voices of praise,
Be proud also that you are a Jew!

The anti-Semitism of great writers such as Dostoevsky and Balakirev proved particularly painful for Jews in Russia; reverence for these figures required a certain internal struggle. The singer Yuliya Abaza, discussing the subject of anti-Semitism with Jascha, once inquired: "Tell me, little boy, are you not ashamed to be a Jew?"[32] Jascha's answer is unknown, and one wonders at how the young genius, constantly smothered by the attention and the adoration of crowds, was affected during his childhood by the sense of inferiority that society tried to impose on Jews.

Soon after his Bar Mitzvah, Jascha and his parents departed again for concerts arranged by Concert-Direction Hermann Wolff. Pauline and Elza stayed home with the governesses—there was a new one, referred to in letters as "the lady"—and Grandfather Israel, who remained in St. Petersburg following the Bar Mitzvah. The Heifetzes passed through Vilnius on January 22 and arrived in Berlin by January 25 (NS February 7); from there Jascha wrote to his sisters: "Dear ones! We are already writing to you for the third time and still we've not received even one of your letters. What does this mean? We are very worried, write to us more often. How are you? Polya! Send me the name and patronymic of the lady. I really don't know how to write it. Is Fraulein Diamant coming to see you? If she is then say hello from me. Today is my concert and tomorrow we leave for Leipzig and Vienna."[33]

In Berlin, Jascha performed at the Blüthner-Saal, and along with some of his usual repertoire, he played the Goldmark Concerto for the first time. The music reviewer for the *Allgemeine Musik-Zeitung*, Kurt Singer, wrote that Jascha lived up to his glowing reputation.[34]

Still in Berlin, the Heifetzes received a letter from St. Petersburg, from a legal representative named Isidor Tsitron.[35] The letter included an offer for Jascha to perform in London. Since there was no time in the schedule, the offer was turned down:

Petersburg, January 26, 1914
To Mr. R. I. Heifetz

Berlin.
    Dear Sir
    Having the proposal of my client in London, director of a local musical
enterprise, I ask you not to delay in informing me whether you agree for
your son to go to London for concerts: the first time for a share of the net
profit and in the future for a set fee.
    With great respect, I. L. Tsitron

Before leaving Berlin, Jascha wrote once more to his sisters back in St.
Petersburg: "Berlin. 9 February 1914.... I'm writing to you after my concert.
Today we leave for Leipzig. I already got a letter from Fraulein Grosse two
days ago, in which she wrote that she'll come to Leipzig and we'll see her.
... How are you? How's Grandfather? Greetings to Vera, Grandfather, and
Katia. Hello to Zinovy Aronovich and the lady. Write to us more often, or
we won't answer!!!"[36]
    The Heifetzes arrived in Leipzig, ready for Jascha's concert on Febru-
ary 12 (os January 30). This was no ordinary event: the boy would perform
at the sixteenth subscription concert under the direction of Arthur Nikisch
at the famous Gewandhaus, a venue once home to Felix Mendelssohn.
Set in the acknowledged music capital of Germany, the venue's illustrious history stretched back to the middle of the eighteenth century. From
1781, the Leipzig orchestra performed in the Assembly Hall of the Cloth
Traders, the Gewandhaus or "Garment House," from where the orchestra
and the venue took their names. Mozart performed with the Gewandhaus
orchestra, Mendelssohn conducted the orchestra from 1835 to 1847, and
in 1887 Tchaikovsky conducted a concert of his own works in the venue.
Nikisch served as conductor between 1895 and 1922. For Jascha, the chance
to perform in this prestigious venue with Nikisch added immeasurably to
his growing profile. He himself recalled later: "I played Bruch's G-minor
in 1913 [*sic*] at the Leipzig Gewandhaus with Nikisch, where I was told that
Joachim was the only other violinist as young as myself to appear there as
soloist with the orchestra."[37] After the concerto, Jascha played two encores
accompanied by Waldemar Liachowsky: Tchaikovsky's *Melodie* and the
Paganini Caprice no. 24.
    Following the concert, Valter quoted the words of the *Leipziger Tage-
blatt* critic Segnitz in the *Den* newspaper in St. Petersburg: "The enormous

technique astonished less than the perfect purity of expression, the beauty of tone in all levels of volume, the somehow self-evident nobility of execution, which is found in such wonderful correspondence with the noble naturalness in performance and in the artist's whole essence."[38] Max Unger, the reviewer for *Die Musik,* wrote, "the crown was claimed by reproductive art, which had a hugely talented representative in the little miracle violinist J. Heifetz (Bruch's concerto in g minor), the future of whom looks bright."[39]

The day after the concert in the Gewandhaus, the Heifetzes left Leipzig and headed for Vienna in preparation for Jascha's next scheduled concert. At the Hotel Tegethoff in Vienna, Jascha received a postcard from Dorothea Grosse: "My dear Jascha! I hope that you and your parents have arrived safely in Vienna. I wish you great success with your concert there."[40] The Heifetzes had crossed the German and Austro-Hungarian borders once before, in the autumn of 1912 when Jascha performed in Prague. This was, however, their first visit to Vienna, the beautiful and impressive Austrian capital so closely associated with the names of Mozart, Beethoven, and Strauss, and of course, it was also the birthplace of Fritz Kreisler.

Jascha performed twice in Vienna during the February 1914 visit, both times at the Musikverein, a hall known for its fantastic beauty. The first performance took place on February 14 in a symphonic concert with the Vienna Concert Society conducted by Vasily Safonov (1852–1918). Safonov was known as a pillar of Russian musical culture. As a pianist he performed for years with Auer and Verzhbilovich, and as a conductor he led symphony concerts for the Moscow division of the IRMO. He taught at the Moscow Conservatory for twenty years and served as director for fifteen of those years, a directorship which led to various controversies, the effects of which rippled far beyond the conservatory. Safonov traveled more than almost any other Russian conductor of the period. He appeared frequently with the Vienna Concert Society, was head conductor of the New York Philharmonic Society between 1906 and 1909, and acted as director of the National Conservatory of Music of America, also in New York.

This was the first time Jascha had worked with Safonov, who was widely known among Russian musicians for his abrupt manner. Was Jascha intimidated by the conductor? Even if he was, it is likely Safonov made a special effort to temper his behavior to ensure the concert's success. Jascha and Safonov performed the Mendelssohn Concerto and, as an encore, Jascha performed the Tchaikovsky *Melodie* and the Paganini Caprice no. 24. Also performing in the concert was singer Elena Gerhardt. Jascha may have heard Gerhardt in October 1912 in Berlin, where she performed with Arthur Nikisch at the piano for recordings by Julius Block. A mezzo-soprano, Gerhardt was considered one of the greatest singers of her time. During the concert with Heifetz and Safonov, Gerhardt sang an aria from Tchaikovsky's *Girl of Orleans* and three songs by Richard Strauss, all of which were accompanied by the orchestra. This star-studded concert attracted a large audience including many dignitaries.[41]

Newspapers showered praise on the boy: "A charming young boy of simple, noble attitude, pretty features and a skill many adults will probably envy."[42] The *Reichspost* described the performance of the Mendelssohn Concerto as unequalled among prodigies.[43] The music reviewer at *Neues Wiener Journal* called Heifetz's performance a highlight of the current concert season, noting that the violinist came from Russia and was of Jewish heritage. The reviewer then pointed out that in recent times, this remarkable people continued to produce magnificent violinists.[44] Berlin newspapers also wrote of Jascha's success in Vienna. Prominent musicologist and critic Richard Specht called the thirteen-year-old violinist a genius.[45]

Just four days after Jascha's triumphant concert in Vienna, the Heifetzes arrived in Budapest, the next stop on the tour. Most notably for the Heifetzes, this was Auer's homeland, but Hungary had also produced many other famous musical names: the composers Liszt, Kodály, and Bartók, along with the conductors Hans Richter, Arthur Nikisch, and Bruno Walter. Of course, many great violinists also came from Hungary, including Joseph Joachim, Jenő Hubay, Joseph Szigeti, Franz von Vecsey, Emil Telmányi, and Carl Flesch.

During this tour Jascha appeared twice in Budapest. At the first recital on February 18, Jascha played the Mendelssohn Concerto with piano accompaniment, the Schubert *Ave Maria*, Cui's *Melodie Orientale*, Kreisler's *Schön Rosmarin*, Handel's Larghetto, and the Paganini Caprice no. 24. The accompanist was Oszkár Dienzl, a local pianist who, it appears, played less than competently. After the recital in Budapest, the Heifetzes returned to

Vienna. They stayed in the Hotel Kaiserin Elisabeth, which to this day is located close to St. Stephen's Cathedral in the city center. A long-anticipated postcard from his sister in St. Petersburg awaited Jascha at the hotel. Pauline had sent the postcard to the offices of the Wolff agency in Berlin, but from there it was redirected to the hotel in Vienna: "I finally got around to writing! How are you? Are you enjoying yourself? I'm practicing hard right now—I have a concert to play soon, what a shame you all aren't here now. Write to me more. . . . Greetings also from Olga Trofimovna and Zinovy Aronovich."[46]

In anticipation of Jascha's second upcoming concert in Budapest, a concerned Ruvin wrote to Waldemar Liachowsky about the unsatisfactory situation with Oszkár Dienzl, the local pianist in Budapest:

> Herrn Liachowsky. Berlin.
> Charlottenburg. Kantstr. 148.
>   Respected Mr. Liachowsky!
>   Please, I ask you to write as soon as possible or send a telegram, has Mr. Wolff spoken with you about the concert in Budapest and will you be coming. I already wrote to him that it is impossible to play with that accompanist, I said this to Mr. Müller, and he said to me that he agrees to pay. Of course, one cannot trust his word and it is necessary that Mr. Wolff demand money from him in advance. The concert is during the day, starting at 11 in the morning. Hopefully you will come the day before and can stop on the way so that here in Vienna you can also accompany [Jascha]. I spoke about this with Mr. Knepler, but he did not want to listen, you know these gentlemen! Although there is a good accompanist here in Vienna, it is nevertheless necessary to rehearse, and Jascha does not feel very well.
>   We received your letter. I apologize that I am writing in Russian, I hope that you will understand me. We leave here on Saturday at 2. It would be nice if you could come by this time and go from here together with us. All the best to you, hello from my wife and Jascha. Greetings to Fräulein Grosse and Mr. Franko.
>   Respectfully, R. Heifetz[47]

Although Ruvin reported that Jascha did not feel well, the second Vienna concert proceeded as planned on February 27 in the familiar Musikverein. With the Vienna Tonkünstler Orchestra conducted by Anton Konrath, Jascha performed the Tchaikovsky Concerto and the Beethoven Romance in G. The *Neues Wiener Journal* reported the following day: "It is rare to hear a virtuoso make music with such clarity and without any gimmicks, as did this young boy, who stands on stage, slim and fresh, guides the orchestra and the conductor just by looking at them and who develops the musical plan . . . infallibly finding its core."[48] In addition to the pieces with orchestra, Jascha played three works with piano: Mozart's Menuet, Popper's *La Fileuse,* and Sarasate's *Zigeunerweisen.* It appears Liachowsky could not arrive in time to accompany Jascha, so the role fell to the Vienna-born composer and pianist Otto Schulhof (1889–1958), described in Ruvin's letter as a "good accompanist." Schulhof accompanied many famous violinists of the era and also performed and recorded with Pablo Casals.

While in Vienna, the Heifetzes became closely acquainted with the Polish-Jewish pianist Leopold Godowsky (1870–1938) and his family. Godowsky grew up in Vilnius and his fame as a virtuoso pianist took him on tours all around the world. In 1911, Glazunov dedicated his Piano Concerto to Godowsky, who had visited St. Petersburg many times and felt at home there. Family and friends nicknamed him "Godos," "Godonius," and "Popsy."[49] The following is a colorful description of Godowsky left by his friend and colleague Abram Chasins:

> Short and round, Godowsky suggested a Slavic Buddha, but with none of the timeless, resolved placidity of a saint. He had an encyclopedic knowledge and a jolly, insatiably curious mind. He loved mental fireworks, and his beaming blue eyes sparkled, his pot belly quivered through the smoke of verbal battle. Pouring out his musical wealth generously and excitedly, he had the rarest capacity to stimulate whoever came, to prod him to sharper insight and searching self-examination. . . . If he invited you to come over "just for a little quiet talk and music," you might arrive to find twenty people who had just dropped in, among them not only . . . musicians . . . but also, likely as not, Popsy's music-loving tailor or butcher, a man he had met the day before who said he liked music, Albert Einstein, or Edward G. Robinson.[50]

Years later in the United States, Godowsky continued to welcome many illustrious names into his home: Rachmaninoff, Stravinsky, Gershwin, Hofmann, Kreisler, Elman, and of course, Heifetz, who would frequently engage in witty exchanges with Godowsky. Back in Vienna, Jascha met Godowsky's daughter Dagmar (1897–1975) for the first time after his concert. In her memoirs, published in New York in 1958, Dagmar recalled the meeting in some detail:

> My governess had taken me to hear him at a recital and I remember so well what I wore. It was a red dress with a square-cut neck and my hair was in corkscrew curls. Jascha was a Botticelli angel. I didn't know which I fell in love with—his playing or his beauty. When I was taken back to meet him, we stood—I in my little red silk, he in his little black velvet suit—and just stared at each other in mute adoration, like the children in *Peter Ibbetson*. He wrote a souvenir on my program, Jascha did. He was barely old enough to write. I was barely old enough to read. I had always remembered.[51]

In the spring of 1914, shortly after Jascha's concert in Vienna, Leopold Godowsky and his family left for the United States. As a result, Jascha did not meet Dagmar again until the autumn of 1917 at the time of his Carnegie Hall debut. The early youthful affection born in Vienna blossomed in New York. At the debut Jascha apparently sent a note to Dagmar: "I am only playing for you."[52]

The Heifetzes departed Vienna on February 28 aboard the daily two o'clock train to Budapest. Accompanying the family was Liachowsky, who had hurried from Berlin after receiving Ruvin's letter. From the train Jascha wrote a letter to his sisters, addressing them with a comical play on the Yiddish word for rags (shmatke, or shmotki in its Russian form) and the truncated German word for butterfly (Schmetterling):

> Dear Schmet-tki! We left Vienna not long ago. In the morning we received your card, in which Polya wrote that tomorrow probably she will play in a concert. What will you play? Do you know this piece well? Polinka, write again after the concert. We will arrive soon in Budapest (I'm writing in the train on the way to Budapest), and from there probably we will come home soon.[53]

Pauline played her student recital on February 11 (NS February 24), for Drozdov's class.[54] She played the Grieg *Berceuse* and the Chopin *Tarantella*. Also appearing in the same student concert was twenty-year-old Aleksandr Gauk, who became a prominent conductor in the Soviet era. Jascha's concerns for his sister were unnecessary—over the past year, Pauline had achieved great success, and this recital was no exception.

Liachowsky and the Heifetzes arrived in Budapest, and on March 1 Jascha appeared in a concert of the National Opera Orchestra under the direction of a young Fritz Reiner (1888–1963), a conductor with whom Heifetz later performed and recorded in the United States. Jascha played the Bruch Concerto in G Minor with the orchestra and five pieces with Liachowsky—the Vitali Chaconne, Beethoven's Romance in G, Mozart's Minuet, Popper's *La Fileuse,* and Sarasate's *Zigeunerweisen.* After the bad experience with the pianist Dienzl, Liachowsky proved both a familiar and reliable accompanist.

With all the planned concerts behind them, the Heifetzes left for St. Petersburg. On their way home they made their usual stop in Warsaw, where on March 5 (os February 20) Jascha gave a recital in the Warsaw Grand Theater accompanied by Professor Ludwik Urstein (1870–1939). The program included the Tchaikovsky Concerto, Schubert's *Ave Maria,* Cui's *Melodie Orientale,* and Wieniawski's *Tarantella* and *Faust Fantasy.* In Warsaw Jascha visited Natan and Fanny and met their newborn daughter Lyusya for the first time. He also met with Uncle Samuil, who at last had the chance to congratulate his nephew on his recent Bar Mitzvah.

CHAPTER FOURTEEN

Spring 1914

JASCHA AND HIS PARENTS returned to St. Petersburg during the second half of February (os). After a short time at home, Jascha traveled to Moscow, where on March 1 he appeared with Isidor Achron at a benefit concert for the Society for the Spread of Enlightenment among Jews in Russia, a charity for which Jascha had performed almost exactly a year earlier. Both performances for this charity were organized by David Shor, a well-known figure in Moscow who had founded the Moscow Trio two decades earlier. Shor ran a private music school and organized many large-scale educational projects. In Moscow and in other Russian cities he gave lectures dedicated to the work of Beethoven, and as the chairman for the Moscow division of the Society for Jewish Folk Music he maintained close ties with his St. Petersburg counterparts. Shor came to know the Heifetzes through his friendship with Zinovy Kiselgof.

For his second concert in Bolshoi Hall at the Moscow Conservatory, Jascha performed the Tchaikovsky Concerto, Handel Sonata in E, Beethoven Romance in G, Mozart Minuet, and Wieniawski's *Faust Fantasy*. In the words of the newspaper *Golos Moskvy,* "the young artist was remarkably successful."[1] The reviewer for the *Russkaya muzykalnaya gazeta* contrasted the young Jascha's achievements with those of twenty-nine-year-old Moscow violinist Mikhail Erdenko, favoring the younger violinist:

> Heifetz has a rare gift of nature with superior artistic intuition, purity of intonation, enormous technique—an abundance even for an adult artist, but Heifetz is still just a youth. May God save this miraculous boy both from losing his childhood prematurely, and from growing coarse, for giftedness is by far not everything, and Mr. Erdenko serves as an example of this.[2]

Upon their return to St. Petersburg, the Heifetzes were finally able to recover from the exhausting flow of hotels, stations, and restaurant food, and for the rest of March the family remained in the city. With Pauline and Elza now reunited with their brother and parents, the whole family could enjoy time together, and Anna no doubt cooked Jascha's favorite meals—chicken cutlets and "herring under a fur coat." Jascha spent time on his collections of butterflies, bugs, and coins, to which he added newly acquired examples from his recent travels. Perhaps most exciting for Jascha was that he began filling the albums he was given for his birthday and Bar Mitzvah, not with photographs, but with the many postcards he had received. Around this time a postcard arrived for Jascha from Fanny in Warsaw, with a painting by Grikke named "Mother's Happiness." Dated March 7, 1914, the postcard reads: "I'm writing to you just a few words. I never have any time now . . . Lyusinka grows not by the day but by the hour! She already laughs loudly, recognizes me, I carry her out on the balcony. When you come to stay for Passover, she will be big already. How did Polinka play at the recital? What's the news with you? Do you study other subjects? Will you have any exams?"[3] The "news" was simple: throughout March, Jascha and his sisters continued to attend music lessons at the conservatory and other lessons at home with Kiselgof and the governess.

On March 22, Valter published an article in the St. Petersburg newspaper *Den* with the title: "Jascha Heifetz: a page from the history of our culture." Reminding his readers of how the conductor Siloti had expressed his disgust at the exploitation of young Willy Ferrero, Valter focused his attention on Jascha's situation:

> . . . Jascha Heifetz has performed in St. Petersburg since the spring of 1911. Everyone is delighted with his playing, but nobody inquires how this boy survives, no one cries that it is necessary to save him. The Society for the

Protection of Children worried terribly about the fate of the Italian Ferrero (whereas Russian children, apparently, are already sufficiently protected), but the fate of Jascha Heifetz hardly worries this society. Ferrero received an enormous honorarium for his appearance in St. Petersburg, whereas Heifetz received fifty rubles for his performance in Pavlovsk on May 13, 1911! They may say to me that no steps were taken because the society and music circles simply did not know that Heifetz was in need. This is disingenuous. As early as 1911 I wrote in *Rech* about Jascha's difficult circumstances and about the sad fate of exploitation by entrepreneurs that awaited him.

Valter emphasized that even the conservatory administration knew about Jascha's material hardship, along with Koussevitzky, who had declared Jascha's playing that of a genius, and Siloti, who had been specially invited to a private home to hear Jascha perform. "And so what happened?" exclaimed Valter. "Not one of the successful concert institutions active in St. Petersburg lifted a finger to come to Jascha's aid." According to Valter, the amount of help needed was relatively little:

Someone needed to become a representative for Jascha without attempting to exploit him, and to secure for him, let's say, six concerts per season—six thousand rubles. This would let such an entrepreneur prevent any exploitation of the boy. But such an entrepreneur was not forthcoming. On the contrary. These large institutions considered it beneath themselves to invite Jascha to participate in symphony concerts which would have immediately raised the boy's public profile. We preferred to leave the honor of Jascha's first performance to the Gewandhaus and to the great conductor Nikisch, who, one supposes, holds no lower an artistic threshold than we here in St. Petersburg. . . . See how we guard Russian children! Since 1911, from the age of ten, Jascha has been supporting his family: father, mother and two younger sisters—very musical girls, and only thanks to the wise cautiousness of the parents managing to escape the seduction of entrepreneurs, the boy performs comparatively rarely, has a healthy appearance, and has time to study a range of educational subjects.

Taking a moment to interrupt Valter's volley of criticism, one wonders whether Jascha's parents were as cautious and protective as he had described. When the sea of concert invitations arrived from 1912 on, the Heifetzes refused many, but Jascha was certainly no stranger to the stage. The previous autumn of 1913, the boy had performed in Berlin, Dresden, Vilnius, Kiev, and St. Petersburg. The start of 1914 proved no different, and between January 18 and February 20 Jascha had played ten concerts and traveled hundreds of miles. Jascha's naturally healthy appearance helped to create the impression that he was unlike the majority of exploited prodigies, and thus his parents acquired a reputation for being caring and nurturing. In response to Valter's observation that Jascha received a full and rounded education, it is natural to question how Kiselgof succeeded in educating the boy who spent every day practicing and was frequently away from home for concerts.

At the end of his article, Valter raised the issue of the inferior instrument Jascha played:

> He needs a first-class instrument just as beautiful and noble as he himself and his playing. But such an instrument costs a great deal of money, ten thousand rubles or more. Once upon a time Vielgorsky bought K. Yu. Davydov a Stradivarius cello. Are there among the wealthy in our age no imitators of this example who would like to place their name in the history of music alongside the name of Jascha Heifetz?

No wealthy patrons emerged, so Jascha continued to support his family with his concert earnings, as well as saving up for a better instrument.

Although Fanny invited the Heifetzes to Warsaw for Passover, Jascha's next paid concert around the same time, this one in Odessa, took priority. The Heifetzes and Isidor Achron arrived in Odessa on April 6. A local newspaper printed a portrait of Jascha with the caption: "Famed violinist Jascha Heifetz—in the upcoming April 9 concert at the Merchants' Exchange."[4] In addition, posters alerted the public to the concert of "twelve-year-old [sic] Jascha Heifetz, described as the little magician of the violin." The press did not mention the canceled concert of the previous April (under contract with G. S. Baltz), but recalled the performance of summer 1911: "Odessites heard little Heifetz four [sic] years ago, when he modestly began his career. Now he comes to us bearing a world-famous name. . . . The wunderkind will receive 2,400 rubles for the concert."[5] The performance in Odessa was organized by the head director of the Odessa City Theater, Anton Eichenwald, a composer, choirmaster, and leader of various opera troupes. As an enthusiastic ethnographer, Eichenwald collected more than four thousand melodies from the people of the Volga Region and Central Asia. He was also an experienced entrepreneur, and Jascha's concert was so successful that Eichenwald continued to work with the Heifetzes on other projects outside of Odessa.

Jascha's Odessa program included the Tchaikovsky Concerto, Handel Sonata in E, Schubert *Ave Maria,* Mozart Minuet, and Wieniawski *Faust Fantasy.* "He is very talented, that is obvious immediately," wrote the conductor, pedagogue, and music critic Boris Yankovsky. "Only genuine talent can so finely, stylishly, with such taste and high musicality, convey the serious Handel Sonata … [and] Tchaikovsky Concerto. … His performance is imbued with life, warmth, all that which comprises the integral character of every artist gifted by God. Yesterday's concert can be counted among the most interesting manifestations of Odessa musical life in recent times."[6] Thirteen years later it was the same Boris Yankovsky who gave Shostakovich a place to stay when the composer arrived in Kharkov to present his Symphony no. 1.

Odessa was a sprawling, bustling city, and local newspapers from the period provide colorful accounts of the general atmosphere. At the same time that critics were writing about Jascha and his upcoming concert, many also focused on another developing story. A thirty-three-year-old elephant named Yambo held in the Odessa zoo had become enraged, and its owners threatened to either tranquilize or shoot the animal. The city-wide debate continued for some time without a resolution. Eventually, as if by magic, everything returned to normal, albeit with a substantial increase in the number of visitors to the zoo. It seems the owners had used Yambo in a devious but hugely effective advertising stunt.

On April 10, the *Odessky listok* printed a lighthearted story about how Jascha and his parents spent their free time in Odessa on the day of the concert:

Although [Jascha] has traveled a great deal, he is unfamiliar with the workings of boats. Finding himself in Odessa with so many boats docked in the port, it seemed unthinkable to Jascha Heifetz that he would not see them. Moreover, Jascha is extremely inquisitive, and has no sailor friends. What to do? Not dwelling long on the issue, Jascha, accompanied by his parents, set out to the port. Seeing a new boat, Jascha climbed up the gangway. Locating the captain, Jascha asked for permission to examine the boat. The captain looked at the little daredevil with surprise: "Jascha Heifetz, violinist," he introduced himself. "I came here to play a concert. Come listen to me." The captain, touched by Jascha's directness, allowed him to look at the boat. The thing that astonished him most of all was the radiotelephone terminal.[7]

Jascha found the terminal fascinating, but if anyone had asked him that day to choose between the career of radio operator or violinist, he would surely not have answered "radio operator," whereas in a similar situation three years earlier, he had told Valter he wished to be "a photographer." The young boy, still only thirteen, already introduced himself as "Jascha Heifetz, violinist."

A day after the Odessa performance, Anton Eichenwald led the Heifetzes to Chișinău (Kishinev), where the entrepreneur organized a concert for Jascha in the Orpheum Illusion-Theater. Eichenwald had overseen a prominent publicity campaign with the concert advertised on posters and in newspapers. The local press described the difficulties facing Jascha's parents, and how they had been persuaded to allow their son to perform just two concerts, in Odessa and Chișinău. "According to Mr. Eichenwald," writes "Bemol," the music reviewer for *Bessarabskaya zhizn,*

> Heifetz is overloaded with proposals from abroad, America and Russia, but, despite the temptations offered by the entrepreneurs, they decline all the proposals. The parents are very careful with Jascha, who at the present time, besides music, is seriously studying other educational subjects. Only thanks to the holidays (Easter break) did his family agree to let him go to Odessa and Kishinev. Despite rare performances Jascha, according to his father, earns up to 30,000 rubles a year, receiving 2,500 rubles per concert.[8]

Despite the alluring publicity, it seems the experienced Eichenwald somewhat misjudged the ticket prices, which were set at between five and fourteen rubles. According to "Bemol," "on April 11, the Hall of the 'Orpheum' Theater was far from full, probably because of the somewhat high prices for regular visitors." Continuing, the reviewer noted Jascha's success and then gave a description of the boy that foreshadowed the adult Heifetz: "Concentrated serious expression of the face, on which there is no friendly smile, nor childish joy . . ." Had Jascha grown up already? Until this point, critics had usually described Jascha as a lovely curly haired little boy with a captivating calm confidence in his own abilities. In contrast to Willy Ferrero and others like him, there was never any overacting in Jascha's stage presence; the high technical and musical level of Jascha's playing had obscured any discussion of his physical connection with audiences. In his child's face one saw the utter absorption in the act of performance, the lack of interest in looking around the stage, and a natural reserve often mistaken for shyness. Music seems to have become a shield, behind which he could hide from the public. The review continues, providing more insight into Jascha's early experience of performance: "Loud applause and cries of delight had long since became an inescapable and ordinary phenomenon for him, which he accepted like something obligatory and hardly concerning him."

This duality between the inspirational violin playing and the reserved stage mannerisms became ever more apparent as Heifetz grew older. Self-confidence and a strong belief in his own musical abilities coexisted with a diffidence that suggested he underestimated himself as a person. Were these features inherent in his personality or did his upbringing have an influence? Was it even possible to separate these two components? In terms of inherited traits, one naturally looks toward Heifetz's somewhat cantankerous father and his more composed mother, but external influences on the young boy prove difficult to ascertain. How, for instance, did Jascha's early family life prepare him for life in St. Petersburg? Unlike other successful figures such as Sergei Prokofiev and Vladimir Nabokov, there was little privilege in Jascha's youth—no impressive family library with antique books or imposing family portraits hanging on the walls.

In many ways, Jascha's parents were helplessly unprepared for life in St. Petersburg and their backgrounds interfered with their assimilation into this new higher circle of friends and acquaintances. In the eyes of early twentieth-century St. Petersburg, Lithuanian Jews held a low position in the social spectrum, a position reinforced by their relatively "unrefined" speech. For Jascha's parents, their spoken language drew on a cacophony of Russian, Polish, Lithuanian, and German words in Yiddish forms, and even with the addition of English later on, there was no hiding their humble roots. The success of Eliza Doolittle in the musical *My Fair Lady* remained firmly out of reach, especially during their first St. Petersburg years. Although it seems that Ruvin considered himself a worldly person, his appearance in photographs from this period tells another story. He seems to strike a proud sculpture-like pose, apparent in the gesture with which he lifts a cigarette to his mouth and with a defiant and presumptuous expression on his face. Might he have provoked an exchange of condescending smirks on the part of conversation partners behind his back?

Might Jascha have noticed these smirks? The adolescent years inevitably produce crises of self-evaluation, and one can imagine the difficulty Jascha experienced as he dealt with the unusual situation facing him and his family. Unlike his parents, Jascha grew up surrounded by great musicians, great teachers, famous composers, and influential entrepreneurs, and he quickly became accustomed to life in the big city. Nevertheless, the absence of a privileged background led him to strive always for self-improvement. These adolescent years in Russia witnessed the start of Jascha's spiritual growth and the development of the desire to perfect himself, both in music and in everyday life. Unlike many artists and musicians, Heifetz's career path followed a direct and unfaltering line toward success; as he himself put it in that succinct but all-encompassing phrase: "Born in Russia, first lessons at 3, debut in Russia at 7, debut in America in 1917."[9] There were no rough patches or disappointments, and he never struggled to overcome physical limitations. Heifetz had an all-encompassing musical memory, an impeccably exact sense of form, and his artistic destiny appeared to have been pre-programmed. In contrast with his professional success, however, his personal life proved far more complicated.

From Chişinău, Anton Eichenwald led Isidor Achron and the Heifetzes back to Odessa. "Jascha Heifetz agreed to give one more general concert in Odessa, which will take place in the Hall of the New Exchange on Sunday, April 13,"[10] explained the *Odesskaya pochta*. No reviews appeared in any Odessa newspapers.

From Odessa, Achron and the Heifetzes headed to Vitebsk where Jascha performed on April 20. At the start of April, the family governess Maria Borisovna found herself back in her hometown of Vitebsk for the Passover holiday. The governess sent a postcard to Pauline in St. Petersburg: "My dear Polinka! I did not manage to visit you before my departure for Vitebsk, where I have come for Passover. Yesterday I spoke with Zinovy Aronovich on the telephone. I heard that Jascha is planning to play in Vitebsk. Is it true, Polinka? I would like to know. Write to me. Address: Vitebsk, Nizhne-Petrovskaya Street, the Koldobsky house. To Boruch Levin."[11] In all likelihood, Boruch (or Boris in its russified version) Levin was Maria Borisovna's father, in which case, Maria's surname would have been Levina. As early as August 1909 the name "M. Levina" appeared on a colorful postcard to Jascha written in the town of Švenčionys.

A pattern can be traced in Heifetz's life, whereby certain people showed up on his path many times, pulled into his orbit. Take, for example, Isidor Achron: he became acquainted with the Heifetzes in St. Petersburg; had his first joint performance with Jascha in Kiev in 1913; and soon after became Jascha's permanent accompanist. In the United States, he and Jascha then performed together for many years. A similar situation occurred with André Benoist: Benoist first heard Jascha as a boy in St. Petersburg, and in the United States they performed together dozens of times and developed a strong working relationship. It is possible that Jascha's relationship with Maria Levina also developed in this manner, given her initial acquaintance with the Heifetzes in Švenčionys in 1909; their meeting in St. Petersburg, probably through Kiselgof; and her work as governess for the Heifetz family in 1913.

Maria Levina was keen to hear Jascha perform, especially in her hometown. No response came from Pauline, so Maria also sent a postcard to nine-year-old Elza: "My dear Elinka! Remind Polinka and write to me yourself, do you hear? Because you already write well. If Jascha plans to come to Vitebsk, then I'll stay to wait for his concert, and then after Passover I'll come to St. Petersburg and will call you."[12]

Replies to Maria's postcards have not survived, so it unclear if she heard Jascha perform in her hometown. If she did, it is likely that the Heifetzes stayed with her father. It is also possible that Maria missed the concert since Jascha did not perform until after the holiday, which had been the reason for Maria's visit. Advertisements in Vitebsk newspapers revealed the excitement surrounding Jascha's forthcoming appearance in this provincial town: "On April 20 in the Tikhantovsky Theater a concert will take place of the young violin-virtuoso Jascha Heifetz, who has already managed to become to a certain degree a celebrity and a favorite of the capital's audiences. . . . It is just a shame that as a result of the extremely high prices not all will have chance to listen to the playing of this little virtuoso."[13] The program for this concert included many favorites: the Mendelssohn

Concerto, Handel Larghetto, Mozart Minuet, Kreisler's *Schön Rosmarin,* the Chopin Nocturne in D, and Wieniawski's Polonaise in A. According to the *Vitebsk vestnik,* the concert passed "with great success, both economically and artistically. Unceasing ovation."[14]

The spring of 1914 is remembered in many parts of European Russia for the destructive weather. A terrible storm struck on the night of February 28 in the Stavropol, Kuban, and Don regions, with heavy flooding that led to many casualties and widespread destruction of property. Charitable events took place across Russia to support the victims; music societies in St. Petersburg also joined the effort. On the night of April 17, another storm hit the central regions, destroying much of the telegraph network and ripping trains from the line on the Moscow–Kazan railroad. The Heifetzes, traveling at that time in the direction of Vitebsk, just barely missed the worst affected areas.

Around this same time, other troubles surfaced in St. Petersburg. On April 18, a meeting of the IRMO board addressed various issues at the St. Petersburg Conservatory. One of the main problems was the status of several students in the conservatory lists, including Ruvin Heifetz. The IRMO directorate marked "this phenomenon as impermissible and expressed the wish that it be abolished in the future."[15] Nikolai Artsybushev, member of the main board of the IRMO and chairman of its St. Petersburg division, wrote to Glazunov, who, as director, was responsible for the conservatory's teaching practices:

> If a student attends classes, then no one can reproach the conservatory for giving residency permits, but on the contrary, if a student does not attend the conservatory for two years, then it means that he is using the residency permit not for the sake of study but for the sake of something else—for the sake of the right to residency. . . . Both the cases of Brian and Papa Heifetz are powerful weapons in the hands of those who say that the conservatory facilitates the right to residency for persons who do not attend it.[16]

Everyone knew about the quasi-students, but such situations would no longer be allowed to continue. Glazunov could hardly object. Artsybushev was right; such situations played into the hands of those wanting to cause trouble.

The name Brian above refers to Maria Brian (Schmorgoner, 1886–1965), a singer who in her younger years studied voice in Paris and attended the Sorbonne, and later sang in St. Petersburg theatres and performed concerts, including some for the Society for Jewish Folk Music. Brian entered the St. Petersburg Conservatory in 1909, and in the spring of 1912 graduated with a small gold medal (second prize) in singing with the condition that within two years she would pass the required musical subjects for the diploma.[17] Two years passed with no changes to Brian's exam record. This was not surprising, since by the spring of 1913 she had gone to perform with Diaghilev's opera in the famous Théatre des Champs-Elysées in Paris. In 1914, she joined Chaliapin in Drury Lane, London, for performances of *The Maid of Pskov* and *Khovanshchina*. In spite of her international success, Brian did not have the right to live in St. Petersburg. Glazunov kept her name on conservatory lists in an effort to resolve the situation, but he could not ask a famous twenty-eight-year-old singer to take an exam. Without Glazunov's assistance, she would have been removed from St. Petersburg by city authorities. Similarly, without Glazunov's support, Ruvin and his family would have faced the same fate. And so, after diffusing the immediate situation with the authorities, Glazunov demanded that Ruvin take some exams during the fall session.

The current exam session began at the conservatory in late April, and on April 22 everyone focused attention on the student piano competition. A graduate of Yesipova's class performed Liszt's transcription of the *Tannhäuser* Overture, along with his own piano concerto; the student's name was Sergei Prokofiev. Prokofiev later played his concerto in an annual public event in the conservatory's Maly Hall on May 11 and was awarded the special prize of a brand new piano from the K. M. Schroeder piano factory. Also performing in the concert was Auer graduate Cecilia Hansen, who played the first movement of the Beethoven Concerto and received the 1,200-ruble Mikhailovsky Palace Prize.

Pauline played her public piano exam on May 10 and was awarded the top grade by Professor Drozdov.[18] Unlike in previous spring exam sessions, Jascha also played. Exam concerts for Auer's class always attracted a large audience from the conservatory and the general public, and the May 1 event was advertised in the St. Petersburg press. Auer wrote three exclamation marks and a 5+, the highest possible grade, in Jascha's exam booklet.[19]

With that, Jascha completed his third year in Auer's class, a significant achievement, since many other violinists considered themselves disciples of the Auer school after much shorter periods. For Jascha, each and every lesson with Auer proved to be valuable. Considering the many times either Jascha and Auer were away from St. Petersburg on tour, the previous summer in Loschwitz had given them important uninterrupted time to work together. In a discussion of Auer's pedagogical influence on students, Carl Flesch wrote: "Auer placed the greatest stress on everything violinistic, e.g., purity of intonation and tone, neatness of technical execution, and taste. Through the fiery force of his personality, he was able to inspire his pupils and wrest top results from them."[20] Flesch's observations came precisely during the time Heifetz was studying in the Auer class. "It was the tone of Auer's good pupils which interested me above all," wrote Flesch.

> It seemed to possess a roundness and mellowness not easily to be found elsewhere. From the outset, I was convinced that the cause of the phenomenon must rest in some inconspicuous peculiarity of bowing or of the actual holding of the bow, and shortly before the First World War I did in fact succeed in establishing by exact observation that Russian violinists place the index finger about one centimeter higher on the stick (wrist-ward) than is customary in the Franco-Belgian school.[21]

Flesch considered that in purely technical terms, Auer's students developed at an advanced pace, but he also felt that something was missing: "If Auer had attached as much importance to a strict musical education as to the perfection of every aspect of violin technique, he might have been the greatest teacher of all times."[22] Flesch made his observations from a distance. Russian violinists, in contrast, knew that the "school of Prof. L. S. Auer is first of all a school of artistic playing. Technique is regarded in it exclusively as a means of artistic reproduction."[23] Auer did not focus on purely technical issues, and in lessons he rarely worked on them. He focused on sound, bow technique, and the "vocalization" of the violin—all largely musical rather than technical concerns. In his book *Violin Playing As I Teach It*, Auer outlines his aesthetic and pedagogical credo: "We do the greatest honor to art when we offer our own very best, not the best we can borrow from someone else. And the communion between the spirit of the music and the soul of the interpreting player must be immediate; it must not be complicated by the player's attempt to express the music by means of someone else's bag of tricks."[24]

Auer attached great significance to the all-around development of his students and always encouraged them to attend concerts and broaden their musical horizons. He also demanded that students study foreign languages, and he expected them to read widely. An amusing story survives in St. Petersburg folklore relating to Auer's desire to discuss the reading habits of his class. According to the story, Auer asked each student what they had read recently. He then turned to Jascha: "So you, Jascha, what are you reading about at the moment?" There was no answer, just a soft mumbling. Auer responded: "By the next lesson, my little friend, be so kind as to read any book and tell me about it." The next lesson arrived. "Did you read a book?" asked Auer. "Yes I did," Jascha answered quietly. "And what was it about?" asked Auer, expecting a musical or historical theme. The young violin star looked toward his teacher, "About lizard reproduction," he whispered even more softly.[25]

The wholly unexpected answer no doubt amused Auer. It is quite plausible that Jascha had been reading a book on reptiles since he already had a deep interest in butterflies, bugs, and the entire living world around him. It is no surprise, therefore, that the personal movie footage Heifetz filmed during his earliest years in the United States and during his earliest international tours includes many clips of animals and the natural world, from majestic birds overhead in Egypt to elephants transporting heavy logs in India.

That spring, the Heifetzes began fresh negotiations with the New York concert manager R. E. Johnston. Previous plans with this agency had ended when it became apparent Jascha was not old enough. The new discussions proposed a tour to the United States and Canada from January 21 to March 21, 1915 (os). It is no coincidence the proposed tour was set to begin the day after Jascha's fourteenth birthday, because the fifth clause in the contract specifically required that Heifetz be at least fourteen years of age in order to avoid "interference on the part of the Children's Society."[26] In contrast to the German text of the previous contract, this one was compiled in English. It contains the following points: a payment of $500 for each of fifteen concerts; payment of all travel expenses for Jascha and his parents to, from, and within the United States; payment of $100 per week for the Heifetz family's hotel expenses; payment of all travel expenses for the accompanist, who would receive a salary of $40 per week and $20 per week for hotel expenses; and a deposit of $5,000 from a New York bank to one in St. Petersburg no later than September 1, 1914 (to cover the last ten concerts—the first five to be paid in person after each one). Finally, the contract states that "in the event of the said Jascha Heifetz being unable in any way through death or sickness to fulfill this contract . . . his heirs or assigns will immediately return . . . the said $5,000.00."

Adding to the sense of excitement at a possible tour of the United States, the Heifetzes received news that Hyman Gerber and his family were already on their way to the New World.[27] Toward the end of April, Jascha had received a postcard from Gerber, sent from the port at Libava (now Liepāja, Latvia), a common point on the emigrant path:

> April 21, 1914
> S.-Petersburg
> Yekaterin[insky] Canal, no. 119, apt. 35
> Dear Jaschenka!
> Tomorrow the ship "Dvina" on which I am going departs for New York, and from there the railroad to Boston. It was difficult to say goodbye to my family for an unknown length of time, but it has to be so, nothing you can do. Write to me, child, at the address: Mr. H. Gerber, 42 Hollanderstr. Rox-bury mass. near Boston, America.
> Write about everything: where and how you have played recently, when you think you'll be in America. It will be wonderful when we see each other there!

Little did Gerber and the Heifetzes know that their meeting on American soil was still more than three years away.

Hall of the Neue Gewandhaus, Leipzig. *Courtesy of the Manuscript Office of the Russian Institute for the History of the Arts.*

Leopold Auer and his students, Loschwitz, summer 1914.
First row left to right: (?), Jascha Heifetz, (?), and Toscha Seidel.
Courtesy of the Historical Archive of the Saxon State Opera, Dresden.

Tour from Loschwitz to Pilnitz, Summer 1914. *Seated left to right:* Anna and Elza Heifetz, (?), Jascha Heifetz, and Kenneth Ray. *Standing:* Pauline Heifetz (*second from right*) and Ruvin Heifetz (*third from right*). *Courtesy of the Heifetz Family. From the Jascha Heifetz Collection at the Library of Congress.*

"In a hot-air balloon," Loschwitz, 1914. *Front,* Max Rosen. *Back from left to right:* (?), Eddy Brown, and Jascha Heifetz. *Courtesy of the Heifetz Family. From the Jascha Heifetz Collection at the Library of Congress.*

Summer 1914 in Loschwitz. *From right to left:* Jascha Heifetz, Pauline Heifetz, Ruth Ray, Elza Heifetz, Kenneth Ray, with Fifi the dog. *Musical America,* November 1917.

Jascha Heifetz and friend, Luga, summer 1915. *Courtesy of the Heifetz Family. From the Jascha Heifetz Collection at the Library of Congress.*

Jascha Heifetz calling card congratulating Viktor Valter on twenty-five years of artistic work. *Courtesy of the Manuscript Office of the Russian Institute for the History of the Arts.*

┌─────────────────┐
│   1915—1916.   │
│   СЕЗОНЪ VII.   │
└─────────────────┘

ВЪ БОЛЬШОМЪ ОПЕРНОМЪ ТЕАТРѢ

при Народномъ Домѣ Императора Николая II

ВО ВТОРНИКЪ, 15 ДЕКАБРЯ 1915 г.

ТРЕТІЙ
СИМФОНИЧЕСКІЙ КОНЦЕРТЪ,

ПОСВЯЩЕННЫЙ ПРОИЗВЕДЕНІЯМЪ

А. ГЛАЗУНОВА

ПОДЪ УПРАВЛЕНІЕМЪ

С. КУСЕВИЦКАГО

ПРИ УЧАСТІИ

Я. ХЕЙФЕЦЪ

и оркестра С. Кусевицкаго.

ПРОГРАММА.

1. „Море" фантазія для большого орк. ор. 28.

2. Концертъ для скрипки съ оркестромъ a-moll, ор. 82.

Исп. Я. ХЕЙФЕЦЪ.

АНТРАКТЪ.

3. Восьмая симфонія Es-Dur ор. 83.

У рояля М. Т. Дуловъ.

НАЧАЛО ВЪ 8 ЧАС. ВЕЧЕРА.

Heifetz concert program, with Serge Koussevitzky, December 15, 1915.
Courtesy of the Manuscript Office of the Russian Institute for the History of the Arts.

Jascha Heifetz, December 15, 1915. *Courtesy of the Manuscript Office of the Russian Institute for the History of the Arts.*

Leopold Auer, Christiania, Norway. *Courtesy of the Heifetz Family.*
From the Jascha Heifetz Collection at the Library of Congress.

Leopold Auer and students, Christiania, summer 1916. *Standing from left to right:* Margaret Berson, Toscha Seidel, Max Rosen, and Jascha Heifetz. *Courtesy of the St. Petersburg Conservatory.*

Snapshot by Jascha Heifetz, captioned: "Beginning of the Russian Revolution, 1917." *Courtesy of Anne Chotzinoff and Lisa Chotzinoff Grossman.*

Jascha Heifetz caricature, *Morgenbladet,* September 5, 1916.

Direktion: Rudolf Rasmussen

Den unge russiske Violinist

Jascha Heifetz

5. Konsert

Logens store Sal
Mandag 25. September 1916 Kl. 8

Ved Flyglet:

Henriette Burgin

I. Jules Conus:		Concert E-moll
		Allegro molto — Adagio — Cadenz et Allegro subito (i en Sats).
II. a. Beethoven:		Romance G-dur.
b. Beethoven-Auer:		Tyrkisk March (Scherzo).
c.	—	Dervischernes Kor (af „Die Ruinen von Athen") Etude.

III. a. Mendelssohn-Achron:		Auf Flügeln des Gesanges.
b. Tartini-Kreisler:		Variationer over et Thema af Corelli.
c. Schumann-Auer:		Vogel als Prophet.
d. Kreisler:		Tambourin chinois.
IV. Wieniawski:		Polonaise brilliante A-dur.

Flygel: Brødrene Hals.

Jascha Heifetz

Heifetz concert program, Christiania, September 25, 1916. *Courtesy of the Heifetz Family. From the Jascha Heifetz Collection at the Library of Congress.*

Jascha Heifetz inscription to Uncle Natan Heifetz, Yekaterinoslav,
April 30, 1917. *Courtesy of the Maltese Collection (Nemirovsky Archive).*

From the album of Pauline Heifetz, captioned: "Train in Siberia," July 1917.
Courtesy of Anne Chotzinoff and Lisa Chotzinoff Grossman.

Siberia Maru, 1917. *Courtesy of the Becker Medical Library, Washington University School of Medicine.*

From the album of Pauline Heifetz, captioned: "Klein Family and we at Newtonville. 1917." *From right to left:* Jascha and Anna Heifetz, Hyman Gerber, Fanny Gordon, Elza and Pauline Heifetz, Ruvin Heifetz, Gertrude Klein, Abraham Klein, and Esther Klein. *Courtesy of Anne Chotzinoff and Lisa Chotzinoff Grossman.*

JASCHA HEIFETZ
NEW RUSSIAN VIOLINIST

AMERICAN DEBUT

CARNEGIE HALL

57th Street & 7th Ave., N. Y. City

Saturday Afternoon

OCTOBER 27th

At 2.30 P. M.

...Programme...

I.

Chaconne . . . . *Tomaso Vitali (1650)*
Arrangements de Leopold Charlier
(With Organ Accompaniment)

II.

Concerto in D Minor . . . . *Wieniawsky*
Allegro moderato
Romanze: Andante non troppo
Finale: A la Zingara

III.

a. Ave Maria . . . . *Schubert*
b. Menuetto . . . . *Mozart*
c. Nocturne in D major . . . . *Chopin-Wilhelmj*
d. Chorus of derviches (Etude) . . . . } *Beethoven-Auer*
e. March orientale (Scherzo) . . . . (From the Ruins of Athens) . . . . . }

IV.

a. Melodie . . . . *Tschaikowsky*
b. Capriccio No. 24 . . . . *Paganini-Auer*

MR. ANDRE BENOIST at the Piano.   MR. FRANK L. SEALY at the Organ.

Tickets: 75c., $1.00, $1.50, $2.00   Boxes: $15.00 & $18.00
On Sale at Box Office.

Management: -   -   **WOLFSOHN MUSICAL BUREAU**

STEINWAY PIANO USED

Heifetz concert program, American debut at Carnegie Hall,
October 27, 1917. *Courtesy of the Heifetz Family. From the
Jascha Heifetz Collection at the Library of Congress.*

From right to left: Robert Heifetz, Anna Sharfstein-Koch, Albina
Starkova-Heifetz, 1998.

Robert Heifetz and Galina Kopytova.

CHAPTER FIFTEEN

Summer–Fall 1914: War

AUER'S SUMMER TEACHING SEASON in Loschwitz be-
gan early that year and students flocked there from all over Russia. The
Heifetzes arrived in May and sent a postcard to Kiselgof. On Sunday, June
1 (NS June 14) he answered them from St. Petersburg:

> I received your letter and was very, very glad. But I'm still in stuffy and dusty
> Piter and I'm not getting out of here until Wednesday. How horrible! But
> I'm glad for you, my friends, that you are already there, in a cultured, clean
> country, and are enjoying the beautiful nature and pleasant surroundings.
> I was in Pavlovsk again, but did not ride my bike—I was too lazy. I saw
> Achronchik [Isidor Achron] and passed along your greetings. He very much
> regrets that he did not see you at the station. Now I will wait from Vitebsk
> for your letter (Generalnaya, d. 3). From there I will write in more detail. Let
> me know your permanent address.[1]

Kiselgof sent the postcard to the home of Dorothea Grosse in Dresden
since she knew how to contact the Heifetzes that summer. Conveniently,
Jascha and his family stayed at the same residence as the previous year:
Kurhaus "Neue Rochwitz," 8 Hauptstrasse, Bergschlösschen. Having already spent a summer in Loschwitz, the Heifetzes quickly settled into the
routine of lessons, forest walks, tennis matches, and trips to the Russian

library in Dresden. Meanwhile, Jascha was never separated from his beloved Leica camera.

Two outdoor photographs of the entire 1914 Auer violin colony survive.[2] Auer is seated in the center of a group of forty-three people, most of whom are likely his students. To the right of the professor sits student Thelma Given with a ribbon around her hair. At the front of the group sitting on a rug are the youngest students, including two in light sailor suits—Jascha Heifetz and Toscha Seidel. The name of the boy in the dark sailor suit is unknown, but he seems to have been friendly with Jascha and appears in various photographs taken during outings with Jascha and others.[3] There was much to do around Dresden, including taking a trip from Blasewitz to Weisser Hirsch by cable car and taking the tram to Pilnitz—the summer residence of the Saxon Royal House. Anna, Ruvin, Elza, and Pauline all appear in the photographs from this time, and it appears the family enjoyed the summer break very much. In one photograph of Jascha and some other students, the impossible inscription reads: "In a hot-air balloon. Over Lake Titicaca. Africa." Such scenes were arranged at the time as tourist attractions. Jascha sits on the edge of the balloon basket holding his camera.

Accompanying Jascha in many of the photographs from this period is a boy of a similar age named Kenneth Ray. Kenneth's older sister Ruth (1897–1999) took lessons from Auer, both in Loschwitz and during the winter in St. Petersburg. There are several pieces of evidence attesting to the friendship between Kenneth and Jascha, including photographs of Jascha and his sisters with the Ray siblings. These same photographs appeared in the American publication *Musical America* following Heifetz's Carnegie Hall debut in 1917, with the subtitle: "Fellow students in the Leopold Auer class."[4] The *Strad* published the photographs again in 1986 accompanied by Ruth Ray's recollections from that time:

> I had the privilege of hearing [Jascha] daily through the summer of 1914. We were both students of Professor Auer. Jascha with his parents and sisters Paula and Elza, and I, with my mother and brother Kenneth, had adjoining apartments in the Kurhaus Bergschlösschen Rochwitz bei Loschwitz, which meant I could enjoy hearing him (and he had to listen to me). Through the month of June he played twenty-one concertos, all twenty-four Paganini

Caprices, all six Bach solo sonatas and many other pieces, plus the daily hour of fabulous scales and arpeggios; also an hour of almost equally beautiful piano. He says I never heard him practise—he was "on vacation" that summer! He was, even then, a kind and considerate friend, never playing the things I was working on until about three days before my lesson. Then he would play them as they should be done. When I could catch my breath, I would start again. If I had understood, I could continue; if I had not, the violin in the next room would interrupt, then I'd try once more. If I showed I understood I could continue. When I thanked him, he said I only imagined the whole thing! But the "Heifetz sound" is unmistakeable. About four in the afternoon our families, as well as Toscha Seidel, with his mother and brother Valodjia, would meet at the tennis courts and then walk through the forest for an hour or so before tea-time—a very happy memory. Heifetz's speed of learning was awesome. One day my mother was practising the accompaniment of the Butler *Ballade* (which she found difficult) when he poked his head around the sun-porch separation asking what it was. She couldn't answer in German so motioned for him to come in. Then he picked out the violin part on the piano, jumping up an octave when the accompaniment came too high. Two days later he played the five pages on his violin, once coming to the sun-porch to ask if one ornament should be a mordent or a short trill. I am in such awe of his memory and think he might still be able to play it![5]

Nothing came between Jascha and his intense violin study, but such dedication did not always apply to his schoolwork. Before the Heifetzes left St. Petersburg, Kiselgof assigned general summer homework to both Jascha and Pauline and received solemn promises they would complete everything. After some time had passed and Kiselgof had heard nothing, he wrote from Vitebsk to Pauline: "It surprises me that you, Polya, don't write anything to me about lessons. Or are they—down the drain? Both history and geography!!!! Anyway, you are a glorious, dear girl, and I care about you, that is why I write."[6] Nine-year-old Elza, free to enjoy the summer, also received a letter from Kiselgof written in large clear letters: "Hello, little snub-nose, blue eyes! I'm doing well, except I miss you, you Elzutka, snub-nose. I'm angry at Jascha and Polya: because of them you haven't written, and I've decided that you've completely forgotten the 'Green' Aronovich." On July 2, Kiselgof wrote to Jascha in a more direct tone: "Are you studying? How many assignments have you completed? How is history, geography? See that 'history' and geography don't leave us! Write more about yourself, about nature, the weather. Be more generous with the letter writing!" Such calls fell on deaf ears. In a heartfelt piece about his father many years later, Heifetz's youngest son Jay explained that the violinist was "a man of few words," who had the ability to express in a short phrase what for others required several pages. And, he added, "so much of what he had to say he said with a violin under his chin."[7]

Kiselgof's postcard to Jascha included an image of a painting by Arnold Böcklin entitled: "The Hermit playing the violin," depicting an old monk playing the violin in the evening twilight, surrounded by attentive angels. Kiselgof continued his postcard to Jascha with news of his own interspersed with a poetic description of the postcard:

> I'm living at the dacha in Dobreiki, I tell fairytales to my little daughter [born 1913]. I read and relax. The summer is hot here by us, the weather is wonderful and the evenings remarkable. And when the hot day changes to evening coolness, it seems that the earth sings to God a quiet prayer and sends him praise on a wonderful little violin, and the angel-stars listen carefully to the quiet wonderful sounds of prayer—the evening song. To the best of my ability, dear Jascha, I have described for you the contents of this Böcklin painting.

Kiselgof carefully selected the postcards he sent to his pupils, always trying to expand their horizons. Jascha saved each one of them, placing them in the albums he had received for his thirteenth birthday from Maxim Olefsky and the Sinelnikovs. During this period, many people collected postcards, which were produced by various companies, including the Riga company Lenz & Rudolf, as well as the St. Eugene Red Cross Society. The Red Cross also published many postcards in Russia in the 1910s and worked closely with various World of Art artists, including Aleksandr Benois, Lev Bakst, Mstislav Dobuzhinsky, Konstantin Somov, and Yevgeny Lansere. For ordinary art lovers and students, these postcards became a guide acquainting them with the works of classic and contemporary artists.

As it turns out, these postcards from Kiselgof to the Heifetz children were to be the last written during peacetime. The threat of war stole up almost unnoticed. Political squabbles had erupted in German and Russian newspapers since the spring, with each side accusing the other of preparing for war. Politicians on both sides, meanwhile, spoke publicly about the "good-natured" relationship between Russia and Germany. There were those who refused to see the coming troubles, but there were also those who foresaw a military conflict between the Triple Alliance of Germany, Austria-Hungary, and Italy, and the countries of the Entente—France, Great Britain, and Russia. The unceremonious annexation of Bosnia and Herzegovina by Austria-Hungary in 1912 further exacerbated the situation and provoked the patriotic indignation of the Serbs.

On June 28 (NS), Archduke Franz Ferdinand of Austria and his wife, Sophie, Duchess of Hohenberg, were assassinated in Sarajevo by Serbian nationalist Gavrilo Princip, a member of the Young Bosnia revolutionary movement, and a month later, Austria declared war on Serbia. At that time, tens of thousands of Russian travelers found themselves in Germany and Austria-Hungary, some treating sickness at prestigious resorts and others filling the concert halls and theaters of Berlin and Vienna. These Russians should have headed home after the assassination, but few expected a Europe-wide war. Events snowballed: within days of the Austrian declaration of war, Germany declared war on Russia, then on France, and subsequently attacked neutral Belgium. Among the many Russian citizens stranded on enemy territory were Auer and his violin colony.

In St. Petersburg, people set ablaze the German Embassy on Isaaki-evskaya Square and removed and destroyed the massive bronze sculpture adorning its roof. Citizens ransacked several German stores. Young men eagerly enrolled in the military, and detachments of mobilized soldiers marched along the streets adjacent to Palace Square. Summertime was usually quiet in St. Petersburg, and the majority of conservatory instructors had departed for summer vacation, either to places near the city or to central or southern Russia. The composer Maksimilian Steinberg had been traveling throughout Europe in May and June, but returned to Russia before trouble began and continued the summer with his family near Luga at the Lyubensk Estate. During a trip to St. Petersburg, Steinberg wrote in his diary simply: "July 1914—war."[8] In addition, he noted that he needed to visit the bank and pay his rent. For some, war was still an abstract concept.

The situation in Germany, however, deteriorated more rapidly. The exchange of Russian money was halted, telegraphs to Russia were cut, and regular passenger train routes were canceled. Subject to repatriation, those

Russians still in Germany besieged the train stations in major German cities. Many Russians, including famous names, faced a tortuous route home; the writer Aleksei Remizov and his family, for example, were stopped for days by the authorities before they could reach Russia. They were forced to take a long and circuitous route home through Denmark and Sweden.

Around the time the German government declared war on Russia, the Heifetzes were no longer in Loschwitz. They had traveled to Berlin to purchase a violin for Jascha from the well-known violin dealer Emil Herrmann. Following lengthy deliberations, they settled on an instrument made in 1736 by the Italian maker Carlo Tononi—the same instrument Heifetz would later use at his Carnegie Hall debut and in his early recordings. A certificate of purchase from Emil Herrmann bears Ruvin's name and the family's Loschwitz address and is dated August 3, 1914.[9] Although the price paid for the instrument is unknown, Emil Herrmann later claimed that he sold the instrument on credit and at a discount.[10] Jascha finally owned his own serious instrument, purchased with money that he himself had earned. Throughout Heifetz's career other valuable instruments passed through his hands, but his attachment to this Tononi remained until the end. He willed the instrument to Sherry Kloss, his former student and assistant.

Despite the excitement over the new acquisition, the onset of war meant that the Heifetzes had to return immediately to Loschwitz, their place of registration. Auer wrote in his memoirs:

> At the beginning of August, 1914, when the World War broke out, some of my pupils took flight, and had much to suffer before they were able to reach their homes in safety. As for myself and the few other Russians in Loschwitz, we remained where we were, seeing that there was nothing else to do, and were subjected to the strictest police surveillance. The English, in particular, were objects of suspicion, and did not dare speak their language in the street. The Americans, since they belonged to a neutral nation, were in no wise molested; but in order to guard against outbreaks of mob hatred they wore little red, white, and blue boutonniers. This precaution taken, they could wait with all tranquility until it was time for them to depart. I myself was looked upon as a Russian spy, since my remaining pupils met in my home to consult together and to ask my advice, and these innocent reunions were thought to be very suspicious. It was due only to the intervention of some of my German friends that I was not seriously molested before I was

authorized to leave the country for Russia, in October. Life was not very pleasant for any of the Russian nationals in Loschwitz during the time they remained there; yet I was allowed to reside unmolested in my little villa, and the fact that I kept my German servants served as a sort of guarantee to the local authorities....

Nevertheless, like all the other enemy nationals, English and Russian, I was forbidden to leave my house after seven in the evening; and when it was necessary for me to leave Loschwitz and go to Dresden during the day I was obliged to notify the police bureau.[11]

All contact with Russia from Germany ceased, so Auer and his students remained unaware of the developing situation back at home. On August 18 (NS August 31) the city of St. Petersburg was renamed Petrograd. This occurred just after heavy losses by the Russian Second Army Division in Eastern Prussia, and after the suicide of its commander, General Aleksandr Samsonov. The general atmosphere in Russia became gloomier. "Art, clearly, is left in the background," wrote Glazunov to one of his students.

... I have no desire to work on composition—who needs it now ... I'm living here at the dacha in Ozerki, where I will stay, probably until the beginning of classes. The train is more infrequent and so it takes much longer to get to the city. Admissions clearly will not be very big, as significantly fewer applications were submitted compared to last year. Our entry standards will be lower for the sake of financial considerations, to the detriment of artistic considerations. Professors Vengerova, Rozanova and Maykapar are stuck abroad. There are also many gaps among teachers of orchestral instruments. An unhappy time....[12]

Auer, one of the conservatory professors stranded abroad, remained with his Russian students under police surveillance in Loschwitz. The professor continued his description of events:

At the beginning of October I was authorized to leave Germany on a train which carried none but Russians, and which disembarked us at the port of Sassnitz, where we went aboard a Swedish ship, after we and all our effects had been subjected to a most rigorous search, the agents even plunging their hands into our pockets. Once aboard the ship which was to carry us to Sweden, whence we could enter Russia by way of Finland, each one of us breathed a great sigh of relief, relief at once more feeling free and unsuspected. Toscha Seidel and his mother were among our company; but the Heifetz party was held back in Berlin, since Jascha's father had not yet reached the age of forty-five, the legal age limit which ensured the repatriation of enemy nationals.[13]

Not long before his departure to Russia, Auer wrote a letter to his friend Artur Abell:

Loschwitz, 10 September 1914
Dear Friend:
just a few words to let you know that I will, pretty soon, travel to Petersburg, with detours, on the "Russians' train" which has to be organized from Dresden. The authorities gave me the choice *either* to travel home soon *or* to stay *here* till the end of the war. I chose the former. And thus, I hope, see you again in better times! Please convey to Mrs. Abell my kindest regards (also from Mrs. v. Stein). To you [I extend] a "shakhand" in friendship.—
L. v. Auer
P.S. I am writing to Wolff in order to continue my subscription to the "Courier."
All my foreign students have departed: only poor Jascha Heifetz is sitting in Rochwitz (Bergschlösschen) and has to stay there till the end of the war because Papa Heifetz has not passed his 45th year, thus is subject to being called up for military service in Russia and not allowed to leave.[14]

Soon after, the Heifetzes managed to move from Loschwitz to Berlin, thanks to the intensified efforts of influential people, namely the director of the Royal Theater in Berlin, Mr. Count von Hülsen-Haeseler. At the start of October Waldemar Liachowsky received a forwarded letter concerning the Heifetz family's status. He immediately sent it on to the Heifetzes:

Sect[ion]—J. No 3944

Berlin C. 2., 3 October 1914
Zeughaus Square 1

Your Excellency
The [military] commanding office feels honored to respond to the well-received letter of 24 of this month by most humbly supplying the information that Mr. Heifetz and family have been granted permission to move to Berlin by the Deputy General Command XII Army Corps.

Nor does the commanding office have any objections against their traveling here.

The Commander
A. B.
pp. M. Stockhausen

To the Managing Director of the Royal Theatre, Mr. Count von Hülsen-Haeseler, His Excellency, here [in Berlin][15]

Once he had sent the document to the Heifetzes, Liachowsky intended to travel to Loschwitz to meet them, but by October 6, Ruvin sent Liachowsky a telegram from Weisser Hirsch, not far from Loschwitz: "Permission granted yesterday arrive Berlin Thursday evening therefore no need for you to come thanks and greetings, Heifetz."[16] The Heifetzes arrived in Berlin on October 8 (os September 25), about two months after the beginning of the war. Fortunately, they were not alone. Liachowsky looked after them, and they were joined by the family of Joseph Schwarz, the pianist who had accompanied Jascha during his first visit to Berlin. In those days of May 1912, Jascha had become acquainted with Schwarz's son Boris, who was now eight. Years later, Boris Schwarz described this wartime experience in his book *Great Masters of the Violin:*

> The whole Auer clan—including the Heifetz family as well as my own—was summering near Dresden when World War I broke out. After a few anxious weeks, the Heifetz family and mine were permitted to return to Berlin. As enemy aliens, we were obligated to visit the police precinct twice a day. Our families became rather close in the face of common problems. Jascha, who played the piano remarkably well, had lessons with my father, while I was taught the rudiments of the violin by father Heifetz. I can still remember Jascha in our music room, playing the finale of the Mendelssohn concerto at breakneck speed while jumping around and mocking the difficulties that were nonexistent for him.[17]

The most worrying aspect of the affair for the Heifetzes was not knowing how long this situation would last. Internees were provided rations, but with the colder autumn and winter approaching, warmer clothes were needed. Buying anything was difficult, since Russian money was non-exchangeable, and the family's supply of German marks was limited. Even with all these complications, the Heifetz family's situation was far from the worst. During the first days of war, Henri Marteau, professor at the Königliche Hochschule für Musik in Berlin, was interned. As a French citizen in Germany and as a person of draftable age (he was forty), Marteau was imprisoned in a fortress where he remained until the spring of 1915. Relatively harsh measures were also taken in the Russian capital against the citizens of hostile states. On the tenth day of the war, newspapers in St. Petersburg wrote that all German and Austrian citizens liable to the draft had been rounded-up and detained in a special building rented in the Peski area of the city.

Decades later from the safety of the United States, Heifetz talked about his family's detention in Germany in 1914:

> ...the outbreak of the First World War caught us. We were, of course, enemy aliens in Germany; we were ordered to Berlin to be registered as such, and there my parents had to report each day. By a lucky chance Count von Moltke, the German Chief of Staff, was a music lover. He had heard me play and liked me. On the strength of this my mother asked him for a safe-conduct for us to neutral Finland, and this the Count was kind enough to give us.[18]

Count Helmuth von Moltke (The Younger) (1848–1916) was a prominent figure in the German army and at the start of the war served as chief of the general staff. In September 1914, Moltke's miscalculations as head commander during the Battle of the Marne, near Paris, led to a bitter defeat of the German forces on the Western Front. Later in September, Moltke was stripped of his duties as chief of the general staff, but he continued to hold enough influence to help the family of the young violinist.

Heifetz's description of these events requires some clarification. There was no "neutral" Finland at that time. Finland was, although autonomous, part of the Russian Empire. It is more likely that from Germany, the Heifetzes ended up in Sweden or Norway, both of which were neutral. Significant streams of Russian refugees from Germany flowed to Sweden and then from there by boat to Finland. Once in Finland, the Russian capital was still a few hundred miles away, and there were no direct routes. As Heifetz explained: "When we got to Finland, railroad transportation to Russia was not available. It was the dead of winter, and we had to travel in a sleigh over frozen lakes. It was great fun for us children, but we arrived in Leningrad [Petrograd] half frozen."[19] Despite all the difficulties that had faced the Heifetzes, everyone and everything reached home safely, including the valuable Tononi. Even the letters and postcards from Kiselgof managed to survive the journey.

St. Petersburg was now Petrograd, but the cold, gloomy winter remained the same. Window frames were firmly caulked, smoke blew from stovetops, and snow covered the ground. In the midst of the winter darkness, the Heifetzes were greeted warmly by all their friends—Viktor Valter, Zinovy Kiselgof, Isidor Achron, Maxim Olefsky, and, of course, Auer. Auer had returned back to Petrograd in October and upon his arrival he heard belatedly the news that his colleague Anna Yesipova had passed away on August 5 (os). Maxim Olefsky also grieved for Yesipova. Although he had only just entered the conservatory in January of that year and had only studied with Yesipova for a short time, his memories of her lasted throughout his life.[20]

The ongoing war disrupted normal city life in Petrograd. The theater and concert seasons opened late, and soldiers drafted into service were quartered in the Theater of Musical Drama, located in the conservatory building, at the start of the season. The patriotic mood of audiences and artists was largely sincere, but occasionally it took on extreme forms. At the opening of the opera season at the Mariinsky Theater, the audience requested six performances of the Russian anthem and two performances of each of the anthems of the allied powers (France, England, Belgium, Serbia, Montenegro, and Japan). Gradually, German music began to disappear from theatrical and concert programs; no more Wagner, Bach, or Beethoven.

To support the continuing war effort, fundraising events took place across the city. Artists from the imperial theaters organized a "tobacco collection" on October 5 and 6, during which 66,158 rubles were collected, as well as around forty boxes of tobacco. The troupe of the Mariinsky Theater agreed to a two-percent pay deduction. Infirmaries funded by both societies and private funds appeared across the city to attend to injured soldiers. The Chaliapin Infirmary opened on October 15, and shortly after, the Artists of the Imperial Theaters Infirmary. The conservatory also used its resources to maintain hospital beds. Despite such efforts, the city remained woefully unprepared to deal with the scale of the devastation. Three weeks after the beginning of war, thirty-eight thousand wounded arrived in Petrograd. Neither Petrograd nor other cities in northwest Russia could manage the influx, so dozens of trains carried maimed soldiers to other parts of the country, even as far away as Siberia. Charity concerts soon became an integral part of Petrograd musical life, and before long Jascha would also appear in such events.

The Heifetzes settled into the new circumstances as best they could. The time came for Ruvin to renew his residency permit, but Glazunov found it increasingly difficult to keep him on the conservatory lists. On July 4, 1914, Glazunov received a letter from Princess Yelena Saxon-Altenburg, chair of the Russian Music Society, who held authority over the conservatory: "Allow me to direct your attention to the danger facing those persons of the conservatory not attending classes. The discovery of such permissiveness on the part of the inspector may result in police involvement."[21] The letter continued, ordering Glazunov to "strictly monitor attendance and expel all students who do not attend classes for more than two months without a valid reason." For the last few months at least, Ruvin had a valid reason for missing classes, one that received press coverage. "Famous young violinist Jascha Heifetz and his family returned to Petrograd," announced one newspaper:

> Last summer he was in Berlin to give concerts and delighted the German capital's public with his playing. The outbreak of war found him still there. The Germans declared Jascha and his parents enemy aliens and for an entire four months did not let them out of Berlin. Only in December did they manage to win their freedom and leave for Petrograd. The Berlin authorities proposed that the young violinist play a concert for wounded Germans. Heifetz's parents rejected this offer, stating that their son, loyal to his homeland, would not render any service to its enemies.[22]

Glazunov of course offered to help Ruvin, but not just out of sympathy for the family's misfortune in Germany, nor as a reward for the manifestation of their patriotism, which was likely invented and then trumpeted loudly by the press. Glazunov worked tirelessly to keep Jascha in the conservatory where he could continue to develop his talent.

CHAPTER SIXTEEN

January–September 1915

THE ARRIVAL OF A NEW YEAR brought no relief to the conflict: Germany had intended to finish the war by autumn, and Russia had planned to fight only on foreign territory and was now dealing with a front line moving toward its own borders. In the words of *Rech,* a popular newspaper in Russian intellectual circles, "to say whether or not the war ends in the coming year, of course, is impossible. Nevertheless, however long the war continues, however much effort it requires, we have enough physical and spiritual strength."[1] Among the artistic elite, some tried to find in the cataclysms of war an opportunity for evolutionary and artistic progress. For example, the composer Alexander Scriabin wrote, "How deeply mistaken are those who see in wars only evil and the results of accidentally formed discord between peoples."[2]

Meanwhile, the Heifetzes began the year in a new home—a rented apartment on Yekateringofsky Prospekt, renamed Rimsky-Korsakov Prospekt in the 1920s. The street starts in a residential area and then stretches southwest through a square that is home to the enormous white and blue St. Nicholas Cathedral; from there both the conservatory and the Mariinsky Theater are visible. The street then continues alongside the Yekaterininsky

Canal before it ends around Kalinkinskaya Square. The Heifetzes settled at this end of Yekateringofsky Prospekt in building 115. This would become the Heifetz family's final address in the city. They lived in this apartment for two-and-a-half years up to their departure for the United States. The walk to the conservatory from this new apartment took twenty minutes, which was longer than before, but a tram stopped outside their building. The neighborhood where they settled was not particularly upscale; it joined the quarter between the Fontanka River and the Yekaterininsky Canal, or the "ditch," as the latter was then unflatteringly called. Apartments in this area were packed together tightly, but unlike the more central streets, the new location was at least quiet and peaceful.

The apartment was in a six-story building that had been completed in 1912 and was owned by a man named Ivan Konoplyov, whose business card stated: "Workshop of molded and sculptural works by I. P. Konoplyov. Yekateringofsky pr. Own home no. 115."[3] Konoplyov's workshop was located in the courtyard wing along with an automobile garage and a stall for horses. He and his family lived in a four-bedroom apartment (number 2) on the second floor of the building. The Heifetzes rented apartment number 3, located on the landing across from the Konoplyovs. Their apartment consisted of an entrance hall and five rooms: a bathroom with a wood-burning furnace, two toilets, and a kitchen.[4] The windows faced not onto the courtyard, but onto the street. By any measure, the apartment provided the Heifetzes with a quite reasonable level of comfort, similar in standard to Auer's apartment. Archival documents connected to the construction of the building and its tax value provide an idea of the rental value of the apartment: 1,440 rubles per year or, in other words, more than ten times what Ruvin had paid for their first place on Ofitserskaya Street.[5]

Jascha turned fourteen on January 20. According to the contract with R. E. Johnston from the past May, Jascha's tour of the United States should have begun, but with the outbreak of war it became impossible. The contract stipulated that the American impresario transfer a deposit of five thousand dollars from New York to St. Petersburg no later than September 1914. If indeed the agency fulfilled its obligation before the outbreak of war, it was unfortunate for the agency, since according to the contract, the deposit was returnable under only two circumstances—Jascha's sickness or death. The boy was alive and well, of course, but the war made the journey impossible.

Despite the disappointment of a canceled tour to the United States, Jascha could still celebrate his birthday; he received a number of greetings cards, including one from Mina Roubleff. Although previous letters from Mina usually arrived from her trips to her father in Theodosia or were sent during Jascha's tours, this one carried the postmark "Petrograd 19.01 1915." Since Mina sent the card and did not deliver it personally, it is possible that their friendship had soured, perhaps as a result of Jascha's long absences or perhaps because of the age difference (Mina was already eighteen by this time). Mina's card sounds almost like a farewell, and it is the last of her letters from the period preserved in the Heifetz archive: "... I wish you to become not only a famous artist, but also a good person, in the fullest meaning of this word: good, kindhearted, sincere, and direct, and the main thing—educated. Only then will all of your enormous talent expand to the fullest. Grow, be good, cheerful, and happy . . ."[6] Mina continued her conservatory studies, attending the instrumentation class of Maksimilian Steinberg and the theory class of Vasily Kalafati, who noted that Mina was "Musical, but lazy."[7] No graduation diploma survives in Mina's file. The name Roubleff later surfaced in 1930 in a letter from Glazunov to Leonid Nikolaev,[8] in whose piano class Mina had studied throughout her conservatory years. Glazunov, finding himself in the United States for concerts, which were then canceled because of his bad health, met with several former conservatory students, including Mina Roubleff. It is possible that Jascha also met with Mina during those years.

The card from Mina was not the only one that arrived. Earlier in January, the Heifetzes had sent birthday greetings to their cousin Anyuta in Vilnius, and now the Sharfsteins wrote back with greetings for Jascha.[9] Still only seven, Anyuta wrote in her best handwriting: "I congratulate you dear and beloved Jaschinka on your special day. I wish you long years and much happiness. . . ." The Sharfsteins had a recent addition to the family; Fanny (or Futka) was born on November 17, 1914 (os). Anyuta's father Isaac also wrote his greetings on the postcard. For now, in spite of the war, everything remained calm in Vilnius.

From Warsaw, the news was more worrying. The German invasion, which had reached the banks of the Vistula the past autumn, resulted in an unending stream of refugees to Warsaw. The hardships of wartime affected the entire civilian population of these western areas occupied by the Russian Empire. For Jews, however, the situation was especially complicated since the war sharpened the issue of national identity and rekindled the idea of their exclusion. Not only was Poland the site of battles between Germany, Austria-Hungary, and Russia, but the three powers all competed for Poland by extending promises of autonomy. Half of the Jews in the world lived on Polish territory. Although only homeless drifters were expelled from Warsaw at the start, Jews began to fear for their safety, thereby increasing the eastward flow of refugees. Heifetz's relatives joined this stream, and in the second year of the war, Natan, Fanny, and little Lyusya left Warsaw. After spending some time moving around Ukraine, the family reached Yekaterinoslav, where they settled for the next few years.

Before long, Vilnius witnessed a mass evacuation of the civilian population; the entire staff of the music school, including Malkin and his family, relocated to Moscow. Isaac and Sonia Sharfstein and their two young daughters ended up in Petrograd with the Heifetzes. They escaped Vilnius on what was almost the last train, discarding most of their belongings and leaving behind only a framed photograph of Anyuta on the wall. Subsequent dwellers in the apartment discovered the photograph, and remarkably, it was returned to the Sharfsteins in the United States in the 1930s.

Anna Heifetz had always looked out for her younger brother's family, and so she now welcomed Isaac, Sonia, Anyuta, and little Fanny into her family's Petrograd apartment. All nine lived there until the Heifetzes left for the United States. With extra houseguests, the apartment became quite crowded. Jascha and Pauline shared a bedroom, which also served as a classroom when Kiselgof came for lessons, and Anna and Ruvin shared their bedroom with both Elza and Anyuta. Anyuta Sharfstein-Koch recalled the situation clearly: "For my father, there was a couch in the living room, and for mama and the baby, a folding bed in the dining room."[10] The family's governess, who taught the Heifetz children German and French, stayed in the remaining tiny room, but later, when Anna let the governess go, Sonia and her younger daughter moved into the spare room.

The apartment impressed Sharfstein-Koch greatly. It was large, with an elevator, a doorman at the main entrance, and an enormous living room, complete with decorated oriental carpets, a piano, and a beautiful fireplace. When at the end of the 1990s Sharfstein-Koch was shown photographs of the same apartment in its present state, she studied the rundown interiors with disbelief. In Soviet times the large apartment was divided into two and became difficult to recognize. The long, unrenovated three-bedroom communal apartment is now known as number 3. Sharfstein-Koch accurately recalled the name of the apartment owners as the Konoplyov family, and she immediately recognized the fireplace in the living room. Jascha used the fireplace mantle as a home for various ceramic figurines of animals and birds that he had received as gifts—his "zoo."

As a child, Anyuta Sharfstein-Koch lived in the apartment almost as a recluse. Although the Sharfsteins were refugees, they were still Jews from the Pale, so living in Petrograd remained forbidden and state aid was unavailable. This applied not only to the civilian population, but also to wounded Jewish soldiers. After recovering in hospitals, those Jewish soldiers not fit enough to return to the front were immediately transported under guard back to the Pale. Local authorities appealed to central authorities to ease the law of the Pale during wartime, but they were unsuccessful. According to the government, war was not a pretext for clogging up the central regions with an influx of Jews.

Without any documents granting them residency rights in Petrograd, the Sharfsteins led a precarious existence. The Heifetzes, whose own rights were tenuous at best, put themselves at serious risk by illegally housing the Sharfsteins. Jascha's mother diligently paid off the building's caretaker for his silence, but to avoid attention, the Sharfsteins rarely ventured outside the apartment. As a result, little Anyuta could not attend school, and so she mastered reading, writing, and mathematics with the help of her father and cousin Elza, who read her Andersen fairytales. Sharfstein-Koch recalled her excitement when one day, in spite of the risks, Jascha's mother took her out to the grocery store. Anna Heifetz always bought groceries herself, and with Jascha's fees, she could shop in expensive stores that stocked everything, even during wartime. Sharfstein-Koch remembered that Jascha's mother bought her teenage son his favorite foods, which included red caviar, salmon, smoked sausage, and poppyseed pies. In general, Anna Heifetz tried not to refuse her children anything, but Ruvin often opposed what he considered his wife's extravagances. Ruvin did, however, send money to needy relatives. According to the recollections of people close to him, he "would write a large cheque for a needy relative but would baulk at giving away so much as a quarter in currency." Ruvin was essentially "a simple man ... with simple tastes, and he saw no reason to squander money."[11]

During the first wartime winter, Jascha and his sisters lived almost as restricted a life as their cousin, with the exception of their walks to the conservatory with Ruvin. Pauline's classmate in Drozdov's class, Vladimir Muzalevsky, recalled: "They made a picturesque trio: proud Papa; curly headed, round-faced and rosy-cheeked Jascha with his violin in its case; and thin, shy Pauline with a folder of music. Always listening to his daughter's playing in the lobby behind the doors of our classroom, Heifetz the father watched what happened in the lesson through the glass spaces in the doors."[12] Muzalevsky continued, turning his focus to Jascha:

> The young conservatory students were a noisy and sociable breed. The violinists of Auer's class stood out from the others. They sometimes went out to the smoking room (next to N. A. Rimsky-Korsakov's classroom, number 23), which they then transformed into a sort of club. Their relations with each other were childishly simple. I remember how in that smoking room, Toscha Seidel, Myron Polyakin, and other young virtuosos repeated various difficult passages from the pieces they studied. Jascha Heifetz, a member of this Pleiades of Auer's students, was also a participant in these musical "conferences."[13]

Aside from time at the conservatory, the Heifetz children stayed at home. They studied French and German with the governess and other subjects with Kiselgof, who came daily for lessons that lasted several hours. The absence of regular lessons from May to December of the previous year had left a mark, and much that had been learned needed repeating. Not in vain did Kiselgof write "Look, Jascha, the time will fly—you can't get it back ..."

Although free time was limited, the Heifetzes made friends with the Schreibers (two sisters and two brothers) who lived on the first floor of the same building. They sent each other postcards with silly messages and invitations to come over and play games. Some of these postcards were saved in albums, and the messages contain amusing references to friends: Katya, who always spelled her name backward; Ida, who called herself "Warsaw"; and Benno, who was nicknamed "New York."[14] A postcard from a girl named Liza, addressed "to glorious Jascha . . . in eternal memory," contained a heartfelt explanation of why she cared so dearly for Jascha; he had promised to take her photograph. The albums also contain a series of postcards with "April Fools" jokes, including a poem by an anonymous author:

> Jascha, you awfully naughty boy,
> There is no end to your pranks . . .
> And your sisters you very often
> Literally drive out of their minds.
> You beat them unmercifully,
> But your hand is not made of fluff![15]

Despite his sometimes "unmerciful" behavior toward his sisters, Jascha was very attached to them, especially to Pauline. Much connected Jascha and Pauline, starting with their nearness in age. Their joint experience at the conservatory brought them even closer, since they loved to share stories and gossip about the administration, the teachers, and classmates. They both idolized Fritz Kreisler and Josef Hofmann, and Pauline had progressed so far with her piano studies that she could now accompany Jascha, not in public, but often at home. The brother and sister shared a joint love of cinema, and often playacted scenes reminiscent of the silent film era. Photos from this time include scenes with costumes, daggers, and various other props.[16] A number of these playacted scenes also appear in the early home film footage recorded by the Heifetzes during their first years in the United States.[17]

Another shared experience for Jascha and Pauline was their time with Kiselgof, who tried to teach the children more than just facts and figures; he wanted to open their imaginations to the natural world around them. Kiselgof's talent for teaching children served him well in the 1920s and 1930s when he taught dozens of Jewish children in the orphanage on Vasilyevsky Island. With good reason, Kiselgof became known as "an outstanding personality and a pedagogue in the highest sense of the word."[18]

Kiselgof's influence on Jascha was great, but Auer's was even greater, and aspects of Auer's character can be found in the adult Heifetz. Just like his professor, Heifetz became known later in life for his insistence on punctuality, and if, for example, a dinner guest arrived a minute or two late, the guest would be refused entry. Jascha, like all of Auer's students, idolized but also somewhat feared his professor. Auer's unpredictability became a behavioral model for Heifetz later in life, and many of those around Heifetz felt intimidated by his personality. This intimidation and fear even applied to Heifetz's accompanists. In the earliest years in Russia, Heifetz's relationships with Isidor Achron and Emanuel Bay were full of respect, but later, Heifetz consciously established a distance from them, evoking a certain amount of fear. To illustrate Auer's unpredictability, Heifetz himself recalled an amusing class scene:

> The days at the conservatoire were hard, but there were amusing scenes. The poor parents, the worried mothers, the anxious relatives, they were all eager to see the great man and to hear what their dear offspring and protégés were doing. They often used to gather in the corridors and the shallow vestibule between the big double doors. Professor Auer pretended not to notice them, but often while encouraging a pupil he crept stealthily around the room, suddenly burst open the doors with a wild whoop and laughed delightedly while a panic-stricken crowd of mothers, aunts, cousins and curious friends fled wildly down the corridor.[19]

As an adult, Heifetz's sense of humor, which could be quite caustic, seemed to resemble that of his professor. Heifetz's daughter Josefa inherited her father's fondness for playing with words. For example, she would sing vocal exercises, replacing the original text with the names and surnames of Russian chess masters or names of dogs. Heifetz loved practical jokes, which he would sometimes play on close friends and family, including his son Robert. As a child, Robert was once delighted to receive from his father a $100 bill for his birthday (a very substantial gift in the 1940s). Poor Robert soon realized that the $100 bill was actually a $10 bill folded cunningly by his father. Heifetz also found himself on the receiving end of humor. In a conversation with the famous Marx Brothers comedians, when Heifetz declared proudly that he had been a "self-supporting citizen" ever since he was seven, Harpo Marx yawned, and replied: "Before that, I suppose, you were just a bum."[20]

Lessons with Auer in early 1915 focused on preparing for Jascha's up-coming solo appearance in the Maly Hall. In contrast to previous years, not one but two concerts were arranged for Jascha. Auer came down with serious neuralgia in his right hand in the middle of February, and for the next two months he could not play the violin. Jascha's lessons continued, but Auer was unable to demonstrate anything on his violin.

The first concert took place on March 1, with the accompaniment of Isidor Achron. The program stated: "Part of the proceeds will go for the benefit of the infirmary for wounded soldiers at Petrograd Conservatory."[21] This was Jascha's first wartime benefit concert, and although he had not performed in Petrograd for the whole year, the overflowing hall proved that the city had not forgotten him. In honor of the recently deceased Anna Yesipova, a display was set up in the hall with items and documents relating to her career; and a large portrait of Yesipova remained on the wall from then on.

Despite Auer's sickness, the professor and his student prepared well for the concert. With the exception of Wieniawski's *Faust Fantasy*, which Jascha had been performing for nearly seven years, the program consisted of works entirely new to him, including *Rêverie*, a lyrical piece by the St. Petersburg composer Aleksandr Taneyev, a high-ranking court official and distant relation of the composer Sergei Taneyev. Jascha also played Tartini's famous *Devil's Trill Sonata* for the first time. Two other works Jascha performed that evening became firm favorites for the rest of his life—Sarasate's *Spanish Dances*. Heifetz recorded *Malagueña* as early as December 1917 and the *Habanera* in 1924 with the accompaniment of Isidor Achron, who was also the accompanist at this Petrograd concert in 1915. Another major work on the program was the Grieg Sonata no. 3 in C Minor, a piece Heifetz performed several more times in Russia and also recorded and performed with Achron in the United States.

After the concert all the main city newspapers wrote glowingly of the boy's performance.[22] Reviews focused on Jascha's expressive and powerful tone and his astonishingly impeccable technique, which was only enhanced by the singing Tononi. "All this," emphasized the reviewer of *Obozrenie teatrov*, "serves as a monumental foundation, on which rests a deeply artistic style of performance and knowledge of the ideal goals of virtuosity . . ."[23] High praise came for the Sarasate pieces, which reviewers believed exhibited Jascha's natural taste and control of rhythm and sound. The reviewer of the *Birzhevye vedomosti* noted that although performers often exaggerate the Spanish pieces, Heifetz captured a more authentic Spanish style.[24] Jascha's intuitive playing of the Grieg also became a focus for reviewers. Grigory Timofeev observed that "in this sonata Heifetz showed other sides of his enormous talent. I do not think that he at his age could relate consciously to everything in the expression. But he understands the artistic essence purely through intuition. Nature itself controls his bow."[25]

Viktor Valter also wrote about the concert, observing how Jascha had developed since his first performance in St. Petersburg in April 1911:

> Four years have passed, and before us on the stage in place of a ten-year-old boy, with his little face and chubby hands reminiscent of Raphael angels, stands a youth, very much grown, slimmed down, not always knowing what to do with his long arms and long fingers. But in his lengthened face is still the same royal calm and simplicity of genius, and his playing is unique, inimitable, without rivals. By the beauty of sound, by the remarkable diversity of timbre in the cantilena and in passages, by the incomparable sonority of harmonics, by the blinding, fantastic, simply incomprehensible technique, Jascha Heifetz is now the only violinist in the world. Generally one very rarely sees in a concert such public excitement as one can observe when Heifetz plays, which in a mysterious way makes this boy the adored master of several hundred people completely unfamiliar to him. The divine power of musical genius![26]

Mark Rivesman gave Jascha another poem, this one entitled: "After the Concert":

> Once again your magic bow!
> Once again, inspired from on high,
> You soared like an angel above the crowd,
> In beauty divine, incorruptible . . .
> At times your melody
> Soothed, like a lovely prayer;
> At times angry, threatening,
> It sounded a summons to the field of battle . . .
> But once again loud sobbing resounds
> From the stage . . .
> One felt like weeping and screaming,
> Making known all one's suffering . . .

And once again the tender entreaty is heard,
Like words of consolation,
And the struggle seems easier,
And all doubts vanish . . .
Oh, be blessed, poet!
Feeling your warm affection,
I want to say, "Thank you!"[27]

Jascha's second concert in the Maly Hall took place a little over a month later, on April 8, 1915, again with the accompaniment of Isidor Achron.[28] The program mostly included works Jascha had played before in public, but not in Petrograd, including the Paganini Concerto, Aulin *Lullaby*, and Auer's Tarantella, all pieces Jascha had performed with Liachowsky during trips around Germany between 1912 and 1914. In addition, the program included for the first time Ferdinand David's edition of Corelli's *La Folia*, Mendelssohn's *Song Without Words* (arranged by Joseph Achron), and Edward Elgar's *La Capricieuse*.

Jascha's final piece in the Maly Hall was the brilliant and virtuosic *Carmen Fantasy* by Sarasate, which he had performed in Germany in 1912 but never before in Petrograd. The final notes of the piece were followed by a roar of applause.[29] Judging from Viktor Valter's review of the concert, however, not all in the audience shared this response:

> In this concert I had to hear talk of the coldness of Heifetz's playing, and for that reason I would like to say the following. For a significant part of the public, Heifetz's playing will probably always be cold. This public wants to see, and not hear, warmth of expression in the performance of music: for them a conductor, not making despairing motions with his arms, is dry, and a violinist, without his hair trembling or with other gestures expressing feelings, is cold. Jascha Heifetz belongs to those violinists giving emotional expression in the sounds of their playing, and not in gestures: Heifetz's pose when he plays is ideal in its noble simplicity.

After defending Jascha from the accusations of coldness, Valter made his own complaint: ". . . the program of the second concert . . . was poor in emotional content: there was not one piece which, like a composition of Beethoven, Chopin, Tchaikovsky, would force the hearts of listeners to beat with a sympathetic trembling. The choice of program from this point of view was unarguably unfortunate." Having written these few lines admonishing Jascha for his choice of program, however, Valter decided against publishing them, making a note on his manuscript: "Not sent to print."[30]

The day after the concert, a lengthy letter from an anonymous source arrived at the Heifetz home:

> Dear highly talented Jascha! I am one of your many admirers, and I would like to tell you several thoughts about yesterday's concert. . . . Yesterday, as always when listening to you, I was overwhelmed by the greatness of your immense talent, which reaches genius. I cannot in a few words express all the captivating, awesome delight which fills my soul when I hear your playing. But, despite that, I left the concert with a feeling of dissatisfaction and sadness.[31]

The reason for the sadness of this anonymous well-wisher closely resembled that described by Valter in his unpublished review: "The program of the concert did not reach truly artistic heights." In the view of the letter's author, several pieces in the concert were superficial and trite, including the Drigo-Auer *Valse Bluette* and the Auer Tarantella. The letter continued: "This concert created for me the impression of a painting by a great artist with astonishing mastery, but of a worthless and banal subject. Was it worth using so much art and talent for such an insipid work? . . . May God save you from playing up to the vulgar tastes of the wide masses—this is humiliating for the true artist . . ."

The timing, style, and content of the letter identify Viktor Valter as the author. Not wanting Jascha to know that it was from him, Valter had someone else write out the letter. He wished to inspire the boy from a distance: "You, Jascha, are an artist by the grace of God. Your mission is to raise our spirit, to tear it from earthly emptiness and point it toward the poetic world of wonderful artistic experiences and feelings. . . . You have achieved the highest technical perfection, and your technique is now only a means to achieve the greatest possibilities in the arena of musical art."

Valter cared deeply for the boy and worried that Jascha was missing out on a more general education, which was not surprising considering that home lessons with Kiselgof were interrupted constantly with concert tours and other events. Of course, the tours and trips widened Jascha's horizons enormously, but Valter believed that Jascha needed to foster the spiritual and emotional aspects of his character. To illustrate this, Valter's published review from the first of the two recent performances reads: "In the Wieniawski Fantasy on the theme from 'Faust' by Gounod, Heifetz performed the lyrical parts too quickly and without sufficient understanding of their emotional content. Probably the boy has never seen 'Faust' on stage and no one ever bothered to explain to him what the motifs used by Wieniawski for his fantasy illustrate."[32] Not limiting himself to mere suggestions, Valter set about widening Jascha's education by gifting him a complete collection of the works of Chekhov. The inscription on the first volume read: "To Dear Jascha Heifetz from his affectionate V. Valter. 13 April 1915." This impressive collection became a constant fixture in Heifetz's life, both in Petrograd and then later in the United States. After Heifetz's death, the Chekhov collection was kept in the home of his close friend Tamara Chapro, but by the mid-1990s, the first volume containing Valter's inscription disappeared without a trace.[33]

Valter's attempts to broaden Jascha's studies seemed to work, for in the coming year the boy was not overburdened with concerts, but rather continued his general education lessons regularly. Auer described this period of Jascha's development in his own memoirs:

> All the time of which I am speaking the Heifetz family remained in Russia, Jascha going to high school at the same time continuing his musical studies at the Conservatoire. During the season of 1915–1916, he made glorious first appearances both in St. Petersburg and in Moscow, at the symphonic concerts, rousing countrywide interest and overwhelmed with flattering offers from every side, offers which were but rarely accepted in view of the fact that his parents did not wish their son to neglect his studies.[34]

On April 14, just a week after his last performance, Jascha took part in a concert in what was previously Bolshoi Hall at the Petrograd Conservatory, but now belonged to the Theater of Musical Drama. The large hall was rented by the Society for Jewish Folk Music for its major annual concert, which traditionally took place in spring. Half of the profits from the concert were given to the Society for the Preservation of the Health of the Jewish Population and for Aid to Sufferers of War.[35] Over recent years, the leadership of the society had been scattered around the Russian Empire: Lazar Saminsky lived and taught in Tbilisi (Tiflis), Mikhail Gnesin in Rostov-on-Don, and Joseph Achron in Kharkov. Each one continued to organize concerts and lecture on Jewish folk music, and despite the wartime difficulties, they still periodically visited Petrograd, where they performed, lectured, and published various works. Around this time, a discussion began on the pages of the Jewish weekly *Rassvet,* between Lazar Saminsky and the Moscow composer Joel Engel, one of the first collectors and researchers of Jewish musical folklore (and a successful music critic— recall his thoughtful review of Jascha's Moscow performance two years earlier). The discussion in the pages of *Rassvet* centered on the question of whether Jewish folk song had its own voice, or, as Saminsky believed, that only the ancient synagogue chants constituted pure, unpolluted Jewish folk music.

The public discussion continued for years. In the midst of heated passions on both sides, a clear methodological problem emerged: that of prioritizing ethnomusicological research. In other words, deciding what to collect and how to collect it. In concerts similar to that in which Jascha participated on April 14, Jewish folk melodies were used successfully in modern compositional styles. The April 14 program included two new pieces by the composer Solomon Rosovsky—*A Nigun on a Sof* for woodwind orchestra and *Chasidic Nigun* for English horn and piano; along with piano arrangements by Ilya Aisberg; and an instrumental suite by Aleksandr Krein, entitled *Jewish Sketches.* Vocal music was represented in the miniatures of Moses (Mikhail) Milner and Lazar Saminsky. The overall performance standard was high, and the event included the world-famous contralto Anna Meichik, and other famous vocalists, such as Joseph Tomars and Maria Brian. Instrumentalists included the concert pianist Esfir Chernetskaya-Geshelina and the well-known accompanist Mikhail Bikhter. Accompanied by Isidor Achron, Jascha performed Joseph Achron's *Dance Improvisation,* and as an encore, the Saminsky *Lullaby.*

Despite the loud applause that greeted the performers in the hall, the sense of excitement normally present at these annual society concerts was subdued, since on the morning of the concert, news arrived from Moscow of the untimely death of the composer Alexander Scriabin. The sudden and premature death of the forty-three-year-old composer shocked Petrograd musicians, and a requiem service took place two days later. A telegram was sent to Moscow: "Students of the Petrograd Conservatory are shocked at the news of the death of dear A. N. Scriabin. The world is deprived of its brightest musical artist . . ."

The exam period at the Petrograd Conservatory, which had started on April 6, continued in spite of the terrible news from Moscow. Jascha's friend Maxim Olefsky received a 5 for harmony, and Pauline passed her piano exam successfully and was promoted to the upper course.[36] Once again, Jascha did not play an exam that spring, most probably because of his recent public concerts.[37] Instead, accompanied by his parents and Isidor Achron, he embarked on his first and only tour of the last half of the year, which took him to Odessa. Here he was scheduled to play a single concert, on April 25, to benefit the Ezras-Choilim Society for Alms to Poor Jews.

After months of war, the normal rhythm of life had been disrupted. Before the war, trains ran relatively punctually, but that now seemed like a luxury. As usual, Jascha wrote postcards from the train, including one to his sisters: "We left from Lida a half an hour ago. We are going [along] well, thank God, and we hope to arrive on time."[38] He sent the postcard at the next station, and a neat oval postmark on the postage stamps reads: "Baranovichi Polessk[aya] railroad 23.4.1915." The town of Baranovichi was approximately half way between St. Petersburg and Odessa. Judging from the stamps on the postcard, the postage price had nearly doubled since before the war.

The rest of the journey continued smoothly, and the Heifetz group arrived in Odessa as planned on April 24. The city's welcome for Jascha was heartfelt, since many people remembered the boy fondly. The next day, April 25, the public filled all the seats in the Dramatic Theater on Khersonskaya Street. Jascha's program included the Vitali Chaconne, the Lalo *Symphonie Espagnole*, Sarasate's *Carmen Fantasy*, and two pieces by Joseph Achron—*Hebrew Melody* and *Hebrew Dance*. The reviewer for the *Odesskie novosti* wrote: "The young concertant was a resounding success. He was greeted with loud applause and was applauded loudly after every piece. For a long while the public, demanding encores, did not disperse."[39]

A more detailed review appeared in the *Odesskie novosti* a few days after the performance: "In the reported concert, especially in the first half of the evening, a certain imprint of fatigue lay on Jascha Heifetz's playing."[40] The reason for this, according to the reviewer, was the outrageous behavior of the audience, which "made noise, yelled, knocked on the doors, did not let the performer begin. In a word what was observed is what happens at charity concerts..." The reviewer noted how Jascha had matured since the Odessa Exhibition concerts of 1911, when he charmed Odessa both with his talent and his childish looks: "Now, still only half-grown, Jascha Heifetz demands completely different treatment toward himself." This treatment, according to the reviewer, required a more objective review of the concert. Elements criticized in Jascha's performance included the interpretation of the Lalo *Symphonie Espagnole:* unfortunate phrasing in the first movement and a slow tempo in the third. Despite this, the reviewer stated that such impressive playing could only come from a true genius, "where talent goes in hand with critical thought, where instinctive sensitivity of musical perception will not dominate over the keen work of musical thought."

The conservatory graduation ceremony took place on May 9 and 10 back in Petrograd. These graduations were the fiftieth in the institution's history and garnered widespread attention. Nalbandian's student Andre Prang, who graduated from the conservatory with the Free Artist diploma and won the Mikhailovsky Palace Prize, attracted particular attention in the press: "For the first time in the conservatory's existence a fourteen-year-old youth has graduated from it. The young laureate entered the conservatory in 1911 and received his general education in the conservatory itself."[41] In purely performance terms, Jascha could easily also have graduated at the age of fourteen, but the absence of general education interfered, something Andre Prang received within the conservatory alongside his musical education. All that stood between Jascha and graduation from the conservatory was either an exam "in scholarly subjects," or a certificate of graduation from another institution of secondary education. As Viktor Valter had noted, Jascha still had some catching up to do.

The school year concluded and on May 21, Ruvin received his usual residency certificate from the conservatory office for the period starting October 1.[42] That summer Auer went to Norway because his usual trip to Loschwitz became impossible owing to the war. The Heifetzes, however, decided to spend the summer closer to home in a place called Luga, eighty-five miles from Petrograd along the Warsaw Railroad. The Heifetzes had passed through Luga each time they traveled by train to Vilnius, to Odessa, or further west to Germany. The area consisted of vast, mossy marshlands and pine forests. Many estates and dachas were located there. The composer Glinka, for example, spent time there in the 1830s, and it was there that he heard a folk melody from one of his coachmen, which he then used for the wedding song in his opera, *A Life for the Tsar* (1836). Rimsky-Korsakov had spent his summers in Luga for twenty-eight years, and, following his death, his son-in-law Maksimilian Steinberg lived there with his family.

According to the date stamped on their conservatory certificate by a local police officer, the Heifetzes arrived in Luga on May 28 and stayed at "House number one on Srednaya Zarechnaya and Malaya, by Yegorova."[43] Among photographs from this period in the Heifetz albums is an image of a two-story log building with a high pointed roof and a forest in the background.[44] On the second floor, directly above the entrance, is a glass-enclosed veranda, and wide windows look out to a lawn and a paved road leading up to the building. Like many of the photographs in the collection, the image is not captioned, but this building was likely the place the Heifetzes stayed in Luga; it was spacious enough to accommodate both the Heifetzes and the Sharfsteins. Anyuta Sharfstein-Koch recalled that the Schreibers (their Petrograd neighbors) also came to their summer house in Luga.

Luga had comparably little to offer compared to Loschwitz: no resort atmosphere, no tennis courts, and no funicular railways. The entire town consisted of just a few streets and a central square, the middle of which was often hidden under an enormous pool of rainwater nicknamed the "puddle triangle." Beyond the railroad was a picturesque park with rough and uneven pathways. Summertime often included children's festivals and amateur concerts, fun attractions, and hot air balloon flights. The town also housed a cinema that employed conservatory violinists to provide background music. In addition to a local summer theater, a circus attracted large audiences and included gymnastic displays, dare-devil jumps, trained dancing horses, and wrestlers.

The children spent their time riding bikes and playing in the pine forest with its June harvest of strawberries, blueberries, and raspberries; Jascha took various photographs of his sisters, cousin, and friends. Anyuta Sharfstein-Koch recalled a particularly unpleasant event that occurred that summer back in the house:

> We were playing tag—running around the house. And Elza ran through the door and she slammed it . . . Jascha was close behind . . . Jascha ran and stuck his hand right in the glass, breaking it and hurting his [right] hand and that was really a serious thing . . . for quite a while there was a lot of confusion and screaming and all that. And they were ready to do something to Elza— something drastic . . . He was lucky because it wasn't a deep cut, there wasn't a lot of blood . . . He was screaming at her, and naturally the whole family. . . . I ran away.[45]

The families remained in Luga for a long time. On August 15, the summer theater hosted a charity concert and the popular Petrograd singer Yakov Levitan performed with the accompaniment of Lyudmila Erbstein, a pianist familiar to the Heifetzes who often performed for the Society for Jewish Folk Music. On September 2, a postcard arrived from Kiselgof in Petrograd sending greetings to the Heifetzes for the Jewish New Year (Rosh Hashanah took place on August 27 and Yom Kippur on September 5). Kiselgof also passed on some news: "Auer returned, communicated with Achron concerning Jascha; he told him that you are in Luga and will soon arrive."[46] It was once again time to return to the city.

CHAPTER SEVENTEEN

The End of 1915

JASCHA HAD NOT SPENT AN AUTUMN in Petrograd for three years: in 1912 he toured Germany; in 1913, after a summer in Loschwitz, he played concerts in Berlin, Dresden, and Warsaw; and in 1914 the Heifetzes were detained in Germany until December. With its changeable weather and abundance of rainy days, September was nevertheless mild in the city. The beautiful yellow color of falling leaves resembled the gilded cupolas of the St. Nicholas Cathedral, which sparkled under the autumn sun, but within a few weeks this pleasant weather turned quickly into winter, bringing with it a mix of rain and snow.

Jascha and Pauline returned to the conservatory in the middle of September, and Ruvin received the customary residency certificate from the police station permitting him and his family to remain in the city until January 15, 1916.[1] After many years of service, Stanislav Gabel had recently resigned as conservatory inspector and was replaced by Professor Nikolai Lavrov, who now gave Ruvin the necessary papers for dealing with the police authorities. It was Lavrov who had examined Pauline back in January 1912 when she entered the conservatory, and he continued to be supportive of the Heifetz family. As director, Glazunov continued to approve Ruvin's enrollment in the conservatory, which allowed the Heifetzes to stay in the city. A significant readjustment, however, is apparent in Ruvin's residency certificates from September 1915 on. Ruvin had previously been registered as a "student of the conservatory," but was now listed as "capital." This change indicated that although he still resided in the city as a student, he was now supporting himself financially. Clearly, Jascha's concerts must have provided the family with enough to live on.

Glazunov turned fifty on July 29 (os) of that year and spent his birthday at his dacha in Ozerki, where he received hundreds of congratulatory messages and telegrams. In response to one of these, Glazunov wrote: "As much as all my friends and acquaintances wish me a 'continuation of your brilliant artistic activity,' this wish sounds somehow like a rebuke: for I left it already two years ago. Over the summer I composed almost nothing new, and did not even start trying to sort out the old things—I'm not in the mood . . ." Glazunov also expressed the opinion that "fifty years of life is not a reason for any kind of celebration."[2] Despite Glazunov's frustration, his music graced the autumn schedules of concert halls across Russia, and many famous musicians played his music, including Jascha, who was invited to perform Glazunov's concerto in various venues.

Around this time, Glazunov was involved in organizing a "Concert of Nationalities" in Petrograd to raise funds for refugees. The concert took place on October 3 and was held in the enormous Hall of the Opera Theater at the People's House. The war had continued to intensify, and by the fall of 1915, the Kaiser controlled not only Warsaw, but also Kaunas, Vilnius, Daugavpils, and Švenčionys. Since people of so many nationalities were in need of support, this benefit concert contained a truly multicultural program. In the first part, Glazunov conducted not only his own works (including a paraphrase of the Song of the Volga Boatmen), but also those of Russian and Polish composers, such as Glinka, Lyadov, Rimsky-Korsakov, Chopin, and Moniuszko. The conductor Alexander Aslanov directed an Armenian part of the concert, which included a performance by Nalbandian of Mikhail Ippolitov-Ivanov's Armenian Rhapsody, for violin solo and orchestra. The third part of the concert included Latvian, Lithuanian, and Estonian folk songs performed by a choir, and orchestral works by Latvian composer Andrejs Jurjāns and Estonian composer Artur Kapp. For the Jewish part of the concert, Glazunov invited popular Petrograd singers, who often appeared in concerts for the Society for Jewish Folk Music, as well as Jascha, who played popular pieces by Joseph Achron, including the *Hebrew Melody* and *Hebrew Lullaby*. Mark Golinkin, who directed the orchestra, was an experienced conductor who had worked with Chaliapin in a number of shows at the People's House.

As newspapers later reported, the event was a great success. People selling programs and flowers dressed up in national costumes and collected donations from the public, and during the interval, the famous singer, Nikolai Khodotov, sang with guitar accompaniment. A significant amount of money was raised, but nothing could solve the growing refugee problem in Petrograd. Men, women, and children overwhelmed the city shelters in search of warmth. As one newspaper wrote in October: "Petrograd is anxious, the people stand in front of stores, worrying about flour, bread, sugar."[3] Nobody knew that this was only the beginning.

In spite of the growing difficulties, musical life in the city continued with a number of special celebrations, including the twenty-fifth anniversary of the start of Chaliapin's career in September. Around the same time, Viktor Valter celebrated the twenty-fifth anniversary of his work. Back in February of that year, when Valter turned fifty, he had received the respected Order of St. Stanislav of the Third Degree. Valter received a letter from the Council for the Encouragement of Russian Composers and Musicians:

> The Council considers it a pleasant duty to send you sincere greetings on the occasion of your completion of twenty-five years of leadership in the quartet of the Petrograd Society for Chamber Music.... The Council highly values its well-established close relations with you and sends best wishes for the success of your further efforts toward the flourishing of chamber music.[4]

Petrograd newspapers wrote of Valter's natural ability to deal tactfully with the volatile politics of the music world, noting that he stayed out of the "squabbles" and "occupied himself only with his own direct business."[5] Jascha also sent his congratulations to Valter, enclosing a gift and a calling card with the inscription: "In honor of the twenty-fifth jubilee of highly respected and dear Viktor Grigoryevich. Petrograd. 1. XI 1915."[6]

At the start of November, Ruvin and Jascha traveled to Moscow for events celebrating Glazunov's fiftieth birthday. The four-hundred-mile journey from Petrograd to Moscow was well traveled by commuters, but Jascha had made the trip only twice before for performances in Moscow, in March 1913 and March 1914. The train departed Petrograd's Nikolaevsky Station in the evening and arrived at Moscow's Nikolaevsky Station the next morning. During wartime, these trains, plagued by delays and cancellations, carried crowds of refugees. One way or another, Jascha and his father arrived in Moscow on the morning of November 8, and took a fifteen-minute carriage ride to the Hotel National on Tverskaya Street. After a short rest at the hotel, Jascha attended a rehearsal in the Nezlobin Theater on Teatralnaya Square, where the next day he performed in a symphonic concert conducted by Serge Koussevitzky.

Toward the end of the first decade of the twentieth century, after securing his international reputation as a leading concert bassist, Koussevitzky turned his attention to conducting. His wife came from the family of the wealthy merchant Ushkov and helped Koussevitzky set up his own permanent orchestra with which he performed all the Beethoven symphonies in Moscow and St. Petersburg. Koussevitzky's subscription concerts in St. Petersburg and Moscow soon became as popular as those of Siloti, which had been held in St. Petersburg since 1903. By 1912, Koussevitzky was considered one of the most promising conductors in Moscow. Following his teacher Nikisch's example of popularizing Tchaikovsky's Fifth Symphony, Koussevitzky championed works by Scriabin such as *The Poem of Ecstasy* and *Prometheus: The Poem of Fire*. After immigrating to the United States in the mid-1920s, Koussevitzky became part of the international musical elite.

The performance on November 9 was the second of eight Moscow subscription concerts conducted by Koussevitzky and was dedicated to the works of Glazunov. The public responded enthusiastically to the event. In addition to the concerto performed by Jascha, Koussevitzky also conducted the symphonic miniature *Idillia*, Symphony no. 8, and the *Sea Fantasy*. Grigory Prokofiev, the famous pianist, Moscow Conservatory professor, and music critic, wrote that the Glazunov Concerto:

> ... was played by Mr. Heifetz, who not long ago at all was still called Jascha and played the role of a "miracle child." It is much to my liking that the gifted youth does not now exploit his age and is establishing himself in the ranks of stage greats, and it is pleasing to observe the public's friendly wel-

come to the artist and his great success. This success is fully deserved by Mr. Heifetz, for his violin sings simply, elegantly, and somehow directly from the depths of the soul. The purity of the young artist's playing is without reproach, his tone is also as flawlessly elegant, delicate, true, but with crystal transparency . . .[7]

Jascha's participation in the Koussevitzky subscription concerts was a significant event. Several years earlier, Valter had written with indignation at how well-funded music establishments in St. Petersburg and Moscow "literally did not lift a finger to come to Jascha's aid."[8] But now, with Jascha's growing fame, the invitation proved beneficial for both Jascha and the concert organizers.

Jascha returned to Petrograd, and soon after, Koussevitzky and his orchestra followed in preparation for a concert on December 15 with the same program as in Moscow. The Koussevitzky subscription concerts in Petrograd were held in the Hall of the Opera Theater at the People's House, the same venue used at the recent benefit concert arranged by Glazunov. The public filled the enormous hall and greeted the performers warmly, especially Glazunov, who was present. In response to the concert, Valter wrote:

> I don't know whether the composer had already heard his works performed in such a way, but he would probably agree if I said that you could not wish for a better performance. Koussevitzky . . . managed to understand and present to the listeners the architectonics of Glazunov's work, being a representative of the apollonic element of music, that is, the beauty of musical forms. . . . Koussevitzky achieves such results thanks to particularly fortunate conditions: he has his own wonderful orchestra with which he can hold as many rehearsals as he finds necessary.

Valter continued, turning his attention to Jascha's performance of the concerto:

> Jascha Heifetz played the violin concerto, and I think that with this enough is said . . . for all who follow the growth and development of this genius boy. By the way, Heifetz is no longer a boy but almost a youth (he will soon be fifteen), tall, who has already lost his childlike beauty and acquired that particular expression of seriousness natural to transitional age, seriousness which undoubtedly includes a shade of melancholy. Heifetz's playing reflects the same qualities that were also noted five years ago: an ideal and

simply fabulous technique which forces violinists to sigh with astonishment, but seeming to the public as if no difficulties exist in what Heifetz plays; an ideal nobility of expression which holds the young artist back from the temptation to impress the crowd with just one passage—Jascha Heifetz plays only for that God who lives in his soul, and it is a great fortune for art that this inborn nobility of character saves even the youth, as it saved the child, from the empty seductions of stage successes.[9]

The concert received relatively little attention in the general press. The critic Karatygin, who usually described Jascha's performances in detail, limited himself to mentioning the "solo movement played wonderfully by the highly talented young artist."[10] Meanwhile, the *Petrogradskaya gazeta* printed a review containing a glaring and telling error: "The soldier displayed complete mastery of the instrument. Despite his youth, he masterfully dealt with the difficulties inherent in the concerto. Great success came to him, and he was forced several times to play beyond the program."[11] The word "soldier" should have been "soloist," but with the war on everyone's mind, the error went unnoticed.

Over the course of the 1915–1916 concert season, Jascha would perform three concerts in the Maly Hall of the Petrograd Conservatory, with a month separating each one. The first took place on December 20 in part to benefit the conservatory infirmary. During these days, newspapers in Petrograd wrote of a bad cold that afflicted Professor Auer, and so Jascha performed without the watchful supervision of his teacher.[12] The hall was filled with enthusiastic admirers, and as Valter explained:

> The name of Heifetz graces symphony concerts with the highest honor; for Heifetz's concerts, one can get tickets only immediately upon their announcement; later on it is already impossible to get into that enchanted world. The large number of listeners who filled the Maly Hall of the conservatory confirms that Heifetz's playing really does transport us to an enchanted, fairytale world.[13]

Taking into consideration Valter's observations made earlier that year, Jascha played a varied and rich program, which included for the first time the Franck Sonata, a piece Jascha had heard Ysaÿe perform in Berlin two years earlier. When teaching the Franck Sonata, Auer focused his students' attention on the form and the thematic connections between the movements. "The whole work may be regarded," he felt, "as four evolutions of the human soul toward the Divine. Its sorrow is mystical: in playing the sonata the violinist has to express at times a feeling of anguish withheld, of tears which cannot flow. And the serene joy of the last movement is not of this earth."[14] The romantic expressiveness of the Franck Sonata and the delicate refined Grieg Sonata no. 3, which Heifetz played in the spring, were steps toward the impressionistic palette of Debussy, whose piano miniatures—in Heifetz's own arrangements and in the arrangements of others—made up an important part of the French composer's later output.

Jascha also performed works that he had not previously played in Petrograd, but were already featured in his repertoire for over a year, including Lalo's *Symphonie Espagnole,* Chopin's Nocturne in D Minor, and Paganini's *I Palpiti.* Jascha had studied this Paganini work with Auer in Loschwitz in 1913, but had not performed it in public before. A new work in Jascha's program was the Tchaikovsky *Valse-Scherzo* (arranged by Bezekirsky). This diverse program allowed Jascha to present many aspects of his remarkable talent. Valter responded positively: "Heifetz's success was exceptional, and the frenetic demand of the public for him to play more and more on top of the program was brought to an end only at eleven thirty when the hall was plunged into darkness."[15]

Two weeks later, another Auer student performed a similar solo program to Jascha's in the Maly Hall; twenty-year-old Myron Polyakin's performance included Sarasate's *Carmen Fantasy,* the Franck Sonata, and the Glazunov Concerto. Polyakin began his studies at the conservatory in 1908 and continued there until 1918 when he left, like Heifetz, on a foreign tour. By the time he left, Polyakin had not formally completed the conservatory requirements. About his playing, a journalist reviewing his Maly Hall concert in 1915 wrote: "At times one feels the drive to outward showiness. But it is impossible to reject the giftedness and ability he commands."[16] The perceived histrionics in Polyakin's playing provided the basis for later contrasts between him and the "Olympian" Heifetz, and several months later when both Polyakin and Heifetz toured the south of Russia, some reviewers identified a lack of "individualism" in Polyakin's playing.[17]

At the end of December a significant event occurred in Jascha's teenage life: he visited the State Savings Bank at 76 Fontanka, where he opened his first personal bank account and received his first bank book. The account was opened on December 29 with a deposit of one hundred and twenty five rubles.[18] From early on, Jascha's parents had set aside a ruble, and later ten rubles, for Jascha from each concert. Though many thousands of rubles went toward the family's living costs and also toward purchasing his Tononi violin, Jascha was proud of the one hundred and twenty five rubles in his own personal account.

On the very last evening of the 1915, the legendary aviator Sergei Utochkin, not yet forty, died from severe pulmonary disease. News of his premature death rang out like a final farewell to the youthful joys of the pre-war era. From now on, humanity would learn to associate the word "aircraft" with "bombing" instead of "progress." By the end of the year, which witnessed Jascha's continued growth and journey toward maturity, Russia had also grown up, losing much of the naïve patriotism that had accompanied the outbreak of the war.

CHAPTER EIGHTEEN

The First Half of 1916

THE ARRIVAL OF A NEW YEAR brought with it another conservatory exam period. On January 20—Jascha's fifteenth birthday— he successfully passed the mandatory viola class, and he received a 5 for both his written work and oral exam in the first level of required harmony.[1] The commission for the harmony exam included the experienced theorist Vasily Kalafati and two younger pedagogues, Semyon Bogatyrev and Aleksandr Zhitomirsky, the latter an active member of the Society for Jewish Folk Music.

For Jascha, the exam period culminated on January 27 with a concert in the Maly Hall, his second of the 1915–1916 season. Also in the Maly Hall shortly before Jascha's concert, Nalbandian had performed a benefit concert for Armenian refugees, with the piano accompaniment of Emanuel Bay and the organ accompaniment of Jacques Handschin. A Siloti subscription concert held at the Mariinsky Theater around this time caused quite a stir in presenting the premiere of conservatory student Sergei Prokofiev's Suite from *Ala i Lolli*. The performance of this new work divided audience opinion, and as newspapers reported, Glazunov "pointedly walked out and returned to the hall only after the end of the piece."[2] Whether or not fifteen-year-old Jascha fully understood the significance of these events is unknown, but Prokofiev's music expanded musical boundaries, flouting the established academic rules of harmony and counterpoint.

Jascha's solo concert on January 27 received excellent reviews, and he once again played without the presence of his professor, who during these days was on tour in Kiev. For the first time, Jascha played the popular Saint-Saëns Concerto no. 3, a piece Sarasate had premiered in Paris in 1881. Auer discussed the concerto with Saint-Saëns himself in Paris and often reminded his students of the composer's wishes. After Jascha's performance, the respected critic Karatygin wrote that "the Saint-Saëns was played magnificently."[3] Although Jascha performed this concerto several times over the coming months, he performed it only a few times as an adult and never recorded it.

Jascha concluded his performance with his first public performances of Paganini Caprices nos. 13 and 20 (arranged by Kreisler). Karatygin continued his review: "To the admiration Mr. Heifetz's playing aroused several years ago, a feeling of surprise is inescapably mingled: he played not only excellently, but considering his age, one might say supernaturally." Karatygin noted that although the boy was growing older, the "element of wonder has in no way weakened."

Jascha's third and final solo concert in Petrograd that season was nearly a month away, so the Heifetzes scheduled a concert tour of southern Russia for the intervening period. The family continued to rely solely on income from Jascha's concerts, and thus Jascha supported not only himself, but also eight other family members, including also the Sharfsteins. The day after the Petrograd recital, Jascha departed for Moscow with his accompanist Isidor Achron and both of his parents. Anna Heifetz gradually became more involved in organizing and planning concerts; her personality suited the role somewhat better than Ruvin's. Her internal strength and external calm had a disarming effect on entrepreneurs and officials; her appearance of detachment proved deceptive, since she was in fact very observant and quick-thinking. Her characteristic imperiousness was softened by her goodhearted sense of humor, which flowed from the same source of strength that allowed her to overcome myriad problems with a minimum of anguish. In later years, for example, when Jascha would arrive late for dinner, Anna would say something like "Well, let's think, what's the worst that could have happened?—Jascha might have died. But now—everyone's at the table. Let's have supper!"[4] Anna maintained a firm and unwavering faith in her son's destiny.

On their journey away from St. Petersburg during the remainder of January and into February 1916, the Heifetzes stopped in Moscow and stayed once more at the luxurious Hotel Palace on Bibikovsky Boulevard. On January 30, Jascha performed in the magnificent Bolshoi Theater. Despite many disruptions that season, concerts continued to be organized:

> Artists of the Bolshoi Theater Orchestra, after performing in symphony concerts for the Philharmonic and the Russian Music Societies, find themselves in the current season "without symphony business" as a result of the suspension of the symphony concerts. But they have found a way out of this situation, and have organized their own symphony concerts in the Bolshoi Theater.[5]

These newly organized concerts were conducted by Vasily Safonov, with whom Jascha had worked two years earlier in Vienna. The Moscow concert at the Bolshoi was dedicated to the works of Tchaikovsky and included the symphonic poem *The Storm,* Symphony no. 6, and the violin concerto with Jascha as soloist. The reactions of critics varied. Although some congratulated the conductor for his efforts, others criticized Safonov for selecting a "ramshackle" program and also complained about the steep ticket prices.[6]

The level of organization for the concerts at the Bolshoi Theater was, unfortunately, below par. A logistical issue on the day of Jascha's concert prevented him from performing the entire Tchaikovsky Concerto with orchestra, and thus he played only the first movement. The problem lay, most likely, in differences in the last movement of the concerto between Jascha's copy, in Auer's edition, and Safonov's score. Auer himself had foreseen potential difficulty with these changes: "I have—*with Tchaikovsky's consent and approval*—deleted a few repetitions. These cuts are exactly indicated. If the soloist is to play it with orchestra accompaniment he should have his own orchestra parts and an orchestra score, in which the cuts have been exactly entered . . ."[7] One wonders at the reaction of the short-tempered Safonov backstage after he discovered that Jascha was to play an altered version of the third movement. The guilty party in this debacle is not known for sure, but reviewers seemed to implicate the Heifetzes: "Mr. Heifetz, who in place of the Tchaikovsky Concerto played some fragments of it, has somewhat saddened us (they say there was no music, but this is not a justification, just an explanation). He disappointed us not because we so wanted to hear this concerto in full—it is not new and unknown—but more from a theoretical perspective, simply out of respect to the composer and the composition. The *Virtuosi* will probably never understand this."[8] Jascha tried to rectify the situation by playing the second movement of the concerto with Safonov's piano accompaniment, followed by Tchaikovsky's *Melodie* and *Valse-Scherzo,* and although the public reacted enthusiastically, the critics still held some reservations. Standing out among the reviews were the words of Joel Engel in *Teatr i muzyka:* "The artist (he is now around fifteen years old) delighted by his astonishing virtuosity, the impeccable purity of his singing tone, and his artistically wonderful musicality. This is certainly a miracle-boy, but in remembering his performance in Moscow two or three years ago, it must be said that Heifetz has progressed more in terms of his virtuosity than his artistry."[9]

During the trip, Jascha had planned to visit the museums in Moscow, but his schedule proved too taxing. "It was not possible to visit the Tretyakov Gallery," he wrote to Pauline, "but next time, in March, I will definitely go."[10] The Heifetzes spent very little time in Moscow—they arrived on January 29, Jascha performed the next day, and a day later they departed for Kiev. At some point during their stay, though, they found time to visit the Malkin family. After evacuating Vilnius, the Malkins now lived in Moscow along with the other teachers from the Vilnius music school in a building on Bolshoi Kozikhinsky Lane. Here, Jascha and Malkin's daughter Marusya agreed to once more correspond with each other.

On February 1, Jascha, his parents, and Isidor Achron arrived in Kiev, which had barely recovered from the effects of preventative evacuations ordered by Russian authorities. Many institutions, including the conservatory, had been moved temporarily to more Eastern regions and were just now returning. The Heifetzes last visited Kiev in December 1913, and at that time they met with Hyman Gerber, but Gerber, his wife, and his daughters Klara and Nyusya were now in the United States waiting for the Heifetzes to follow. After the previous year's summer invasion by the German army, which resulted in the loss of Warsaw, Kaunas, and Vilnius, the Russian command decided to begin evacuations in Kiev early, and by the start of autumn, many institutions in the city were transferred to the eastern borders. The conservatory started the academic year in Rostov-on-Don, but by the end of 1915, when the situation stabilized and the front settled along the Riga-Dvinsk-Baranovichi line, various Kiev institutions gradually began to return.

Jascha's tour included performances in Kiev on February 2 and 5, both in the Merchants' Club, a venue Jascha knew from his previous trip. Other famous names to perform in Kiev around this time included Sergei Rachmaninoff, who played a program of his and Scriabin's works, and Auer, who in the same hall on January 26 performed the sonatas of Grieg and Beethoven with a young pianist named Irina Eneri. "It was somewhat strange to hear L. S. Auer without Yesipova," wrote a Kiev newspaper. "Their relatively recent performance in the same hall is still in memory. But it would be unfair to say that the new ensemble turned out badly. . . . Let some unsatisfied people say that Mr. Auer's sound has become less pure, that the years make themselves felt and his arm does not command the bow as freely. . . . He is young, his playing has become younger and fresher than before."[11]

For his first Kiev performance, scheduled for February 2, Jascha played a similar program to the one he had recently presented in Petrograd, including the Lalo *Symphonie Espagnole*, Tchaikovsky *Valse-Scherzo*, and Chopin Nocturnes, adding other familiar pieces such as Corelli *La Folia*, and pieces by Aulin. Newspaper reviews reported the extremely positive reaction of the Kiev public: "The violinist's double and triple stops, double trills and quick-moving octaves, and harmonics astound in their captivating precision."[12] Reviewers noted that Jascha had matured over the last two years, and had developed "a thick, unusually warm and intimate tone, amazing and charming in the softness of sound."[13]

A surprisingly large number of reviews appeared in the Kiev newspapers, especially considering that much general attention was focused on military events that occurred the day after the concert. On February 3 (NS February 16), troops from the Russian Caucasian Army led by General Nikolai Yudenich took control of the Turkish city of Erzurum. All the newspaper front pages were dedicated to the military victory, including the usually music-oriented *Kievsky teatralny vestnik*. During the battle at Erzurum, the Turkish army lost over sixty thousand troops, including many who were captured. In contrast, the Russian army lost only a few thousand. This victorious operation inspired the Russian soldiers, filling them with pride and hope for the future.

This atmosphere of hope and jubilation greeted Jascha at his second Kiev performance on February 5, though the reviewer for *Vechernyaya gazeta* felt that the boy was "less on form than at the first concert." Jascha played a Handel sonata and the Saint-Saëns Concerto no. 3, which in the words of the reviewer, "remained foreign to the young artist, and only where he was permitted the possibility to shine with his exceptional technical gifts, for example the purity of harmonic notes in the second movement, did Mr. Heifetz accomplish with his task with unfathomable ease."[14] A review in *Kievlyanin* addressed the concerns of some in the audience: "Some observers claim that for all his technical virtues, Heifetz plays coldly. It is impossible to agree with this.... First of all he comprehends beauty, he has an excellent feel for dynamic nuance, the need for speeding or slowing of tempos, showing this child's instinctive impulse for musical feeling. The brilliance of his musical career still lies ahead."[15]

On the day of the concert, Jascha fulfilled a promise he had made to Pauline before leaving Petrograd. He sent her a postcard bearing an image of the famous Kiev Chain Bridge. "Dear Polyusya!" wrote Jascha, "... this is the huge bridge across the Dniepr (very beautiful, especially in summer, as you can see in this shot)."[16]

The next stop on the tour was Kharkov. Fortunately for the Heifetzes and Achron, they left Kiev on February 6, since the next day an unprecedented snowfall fell upon that city. Gusts of wind damaged roofs, power lines collapsed, and telephone lines stopped functioning. "Yesterday evening we left from Kiev," Jascha informed Pauline upon arrival in Kharkov, "we arrived here today in the morning with a delay of an hour and a half. Still, thank God. It could be worse!" The group stayed in the Hotel Metropol in the city center on Nikolaevskaya Square; despite having arrived safely, they worried at the lack of correspondence from Pauline in Petrograd.[17] "Why don't you write to us?" Jascha wrote bluntly to his sister. "I'm writing for the third time already. If you're not going to write, then I won't send you any more postcards. Mama is very worried and really wants you to write . . ." Jascha then resorted to harsher words: "Dear grouch! You think I'll keep writing to you? No, excuse me—this is the last time. It is clear you are a pig—not a holy one, just a stupid one. . . . Why doesn't anyone write to us? We hoped to receive a letter from you in Kiev, but there wasn't anything, I don't understand—why?[18] Pauline's silence was hardly intentional; wartime interrupted everything, including the mail.

On February 8, Jascha appeared at the Kharkov Opera Theater of the Merchants' Club, and performed the Tchaikovsky Concerto, Schubert's *Ave Maria*, Paganini's Caprice no. 24, Sarasate's *Carmen Fantasy*, and Kreisler's Sicilienne and Rigaudon. The audience reacted to Jascha's first Kharkov appearance with standing ovations and ceaseless applause: "Heifetz is a sensational phenomenon, there is no exaggeration in his glory, no hint of the 'margaric' halo of a miracle-child; his talent is a brightly shining precious stone, which has an equally valuable setting—fifteen years of age and excellent schooling. . . . Heifetz's noble phrasing forces the listener to involuntarily call this boy an aristocrat of his art . . ."[19] At the end of the concert the organizers repeatedly raised and lowered the curtain and turned the hall lights on and off for effect; critics described this as unnecessary sensationalism.[20]

During their time in Kharkov, the Heifetzes and Isidor Achron met with Isidor's older brother Joseph. On February 9, the day after Jascha's concert, Joseph Achron performed his recently published Violin Sonata in D Minor, op. 29, in the chamber gathering of the local division of the IRMO. Reviewers called the piece a "rich contribution to chamber violin literature," and noted Achron's inclination toward "the newest currents of musical modernism [and] contemporary harmonic daring."[21] Joseph Achron was also a successful pedagogue. He taught violin at the music school in Kharkov, and at the start of February newspapers in Petrograd wrote about the decision of the director of the IRMO to accept Joseph as a junior violin teacher at the Petrograd Conservatory, an offer he, however, never took.[22]

From Kharkov, Jascha, his parents, and Isidor traveled farther south to the city of Yekaterinoslav, almost a thousand miles from Petrograd. There they finally received news from home that all was well; a homesick Jascha wrote back to Pauline, also sending his greetings to Kiselgof, and to his beloved city: "Kiss Petrograd for me ..."[23]

Jascha performed only once in Yekaterinoslav, on February 11, in the Winter Theater, in a concert organized by Yosif Bakk. The program was the same as in Kharkov, and the reaction of the crowd proved just as enthusiastic. The visit to Yekaterinoslav also gave the Heifetzes the opportunity to see Uncle Natan, since after the onslaught of the German army in 1915, Natan and his family had relocated there from Warsaw. Natan taught music in an evacuated gymnasium and directed two local school choirs, and he also became involved with the local division of the Society for Jewish Folk Music.[24] Unfortunately for Jascha and Ruvin, they did not see Natan's wife Fanny or his two-year-old daughter Lyusya, since at this time both were staying in the Heifetz family's apartment in Petrograd. It is unclear how long they stayed in Petrograd, but at some point the apartment held even more undocumented people than usual.

From Yekaterinoslav the tour continued by train to the southern-most borders of the European part of the Russian Empire—the Caucasus—passing through Taganrog and Rostov-on-Don, and on to Vladikavkaz. From there the group took horse-drawn transport along the treacherous Georgian Military Road to the city of Tbilisi. This 120-mile road through the Caucasus was Jascha's first serious trip into the mountains. On leaving Vladikavkaz, the Heifetz party was presented with the astonishing sight of the Caucasus Mountains and Mount Kazbek with its snowy cap. Passing through the Dariel Ravine, the party eventually arrived at the pass, where a steep ascent took the travelers up to the highest peak of the journey, Krestovaya Gora. The road then continued along the mountain ledge with imposing cliffs on one side and breathtaking drops on the other. The descent passed along the cliff banks of the River Aragvi to its confluence with the River Kura and on to the city of Mtskheta, the ancient capital of Georgia. The banks of the Kura then led the travelers down through green slopes and into Tbilisi.

Located between mountains and rivers, the sprawling city of Tbilisi was an impressive sight: European-style streets in the newer areas contrasted with older streets filled with the cheerful hubbub of bazaars and dotted with brightly colored caravansaries and bustling taverns (dukhans). After the snow in Kiev and Kharkov, the group found Tbilisi vivid and spring-like in its relative warmth. They stayed on Golovinsky Prospekt, one of the most beautiful streets in the European quarter of the city, in a hotel neighboring the Artistic Society and the State Theater, where Jascha would perform.

Announcements for Jascha's concert appeared in the local newspapers, and a week before the concert the *Tiflissky listok* published a large article on the theme of child prodigies: "The upcoming performance in Tiflis of the genius boy-violinist Jascha Heifetz, who has managed, despite his young age, to become a celebrated virtuoso in Europe, evoked both joy for the coming enjoyment, but also a swarm of melancholy over the fates of other child prodigies."[25] Among these unfortunate prodigies, the author identified the violinist Konstantin Dumchev, who "did not manage to survive his talent, [and] not so long ago ended his own life." Here the author brazenly misrepresented the story for effect because in reality Dumchev had graduated from the Moscow Conservatory in 1902, toured Russia, China, Japan, and the United States from the age of eighteen, and he eventually passed away of natural causes in 1948 at the respectable age of sixty-nine. The author for the *Tiflissky listok* then turned his attention to Willy Ferrero, and with an exaggerated tone wrote of the conductor suffering because of "the monstrous greed of his parents and guardians." The author used the exaggerated stories to contrast with examples of prodigies who succeeded, including Josef Hofmann, and Heifetz, "... a genius lucky child receiving a proper and wise spiritual upbringing." As the author continues, in Heifetz's fortunate case, "we already without fear read recent reports, full of delight, from professors, famous musicians and critics regarding his recent concerts in St. Petersburg."

In the days leading up to Jascha's performance on February 16, the *Tiflissky listok* and the *Kavkazskoe slovo* published extensive biographical information about the boy and quoted the glowing comments of critics and musicians.[26] By the day of the concert despite the "highly inflated prices," the public filled the enormous Hall of the State Theater; many were turned away.[27] Although at a distance from other major cities, over the years, Tbilisi had attracted many famous musicians, including Tchaikovsky, Auer and Yesipova, Hofmann, and Rachmaninoff. The concert in which Jascha participated was part of the symphonic series organized by the Pouishnoff and Schweiger Music School, directed by Leff Pouishnoff, a young but prominent figure in Tbilisi musical life. After studying piano with Yesipova at the St. Petersburg Conservatory, Pouishnoff graduated in 1912 and began working as a piano teacher in the school of the Tbilisi division of the I R M O.[28] In addition to his talents as a pianist, Pouishnoff set up a concert bureau and a private music school with his pianist friend Adolf Schweiger. The well-respected concerts of the Pouishnoff and Schweiger Music School drew large audiences.

The February 16 concert included performances of Rimsky-Korsakov's *Scheherazade* and excerpts from Glazunov's ballet *Raymonda* and was conducted by Pouishnoff. For the first time, Jascha performed two large works in one concert, the Mendelssohn and Tchaikovsky concertos, with encores by Handel, Kreisler, and Popper. Applause filled the hall and the audience covered the stage with flowers. "Perfection—that is the word distinguishing the playing of the young violinist J. Heifetz," wrote the reviewer of the *Kavkazskoe slovo*. "Something unearthly, deeply touching," he continued, "is concealed in the singing softness of tone, in the remarkable strictness of rhythm, in the virginal purity of the smooth flowing sound—neither affect, nor effect, simply a prayer from a chaste soul. Like a river—wide, peaceful . . ." The reviewer saw an element of restraint in Jascha's performance style, but noted that

> this is not nonchalance; this is—passion, not willful indignation. Without feeling, pure and controlled, it is impossible to touch as Mr. Heifetz touches with his performance of the Andante in the Tchaikovsky and Mendelssohn concertos, in the Handel Largo. . . . He plays the finale of the Mendelssohn

Concerto not with the usual brio of a finale, but weaves a perfect transparent web of Mendelssohn's scherzo: it is reminiscent of the playing of the elves in A Midsummer Night's Dream. He plays the Caprice Viennois not with the usual Kreisler zeal, but with his restraint he reveals inexpressibly tender elegance. . . . Listening to the bewitching simplicity and beauty of this music, you see this wonderful character: rarely does nature endow even its chosen ones so richly . . .[29]

The reviewer for the *Zakavkazskaya rech* wrote:

The great beauty of Jascha Heifetz's performance lies in the confluence of an especially disciplined spirit, seriousness and internal obedience to the god of art who lives in his soul, with childish purity and radiant clarity of musical perception, not afflicted by any trait inherent to the adult performer, who already knows the poison of posing, that unnatural expression so beloved of the masses.[30]

The author of these words, Lazar Saminsky, was well-acquainted with the Heifetzes; a former student in the St. Petersburg Conservatory, Saminsky headed the musical committee of the Society for Jewish Folk Music after its founding in 1908 and oversaw composition work in the society. He settled in Tbilisi in 1911, where he taught at the local conservatory and the following season he became its director. He performed frequently in the Caucasus as a conductor, lecturer, and promoter of Jewish music, and maintained ties with his Petrograd colleagues in the society. The previous February he had written a report on biblical music and the past fall he presented a paper entitled: "Jewish Music, Its Past, Present, and Prospects" which was printed and used as concert notes in many Russian cities.

The Heifetzes met with other long-held acquaintances in Tbilisi, including the violinist and conductor Mikhail Wolf-Israel, who was now a soloist and concertmaster with the Tbilisi Opera Orchestra; Nikolai Nikolaev, the pianist, conductor, and director of the IRMO music school; and the Amiradzhibi family, the members of which, despite their aristocratic background, taught in the music school of the Georgian Philharmonic Society.

Amidst the many meetings with acquaintances and local establishment figures, Jascha found time for other more enjoyable activities, such as riding the funicular railway to the top of David Mountain, which looks out over the entire city. After his recent concert Jascha received a three-page letter that he now opened: "Read this letter when you are completely alone," wrote an unknown girl,

> and if it says to you even a small part of what was so radiant, bright and wonderful in my thoughts, I will be glad. Long, long ago, when I was still a young girl looking at the world in surprise, I loved fairytales. On long winter evenings I loved to sit and remember what I read in books—big ones, with colorful covers and beautiful drawings. In my imagination, reality was interwoven with dreams, and fairytales came to life, coming to life and then melting away again in the silent air. . . . A long time has passed since then. The fairytales have lost their luster and are in the past. In their place came life with its sadness and melancholy, doubts and tears. But somewhere there, in the depth of the soul, where even thought cannot penetrate, a fire of dream continued to burn. It called me to the unknowable, the nonexistent. . . . It promised that which is wonderful. And then came the day, the Day, that I will never forget . . . Scheherazade flashed by in a stormy dream. And I saw you—a slender young figure and face with sad eyes, sad like my fairytales. Why is there such grief in your violin playing, quiet and velvet, penetrating into the soul with inexpressible tenderness? Why did it awaken the sleeping fairytales of childhood within me?—I do not know. Are you really not a fairytale come to life? And have you not come into the world to force people to believe in beauty? I want, I dream, to see my fairytale face to face. To see a fairytale in real life. And although you are a young genius, and I am just a girl, who has only beautiful dreams, I ask you to fulfill my wish. Come on the 19th at 6 in the evening to the Kadet building.[31]

The girl with the beautiful dreams in Tbilisi was not the only one besotted with the sound of Jascha's violin. During those days he received yet another message: "Jascha! You surely received my awful flowers at the first symphony concert, and now I have composed a poem for you. I generally write poems, but I like my cello much more. We will probably never meet again and that makes me very sad. Farewell. Yuliya Reiman."[32] A poem attached to the letter bears the title "Music" with the note "dedicated to Jascha":

> Both grief and melancholy you express,
> You in the sounds of a golden string,
> Over a song you quietly weep
> And immediately your soul flies away
> Into your miraculous unearthly world . . .

On February 18, two days after his first Tbilisi concert, Jascha played in the Hall of the Artistic Society, not far from the State Theater. The program included familiar repertoire such as the Corelli *La Folia*, Lalo *Symphonie Espagnole*, Schubert *Ave Maria*, Paganini Caprice no. 24, and Sarasate *Carmen Fantasy*. "It is difficult to achieve greater success than that which the violinist had with the public. The hall trembled from the applause and demanded encores," attested the reviewer from *Kavkaz*.[33] "After Jascha Heifetz's second performance, impressions from the playing of the young violinist grew in width and depth," wrote the *Kavkazskoe slovo*:

> The acoustic conditions of the Hall of the Artistic Society were more favorable, in which the artist's tone seemed still deeper, fuller, clearer, the sound more varied, the nuances richer. . . . The emotional aspect also received a significant deepening this time, and again immediately, with the Corelli Variations, with their change of mood. Schubert's "Ave Maria" cannot be interpreted better: it reaches the boundaries of sound purity. . . . In the whole figure of the young artist, in the absolute restraint of movements, in the dispassionate and wonderful expression of his face this purity of emotion pours out . . .[34]

"I listened to you," again wrote the unknown girl, "and it seemed to me that everything around became better, more wonderful. I saw your sad face, and so wanted, torturously wanted, for a smile to sparkle on it, young, spring-like, like a ray of sun in the early morning. Did my violets say anything to you? I will never find this out. 'Never' is such a big word, and how much meaning is in it now for me . . ." Lamenting sorrowfully, the girl continued: "No! You didn't come. . . . And you, living fairytale, and you in the fetters of reality. . . . If sometime in the future we meet and you need support or you are suffering and lonely, remember that there is a girl who would consider herself lucky to help you. But for now farewell, living fairytale!"[35] In the starry velvet darkness of the southern night, the ecstatic dreams of the unknown girl were born and left unrequited, since for Jascha, it proved easier to stand before an audience of thousands than to find himself one on one with the unknown admirer.

Jascha played his third and final concert in Tbilisi on February 21, and that same day he remembered the promise he had made to Marusya Malkina in Moscow. On a postcard with a view of Kharkov he wrote: "Better late than never—isn't that right? I'm writing with a disgusting pen, and you'll probably have to struggle to read this. I'm writing to you from Tiflis, I unfortunately didn't manage to buy a local picture. . . . From here I soon leave for home and will write to you from there. Here it's very warm, 12 degrees, and in Petrograd –12 degrees [in Celsius]."[36] No further traces of their correspondence remain, and the next mention of the name Marusya appears thirty-seven years later in her father's obituary.[37] Ilya Malkin died in Brooklyn on July 18, 1953, at the age of eighty-seven, and according to the American newspapers, Malkin's daughters attended the funeral: Mrs. Margaret Malkin-Pierce (known as Ritochka in Russia), living in New York, and Mrs. Mary Gorshkova from Montreal (this was Marusya).

Jascha's third and final Tbilisi concert included Mendelssohn's *Song Without Words*, a Handel Sonata, Paganini caprices, and the Saint-Saëns *Havanaise* and Concerto no. 3. Reviews from the event attest to Jascha's success: "An enormous number of people gathered to hear this phenomenal artist,"[38] wrote the music critic for the newspaper *Kavkaz*. Nevertheless, the reviewer for the *Kavkazskoe slovo* felt that Jascha underperformed:

> Jascha Heifetz's farewell performance was not the best. The young artist spoiled us with the ideal perfection of his interpretation, and, listening to the harmonics in the Andantino of the Concerto in B Minor by Saint-Saëns or several passages from the Capriccio XX by Paganini, we knew that Jascha Heifetz could produce even more tender and singing harmonics, and neater passages. . . . Much, even very much, was good, but it was not the best that the artist has given during his visit.[39]

Even so, "the overflowing hall gave J. Heifetz an enthusiastic ovation," and he received a beautifully decorated dagger as a gift. Once again a sea of flowers covered the stage, among which may have been yet another bouquet of violets from the unknown girl.

With the concerts completed, the train carried Jascha and his party northward to cold and snowy Petrograd. A letter awaited Jascha on his return. It was addressed simply to "Petrograd. Conservatory. J. Heifetz," and was written by the same unknown girl from Tbilisi: "I saw how you left, I saw your face close with your big dark blue eyes and a smile fluttering about your lips, peaceful and clear. Your smile..." A return address appears at the end of the letter: "Tiflis. Krylovskaya, 8. Princess V. N. Amiradzhibi. To give to L." The letter continued: "My life before our meeting was very simple," wrote "L":

> A quiet and calm existence, outward peace and satisfaction, but inside, inside a fever of doubts, melancholies, disappointments and mistakes. Everything—exaggeratedly torturous, everything—woven of illusions. ... Now, at 18 years old, I can say just one thing: I'm too tired to turn away from beauty when I feel its breath on my face, when I see its radiant image. This is not just a saying. I am truly tired. I have been thinking a great deal, and those who think much tire early.... Between us is a great distance, but if you feel anything at all reading this letter, you'll answer me. It's difficult and awkward to write back to unknown people—you don't know what to write about... isn't that true? Yes, of course. But if a word, however simple, is valuable, if it gives many bright, wonderful minutes?... Write about your life. How was your trip? What are you up to? What are you reading?[40]

What was Jascha doing back in Petrograd? The usual—studying and preparing for his upcoming concerts in the city. What was he reading? Great works from the Russian language by authors such as Tolstoy and Nikolai Gogol and translations of foreign authors such as Dickens, Twain, Thackeray, Shakespeare, and Byron. On the family's bookshelves by the fireplace, next to the collection of Chekhov works from Valter, stood eighteen volumes of Dmitry Merezhkovsky. Jascha loved to recite poetry aloud and knew many poems by heart, especially those of Pushkin. After reading several verses, Jascha would then begin making puns out of the poetry, changing accents, playing around with the words and twisting their meanings. Similar fun and games took place also in the United States, where parties at the Heifetz home continued late into the night: "Jascha would sit on the kitchen stairs and recite nonsense verse in Russian, which he made up on the spot. Everyone was amused, even those... who spoke no Russian." The most attentive listener was often Jascha's mother, who laughed heartily at everything he said. Samuel Chotzinoff gave his own reaction: "For me, these deadpan, childlike performances were both amusing and touching. I had the feeling that Jascha set greater store by his success in the kitchen than in the concert hall."[41] Meanwhile, the eighteen-year-old girl in Tbilisi waited and waited, but it seems Jascha did not answer her. No more letters exist from the hand of the dreamy Tbilisi girl.

Heifetz's tour to Tbilisi brought about an unforeseen consequence. Lazar Saminsky published an article in the Petrograd journal *Yevreiskaya nedelya* entitled: "Jewish Musicians and their 'stage exoticism' (on the Concerts of Jascha Heifetz),"[42] in which he analyzed Jascha's Tbilisi performances. In the article, Saminsky set about addressing the growing mischaracterization of Jewish musicians and the so-called "Judaization" of European music. Essentially, Saminsky responded to those who believed that melodramatic acting and "stage exoticism" were traits inherent to the Jewish performance psyche. As an example of this mischaracterization, Saminsky quoted from a book by the author Wolfing, *Modernism and Music:* "All of these Osips, Yevseis, Grishas and Mishas are alike, like one great violin after another . . . the brightest of them, aware of the public's love for the 'exotic,' roll their eyes back or make prominent facial gestures while playing the cantilena; moreover, as a last resort, they over-do the vibrato to create a most sickly sweet southern passion, which is extremely unartistic and barbarically violates the European style."[43]

The book cited by Saminsky, *Modernism and Music,* is a collection of articles by the music critic and author Emil Medtner (1872–1936) writing under the pseudonym Wolfing. Emil Medtner was the older brother of the pianist and composer Nikolai Medtner and a close friend and confidant of Russian poet and writer Andrei Bely. In 1909, Medtner was one of the founders of the Moscow publisher Musaget, which published many works of the Russian Symbolist movement. Musaget published Medtner's *Modernism and Music* in 1912, but it contained articles that had appeared between 1907 and 1910 in the journal *Zolotoe runo.* In these articles Medtner criticized aspects of modern culture, which in his opinion had squandered its higher calling. He contrasted what he saw as the current decadence of art with the positive potential of symbolic art; he held the music of the old masters over that of modern composers. Against the musical modernism of Reger, Richard Strauss, and Vladimir Rebikov, Medtner contrasted German music of the so-called great era (from Bach to Wagner). Also, in the field of performance, Medtner placed the German "greats" above what he called "musical Judaism." According to Medtner, Jewish musicians failed to grasp the values of Aryan composers, and were responsible for the transformation of European art into "a hideous monster of the musical bazaar."[44]

Medtner was angry about the growing influence and importance of advertising, celebrity, and the increasing transformation of performance art into no more than a profit-making business. Of course, in a capitalist society, such a situation was inevitable. Only in a non-existent social utopia could the realm of performance art flourish, entirely away from the pressures and influences of profit and loss. Blinded by his virulent anti-Semitism, Medtner arrived at the conclusion that to resolve the situation would require a significant decrease in the number of Jews employed in the artistic sphere (by giving them a broader choice of profession). He also suggested replacing current performance institutions with amateur and community performing groups that would more closely represent the ethnic core of the nation. As much as Medtner foresaw and tried to deflect accusations of anti-Semitism, it is impossible to take anything else from his writings. Medtner's suggestion that the fight for true art required the removal of an entire group of people foreshadowed the ideas that led to the atrocities of the coming decades.

Russian society as a whole responded negatively to the release of *Modernism and Music* in 1912, and Jewish musicians in particular took great offense. In his 1916 article following Jascha's Tbilisi tour, Saminsky advanced claims made by the Moscow music commentator Leonid Sabaneev. Sabaneev wrote in 1912 that it was not Jews who were guilty of "stage exoticism," but Romanians, Hungarians, and Roma, with their "primitively exotic, black-eyed and materialistically passionate audience, posturing as the purest Aryan tribes."[45] Although Sabaneev and Saminsky set out to defuse Medtner's vicious attacks, they in turn ended up committing a similar offense.

Several lines in Medtner's 1912 book are dedicated to Heifetz: "I would be overjoyed if all that I say about Judaism was, if only for now, theoretical, and could be disproved. I would be even more overjoyed if out of Heifetz grew a Jewish, American, or Russian Beethoven. I would then unashamedly acknowledge that I made a mistake . . ."[46] Saminsky's 1916 response also drew on Heifetz's performance manner, referring to his restraint, his classical "objectivism," his artistic taste, and his noble appearance: "Such a phenomenon as Jascha Heifetz, from among the current Jewish performers, is an example of our new musical culture ... striving to reach the pure national-spiritual environment of our people. ... Heifetz ... is certainly the pride of our nation."[47]

Raised on a wave of resurgent interest in professionally oriented Jewish musical culture, Heifetz soon earned his place in its ranks, and on leaving Russia he became a prominent figure in the circle of famous Jewish artists. Rather poignantly, Wolfing's (Medtner's) biting words from 1912 were unwittingly paraphrased by George and Ira Gershwin in a humorous short song composed in the 1920s, "Mischa, Jascha, Toscha, Sascha ...";[48] otherwise known as Elman, Heifetz, Seidel, and Jacobsen. By the 1920s, all of these violinists were prominent on the American concert scene. Placed into a cosmopolitan and largely secular environment, however, many of these Jewish musicians grew apart from their traditional roots.

On February 29, 1916, just over a week after the farewell concert in Tbilisi, Jascha once again stepped onto the concert stage. He played his third and final performance for that 1915–1916 season in the Maly Hall of the Petrograd Conservatory. The program included the Tchaikovsky Concerto, Saint-Saëns's *Introduction and Rondo Capriccioso*, Bach's Chaconne, Schubert's *Ave Maria*, and Bazzini's *La Ronde des Lutins*. Viktor Valter's files contain a fascinating item from this performance—a calling card printed with the name "Jascha Heifetz," and on the reverse, a handwritten note: "Invitation. To the concert 29th of February 1916. 1st row, no. 4."[49]

A few weeks after the concert, a courier arrived at the Heifetz home with a letter for Jascha. The letter was a formal invitation from the "Director of the Petrograd Conservatory":

16 March 1916
    Dear Jascha Heifetz,
    The Russian Society for the Study of Jewish Life is organizing a musical and literary evening on March 22 in the Theatrical Hall of the Petrograd Conservatory and has authorized me to ask you to take part in it, in a performance with orchestra or with piano, with pieces of your choosing. It would be awkward for you to refuse, since the best literary and musical names are participating in the evening: M. Gorky, Kuprin, Merezhkovsky, S. Koussevitzky with his orchestra, Cherkasskaya, Tartakov, Siloti, and your humble

servant. I just called L. S. Auer by telephone, who informed me that you have only just left. He also advises you by all means to perform at the evening event on 22 March.

I will wait in the conservatory for your answer.

Sincerely devoted, A. Glazunov.[50]

The recently assembled Russian Society for the Study of Jewish Life was founded by representatives of the Russian intelligentsia to counterbalance the growing public antagonism toward Jews and their perceived dominance in musical circles and in the Russian world of business. (Russian businessmen profiting from the war apparently did not upset people as much.) Despite its sincere intentions, the very name of the new society created some friction. An article in the society's defense by the popular writer Maxim Gorky, "A Russian—to a Jew,"[51] appeared in the journal *Yevreiskaya nedelya* in 1916, presenting itself as an open letter to the publicist Baal-Makhshoves. The article was reprinted in many newspapers across Russia, reaching a large audience of Jews and fellow Russians. In the article, Gorky clarified and defended the goals of the new Society for the Study of Jewish Life. Gorky believed that since Russians were reasonable people, they would, once free from the dominance of foreign influence, accept Jews as fellow citizens. The efforts and achievements of the Jews should be valued in a country "as disorganized and stagnant as our Russia." And anyway, Gorky wrote, "humanity is united in the spheres of science, art, and on the basis of thought about the world . . ."

Jascha accepted the invitation of the Russian Society for the Study of Jewish Life, whose profits from the evening of music and literature would go strictly to charity. "The evening passed with remarkable success," Karatygin wrote in *Rech*. "Two orchestral pieces framed the program: Tchaikovsky's symphony poem 'Francesca da Rimini' under Koussevitzky's direction and, in the finale, the colorful 'Stenka Razin' by Glazunov under the direction of the composer."[52] The prima ballerina of the Mariinsky Theater, Olga Preobrazhenskaya, danced fragments from a Glazunov ballet, accompanied with four-hand piano played by Glazunov and Siloti, and Ivan Alchevsky sang romances by Gnesin and Rachmaninoff.

The literature part of the program should have included Maxim Gorky, but according to newspaper reports, the author was absent because of sickness. Pavel Milyukov proposed that all those present at the evening send a greetings telegram to Gorky. The famous lead actor of the Aleksandrovsky Theater, Pavel Samoilov, read Gorky's "Song of the Falcon," and Aleksandr Kuprin read his own "Demir-Kaia." Jascha participated in the musical section of the evening, performing Tchaikovsky's *Melodie* and Debussy's *La plus que lente,* both with the famous accompanist Mikhail Bikhter, whom Jascha had already heard in concert with Auer, Kreisler, and Chaliapin. This was Jascha's first performance with Bikhter.

For Jascha, meeting so many influential and important figures that evening proved unforgettable, and for the first time, he saw the chairman of the Kadets (the Constitutional Democrat Party)—an important reformist political party. Jascha had heard about the Kadets from Valter, since for many years Valter had worked for the *Rech* newspaper, a Kadet mouthpiece. His only disappointment that evening was not meeting Maxim Gorky.

The following months revolved around conservatory work for Jascha. Comprehensive exams took place between March 30 and April 1. Some confusion arose in the conservatory records, since at the time there were several students with the name Heifetz in the conservatory, including a full namesake, albeit with a different spelling of the surname—Heifitz.[53] In between his various travels, Jascha studied for his comprehensive exams with Viktor Belyaev, who had become an instructor at the conservatory immediately following his graduation from the same institution two years earlier. The comprehensive exams required knowledge of music history and the characteristics associated with each era, an understanding of counterpoint, an ability to analyze musical form, and knowledge of the acoustic characteristics of various musical instruments. Belyaev noted the results for Jascha's exam: for his written answer, a 5 -, for his oral analysis of musical forms, a 5.[54]

A textbook from Jascha's childhood kept in his archive is titled: "Instrumentation: Description of instrument pitch ranges used in modern symphonic and military orchestra. Compiled by Prof. of the St. Petersburg Conservatory A. Petrov."[55] Published in 1913, Russian conservatories and schools used this book as a methodical approach to learning the basics of instrumentation. Jascha scribbled notes and doodles in the margins. Near to the summary of instrument pitch ranges, Jascha wrote: "Learn it well!!!"

and on the same page is an unfinished line: "Ah, my friend . . ." Next to that, a sketch of a tearful face. Despite the humorous doodles, Jascha certainly must have worked hard. The inside of the back cover contains the course schedule: Thursday: seven in the evening; Sunday: eleven in the morning; Monday: eleven in the morning, and so on.

At the end of April Jascha took yet another exam, this time in mandatory piano, with a positive outcome: "excellent [5] . . . graduated with a diploma." In all, between January and April, Jascha completed exams in four required musical fields: harmony, comprehensive studies, viola, and piano. That spring, Jascha also completed an exam in his primary subject of violin playing. Next to Jascha's surname in Auer's class exam list for May 1916 stands the customary "5+."[56]

During the last week of May, the Heifetzes made a short trip to Odessa, where Jascha was scheduled to perform on May 26. This was already his fifth visit to Odessa. Just as it had the previous year, Jascha's solo concert took place in the Dramatic Theater on Khersonskaya Street, and was again a benefit, this time for the Society for Aiding the Needy Studying at the Wasserman School. Jascha performed with the local accompanist A. Benditsky, and the program contained works he knew well, but had never played in Odessa: the Saint-Saëns Concerto no. 3, the Chopin Nocturne in D, two Paganini caprices (nos. 13 and 20), the Bach Chaconne, Schubert's *Ave Maria,* Sarasate's *Malagueña* and *Habanera,* and Debussy's *La plus que lente.*[57] "The concert was an enormous success," wrote the *Odessky listok.*[58] A review appeared in the same paper the next day, beginning with a recollection of Jascha's earlier performances in Odessa:

> Never will we forget those evenings, when the whole public, like a single being, flocked to this miraculous child, who was able to make them rejoice, make them cry, pray, or to deeply sense the truly wonderful. . . . Only six years in all have passed. The power of time! . . . It is now no longer that Jascha who made the seasoned conductor Wolf-Israel in ecstasy lift him in his arms publicly to kiss him. . . . Now before us on the stage is Jascha Heifetz— already a young man with all the attributes of his age, starting with a man's suit.

According to the reviewer, these changes occurred not just externally; the clarity and calm that had distinguished Jascha as a child were replaced with maturity and awareness: "The drama of emotional experience is also close to him, just as clear as the romanticism of Chopin. And as with a genius artist, for him everything difficult and complicated comes out easily, freely, and wonderfully."[59]

Returning to Petrograd at the end of May, the Heifetzes spent the next month in the city, and on June 27, Jascha visited his bank. Since opening his account six months earlier, Jascha had stopped at the bank several times. According to the bankbook, on February 29 Jascha deposited 375 rubles from his tour of Moscow, Kiev, Kharkov, and Tbilisi.[60] On May 21, not long before his departure for Odessa, Jascha withdrew one hundred rubles. Now, at the end of June, Heifetz deposited 175 rubles, bringing his total to 575 rubles—not bad, for a teenager!

CHAPTER NINETEEN

The Second Half of 1916: Norway and Denmark

THE HEIFETZ FAMILY'S DECISION to spend the summer in Norway with Auer's violin colony was finalized in April when Ruvin received the necessary departure documents.[1] In Auer's book *My Long Life in Music,* he described his time in the suburbs of Christiania (now Oslo), the Norwegian capital:

> Beginning with the summer of 1915 I spent my vacations, until 1917, entirely in Norway, amid the gorgeous scenic surroundings of Christiania. One of my pupils, Maia Bang, a Norwegian who had gone to Russia to study with me despite the incertitude of the war times, persuaded me to go to her native land for my summer holidays, and I could only congratulate myself upon having followed her advice. Some of my English and American pupils who had remained in St. Petersburg, together with some Russians, a few Scandinavians from Stockholm and Copenhagen, and some Norwegians, gathered around me there in order to continue their studies. I was very comfortably established in the hotel-sanatorium "Voxenkollen," situated some 1,500 feet above sea-level, with a view over the mountains which seemed too beautiful for anything but a fairy tale. The mountain peaks were covered with snow and, together with the innumerable small lakes which glittered in the distance and the blue fjords round about Christiania, formed a picture, especially in the moonlight, which once seen could never be forgotten. There probably were a hundred guests in all at the "Voxenkollen," Russians,

Englishmen, Germans, and Scandinavians. In spite of the war raging over the entire world, we lived peacefully and contentedly, in good comradeship though without mad gayety, in this delightful retreat planted on the summit of a mountain verdant with pine and evergreens.[2]

Located on the banks of an enormous fjord, Christiania enjoyed cooler summers and milder winters than Petrograd. The area benefited from the warm Gulf Stream, and the Scandinavian mountains to the west defended it from the cold winds of the North Sea. As a result of frequent summer rain, Christiania boasted a luxuriant green countryside and parks that attracted many visitors. At this time the city was home to approximately 250,000 people. Developments during the second half of the nineteenth century gave the city an aura of modernity interspersed with reminders of its older history, such as the Old City and the Akershus Fortress. Foreign tourists packed the main thoroughfare, Karl Johans gate, which led to the Royal Palace. In addition to the beautiful parks and squares, other places of interest included the city's university, the National Theater, and the Historical Museum, located near three Viking ships in specially covered barns. The city suburbs also proved pleasant, and a stunning view of the city could be enjoyed from the slopes of Holmenkollen and Voksenkollen.

Norway's neutrality since the outbreak of war guaranteed security and peace to foreigners, including Russians. In contrast with Russia, where overfilled trains ran inconsistently, transportation in Norway functioned normally. The effects of the war in Norway were felt in the absence of expensive delicacies, but there was no shortage of general supplies. As Auer had predicted, conditions in the Norwegian capital were ideal for the summer vacation.

That summer, Toscha Seidel and his mother also received an invitation from Auer. The Seidels had been to Norway before, and Petrograd newspapers had written about that trip earlier in the year: "Seidel recently returned from Scandinavia, where he gave twenty-two concerts with great success. In Stockholm he played in the Royal Opera in the presence of the King, and in Christiania the Royal couple visited two of his concerts."[3] A new contract was concluded for a tour around Scandinavia for the coming autumn.

For the members of Auer's violin colony, the month of July involved both hard work and the chance to enjoy the beautiful surroundings. In August Auer made plans to acquaint the Norwegian public with Jascha and called on the help of an experienced impresario.

> It was then that a strange thing occurred. Toscha Seidel was returning to a country where he was known; his concerts for the autumn had been fixed long before. The name of Jascha Heifetz, however, was totally unknown to the great mass of the public yet his manager discovered in the library of one of the most important Christiania dailies a Berlin article of 1914, which gave a very enthusiastic account of Jascha's sensational début in that city at a symphonic concert conducted by Arthur Nikisch. It had been written by a Norwegian musician of high repute who chanced to be in Berlin at the time. This article, coming from an altogether unprejudiced source, aroused the interest of the public to such a degree that the house was entirely sold out when Heifetz gave his first concert, and the same held good for his succeeding ones.[4]

Auer forgot that Jascha's Berlin appearance with Nikisch had actually taken place in the autumn of 1912; Jascha did perform with Nikisch in 1914, but at the Gewandhaus in Leipzig. Regardless of which concert review the impresario found in the library files, the public was clearly interested. A week before Jascha's concert, the influential *Morgenbladet* wrote about Auer and the arrival in Christiania of three of his excellent students: Heifetz, Seidel, and Max Rosen.

On August 28 (os August 15), Jascha made his debut in Christiania at the Brødrene Hals' Konsertsal, and, with the accompaniment of Henriette Burgin, he played the Tchaikovsky Concerto, the Vitali Chaconne, and various short pieces from his ever-expanding repertoire. Many local newspapers wrote about the concert, including *Tidens Tegn, Socialdemokraten,* and *Dagbladet:* "His technical ability and security is exceptional, his easy and refined virtuosity was dazzling."[5] Of particular interest is a review in *Aftenposten* written by the famous Norwegian composer Hjalmar Borgstrøm:

> His technique must, without doubt, be considered perfect. With total ease Heifetz performs the most breakneck passages, fast runs in thirds, difficult octaves, high harmonics and everything else that normally poses problems to a violinist. And every single note can be heard, pure and in tune. But al-

though Heifetz masters all the virtuosic tricks, they are nevertheless not the focus of his performance. One soon notices that the young violinist is a sensitive musician. His playing is, in fact, not very fiery, nor does he have a big tone. But there is a quiet glow in his playing, which thus has a special depth to it. . . . His interpretation is full of beauty and poetry.[6]

A similar reaction followed Jascha's next two performances on August 30 and September 4 in the Logens Store Sal. The concerts included pieces Jascha knew well, such as the Mendelssohn Concerto, Lalo's *Symphonie Espagnole,* Chopin nocturnes, Paganini caprices, and Sarasate's *Malagueña* and *Habanera.* Jascha also played several new pieces, including *Arva* by Paul Juon, a professor at the Königliche Hochschule für Musik in Berlin whom Jascha had met in 1912. Swiss by nationality, Juon was born and raised in Russia, and his music contained not only Russian and German themes, but also Scandinavian ones. In the coming months Jascha played Juon's *Arva* several times in Norway, then in Denmark, and finally in Petrograd. Among the new works in Jascha's first Norwegian performances were compositions by Kreisler, including the Minuet (in the style of Nicola Porpora), and the Sicilienne and Rigaudon.

The *Morgenbladet* reported that "the extraordinarily talented virtuoso Jascha Heifetz played his second concert in Logesalen, whose seats were well occupied. This master of genius made an even stronger impression than last time."[7] At the third concert, Jascha played many encores, and the audience left only after the lights were switched off.[8] After the third concert, a pencil sketch of Jascha appeared in the pages of the *Morgenbladet,* which showed Jascha with a youthful long neck, tousled hair, and a sharply delineated profile—a far cry from the chubby cheeks and soft oval face so often described by earlier reviewers.

Toscha Seidel also performed in Christiania during this period, and as Auer wrote in his memoirs, "it is worthy of note that these two boys, Seidel and Heifetz, were not regarded as rivals, but shared equally the general favor accorded them. Their numerous concerts were given turn and turn about, and every seat in the hall was always filled by an enthusiastic audience."[9] Although the two boys were not necessarily considered to be rivals, the press did nonetheless make comparisons and even published rumors: "Jascha Heifetz is hardly as temperamental as his compatriot Toscha Seidel, he is less distinctive and 'Russian,' but, nevertheless, he is an exceptional masterplayer, and one can easily understand that the young Seidel, according to rumors, considers Jascha Heifetz as his complete superior when it comes to virtuosity."[10]

The King and Queen of Norway attended concerts by both Heifetz and Seidel, and invited the young musicians to perform at the royal summer residence. The previous year marked the tenth anniversary of that particular King's reign. Ten years earlier, the union joining Norway and Sweden under the authority of the Swedish king had been dissolved, and Prince Carl of Denmark, as he had been known, became King Haakon VII of Norway. By 1916, the forty-three-year-old Norwegian King was married to Princess Maude, daughter of English King Edward VII. Not long before the outbreak of war, in February 1914, Haakon VII had visited Russia, and photographs from the trip show him with his wife and his heir, the crown prince. In comparison with Russia under the Tsar, Norway boasted a more equalized society with a strong representative parliament.

The initiative behind the royal invitation to Heifetz and Seidel came from the Queen, a great music lover, so the Russian Ambassador Konstantin Gulkevich called Auer by telephone to pass along the invitation.[11] The Queen accepted Auer's proposal that his two students play the Bach Concerto for two violins (the same concerto they had performed successfully in Loschwitz), but she also insisted that the boys play alternate solo pieces, "somewhat in the style of a competitive concert." Both Heifetz and Seidel were excited by the invitation and as Auer recalled, "since they were good, amiable lads, they cheerfully agreed to do so rather than be spoilsports."[12] They were accompanied by Auer's accompanist and future wife Wanda Bogutska-Stein.

The lavish reception at the royal residence took place on September 6. "When the great day dawned," wrote Auer, "the Russian minister came in his car to call for Mme. Stein and the artists whom she was to chaperon and whose accompaniments she was to play." The car headed to the royal villa in the other suburb of Christiania. Auer recalled that the "royal couple received their guests in the most cordial manner." During intermissions, "the two boys ran races with the Prince Royal" in the beautiful gardens of the royal villa.[13] Prince Royal Alexander Edward Christian Frederick was just two and a half years younger than Jascha and was a willing participant in the games. The prince acceded to the throne forty years later in 1957; Jascha went on to perform several times in Norway in the intervening decades, in the presence of the royal couple and the prince. Both Heifetz and Prince Olav, as he was known, joined the allied efforts in World War II—Heifetz playing for the troops in Europe, and the Prince in the position of Chief of Defense of Norway.

After a few days of rest following the Christiania performances, Jascha headed westward to Bergen, Norway's second largest city, situated on the coast. Reports of the double violin performance at the royal residence spread throughout Norway, and, as Auer wrote in his memoirs, "the enthusiasm of the inhabitants in the capital and throughout the country for their playing was, if anything, increased."[14] As a result, Jascha's concerts in Bergen on September 15 and 19 both sold out. At the first Jascha performed the Tchaikovsky Concerto, and at the second he played the Mendelssohn Concerto, and in addition, both concerts included pieces by Schubert, Paganini, Chopin, Sarasate, and a number of Kreisler arrangements. Jascha toured the city and visited the Bergen Museum between the two concerts. After the second concert in Bergen, Jascha departed almost immediately for Christiania to prepare for a second series of performances in the capital.

This second series of concerts, as with the first, consisted of three evening performances, two in the Logens Store Sal, September 21 and 25, and a farewell concert on September 27 in the National Dramatic Theater. At the second of the concerts, for the first time, Jascha performed Auer's arrangements of both the *Chorus of Dervishes* and the *Turkish March* from Beethoven's music for *The Ruins of Athens*. These pieces appeared again in the coming months; he recorded both of them a year later during his earliest American recording sessions. Both pieces became important parts of his recital repertoire.

With the farewell concert completed successfully, the time came to leave Voksenkollen and head to Denmark for further concerts. Although the quickest route from Christiania to Copenhagen was by sea, during wartime such routes posed significant risks, especially after the destruction of the British passenger liner Lusitania, sunk off the coast of Ireland by German submarines just a year earlier. The safer route by rail between the two cities took the Heifetzes along the south of neutral Sweden, past Lake Vänern and through the port city of Gothenburg.

In contrast to neutral Sweden's pro-Germany position, and neutral Norway oriented toward the Entente, Danish neutrality proved to be somewhere in between. Close ties developed between Denmark and both English and German manufacturers, and though German submarine warfare negatively impacted the Danish economy, living standards in the country remained higher than in other warring nations.

The Heifetz family arrived in Copenhagen by October 1 and stayed for almost a month and a half. During that time, Jascha gave a total of eight concerts with the accompanist Henriette Burgin, six in the Odd Fellow-palæts Store Sal (October 2, 12, 19, 23, 26, and 30), and two in the Hall of the Royal Music Academy (October 9 and 17). Jascha's programs varied greatly; he performed concertos by Mendelssohn, Paganini, Tchaikovsky, and Bruch (G Minor), and the Lalo *Symphonie Espagnole*.

During their stay in Copenhagen, the Heifetzes entered into negotiations with the Haensel & Jones concert agency in New York for a possible tour of the United States and Canada between November 1917 and January 1918. This was already the third attempt to organize an American tour for Jascha. According to the wording of the contract, written in English and dated October 11, 1916, the concert agency entered into an agreement with "Mr. R. Heifetz, of Petrograd, Russia, the Father and duly authorized guardian and agent of Sasha [sic] Heifetz, a minor, hereinafter referred to as the 'Artist.'"[15] The contract stipulated a tour of at least ten performances (at $500 each) and as many more as possible during the period of the contract. Additionally, the agency offered a payment of $1,000 to cover hotel and travel expenses incurred as a result of the tour. To cover the expenses and the first ten concerts, the concert agency agreed to deposit an advance payment of $6,000 with the New York branch of the Crédit Lyonnais of Petrograd. The contract stipulated that the agency had the "sole right to negotiate and close contracts for the artist for Phonograph or Talking Machine Records," and they would take fifteen percent of all income made in the first year, and ten percent of subsequent royalties. Finally, the agency required that it have first refusal on engaging the artist for a second and third tour, with a commission of five percent from all payments. The signatures of the agency officials appear on the third and final page of the contract, just below the corporate embossed stamp. Ruvin's signature is missing. For whatever reason, the Haensel & Jones agency failed to convince the Heifetzes to sign.

With eight concerts scattered throughout October, the concert schedule in Copenhagen gave the Heifetzes at least some time to enjoy the city. By now, Jascha was used to turning up in a city by train, playing a concert, and returning home within a few days; in comparison, the trip to the Danish capital felt like a vacation. Located across two islands, Zealand and Amager, Copenhagen boasted many beautiful waterways and bridges, and the history of the city dated back to about five centuries before St. Petersburg-Petrograd. In addition to its rich history, the city offered its visitors a vast selection of stores and antique shops full of Danish porcelain, which at the time surpassed any other in Europe. Jascha paid particular attention to the many glazed figurines of birds and animals which he continued to add to his "zoo" on the fireplace mantel back in Petrograd. Also during this time in Copenhagen, Jascha began a new collection that would last into adulthood—souvenir silver teaspoons engraved on the handle with the year of purchase. In addition to the Copenhagen teaspoon from 1916, Jascha purchased others in 1932, 1938, 1940, 1943, and 1947.

After Jascha's final Copenhagen concert on October 30, the family departed for Petrograd. The two-week train journey took them through Sweden and Finland, and they arrived home at the start of November (os). Although the academic year had been scheduled to begin on September 9, the conservatory buildings were temporarily occupied for military purposes, so classes were postponed until the end of September.[16] Jascha and Pauline missed some classes, but not many.

Horrific changes occurred during the four months that the Heifetzes were absent from Petrograd. Inflated prices, worsening food scarcity, and the crumbling economy led to increasing hostility toward the war and the authorities. Anger grew in industrial and intellectual circles and was directed at those in power who exhibited an inability to manage the worsening situation. The Petrograd intelligentsia was reduced to poverty, and endless directives and pronouncements regulating the financial and economic life of the capital resulted in ever greater frustration and resentment.

Since the conservatory did not receive funds from the state, the directives did not apply to it. Nevertheless, a directive published at this time related to much-needed pay increases for government workers to match the substantial increase in living expenses. Since the conservatory faculty members were not technically covered by the directive, Glazunov tried to transfer the conservatory into the category of government agency, but faced a number of bureaucratic hurdles. While negotiations continued, some of the professors of the conservatory, according to the existing payment scheme, were being paid two and a half times less than voice teachers at the lowest level of the state school system.

Despite inflation and worsening overall conditions, the Heifetzes lived comfortably on the fees Jascha received from his concerts; the boy's personal savings continued to grow. That autumn, Jascha twice visited his bank on Fontanka. Though he withdrew three hundred rubles on November 18, on November 30 he deposited seven hundred—his share from the tours to Norway and Denmark. This left a balance of 975 rubles. Considering the considerable amount in Jascha's personal savings, one is left to wonder at the impressive state of his father's account at the Crédit Lyonnais in Petrograd.

That autumn, for the first time, Ruvin did not receive a residency certificate from the conservatory. The final such certificate was issued a year earlier and covered the period from September 2, 1915 through January 15, 1916, with an extension for another half-year until June 1, 1916. This document was Ruvin's last in the conservatory files, and with good reason. The military authorities undertook a rigorous investigation of students of draft age in all Petrograd educational institutions, including the conservatory. At the official request of the Town Governor, in January 1916 the conservatory produced a list of male students with an indication of their class, date of birth, and year of entry into the conservatory. Jascha and his father appear in the list as numbers 859 and 861.[17]

Ruvin's continuing presence on the conservatory lists became impossible during this period. Lore says that the Heifetzes obtained residency rights in Petrograd thanks to the assistance of various well-connected people. Among Auer's private students was the illegitimate daughter of the Grand Duke Nicholas Konstantinovich, Darya Chasovitina, who had also spent the summer in Christiania. To the envy of all the other Auer students, Darya played on her very own Stradivarius, and according to several accounts, it was she who out of admiration for Jascha and his talent helped the Heifetzes obtain a medallion from the Grand Duke with the engraved command: "To render any assistance to the bearer."[18]

Meanwhile, musical life in the capital continued. The coming season included six symphonic events by the IRMO, ten subscription evenings with the Court Orchestra, and a concert cycle by the orchestra of Count Sheremetyev. The Siloti Concerts began on September 24, and Siloti also organized chamber music evenings, organ recitals, and free daily folk concerts in the Hall of the City Duma. As a result of the ongoing war, European musicians no longer made the trip to Petrograd, and although this somewhat weakened the city's concert schedules, it opened up opportunities for local performers, including some of the conservatory instructors. Another peculiarity of the current concert season was the involvement of military personnel. The wartime draft included many young musicians, who on their arrival in Petrograd joined various military ensembles. The previous spring witnessed a concert by the symphony orchestra of the Izmailovsky Lifeguard Regiment, a division of the Imperial Guard, and the current season included performances by the orchestra of the Grenadier Regiment directed by Samuil Samosud and the orchestras of the Volyn and Preobrazhensky regiments.[19] Jascha's upcoming Petrograd performances were connected with the two latter groups.

In contrast to many of these new ensembles, the orchestra of the Preobrazhensky Lifeguard Regiment had performed concerts for many years. The orchestra included many talented musicians, even a conservatory gold medalist, former Auer student and old acquaintance of the Heifetzes, Mishel Piastro. Another prominent member, conductor and violist Vladimir Bakaleinikov, would later correspond with Jascha in the United States, sending humorous poetic verses in Russian and English. In the current season, the orchestra under Bakaleinikov's direction staged a series of folk concerts in Aleksandrovsky Hall of the City Duma and a cycle of six concerts dedicated to the work of Glazunov. Jascha performed in the first concert of the Glazunov cycle on November 29 in the Opera Theater of the People's House, with Glazunov guest-conducting. In addition to the

Glazunov Violin Concerto, the concert included the composer's first and second symphonies. Given that Glazunov invited Jascha to perform with him again and again, the boy's interpretation of the concerto no doubt impressed the composer greatly.

Reviews of the concert were mixed, with critics noting the clean but uninspired performances of the two Glazunov symphonies. According to one review, "the greatest success was the Violin Concerto performed by J. Heifetz. And not surprisingly, the inspired, bright music of this Concerto, in combination with the wonderful qualities of the performance, full of nobleness and artistic initiative, enlivened the mood of the public after the somewhat listless impression from the previous pieces."[20] Owing to the effects of wartime, the enormous hall at the People's House was almost half empty, but the audience still welcomed the soloist warmly, and requested many encores.[21]

The second ensemble Jascha performed with during the current season was the orchestra of the Volyn Lifeguard Regiment conducted by the recent conservatory graduate Mikhail Steiman. The orchestra's first concert took place on December 11 in the Hall of the Army and Navy on Liteiny Prospekt, and included a performance of Glazunov's Sixth Symphony.[22] The composer accepted applause after the symphony and then witnessed Jascha perform the Mendelssohn Concerto, which in the opinion of the press was played with a sense of style that kept Jascha from "the exaggeration of tragedy where there is none. One does not frequently come across an artist who so clearly understands the meaning of noble simplicity and clarity of performance."[23] Jascha played encores by Schubert, Corelli, and Beethoven, with the piano accompaniment of Rudolph Merwolf. Although this was the first time Jascha and Merwolf performed together, Jascha had seen Merwolf accompany both Kreisler and Ysaÿe in concert. The encores received a rebuke by reviewers who considered them disruptive to the atmosphere; rather unfairly, Jascha was blamed for encouraging the "great frenetic delight of the public."[24]

Performances with orchestra proved exciting for Jascha, but the current season also included no fewer than six solo recitals in the conservatory's Maly Hall. No other Auer student had performed so many prominent concerts in one season in the city; the large number of appearances reflected the ever-increasing demand to hear Jascha. The first of the six appearances took place on December 22: "Those wishing to listen turned out to number significantly more than the Maly Hall could hold," wrote the press. "Such determination by the public, by the way, was understandable, because J. Heifetz at the present time is an exceptional phenomenon."[25] In the absence of Isidor Achron, Jascha was once again accompanied by Mikhail Dulov. The recital consisted of works Jascha had performed before, including the Ernst *Concerto pathétique*, Beethoven Romance in F, and two pieces by Kreisler—*Tambourin Chinois* and Menuet (in the style of Porpora). The new pieces included Wagner's *Album Leaf* (Romance), Weber's Larghetto, the impressive "La Campanella" from the finale of Paganini's Concerto no. 2, and the Handel Sonata in D.

The choice of program evoked a variety of reactions from the critics. Some praised the Ernst Concerto for its technical and musical value, but others considered it musically meaningless and lightweight. Critics were similarly divided over the Kreisler pieces. The reviewer of *Muzykalny sovremennik* took the view that Jascha was not responsible for the choice of repertoire: "We will not subject the program of the concert to a particular critique, or use it to determine J. Heifetz's personal taste, because as a result of his young age, its compiler could hardly have related completely consciously to the selection of one or another piece, and, therefore, does not hold full responsibility."[26] In reality, Auer only partially interfered in the process of selecting repertoire for his students' concerts, so the reviewer's comments were slightly unfair and inaccurate. Besides, the program did contain a rich combination of repertoire by a large selection of composers of many nationalities, including German. On this particular point, Jascha was not criticized; the overly nationalistic feeling during the first months of the war, when Beethoven and Wagner were banished from concert programs, had long since dissipated. In this sense, Jascha was, already at this young age, holding music higher than politics, something he continued to do throughout his life.

There was no shortage of praise for Jascha, with many reviewers focusing on his technical abilities:

A distinctive feature of the performance of J. Heifetz is precisely his lightness and technical completeness. For him, scales and arpeggios to the highest registers on all strings sound identically clear and pure. Double harmonics ("La Campanella"), with which he brought the greatest delight to the public, sound like two flutes, but at the same time with a soft violin sound, like no flutes can do. But besides the technical side of Heifetz's playing, there is such beauty of sound and completeness of phrasing. The absence of rude strokes or cheap and tasteless nuances is also captivating.[27]

The responses attest to the high artistic level of Jascha's playing and to a performance style in which technical perfection was no longer dominant: "To acquire such technique as Heifetz has, so organically tied to the artistic possibilities of violin playing, so closely uniting the concrete tone with the spiritual element of music—here even the best teachers and years of study fall short . . ."[28]

Viktor Valter also commented in his own inimitable style: "Just as five years ago I considered the miraculous boy Jascha Heifetz a 'unique' violinist, so even now this youth, approaching adulthood, remains 'unique,' an artist beyond compare."[29] Valter felt convinced that no other violinist could play such octaves and double stops, and most importantly, that his faultless technique was not an end in itself, but "only a means for the re-creation of ideal beauty and expressiveness in music." Over the last five years, Valter had witnessed Jascha grow from a chubby-cheeked little prodigy into a thoughtful and masterful young artist, and under Valter's caring and steady influence, Jascha had broadened his intellectual and musical knowledge. For this, the boy would be forever grateful.

CHAPTER TWENTY

The First Half of 1917:
February Revolution

NO ONE COULD HAVE PREDICTED just how the political
and social unrest would develop during 1917. Military successes during the
previous year had created a sense of optimism; the hardships of the first
two years of the war were not felt as sharply in the expanses of the Russian
Empire as they were in other warring European countries. The autumn 1916
draft of thirteen million farmers, factory workers, and transportation workers, however, left the economy in total ruin. The Tsar, taking upon himself the responsibilities of commander-in-chief, was overburdened with
wartime affairs. Empress Alexandra Fyodorovna, meanwhile, mourned
the death on December 16 (os) of the controversial Russian Orthodox
mystic, Grigory Rasputin. He had served as her confidant and had been
successfully treating the bleeding episodes of her son, who was afflicted
with hemophilia, a condition the boy inherited from his mother. High-
society, monarchist conspirators, afraid of Rasputin's growing influence
on the royal family, murdered Rasputin, thus depriving the Empress of her
last hope in the fight with her son's illness.

For good reason, the country followed the reshuffling of the government with great apprehension. They had already witnessed a quick succes-
sion of prime ministers: after Ivan Goremykin, Boris Stürmer lasted only

ten months, then Alexander Trepov for just forty-eight days, followed by Prince Nikolai Golitsyn, who took the position shortly before the end of 1916. The government found itself in complete disarray. A modicum of hope rested on the State Duma, in which progressive forces gathered strength, including specifically the Kadet Party, the party favored by professors and industrialists alike. The famous Kadet publicist and ideologue, Yosif Gessen, wrote in *Rech's* New Year edition about the need to unite all of the political and social powers opposed to the Tsar's government, for "... only under such conditions is it possible to look the future in the eye bravely and not feel the harsh reality—however dismal and intolerable it be." The tumultuous events in Petrograd during the winter and spring of 1917 spared nobody, including Jascha. In the coming months he would perform at one of the concert-rallies amidst the leaders of the Kadets and the ideologues of the social-democratic movement, with the leaders of the General Jewish Workers' Union (Bund), and with representatives of the Councils (Soviets) of Workers' and Soldiers' Deputies.

Jascha turned sixteen in January. Seven years had passed since he had turned nine and had entered the conservatory for the first time. Following his debut in April 1911, Jascha had performed solo concerts in the conservatory's Maly Hall every year except during the 1913–1914 season. The season before last, there were two appearances at that venue, and three in the last year. The challenging task for Jascha this season was to put together a series of six programs. His repertoire had grown considerably, new works were added, and at his second performance, on January 9, he played for the first time the Mozart Concerto in A and the Wieniawski *Scherzo-Tarantella*. He never again played these pieces in Russia, but he would play them frequently in the future. His program on January 9 also included the *Grand Adagio* from Glazunov's ballet *Raymonda* and Paul Juon's *Arva*. The concert also featured the return of Isidor Achron, who had been away from Petrograd for almost a year, most probably as a result of the military draft. Jascha had developed a successful partnership with Achron over many performances, so his return prompted much pleasure for the Heifetzes.

Almost immediately after the Petrograd performance, Jascha and his entourage traveled to Estonia's second largest city, Yuryev (now Tartu), for a solo concert at Vanemuine Hall to benefit a Jewish primary school.

The January 12 concert included many well-worn pieces: the Mendelssohn Concerto, Schubert *Ave Maria,* a Chopin Nocturne, a Paganini Caprice, the Tchaikovsky *Melodie,* and a few Kreisler miniatures. This was Jascha's first appearance in this old university city and, despite the high admission prices, the hall was full. In the words of the music reviewer for the *Rizhsky vestnik:* "The performance of a talented concertant is a phenomenon far from commonplace in our musical life and therefore was met with delight by the gathered public."[1] According to both the public and the critics, this "young man, modest and shy," in no way resembled those nerve-wracked and sickly narcissistic characters, into which child prodigies "of the usual type" transform.

Jascha returned to Petrograd and on January 31 played his third Maly Hall concert of the season with a program of new works, including *Burlesque* and *Un poco triste* by Josef Suk, Gluck's *Melodie* (from the opera *Orpheus and Eurydice*) arranged by Kreisler, Gavotte-Rondo by Bach (likely from the Partita in E for solo violin), and a Scherzo by Tchaikovsky-Auer (probably from the cycle *Souvenir d'un lieu cher,* from which he had already performed the *Melodie*). The major piece on the program was the impressive Conus Concerto, a piece he had performed previously, but never in Petrograd.

Interest in Jascha's performances continued to grow, and, according to reports, tickets were sold out by the day of the concert.[2] The diverse audience at the Maly Hall included the Petrograd intelligentsia, music lovers, and conservatory teaching staff and students, many of whom managed entry into the hall without tickets. After the concert, Jascha received a handwritten letter from a female admirer:

> Tuesday Evening
>> Dear Jascha!
>> I'm writing to you having returned from the concert; you played incomparably, and I'm so thankful to you for that feeling of joy which I experience when I listen to you.
>
> I fear that our last meeting made a bad impression on you . . .[3]

Frustratingly, here the letter breaks off and no other pages survive. The admirer was a person of high royal rank, since a circular stamp with the letter M inside topped with an imperial crown adorns the left upper corner of the page. Unlike in Vienna, where the newspaper *Die Zeit* listed prominent attendees at concerts, the Russian press did not, and so the identity of the letter's author remains unclear. There were several females in the Russian imperial home at the start of 1917 whose names began with the letter M, including the Grand Duchess Maria Nikolaevna, the seventeen-year-old daughter of the Russian Tsar. She is unlikely to have been the author of the letter, since the children of the Tsar were raised under strict conditions in which socializing and corresponding with a musician and a commoner, not to mention a Jew, would have been enormously difficult. Another possibility is Maria Pavlovna the Younger (1890–1958), the cousin of Nicholas II. She married in 1908 but was divorced in 1914. Others with a name beginning with the letter M include the dowager Empress Maria Fydorovna and the Grand Duchess Maria Pavlovna, the wife of Grand Duke Vladimir Alexandrovich and the aunt of Nicholas II. Both of these women were enthusiastic music lovers. The first was seventy years old at the time, the second, over sixty; therefore both were allowed freer rein socially.

Irrespective of which member of the royal family jotted down the words, Jascha in later life never prided himself on his proximity to this powerful aristocratic world. He kept various documents relating to the political tensions of early 1917, but none as personal as the letter from the female royal known only as, "M."

Despite the countless protests and strikes sweeping through Petrograd, life in the conservatory continued as usual, and winter entrance exams took place in January. Ninety-five new students joined the conservatory, the majority of who, as a result of war, were female. Jascha's youngest sister Elza was among the new entrants.[4] Elza's entrance exam committee included Aleksandr Zhitomirsky and Nikolai Lavrov, and in the exam record under the column "General Musical Abilities," the committee noted: "Musical ear very good. Musical memory very good." As for Elza's piano playing, the committee wrote: "Excellent. Lower course. In Drozdov's class."[5] Now, no fewer than four of the Heifetz family could consider the St. Petersburg-Petrograd Conservatory their alma mater.

Although there were traditionally more girls than boys in the conservatory, especially in the piano class, the draft claimed many of the male students born in the 1890s and increased the customary imbalance. Of the ten students performing at a musical morning of Professor Drozdov's piano class held in the Maly Hall on February 2, 1917, seven were girls, including Pauline.[6] Her continuing development might not have received as much attention as that of her brother, but her program included impressive and challenging works such as Liszt's *Consolation* and his *Paraphrases de Concert* on a theme from Verdi's *Rigoletto*. The entire Heifetz family attended the concert. Another significant name appeared in the program, eighteen-year-old Maria Yudina, who later became one of the great pianists of the twentieth century.

The month of February 1917 was also rich with experiences for Jascha. On February 12 he participated in an evening of music and literature held in the studio of Nadezhda Dobychina. Dobychina founded her Art Bureau in 1911 to serve as a link between artists and the public. It represented the merging of an artistic workshop and an exhibition, where modern artists such as Chagall, Roerich, Goncharova, Dobuzhinsky, and Petrov-Vodkin displayed and sold their work. Dobychina's ten-room apartment by Petrograd's Field of Mars included six rooms set aside as exhibition spaces for gatherings that were attended by many famous names from literature and music, including Maxim Gorky, Chaliapin, and the young Prokofiev. The program from the February 12 event, to which Jascha was invited, included an impressive list of names.[7]

The program opened with Maxim Gorky reading the first chapter from his autobiographical tale *Childhood*—a novelty, since up to then it had been published only in newspapers. After Gorky, the actress Henriette Roggers of the French troupe of the Mikhailovsky Theater read Alfred de Vigny's poem *La Mort du Loup* (amusingly listed in the program as *l'amour du loup*). Then came the music of Wagner, with pianist Sofya Polotskaya-Yemtsova performing the "Magic Fire Music" from *The Valkyrie* as transcribed for piano by Louis Brassin. At that point, Jascha played Paganini Caprice no. 24 and a Chopin Nocturne. The second half of the event included the works of Prokofiev, and the entire experience made a strong impression on Jascha. Few teenagers could boast of such an opportunity: meeting a literary giant such as Maxim Gorky and the theater star Henriette Roggers, as well as hearing Prokofiev perform his own music, all in the space of one evening.

Other events during those February days, far from the sphere of art, took on a more sinister guise. The State Duma reconvened its session in mid-February, and although the authorities feared social unrest, it passed relatively peacefully. The first signs of tension appeared a week later, though, on February 23, when crowds gathered on the Vyborg side of the Neva River, on Nevsky Prospekt and the surrounding streets, to chant slogans, such as "Down with the war!" and "Bread, bread!" Meanwhile, the authorities assured the public that the city's stores of flour were sufficient and that shortages were occurring only as a result of panic buying and hoarding. These explanations failed to placate the crowds, and police arrived on foot and on horseback to disperse the growing numbers. The first fatalities were reported on February 24, and on February 25 the clashes escalated further. The city came to a standstill as people flooded the central streets. The Heifetzes felt grateful that they lived in a quiet neighborhood away from the center, even though various demonstrations and marches did pass through their area. From Admiralty Wharf, located close to the Heifetz home, large groups of striking workers moved toward Nevsky Prospekt. No shooting occurred in the Heifetz family's neighborhood, but a rifle and machine-gun cannonade on February 26 from the city center sent shudders of fear throughout the city. Early on February 27, reports emerged of mutinous soldiers, who by noon were already occupying the arsenal at the Peter and Paul Fortress and had released prisoners from the infamous Kresty prison and other jails. The Tsar, who had been at the military headquarters in Mogilev during the previous days, sent telegrams to Petrograd demanding that the government restore order to the city. By evening, however, groups of rebelling soldiers were already patrolling Petrograd streets.

Jascha's fourth Maly Hall concert of the season should have taken place that same day. From the middle of February, announcements for the concert had appeared in several local newspapers, and a program had been printed. Permission from the censor for the concert program was signed by the assistant to the town governor, Chamberlain Vladimir Lysogorsky, on February 23, 1917, the first day of disturbances, but prior to the shootings. The Heifetzes and others may have felt at that moment that the disturbances would gradually die away and that the concert would go ahead as planned, but by February 27, theaters and concert halls were all closed, newspapers ceased to circulate, and the city was declared under siege.

Although Jascha did not keep a copy of the February 27 printed program in his own archive, it was found in the collection of Valter, who on the cover crossed out the date and wrote: "Concert postponed—revolution. Concert given two weeks later, March 13th, under the new order."[8] The bloody and violent clashes that broke out that day led to the inevitable abdication of the Tsar and his heir Aleksei on March 2.

On March 5, newspaper headlines all read the same, whether from the anti-autocracy *Rech* or the royalist *Russkaya volya:* "The Old Power Has Fallen. Long Live Freedom! Long Live the Republic!" An agreement with the Petrograd Council of Workers' and Soldiers' Deputies led to the installment of the Provisional Government in the State Duma, and a measure of normality was reestablished. By March 7, tramlines in the city were restored, and educational institutions in Petrograd resumed classes on March 9. In an emergency meeting, the administration of the Petrograd Conservatory resolved to send a welcome telegram to the Provisional Government, in which it promised "to direct all efforts in service to the glory of the arts of our free and great homeland."[9]

On the day conservatory classes resumed, Jascha received a handwritten note:

> To Mr. Jascha Heifetz
> Yekateringofsky Prospekt
> no. 115, apt. 3.
> 9 March 1917
> We all sincerely greet you as a free citizen and wish you much, much happiness on your new path.
>
> Free citizens: Ida, Vera, Mary, Kitty, Lilly, Lyusya, Ira, Nina.[10]

The free citizens rejoiced, but for Jascha and his family the celebrations were tainted by a criminal event that occurred during these days. During an interview in the 1920s, when asked about this period of political turmoil in Russia, Jascha explained that his family had "experienced some difficulties." He continued:

... the lives of people and their property [in Petrograd] were in constant danger of pillagers and ordinary burglars, who, pretending to be political emissaries for the purpose of preserving the "safety of the Republic," invaded the homes of well-to-do citizens. One evening three criminals, dressed as soldiers, suddenly entered our apartment and requested to search it for a political fugitive. There was no alternative. The "soldiers" drove the family at revolver point into one of the rooms and threatened to shoot, if anyone ventured out. Half an hour later, when all the noise had died away, we came out of our enforced prison, to find that the place had been thoroughly ransacked and many valuables taken.[11]

With the opening of the city's jails, political prisoners and also criminals roamed the streets, and it was probably the latter that were responsible for the robbery. Further details appeared in a letter Jascha received from Lyudmila Erbstein on March 9, 1917. Erbstein was a pianist and accompanist who had visited Luga for concerts in the summer of 1915 while the Heifetzes vacationed there, and she often performed for the Society for Jewish Folk Music. She and her husband, a successful doctor specializing in diseases of the throat, lived in the center of Petrograd, on Kuznechny Lane, not far from Vladimirsky Square, and the tumultuous days and nights of the February Revolution also brought them considerable worry. Nearby, on Nikolaevskaya Street, the apartment of the tsarist War Minster Belyaev was raided and looted, and other nearby apartments of the wealthy on Razyezhaya Street and Nevsky Prospekt suffered similar fates. "Dear Jascha!" Lyudmila began.

Yesterday I found out about the unpleasantness that befell you. Horrible, simply horrible, that these moments of bright, happy liberation from under the yoke of our former *oprichniki* have been darkened for you by this ugly act of hooliganism. I also regret that you have lost your watch, the souvenir and gift you received in childhood. I can easily imagine the fright and worry of your parents! ... That which awaits you in life, I think, will reward you a hundredfold for this small sacrifice to the great revolution; and let it be a comfort to you, that in these historical days of unusual sufferings, you were no stranger to both the joys and the sorrows connected with them. ... Nature and fate have given you so much personally, Jascha, and your parents, that you have to make some kind of sacrificial offering to fate itself. Just think for a minute what danger you were all in during the time of scarlet fever in your home! If one of you had become ill with even the lightest scarlet fever—that would have been a hundred times worse. ... I have no doubt that you will soon forget about this grief. When only I can—I will come to you. Sincere greetings to all your family. Tonya and Mirushka are terribly grieved over what has happened with you. With my whole heart loving you like my own son,

L. Erbstein[12]

This was hardly the first time in his young life that Jascha had confronted the duality of joy and sorrow, but this time he lost something special and symbolic—the souvenir watch given to him by a monarch at just ten years of age. Regardless, Jascha and his family escaped any serious physical harm. Meanwhile, the revolution had forced the Tsar and the rest of the imperial household out of Petrograd.

Public entertainment in the city began again on March 12, and, as the capital's newspapers triumphantly announced, all the halls and theaters were full. Soldiers filled the first rows and the director's box of the former Imperial Aleksandrinsky Theater, now called the State Aleksandrinsky Theater. Several days later, the same newspapers lamented that an antique bronze timepiece in a case had disappeared from the director's box.

Jascha's fourth concert, canceled because of the revolution, was not rescheduled, so of the six performances planned for that season, only five took place—three before the revolution and two after. To use the words of Lyudmila Erbstein, the missed February 27 concert, along with the sto-len watch, became a "sacrifice to the great revolution." The unplayed program included Sarasate's *Zigeunerweisen* and various new works, such as the Bruch Concerto no. 2, Tartini-Kreisler Fugue, and Kreisler's Scherzo (in the style of Dittersdorf). During the few remaining months in Russia, Jascha did not perform any of these pieces.

Despite the unfortunate incident, the Heifetzes could not avoid the atmosphere of joy and optimism surrounding them. The main and only source of reliable information during this period continued to be the printed press. By the age of sixteen, Jascha knew the political affiliations of the most popular publications. *Rech*, which published Valter's reviews, was a mouthpiece for the Kadet Party, whose members now formed three-quarters of the new Provisional Government. Another popular newspaper, *Den*, also took a left-liberal position, albeit with a different focus: it supported the views of the social-democratic Mensheviks and Socialist Revolutionaries (SRs). Owing to the turbulent events in the city, the distribution of Petrograd newspapers ceased entirely between February 28 and March 5, and during the first week of the February Revolution, only *Izvestia* was published. It served as the print organ of the recently founded Petrograd Council of Workers' and Soldiers' Deputies, in which the Mensheviks and SRs played a prominent role. Jascha kept the twelfth issue of *Izvestia* (March 11) among his souvenirs.[13]

Jascha's two post-revolution concerts took place on March 13 and 20. He played the Vitali Chaconne, Wieniawski Concerto no. 2 and *Faust Fantasy,* as well as new pieces such as Paganini's "God Save the King" Variations, and Bruch's *Scottish Fantasy.* He had begun studying the *Scottish Fantasy* as early as 1913, but this was the first time he performed it in concert. Another new work was the Joseph Achron Suite (in the old style), op. 21, a piece written long before the composer's most popular pieces on Jewish themes.

Reviews of these two post-revolution concerts did not appear in the pages of Petrograd newspapers because there was neither space for, nor widespread interest in, musical life. Since the end of February, the bodies of those killed during the revolution had remained in the morgues of the city hospitals, but on March 23, the city buried these victims. Accompanied by a gun salute from the Peter and Paul Fortress, 184 coffins were deposited into a communal grave on the Field of Mars. A red flag flew nearby, and a banner carried the slogan: "Let your holy blood be spilled to the last for the freedom of the motherland!" Despite the gloomy weather, more than three hundred thousand Petrograd citizens joined the funeral ceremony. Throughout March, cinemas showed a film entitled *Great Russian Revolution of 1917 in Petrograd.* A week later another film began showing, *Funeral of the Victims of the Revolution.* These films, which included images from the days of the revolution, were shown in every major Russian city.

After such turbulence, the country thirsted for renewal. The Orthodox Church started this process by removing the prayer for the health of the Tsar and his family from the church service. Debate then began over the issue of a new national anthem; various possibilities were suggested, including a version of Dmitry Bortnyansky's "Kol Slaven," Mikhail Glinka's chorus "Slavsya" (from his opera *A Life for the Tsar,* 1836), and the folk song "Dubinushka." New works were also composed, including music by Alexander Grechaninov to the words of the poet Konstantin Balmont. A concert-rally took place at the Mariinsky Theater on March 26, during which Chaliapin sang his own composition, "Song of the Revolution," accompanied by choir and two orchestras. Debate also raged over the renaming of streets and squares, and by the start of April, the Petrograd City Council, commissioned by the City Duma, put forward several proposals. These included changing Palace Square to 28th of February Square, Palace Embankment to Embankment of Freedom, and Mikhailovskaya Street to the Street of Brotherhood. A proposal arose to rename the Court Orchestra as the National Orchestra, but it eventually became simply the State Orchestra.

Regardless of such regenerative efforts, the economy remained in a state of exhaustion and near-collapse, and serious problems plagued the worsening transportation system. Owing to the impact these difficulties had on Jascha's ability to earn concert fees—the family's sole source of income—the Heifetzes decided to undertake a tour around the cities of southern Russia. At the start of April, Jascha departed Petrograd with his parents and Isidor Achron, unaware of the difficulties that would await the group.

They headed south, stopping in Moscow, where on April 6 Jascha gave a solo concert in the 900-seat Bolshoi Hall of the Polytechnic Museum (Museum of Applied Knowledge). The concert was held to benefit the Fund for Mutual Help of Jewish Students of the Riga Polytechnic Institute, and Jascha performed much of his tried and tested repertoire, including the Vitali Chaconne, Paganini Concerto no. 1, Beethoven *Chorus of Dervishes, Turkish March,* and Romance in G, Chopin Nocturnes, Kreisler *Tamborin Chinois,* and Wieniawski Polonaise in A. During the following twenty days, Jascha would give eleven solo concerts, in which he performed concertos by Tchaikovsky, Wieniawski, Paganini, and Mendelssohn, and many miniatures.

From Moscow, Jascha, his parents, and Achron headed for Kiev for two performances at the Merchants' Club, a venue in which Jascha had previously played twice. Announcements for the two present concerts began appearing in the local newspapers on March 21, and by the day of the first performance, April 9, all the tickets were sold.[14] A ferocious snowstorm hit the city on the day of the concert. This was of course not the first time the Heifetzes had experienced bad weather in Kiev. Jascha's second concert in Kiev took place two days later, on April 11. Unable to enjoy the city because of the bad weather, Jascha spent time during his free day writing letters home to Petrograd. An incomplete postcard written in French to his French language teacher Augusta Girardot survives:

> Mademoiselle Augusta Girardot
> Gorokhovaya St., 19, Apt. 4.
> Petrograd.
> Kiew. 10. Avril.
>   Je me donne la peine d'écrire a vous. Cela ne me plais pas beaucoup, mais il faut tenir . . . [I'm taking the time to write to you. It doesn't please me much, but I'm doing it anyway . . .][15]

Although Jascha struggled with his letter to Madame Girardot, over time his French improved, and in later years newspapers commented upon his language skills: "This extremely erudite person speaks an impressive number of foreign languages: French perfectly, and especially French slang, which he is always trying to perfect."[16]

Following the second Kiev concert, on April 12, the Heifetzes and Achron left the city, and not a moment too soon. The flooding worsened dramatically, and by the evening, power to most of the city had been cut. They headed southeast to Yekaterinoslav, where they were greeted by Uncle Natan and Aunt Fanny. Jascha was scheduled to perform in the local Bolshoi Theater on April 14, and on the day of the concert, the *Pridneprovsky krai* wrote: "Jascha Heifetz has arrived from Kiev, where he had two concerts playing to full houses."[17] By the evening of April 14, with the Dniepr River more than six-and-a-half meters higher than usual, flooding also engulfed Yekaterinoslav, and Jascha's concert was canceled.[18] The flooding even threatened to surpass the previous record set in 1845, when flood waters caused significant destruction and left many victims in its wake. The waters continued to rise dangerously until noon the next day. Jascha's concert was rescheduled for April 15, after which a reviewer wrote: "the concert went very successfully; the gifted violinist showed himself at his best and introduced the public to his brilliant technique and intonation, rare in its purity."[19]

The Heifetz party left Yekaterinoslav on April 16 with a plan to return to the city toward the end of the month so that Jascha could give another concert, but unforeseen circumstances would make that impossible. They continued to Kharkov, the city that had welcomed Jascha so warmly back in February 1916, and the home of Joseph Achron. Unlike Kiev and Yekaterinoslav, Kharkov was free of flooding, but daily life in the city had worsened considerably as a result of the ongoing war. At a recent joint meeting of the city coal production commission and the production commission of the Council of Workers' and Soldiers' Deputies, participants had discussed the introduction of bread ration cards as a last resort to combat growing hunger, and it was determined that each person would receive one pound of bread per day.

The Heifetzes and Achron arrived in Kharkov on April 17, and that same evening Jascha performed in the local Maly Theater. A second performance in Kharkov was scheduled for April 21, and in the intervening days, Jascha and the group headed to the city of Poltava for yet another concert. This was Jascha's first visit to Poltava, an important regional capital with a long and impressive history. In 1709, Poltava had witnessed the victory of Peter the Great over Swedish forces, an event that remained firmly fixed in the minds of the locals. The city also boasted links to many literary figures. Gogol had studied in the city a century earlier, and it was now home to the famous Russian-Ukrainian author and poet Vladimir Korolenko, who in recent months had appealed to his countrymen with articles in all the major Russian newspapers: "Let us forget factions, set aside arguments about the future. Down with party factionalism! Let all look in one direction, where the tread of the German and the din of his guns resounds."[20]

The Heifetzes arrived in Poltava on April 18 (N S May 1). Local newspapers declared: "Today is the celebration of May 1. The celebration of labor!" The city hosted a colorful procession, and among those involved were the Sisters of Mercy and local musicians. The largest group in the procession consisted of workers carrying countless colored flags and banners, and the festivities continued until evening. With the war still raging, this celebration had a peculiar feeling to it.

The next day, Jascha gave his only concert in Poltava at the Hall of the music school, and according to a program preserved in the archive, he played the Mendelssohn Concerto, Schubert *Ave Maria*, Chopin Nocturne in E Minor, Paganini Caprice no. 24, Kreisler miniatures, and Tchaikovsky *Melodie*. Nothing is known of the event, since not a single review appeared in the newspapers, and the last reference to the concert had appeared a few days earlier in the *Poltavsky vestnik*. The day after the concert, the Heifetzes returned to Kharkov, and that same day Jascha wrote a card to his cousin Emma with a note about his travels: "Dear Emusya, I just recently arrived from Poltava.... Been to Yekaterinoslav. The day after tomorrow I'm going there again, and from there to Rostov, Gomel and home . . ."[21]

Newspapers in Yekaterinoslav announced Jascha's second concert set for April 24, but for some unknown reason, the Heifetzes did not return there and did not succeed in making a visit to Natan and Fanny. After the Kharkov concert on April 21, the Heifetzes and Achron headed north to the city of Gomel in Belarus. Although it was their first visit to this small and very old city, located on the high rocky banks of the river Sozh, they knew of it through the stories of Anna's brother Isaac Sharfstein, who had worked there in 1915 for the *Vilensky vestnik* after it was evacuated from Vilnius.

It was in Gomel that the Heifetzes first dealt with the Council of Workers' and Soldiers' Deputies. The most prominent work of the Gomel Council was to lead rallies and meetings, during which important issues were discussed concerning the war, industry, and the introduction of the eight-hour workday. From April 11, the popular newspaper *Gomelskaya kopeika* began printing advertisements for Jascha's concert, which took place on April 24 in the Theater of the Arts. As the newspaper indicated, "the entire proceeds . . . will be put at the disposal of the Gomel Council of Workers' and Soldiers' Deputies."[22] The review of Jascha's concert in the *Gomelskaya kopeika* revealed that the income from the event came to 4,528 rubles and 58 kopecks, with a net profit of 2,342 rubles and 6 kopecks, which was indeed given to the Council of Workers' and Soldiers' Deputies.[23]

The day before the concert, Jascha sent a postcard back to Petrograd: "Dear Elzochka! I completely forgot that I had still not written to you . . . forgive me? I hope that you're already healthy and feeling better again. Today I arrived in Gomel. From here we have to go to Rostov and from there home. . . . Hello from Papa, Mama, Achron. Be well and safe . . ."[24] The day after the concert, Jascha wrote home again, this time addressing all the inhabitants of their apartment, Pauline, Elza, Uncle Isaac, Aunt Sonia, Anyuta, and three-year-old Fanny: "So we left Gomel for Rostov. I don't know what will come after that. Anyway, at the beginning of May we'll be back in Piter."[25]

Planning ahead became difficult. Many unforeseeable events had already occurred over the course of the present tour, from the postponed concert because of the Yekaterinoslav floods to the changed route to Gomel. And now, in Rostov-on-Don, another change became necessary— the rescheduling of the concert from April 28 to April 27.[26] Local newspapers responded positively to the concert, and a review in the *Rostovskaya rech* turned out to be the last from the present tour. The review contains countless typographical errors and other mistakes (incomplete sentences, misspelled words), suggesting the work of non-professional typesetters, a sure sign of the ongoing struggle to maintain normalcy during a time when thousands of people perished as a result of the flooding and the war.[27]

After a second concert in Rostov, on April 29, the Heifetzes and Achron made the four-hundred-mile journey back to Gomel on a train filled with soldiers, the homeless, the jobless, and civilians displaced by war and revolution. Trains ran with frequent and unavoidable delays. The final concert of the current tour took place on May 3 in the Gomel Theater of the Arts, and Jascha played the Paganini Concerto, Achron *Hebrew Melody* and *Hebrew Dance,* Mendelssohn *On the Wings of Song,* Beethoven *Chorus of Dervishes* and *Turkish March,* and the Wieniawski *Faust Fantasy.* From Gomel, a daunting 650-mile journey awaited the travelers on their route back home to Petrograd.

After arriving safely back in Petrograd, the Heifetzes attended the conservatory's concluding event on May 9. With Glazunov at the head, the entire faculty gathered on stage at the Maly Hall to hear the annual report read by Inspector Lavrov. The *Petrogradsky listok* noted that "in a monotonous, quiet, completely unintelligible voice [Lavrov] began to read something out. At first the public tried to listen to Mr. Lavrov, but, despairing, gave way to peaceful conversation."[28] For those close enough to Lavrov, they heard that during the past 1916–1917 academic year, the conservatory had been home to 2,509 students, of whom 133 graduated the full course with diploma, 92 in piano, 9 in voice, and 26 from the orchestra division. At that point, during the celebratory concert, a student in Auer's graduating class, Vitold Portugalov, played the Conus Concerto. The year had been productive for Jascha. He had passed exams in many required subjects, including two harmony courses, comprehensive studies, viola, and piano. In the exam lists for spring 1917, however, his name does not appear even once.[29]

Soon after the conservatory event, Jascha received an invitation to participate in a concert-rally in the Theater of Musical Drama. "The joining of a symphony concert and a rally is a characteristic phenomenon of the revolution," *Rech* wrote in its report.[30] The large-scale event, organized for May 12, took place for the benefit of the Central Committee of the Bund.[31] The full name of this organization was the General Jewish Workers' Union (Bund) in Lithuania, Poland, and Russia; it was organized in Vilnius in 1897 as a vehicle to support the interests of Jewish craftsmen in the western regions of the Russian Empire. It was clear why the Bundists invited Jascha to participate in their event: he was a Jew by nationality, from Vilnius by birth, and his name drew big crowds. The event also included the participation of other political activists, including the leader of the party of the Kadets, Pavel Milyukov, whom Jascha had met a year earlier at a rally. From their position in the Provisional Government, the Kadets tried unsuccessfully to control radical elements in the public. In May, the leaders of the Mensheviks joined the Provisional Government, and since they also held leading positions in the Petrograd Council of Workers' and Soldiers' Deputies, they appeared to be growing in power.

In attendance at the May 12 concert-rally were all the main figures from the Menshevik movement with which the Bund was closest ideologically. Among them were the chairman of the Mensheviks in the State Duma and the chairman of the Executive Committee of the Petrograd Council of Workers' and Soldiers' Deputies, Nikolai Chkheidze, and Chkheidze's deputy, Matvei Skobelev. Also invited were Irakli Tsereteli, who under the authoritarian tsarist regime had undergone a decade of hard labor in Siberia and now occupied a ministerial post in the Provisional Government, and Fyodor Dan, a member of the Executive Committee of the Petrograd Council. No less prominent was the name of the leader of the SRS, Aleksandr Kerensky, who occupied the post of Minister of Justice in the Provisional Government and since May had also served as Minister of War.

The list of orators at the event started with Émile Vandervelde, a Belgian political activist and chairman of the International Socialist Bureau of the Second International, who traveled to Russia to press for the continuation of war. Other speakers included representatives from the Mensheviks, the Bund, the Peasants' Union, and sailors from Helsinki. As reported in *Rech*, the impassioned speeches called for the salvation of the homeland and resistance to the enemies: "In the masses a great lift was felt—and one wanted to believe in a better future."[32]

The concert-rally included a performance of Tchaikovsky's Sixth Symphony by the Orchestra of the Theater of Musical Drama with Arnold Margulian conducting. The orchestra also accompanied Jascha in the Beethoven Concerto, the first time he had played the piece since December 1913 in Vilnius. The deep pathos of Beethoven's masterpiece corresponded as never before to the atmosphere of political struggle and societal fervor present at the rally, and the large audience listened, spellbound by Jascha's performance: "His violin sounded so fully, deeply, his phrasing was so elegant, the brilliance of his interpretations so captivated, that in a minute reality was forgotten, another world was uncovered."[33] Along with the applause, Jascha received a laurel wreath with an inscribed ribbon: "To the inspired artist Jascha Heifetz from a group of grateful organizers of the evening. 12. V. 1917." He kept the ribbons from this wreath his entire life.

Jascha performed again in May, this time for a concert in the city of Saratov. The Heifetzes had planned to visit Saratov back in April, but as a result of revolutionary turmoil, Jascha's appearance with Isidor Achron was postponed by more than a month.[34] On the program for the Saratov concert, above the printed date April 3, 1917, is a handwritten note: "May 17." The city of Saratov boasted a long and rich cultural history, and many leading figures of Russian theater began their careers there. The Radishchev Art Museum in Saratov, founded by the grandson of the author Aleksandr Radishchev, was widely considered one of the greatest in Russia. The city also housed the first Russian provincial conservatory, which celebrated its fifth anniversary in 1917. The thousand-seat Saratov Concert Hall hosted many important musical events that season: Rachmaninoff performed his then-unpublished *Etudes-tableaux,* Koussevitzky played a bass recital, and Prokofiev performed his own compositions.

The economic difficulties of wartime resulted in the closure of many newspapers across Russia, and by 1917 only two remained in Saratov, the *Saratovskie gubernskie vedomosti,* which at this time printed only official information, and the *Saratovsky listok.* Since the *Saratovsky listok* was not archived during the period between March 31 and May 30, 1917, no reviews survive. Fortunately, a program preserved by Jascha himself reveals the repertoire performed that evening: the Tchaikovsky Concerto, Schubert *Ave Maria,* Mozart *Minuet,* Gluck *Melodie,* Kreisler *Tambourin Chinois,* and Paganini Caprice no. 24.[35]

This was the last solo recital of the current season for Jascha, but neither he nor his parents could have known that this would actually be his final concert performance in Russia. That this final concert occurred in Saratov was significant; though Jascha had visited countless countries and regions over the last six and a half years, the trip to Saratov and the Volga River was his first. The Volga was not just another river—it was a symbol of Russia. Jascha had often heard the voice of Chaliapin singing the folk ballad of the Cossack hero Stenka Razin: "Volga, Volga, native mother, Volga, mother-river," and finally, on this trip to Saratov in early 1917, he saw the majestic river with his own eyes. Russia, meanwhile, yearned for help; all around were only war, hunger, and devastation.

CHAPTER TWENTY-ONE

Summer 1917: Departure for America

UPON RETURNING FROM SARATOV, the Heifetzes found the capital in a political fever: "Revolution or anarchy?" asked the front page of *Izvestia* on May 21. The Kronstadt Council of Workers and Soldiers' Deputies had refused to recognize the Provisional Government. The First Congress of the Councils (Soviets) assembled on June 3, at which time the Bolshevik faction of the RSDRP (Russian Social-Democratic Labor Party) demanded the end of the war, but the Mensheviks and SRS blocked this demand. Problems worsened, resulting in countless strikes, political rallies, and demonstrations.

Surrounded by growing turmoil, the Heifetzes began once again to contemplate a possible tour to the United States. Later that year, Jascha explained the motivations behind their decision in an interview:

> All Petrograd was put to worrying about food and fuel. Such things as artistic aspiration had been forced into the background . . . I had been thinking for more than five years of a trip to America, and had been negotiating for most of that time, but it is true that if conditions were not so tragic in Russia I wouldn't have made the perilous trip at this time. Money no longer can get the necessities in Russia. The whole country faces starvation and the most terrible sacrifices. So I finally decided that we had better make the attempt

to get to America, come what might. The family came with me, father and mother and my two sisters.[1]

The logistics of such a tour had become easier as a result of recent foreign policy developments, namely the entrance of the United States into the Great War on the same side as Russia. Russia and the United States became allies on March 23 (NS April 6), 1917. This not only buoyed the Russo-American relationship, but made it easier for ordinary citizens to move between the two countries.

The Heifetzes began what was now the fourth round of American tour negotiations. Previous attempts included discussions with the concert bureau of R. E. Johnston in the fall of 1913 and the spring of 1914 and with the Haensel & Jones agency in October 1916. The latest negotiations were with an entirely new American firm, the prominent Wolfsohn Musical Bureau in New York, which proceeded to fight bitterly with Haensel & Jones for the exclusive right to present Jascha to the American public. Following lengthy deliberations, the Heifetzes decided in favor of the Wolfsohn Bureau, but according to reports in the American press, Haensel & Jones refused to back down: "A controversy has arisen between the Wolfsohn Bureau and another firm of managers, Haensel & Jones, each concern claiming to have an exclusive contract with the young genius. Interesting developments may be expected when Heifetz arrives from Russia."[2] In reality, following lengthy "negotiations by cable and letter," the contract between the Heifetzes and the Wolfsohn Bureau was already completed during the first half of June.[3] After setting their departure date, Jascha wrote a letter to Valter, who was away on vacation:

> 20 June 1917
> Respected Viktor Grigoryevich!
> I am very sorry that I took so long to answer. This whole time I've been preparing seriously for my departure to America. We finally decided to go there and we leave on June 27. The trip will be very long and probably exhausting. When we will return is still uncertain for now. We will possibly be back here in the winter.
> I will definitely write to you along the way. In any case I'm giving you my address: Mr. Jascha Heifetz. New York. Wolfsohn Musical Bureau. Viktor Grigoryevich, if you want to write to me—I will be very, very glad!

In Petrograd it is very tumultuous now. There are rallies and gatherings on the streets—there are all kinds of rumors going around. It's terribly hot and dirty; I envy you, that you are at your dacha. I wish you a good summer. Sincere greetings to your wife. When you write to [your sons] Shura and Volodya—be so kind as to say hello to them for me. All of us send our best wishes.

Yours affectionately, Jascha.[4]

During those same days, Jascha received an invitation to play at another concert-rally, and an announcement appeared on the front pages of the Petrograd papers:

Theater of Musical Drama. On Sunday June 18 a big concert-rally in support of the Society for the Distribution of Literature of the Party of Socialist Revolutionaries under the honorable chairmanship of E. K. Breshko-Breshkovskaya. Participants: ministers A. F. Kerensky and V. M. Chernov, political activists M. A. Spiridonov and N. D. Avksentyev, A. R. Gotz, N. S. Rusanov; in the concert part—Jascha Heifetz (performing for the last time before his departure to America) and the orchestra of the Theater of Musical Drama under the direction of Grigory [Grzegorz] Fitelberg. Beginning at 8 PM.[5]

The event was postponed, however, owing to a huge, 500,000-person political rally by the Bolsheviks that same day. Demonstrators carried slogans such as "All power to the Soviets!" and "Down with the 10 Capitalist Ministers!" The postponed concert-rally took place five days later, on June 23. It embraced all parts of the Social-Revolutionary movement and was attended by one of the leading political activists among the SRs, Yekaterina Breshko-Breshkovskaya, who, for her long-time revolutionary efforts, was sometimes called the "Grandmother of the February Revolution." Also present at the rally was Maria Spiridonova, the leftist SR member who had been sentenced to death in 1906 for the murder of one of the Black Hundreds (an extremist far-right political movement), but was then sent indefinitely to a Siberian hard labor camp. Following the February Revolution, Spiridonova and other sworn enemies of the autocracy were released and returned quickly to their political activism. But this did not last long. Over the coming months, all the leaders of the SRs and the Menshevik movement present at the concert-rally would turn out to be both ideologically and militarily opposed to the Bolsheviks. Most of those who did not perish as a result of the Bolshevik coup in late October 1917 (os) were forced to emigrate.

Continuing bolshevization of the Russian Revolution occurred after the Heifetzes had left, but back in June 1917, Jascha was proud to serve the cause of freedom and equal rights with his music. In April at the Menshevik rally he had played the Beethoven Concerto, and now, three days before leaving Russia, he played the Tchaikovsky Concerto.

With that, the entire Heifetz family bade farewell to their friends in Petrograd and left the Sharfsteins in the apartment on Yekateringofsky Prospekt. After the February Revolution the Sharfsteins were legally allowed to reside in the city. Little Anyuta was hospitalized with Scarlet Fever in the days leading up to the departure. When Anna Heifetz went to visit her niece, however, she was refused entry into the infections ward. Years later, Sharfstein-Koch spoke about the situation: "Aunt Anna taught me to go to the courtyard and look out the window of the second floor. That way we could see each other and say goodbye. She left me a box of candy and the book 'Joseph in Egypt.'"[6]

With such a long and difficult journey ahead, the Heifetzes took only the most essential items, leaving behind many things dear to Jascha, including his books, albums, and various collections. All of this remained in the apartment with the Sharfsteins, who would also eventually set out for the United States. As Sharfstein-Koch described years later: "We were only supposed to stay on for three months until they came back. But they never came and we stayed on for five more years."[7] Unlike the Heifetzes in 1917, the Sharfsteins knew they would not return, and so when they left in December 1922 they took as much as possible, including items that belonged to the Heifetzes. They wanted to take more, but their fear of Soviet authorities stopped them. This is why some things are missing; for example, part of the letter from the Grand Duchess with the name beginning with the letter M. They did take a risk in bringing just a single newspaper relating to the February Revolution—a copy of *Izvestia*.

Traveling to the United States through war-torn Europe remained unthinkable in 1917, so on June 27 (os), the Heifetzes departed for Moscow from where they caught a train heading toward the distant eastern borders of Russia. The first thousand miles of the route took them through Ryazan and on to Samara, where the railroad crossed the Volga, and then farther along the Bashkir steppe to Ufa and through Zlatoust to Chelyabinsk. From Chelyabinsk, the next stage of the land journey stretched more than four thousand miles across the border between Europe and Asia and then along the great Trans-Siberian Railroad, which connected Europe with Siberia and the Russian Far East.

In an interview conducted later in life, Heifetz said: "I don't see how a young musician can find the time to grow at today's tempo. Of course, I played a great deal when I was younger, but there was always time for reflection. We didn't travel in jets. We used trains and ships, and we had time between engagements, no matter how many we filled, to think, to study music, to read books."[8] This journey during the summer of 1917 was no exception; the train car became a home for the Heifetzes, and there was plenty of time to think about what they might find in the United States.

The train continued its march across the boundless expanses of western Siberia—from Omsk, through Irtysh, through the deep taiga forests to Novosibirsk and then to Krasnoyarsk. It eventually took a southeasterly path toward Irkutsk, up along the eastern shores of Lake Baikal, and then east through Verkhneudinsk (now Ulan-Ude) and Chita, to the Manchuria railroad station situated on the Russia-China border. From there, on what was already the eleventh day of the trip, Jascha sent a note to Valter on a black and white postcard with a view of Baikal:

> In the train car. 7th of July 1917
> Dear Viktor Grigoryevich!
> I am writing to you from Manchuria. Tomorrow we will be in Vladivostok. We already crossed the border—Manchuria, and in several days we'll be in Japan. . . . I will write to you from Vladivostok and Japan. The journey is wonderful. I've seen quite enough of darkness![9]

The train took the Heifetzes across the Russia-China border and into the region of Manchuria. During this part of the journey through China, the train stopped at various places, including Anda and Harbin. At these stops passengers were allowed out onto the platform. The Heifetzes mingled with the Chinese, and they took photographs, including some of Jascha and Pauline with an officer and locals.[10] They continued on the route through China, before once again crossing back into Russia. The Heifetzes were probably unaware at the time that during those July days the Provisional Government had ordered the complete closure for entry and exit of all Russian borders, an order made following the severe worsening of the political situation. Waves of rallies had erupted across Russian cities, and in Petrograd the military was forced to intervene against protesters. As in February, many were killed and wounded in the fighting. Granted unlimited power from the government, Kerensky led the fight against the Bolsheviks, accusing them of military conspiracy. The borders were ordered closed between July 15 and August 2, mainly to prevent the flight of Bolshevik leaders, including Lenin. Had the Heifetzes departed just a week later, they would have been trapped on either the Russian or Chinese side of the border. Fate was firmly on their side.

According to an account of the trip Jascha gave soon after to a reporter from *The World Magazine* in New York, other unforeseen events helped them on their way:

> We were eleven days going from Petrograd to Vladivostok, and at that we seized the favorable opportunity of travelling in the wake of the train bearing the Root Commission. Bridges were burnt down in our path and had to be speedily reconstructed out of flimsy materials to let the American Commissioners through on their way home. At another place the rioters—who knows of what complexion or party?—had set fire to buildings along the track and destroyed the right of way, so that both trains had to make a long detour.[11]

In the same interview, Jascha gave a detailed account of the severe risks facing the family as they headed across Russia:

> ... there was danger all the way that mobs would break into the train and rob the passengers of whatever they carried—a serious matter, since we had with us in gold whatever we thought we needed for the trip and our stay in America. All along the way we saw engines and coaches wrecked by the rebels. The whole country was in a pitiful state of anarchy and poverty. What a relief it was when we finally got to the Pacific!

The Trans-Siberian Railroad took them all the way to Vladivostok, a port city on the Golden Horn Bay connecting Russia with the countries located on the Pacific and Indian Oceans. By this point on their journey, the

Heifetzes had already traveled over five thousand miles under the hot July sun, and, although they did not realize it at the moment, they were leaving Russian territory for the last time. From Vladivostok the intrepid travelers began a new stage of their journey which also, symbolically, saw them convert permanently to the New Style or Gregorian calendar observed by the rest of the world, but not yet by Russia. They sailed to the west coast of Japan, an experience Jascha described colorfully and with a healthy dose of youthful bravado:

> ... the voyage through the Sea of Japan was a thriller. The waters are said to be sown with mines and we constantly encountered mine sweepers at work for the Japanese. Finally we landed on the west coast of Japan and made the trip to Yokohama by train. ... You know, one really isn't in such terror of mines and U boats. You feel that if it happens there are all these others to go down with you. It makes you feel better, somehow.[12]

In the Japanese port of Yokohama, the Heifetzes transferred to the ocean steamer the Siberia Maru (of the Toyo Kisen Kaisha Oriental Steamship Company) on its route from Hong Kong. The family spent several days in Japan simply as tourists before departing from Yokohama. The revolution was behind them, and the concert tour in the United States still lay some distance ahead. The family enjoyed their stay in Japan, marveling at the unfamiliar language, riding on rickshaws, visiting souvenir stands, learning how to open and close hand fans, and trying to eat with chopsticks. Jascha bought himself a traditional Japanese outfit, which he later wore in various informal press photographs taken in the United States.[13]

The Siberia Maru departed Yokohama on August 8 and headed east across the wide expanse of the Pacific Ocean. On the manifest for First Class passengers, the Heifetzes listed their home contact as Isaac Sharfstein at 115 Yekateringofsky Prospekt, Petrograd, a home they would never see again. Including the souvenirs they had purchased in Japan, the Heifetz family's luggage now totaled thirteen pieces, remarkably little considering the length of the journey and the number of people in the family. Most of the passengers aboard the ship were Asian emigrants on their way to the United States in search of a better life, who sailed in extremely crowded conditions. For the Heifetzes and others traveling in first class, the journey was significantly more comfortable: there were cabins, beautiful and spacious salons, swimming pools, tennis courts, and lots of open space on the decks.

While on board, the Heifetzes met a young Cuban tourist in her twenties named Antonia Mariano, who was on her way back to Havana. They also befriended a fourteen-year-old British girl named Edina Elisabeth Davis, another first class passenger, who was traveling with her father Edward, a businessman, and her mother Clara. Dozens of photographs from the trip saved in Pauline's personal album show the Heifetzes and their new-found friends relaxing on the long journey. They played games, clambered around the decks, took photographs of the ocean, admired the sunsets, met with and took photographs of the ship's captain, and participated in various organized sports and "obstacle races." They particularly enjoyed spending time outside on the decks; below one windswept scene Pauline added the inscription in English: "Edina, myself, and the wind." The fun and games even include dressing up. A photograph of Jascha in a dress carries the caption "Jascha as a female."

After ten days of sailing, the ship arrived in Honolulu, Hawaii, which was by then already American soil. The islands were annexed by the United States in 1898 and were home to the Pearl Harbor Naval Base. Although the ship did not stay long in Hawaii, the passengers were allowed to disembark, and photographs show the Heifetz siblings enjoying the island. As an adult, Jascha returned frequently to Hawaii, both as a stopping point during world tours and also as a holiday destination.

After sixteen days and many thousands of miles, the passengers aboard the Siberia Maru finally reached the North American coastline. Before the Heifetzes and other immigrants were allowed to disembark in San Francisco, they were sent to Angel Island for customs and immigration procedures. According to the official registration documents, the Heifetzes arrived on August 24, 1917. The document gives their names and ages: "Ruvin—45, Mrs. Haia [Chaya]—43, Joseph—16, Pecia—14, Elka—11."[14]

In San Francisco the Heifetzes were met by John "Jack" Trevor Adams (1891–1962) of the Wolfsohn Musical Bureau and by an older gentleman named Sir Henry Heyman (1849–1924), a violinist and a prominent figure in the local music scene.[15] The family spent a few days in the city, reveling in the California sunshine and marveling at the new country. Photographs in Pauline's album show Ruvin, Sir Henry, and Jack together in San Francisco. As the son of Avon Franklin Adams (1862–1924), the proprietor of the Wolfsohn Musical Bureau, Jack had been sent to San Francisco to meet with the Bureau's precious new "cargo." Jack developed a warm relationship with the Heifetz family and maintained ties with them for some time.

The violinist Sir Henry Heyman, who also greeted the Heifetzes, was a native of California and had studied in Europe during his youth. He reportedly took lessons with the great Ferdinand David and had studied at the Leipzig Conservatory during the 1870s, where he won the Mendelssohn Prize and played in the Gewandhaus Orchestra. During a tour to Hawaii in 1884, Heyman was awarded a knighthood by King Kalākaua and used the title from then on even though he was sometimes teased about it by his friends and colleagues. Perhaps Heyman's most important talent was his ability to draw people together. As a member of the San Francisco Bohemian Club, he developed ties with important musical figures such as Paderewski, Rachmaninoff, Wieniawski, Ysaÿe, and Saint-Saëns, who dedicated his *Élégie* for violin and piano, op. 143, to Heyman.[16] Heyman passed away in 1924, before Jascha reached his full musical maturity, but the two had managed to meet again in New York in 1919 after Jascha performed at Carnegie Hall. At this meeting Jascha gave Sir Henry a signed photograph with the inscription: "To my dear friend Sir Henry—the artist and gentleman who has my highest esteem."[17]

For the Heifetzes, San Francisco represented the New World, and the city, rebuilt after the 1906 earthquake, left them awestruck. The famous cable cars ran along the streets, and from the windows one could see sights such as Chinatown, the Italian quarter, the church of the Mission Dolores monastery, and the imposing new building of the Palace of Fine Arts.

After some rest, sightseeing, and clothes shopping, the Heifetzes set off by train across the United States. On their arrival in New York, a reporter from *Musical America* noted that "when the artist and his family alighted in the Grand Central Station a few days ago they might easily have been mistaken for an American family returning from a summer vacation. Aside from their baggage, there was no suggestion of the fact that they had just completed a ten-thousand-mile journey from their Petrograd home. The customary 'foreign look' was lacking."[18] Not surprisingly, the reporter focused his attention on Jascha:

> He is tall and well proportioned, of rather fair complexion and decidedly attractive features. The arduous trip had apparently weighed but lightly upon his youthful spirits and he expressed the greatest interest and pleasure in everything he had so far seen in America; as yet he speaks but little English, so his conversation was carried on chiefly in French, Russian and German. The subject of his New York début naturally aroused his enthusiasm and he was delighted at the prospect of appearing with several of the leading symphony orchestras during the season. The announcement is now made that the violinist's first appearance in America will be in a recital at Carnegie Hall, New York, on Saturday afternoon, Oct. 27.

Prior to the debut, the entire Heifetz family resided in Newtonville, Massachusetts, a suburb of Boston, and was hosted by Ruvin's sister Mary (Malka-Chaya) (b. 1865), who had immigrated to the United States in the early 1890s. She was married to another Russian-Jewish immigrant named Abraham Klein (b. 1866), a tailor, and together they had three daughters—Fanny (b. 1896), Esther (b. 1898), and Gertrude (b. 1900). Fanny was married to a physician named Louis Gordon (b. 1892), but both of them lived in the house with her parents. The two younger sisters were much closer in age to Jascha and Pauline. There is no evidence that Jascha and his family had corresponded with the Kleins during the time they lived in Russia, but it is likely Ruvin kept some contact with his sister. Reunited in Newtonville after decades apart, the two families became close; in the 1930s Ruvin taught the violin to Gertrude's daughter Elza Mimi, and in old age he was cared for by Esther.[19]

In an interview with *The Strad* in 1986, Gertrude (Klein) Reed, Jascha's first cousin, recalled the days when the Heifetzes first arrived at her family's home in Newtonville:

> They arrived with a vast collection of items—trunks of books including classical literature of all sorts, a large library of music, and violins. I especially remember their select wearing apparel—heavy fur coats and my uncle's cane, his waxed moustache and fancy cigarette lighters and holders for smoking. They all had such elite personalities and Jascha and his sisters spoke English so well.

What a thrill it was to our family! . . . We had a piano and our life-style was immersed with music and studies. For those months the walls of our simple nine-room house rung with music.

It was a very hot summer. We had a huge screened porch surrounded with honeysuckle vines and Jascha would relax there on a large leather couch and imbibe the unusual aromas of the nasturtiums and pansies. Jascha would always love to take an early morning walk before breakfast in the back of our house, which was a vast meadow surrounded by apple trees, berry bushes, and both wild and cultivated flowers. When I think of those days I picture Jascha not as the world-famous violinist he became, but as a young boy of refined and majestic stature. Even at that young age he had elegant mannerisms—words cannot express the aristocracy which he exuded. He was always appreciative, and his modesty and humility were beyond description. He never bragged about his great accomplishments and never had to struggle with his practicing. I remember his father, with a bunch of keys and a gold watch hanging from his trouser pocket, supervising Jascha's systematic routine of study. The daily programme was conducted like clockwork.[20]

The house in Newtonville, at 47 Kensington Street, provided Jascha with a small piece of Russia. Where better to familiarize himself with the new country than under the guidance of his Russian-speaking relatives. A familiar face also came to visit—Hyman Gerber, Ruvin's friend from Vilnius who had known Jascha from his earliest years. Gerber had immigrated to Boston in 1914 and in the intervening years had always hoped to see Jascha visit the United States. He also helped the Heifetzes get settled.

Preparations for the big debut moved ahead. A representative of the Wolfsohn Bureau, Charles "Charlie" Nelson Drake (b. 1882), and other business managers from the Bureau often visited the house in Newtonville. Publicity photographs were required, so Jascha was taken to the Horner Photography Company in Boston. The iconic images from this visit would grace the cover of the debut program and would appear in the press during the coming season and for many years to come. The representatives of the Wolfsohn Bureau and Jascha's mother spent a great deal of time discussing the details of the debut and the upcoming tour. Meanwhile, Ruvin and Jascha planned the concert programs.

Earlier in the summer, before the Heifetzes arrived, the Wolfsohn Bureau had engaged the talented pianist André Benoist as Jascha's accompanist for the upcoming debut and subsequent concerts. The two musicians had already met in 1913 in St. Petersburg when Benoist and Albert Spalding visited the Auer class at the conservatory. Benoist and Spalding continued to work together after that tour and became great friends, but when Spalding voluntarily enlisted in the military in 1917, Benoist was left without a permanent partner and without a close friend. Shortly after, still feeling saddened at Spalding's departure, Benoist was approached by Richard Copley (1874–1939), the manager at the Wolfsohn Bureau. In his memoirs, Benoist recalled Copley's words: "come to the office with me now and sign up with another violinist immediately." Benoist at first refused, but when Copley explained that it was a certain "young Russian violinist," Benoist replied: "What? That can only be little Jascha Heifetz! . . . So along I went, still feeling a bit disloyal to my old friend, but nevertheless touched by the cordiality of the offer before me."[21]

During the weeks Jascha spent in Newtonville, Benoist visited regularly to rehearse for the upcoming performances; the musical relationship between the two turned out to be highly successful. On Benoist's first visit he recalled being "steadily examined through fishy and suspicious eyes by both Mama and Papa." But after he and Jascha had played through a few pieces together, "everyone loosened up . . . and the ice was broken. Mama even went so far as to offer tea!" Benoist continued, describing his experience working with Jascha:

> It took a good many days before I was able to break through Jascha's natural crust of distant coldness; but when I did, I found a boy with the nature of the friendliest puppy: shy, but full of fun, pranks and practical jokes. Of course, he played the violin like a young god, but never referred to it in action or conversation. Conceit was so foreign to him that I believe he did not know the meaning of the word. In playing together we got along from the very first. His playing was so clean, so sane and sound, and throughout so rhythmical, that there was no difficulty in accompanying him . . . except when he would suddenly take the bit in his teeth and start on a spurt of staggering speed. But even then his rhythm never faltered.[22]

In early October, with the debut just a few weeks away, Jascha and his parents headed to New York. Pauline and Elza remained in Newtonville under the supervision of their Aunt Mary, and the girls enrolled at Newton

Classical High School where they would stay until being reunited with the others in New York during the Christmas vacation. As Gertrude Klein later noted, thanks to their illustrious brother, the Heifetz girls "were already celebrities."

In New York, Jascha and his parents found a place to stay located somewhere in the nineties of upper Manhattan.[23] The Godowsky family, with whom the Heifetzes had become acquainted back in 1914, took time to welcome the visitors to the big city. Before long, the much-anticipated event arrived: Heifetz's American debut, at 2:30 p.m., on Saturday, October 27, at Carnegie Hall—the heart of music in America. The famous concert venue consisted of two halls, the main one with approximately three thousand seats and a smaller one with a few hundred. Heifetz's debut was in the impressive main hall. This prestigious venue was known around the world; Tchaikovsky had traveled all the way from Russia a quarter of a century earlier to conduct his own works at its inaugural concert in 1891.

On the day of Jascha's concert debut, people filed into the building until they were turned away: "The audience that witnessed the debut at Carnegie Hall Saturday afternoon was not only very large," wrote Pitts Sanborn in the *Commercial Advertiser and Globe*, "but notable for the number of professional violinists it included—apparently every disengaged man and woman in town that ever drew a bow for money."[24] According to a report in the *Violinist* journal, the many prominent violinists present at the debut included: Fritz Kreisler, Mischa Elman, Maud Powell, Franz Kneisel, Sam Gardner, David Hochstein, David Mannes, Nathan Franko, Albert Greenfeld, Leopold Lichtenberg, Geraldine Morgan, Louis Siegel, Sam Franko, Gustave Saenger, Emily Gresser, Edith Rubel, Edwin Grasse, Helen Ware, Maurice Kaufman, and Victor Kuzdo.[25]

With such an intense atmosphere developing in the auditorium, the experienced Benoist began to feel a little nervous: "no matter how inured one may be to such occasions, it is almost impossible to remain entirely indifferent to them. I must confess that, in spite of many experiences of the same kind, I felt a bit aflutter myself." It seems, however, that Jascha did not share the feeling of nervousness. As Benoist recalled: "When I reached the old Green Room at the hall, I found Mama and Papa [Heifetz] sitting about, as calm and unconcerned as if they were about to witness a Christmas party. As for Jascha, he ran up to me in high glee and said, 'Look! Look! Fine long pants! Fine cutaway coat! Fine new necktie! I look fine, no?'"[26]

When the time came, Jascha walked out onto the stage to face an electrified public, and a deafening wave of applause broke out all around. As a reviewer in *The World* noted: "Some measure of the advance estimate in which this Russian youth is held was shown when he first appeared before his anxious throng. No sooner was he sighted than a wave of applause sounded through the big auditorium: a greeting so spontaneous, so sincere as to cause the seasoned concertgoers to exclaim involuntarily."[27] Jascha started with the Vitali Chaconne, with organ accompaniment provided by Frank L. Sealy, and as one reviewer noted, "long before the completion of the Vitali Chaconne it was apparent that a master violinist superlatively endowed had come to disclose the measure of his worth." After each subsequent piece, the delight and excitement in the audience continued to grow. Jascha then played the Wieniawski Concerto no. 2, Schubert's *Ave Maria*, Mozart's *Minuet*, Chopin's *Nocturne in D*, the Beethoven *Chorus of Dervishes* and *March Orientale*, Tchaikovsky's *Melodie*, and the Paganini *Caprice no. 24*. Another reviewer noted that "this boy was establishing new violin marks; that in every department of his art he was the superior of any fiddler this country has known in at least fifteen years."[28] It was at this debut that a very well-known anecdote between a famous violinist and pianist came to life: "It's hot here, isn't it?" said Mischa Elman to Leopold Godowsky, who was sitting in the same box. "No, Mischa. Not for pianists," Godowsky quickly responded.[29]

The calm and unconcerned behavior of Jascha's parents before the debut attested to the unwavering faith they had in their young son's incredible talent. After all, they had seen and heard him conquer every stage on which he had set foot, throughout the Russian Empire and Europe. Just as elsewhere, the crowd in Carnegie Hall cheered and applauded and rushed the stage at the end of the recital. In this sense, Carnegie Hall was just one more venue to add to the burgeoning list of accomplishments in Jascha's career. His overwhelming success on October 27, 1917, however, provided him a special place in the hearts and minds of the American public, and ultimately resulted in the family's decision to remain in the United States. Political circumstances far out of their control had led the Heifetzes to make the epic journey to New York, leaving behind the country that had raised Jascha and contributed to the formation of his musical character. With years of preparation behind him, Jascha was ready for this next stage of his life.

Certainly, this move was not easy for Jascha. He left behind the country that had been his home, and he left behind many friends: people from the conservatory, including Glazunov, who had facilitated the family's stay in St. Petersburg-Petrograd; Viktor Valter, his constant supporter; beloved Professor Auer, the man responsible for Jascha's artistic training; and Kiselgof, who had worked tirelessly to broaden Jascha's education. The Heifetzes also left behind the Sharfsteins, who would eventually join the Heifetzes in the United States, but not for another five years. Others in the wider Heifetz family ended up staying in Russia, including Natan and Fanny and their daughter Lyusya, Ruvin's other siblings, and Jascha's grandparents. Some of these people Jascha would never see again.

Despite the sacrifices, if Jascha and his parents needed proof that they had made the right choice, back in Petrograd, just days after the debut in New York, the Bolsheviks seized power in the October Revolution (on November 7 in New York City, but October 25 in Petrograd). A lengthy and brutal civil war ensued. No one in Russia knew how and when the situation would end. The Heifetzes, at least, were safe in the New World.

Reviews of Jascha Heifetz's Debut at Carnegie Hall, October 27, 1917

IN THE MONTHS FOLLOWING Heifetz's debut, the following reviews were collated and reprinted in various newspapers and publicity brochures.

Max Smith, "Boy Violinist Wins Triumph," *The New York American,* October 28, 1917:

The American debut of Jascha Heifetz yesterday afternoon in Carnegie Hall will go on record as one of the most notable incidents in the recent musical history of New York.

This Russian youth is said to be only sixteen years old, though he might be eighteen or nineteen, to judge from his appearance, and forty, to judge from his extraordinary poise. Yet already his mastery of the violin is such that one can compare him only to the greatest virtuosi of the present and the past.

Comparisons are often odious, but the writer for the American does not hesitate to assert that in all his experience he has never heard any violinist approach as close to the loftiest standards of absolute perfection as did Jascha Heifetz yesterday.

It was an occasion not soon to be forgotten, this sweeping triumph of a boy who, without pose or affectation, cast a spell of utter amazement over every professional listener.

To dilate upon the mechanical proficiency Jascha Heifetz has obtained on his instrument—to discuss in detail the extraordinary dexterity and precision of his slender fingers, and lightness, elasticity and supple firmness of his bowing—seems almost superfluous, when it can be described by one word: perfection. Verily, his command of the technics of the violin is nothing short of transcendental.

The tone he draws from the strings—a tone exquisitely pure and precise to the pitch at all times—is not only mellow, vibrant, intense, but breathes a delicately refined expressiveness that can only come from the soul of a poet....

Sigmund Spaeth, "Perfect Violin Playing at Last," *The Evening Mail,* October 29, 1917:

Superlatives do not flow easily from the pens of reviewers. Extravagant eulogy can scarcely be habitual with any one who, for even a few seasons, has observed the music of New York and has realized how much of it is good without being great, and how much of it pretends to greatness without being even good. Therefore when Jascha Heifetz is called the perfect violinist, the words are used advisedly, and by no means in the first flush of hysterical enthusiasm.

It has always seemed to the writer that it ought to be possible to play the violin with every note clear and in tune, with a correct rhythm in fast as well as slow passages, and with a pure, musical tone, neither scratchy, nor shaky, neither lifeless nor maudlin.

Until last Saturday afternoon he had never heard any one actually do it. Then a tall Russian boy with a mop of curly hair walked out on the stage of Carnegie Hall and made the ideal a reality.

Jascha Heifetz plays the violin as it should be played, as every serious violinist must dream of playing it. That his greatness should have been instantly recognized by a New York audience is a credit to local intelligence and musical taste.

To say that Heifetz is a complete master of his instrument scarcely conveys the ease with which he accomplishes what has heretofore seemed superhuman. His astounding technic seems to him a matter of course. He never uses it for mere display, but always as a legitimate and necessary feature of his interpretations....

This new prodigy of the violin is by no means a jangler of the heart-strings, a whipper of the emotions. He depends upon sheer musical beauty for all his effects, and the result is a practically flawless art. Once more let it be said emphatically, Jascha Heifetz is the perfect violinist.

"A New Violinist Plays," *New York Times,* October 28, 1917:

Another was added yesterday to the number of remarkable violinists who have come to this country out of Russia, in Jascha Heifetz, who made his first American appearance in Carnegie Hall. There was a large audience, in which there were many musicians full of enthusiasm which was eminently justified.

Mr. Heifetz is a pupil of Leopold Auer, who has sent many excellent violinists out into the world. He is young; he is said to be only eighteen years old; but in his art he is mature, and there is no suggestion, in his appearance or his manner or his performance, of the juvenile or the phenomenal. There was never a more unassuming player who demonstrated great abilities, or one more intent upon his art and so oblivious of his listeners as he stands upon the platform.

Mr. Heifetz produces tone of remarkable beauty and purity; a tone of power, smoothness and roundness, of searching expressiveness, of subtle modulation in power and color. His bowing is of rare elasticity and vigor, excellent in many details; as is his left hand execution, which is accurate in all sorts of difficulties. In his technical equipment Mr. Heifetz is unusual.

He plays with great repose and dignity, with simplicity and directness, with purity of taste, shown in the Chaconne by Vitali so often heard here in recent years, perhaps oftener than its real value would warrant, and in some of the smaller pieces that followed. There was real breadth and warm sincerity here and in many another number of his program. There was the true feeling for the finish and effect of detail. . . . In all his passage work, in his up-bow spiccato, his singularly pure harmonics, his double stoppings, there was much to admire; and it was all so easily accomplished and with such perfect taste.

"Boy Violinist is Acclaimed Here," *New York Sun,* October 28, 1917:

. . . It was the custom many years ago to enumerate all the constituent parts of violin technic when describing the playing of such an artist as Heifetz, but the musical public, as well as the commentators, has been educated to a higher outlook. Furthermore, it would be the grossest injustice to this young artist to represent him as a "phenomenon" or a "wizard." He is a troubadour, not a jongleur, of the violin.

He has a technic which must make him the admiration and the despair of all the other violinists. His finger work is almost unerring, whether in rapid flights or in intricate passages of double stopping. But better than this is the exquisite finish, elasticity and resource of his bowing, which gives him a supreme command of all the tonal nuances essential to style and interpretation.

But his merits do not end here. Young Mr. Heifetz has been endowed with a sound musical temperament, one which appreciates with the deepest sensitiveness the real beauty of the music to be played, and which moves him to publish it with finish, with repose, with taste and with a genuine feeling, always guided by intelligence. In short, he is a musician whose respect for his art and his instrument forbids anything tending toward sensationalism. Even in the compositions calling for the most brilliant displays of pure dexterity, he played yesterday with elegance and poise and with musical sincerity. His beautiful tone he carried into every bit of passage work and he made eloquent such easily sentimentalized fiddler's bits as the transcription of Schubert's "Ave Maria." ...

"Another Great Violinist Comes Out Of Russia," *New York Herald,* October 28, 1917:

Another great violinist has come out of Russia. Jascha Heifetz, younger than Mischa Elman or Efrem Zimbalist, and just as individual as either one, made his American debut at a recital in Carnegie Hall yesterday afternoon. An audience that crowded the hall heard his program and applauded him unrestrainedly.

At the first few bars of Vitali's Chaconne, with which the program began, the audience seemed to sense a rising star. There is nothing that moves a habitual concertgoer as does the discovery of new talent. The first hearing of a new genius brings a joy not to be equaled by the performance of a familiar idol.

Mr. Heifetz, tall and of slight build, plays without affectation. His playing is as straightforward as his manner on the stage. His first notes disclosed a penetrating tone, full of vitality. His technic is clean; his intonation is almost faultless. There is a refinement, a delicate finish to everything he does. He can stand on his own merits. ...

Pitts Sanborn, "Enter a Genius: Jascha Heifetz," *Commercial Advertiser and Globe,* October 29, 1917:

... To undertake analysis of such playing seems futile and rather silly. But if anyone wants it, here is a very fragmentary beginning, submitted cheerfully: Heifetz has a broad, firm tone, edged with the silver resonance that rings in our ears from fiddler or human voice as right. And the purity of this tone, from the open G string to the top-most harmonic, whether proclaimed in a lordly fortissimo or fined down to the faintest whisper, alike in flowing cantilena and in complicated passage work, is a modern miracle.

To chatter about technic were an impertinence. Through sheer perfection the mechanics of the instrument cease to exist—double stopping can never grate, every scale is of those matched pearls, every staccato a point of light. Infinite finish of detail has its just place in the composition of the picture, but no more. Heifetz displays the sense of large design we find only in the greatest musical interpreters—a Paderewski, an Ysaÿe, a Casals, and the feeling, musical and emotional, that suffuses the design is the right and only feeling.

Moreover, anything he touches turns to gold. Ysaÿe can make a Vieuxtemps concerto sound as if Beethoven wrote it. Heifetz did the same for the Wieniawski D minor. One might point out that he played Vitali's Chaconne grandly, nobly; one might dwell on the grace, the hauteur, the aristocratic sentiment that sounded in Chopin's D major nocturne (arranged by Wilhelmj), and so ramble on about the Faubourg and twilight and countesses and Georges Sand; one might seek the unique word for the tenderness of Schubert's "Ave Maria," the chiseled delicacy of a minuet by Mozart, the yearning Slavic melancholy of Tchaikovsky's "Melodie," the jeweled splendor of two transcriptions by Professor Auer from Beethoven's "Ruins of Athens" music and the same authority's arrangement of Paganini's twenty-fourth caprice, but to what avail?

What the grave-faced youth puts into it all another cannot say; to know you must hear his violin. At least Zarathustra has fiddled!

Essential to the record of so extraordinary an occasion is the behavior of the audience. It greeted Heifetz cordially on his entrance, and after his first number, the Vitali Chaconne, it gave him an ovation. The ovations recurred relentlessly after every number, and at the end of the program there was a mad rush to the stage of an avid, noisy crowd which, when throats tired, waved handkerchiefs and hats. This crowd made the youth, already drooping visibly with weariness, play again and again, and dispersed only when some one resorted to turning off the lights.

Pierre V. R. Key, "Jascha Heifetz Scores Triumph," *The World,* October 28, 1917:

. . . As for Jascha Heifetz' art—that is a supreme thing. He plays with a bearing so modest, so devoid of assurance that one instantly realizes how deep is this boy's sincerity in his desires to interpret all the composer created. Though technic is ordinarily the last thing to consider, it invites primary consideration because, in this instance, it is so perfect and so perfectly used as to stand forth like a gem stone.

Thus equipped, Heifetz is enabled to approach any interpretative task without thought for the mechanical means employed. He played yesterday with the maturity of a man of forty, a maturity difficult to regard as an element that can grow. His breadth, poise and perfect regard for the turn of a phrase constantly left his hearers spellbound.

Nothing that he undertook was without a finish so complete, so carefully considered and worked out, that its betterment did not appear humanly impossible. In cantilena Heifetz played with an evenness that was almost mathematical in exactness; yet there was nothing mechanical, nothing wherein freedom did not appear to the utmost. His tone—big, luscious and impeccable in purity and intonation—was of oily smoothness. And whether the tempo was fast or slow, this beauty of quality ever remained.

But if both tone and technic were superlative, it was from an interpretative standpoint that Heifetz appeared supreme. His mood was one susceptible to constant change. Now grave, now light, shifting to meet each new demand of phrase, this element was of outstanding importance. And by right of this possession the Russian youth was enabled to appear at his greatest, no matter what character of composition he undertook to play.

We cannot complete in a single review the estimate of Jascha Heifetz' greatness. Further opportunities are required, and in them more detailed consideration of his abilities will be set forth. For the moment it is sufficient to say that he is supreme; a master, though only seventeen, whose equal this generation will probably never meet again.

H. E. Krehbiel, "The American Debut of a Violinist Who is a Musician," *New York Tribune*, October 28, 1917:

Of course, we ought to have known all about Mr. Heifetz, since he effected his debut in Russia four or five years ago, but we didn't; and therefore he came as a surprise—as a surprise of an unusual character, because there was nothing sensational about him or his playing. We are used to sensations, but there was none in his playing, because in it there seemed summed up all the fine qualities which we have admired in the older artists, some of whom we have mentioned. In their cases we took the great qualities for granted, because they were not only violinists, but musicians as well. There was so much beauty in the playing of Mr. Heifetz that we did not care to think about his impeccable intonation, his loveliness of interpretative phrase, his gracious attitude on the stage, as if a musician might be an unobtrusive gentleman who had concluded that extravagance of conduct was no more essential to music than long hair and violence of gesture; his intellectual as well as his emotional poise, even his exquisite loveliness of tone, though that is a quality which is usually bestowed by genius. . . .

He appeared a stranger before a strange audience; but his extraordinary ability won speedy recognition. He will not need to stand again the test which he stood yesterday. He is now in his own shoes, and we are not sure that any violinist now before the public can fill them as well as he does.

Jascha Heifetz's Repertoire in Russia

THIS LIST WAS COMPILED using source materials such as concert programs and published notices. It also takes into account works that were not listed in programs but that Heifetz played as encores. Those works marked with an asterisk were first performed on recordings and those marked with two stars were written about but not performed publicly. Conjectures for what the incomplete titles should be are in brackets. The pieces are listed in order of first public performance. Dates are given according to the Old Style calendar, except where performances took place outside of Russia, for which the New Style date is also given.

1906
December 7
   Singelée, *Fantaisie Pastorale,* op. 56

1907
December 12
   De Bériot, Aria with Variations

1908
March 27
   De Bériot, Concerto no. 7 in G, op. 76

May 17
   Dont, Etude [Dont-Auer, Etude, op. 35, no. 15]
   Vieuxtemps, *Ballade et Polonaise,* op. 38
November 2
   Sarasate, Fantasy on a theme from Gounod's opera *Faust*

1909

May 2

Mendelssohn, Concerto in E Minor, op. 64

May 29

Wieniawski, Concerto no. 2 in D Minor, op. 22

1910

November 5

Paganini, Concerto no. 1 in D, op. 6, ed. Wilhelmj

December 9

Chopin-Sarasate, Nocturne in E-flat, op. 9, no. 2

Paganini-Auer, Caprice, op. 1, no. 24

1911

April 17

Saint-Saëns, *Introduction and Rondo Capriccioso,* op. 28

May 13

Popper-Auer, *La Fileuse* (Concert Etude), op. 55, no. 1

May

*François Schubert, *The Bee,* op. 13, no. 9

*Kreisler, *Caprice Viennois,* op. 2

*Dvořák-Wilhelmj, *Humoresque,* op. 101, no. 7

*Auer, Romance in F, op. 4

*Drdla, *Souvenir*

*Drdla, *Serenade* no. 1 in A

July 31

Alard, *Symphonic Duet for Two Violins,* op. 31

1911 *continued*

September 1

Glazunov, Concerto in A Minor, op. 82

December 29

Sarasate, *Zigeunerweisen,* op. 20

1912

January 14

Bazzini, *La Ronde des Lutins,* op. 25

January 28/February 10

Bach-Wilhelmj, Aria (on the G string) from Suite in D for String Orchestra

Cui, *Melodie Orientale.* From the cycle *Kaleidoscope,* op. 50, no. 9

February 3/February 16

Wieniawski, Caprice [*Capriccio-Valse,* op. 7]

February 10/February 23

Tchaikovsky, Concerto in D, op. 35 (first two movements)

April 8

Tchaikovsky, Concerto in D, op. 35

Bach, Chaconne, from Partita no. 2 in D Minor for solo violin

Schubert-Wilhelmj, *Ave Maria,* op. 52, no. 6

Kreisler, *Schön Rosmarin*

Kreisler, *La Chasse* (in the style of Jean-Baptiste Cartier)

Chopin-Auer, Nocturne in E Minor, op. 72, no. 1

Wieniawski, *Souvenir de Moscow,* op. 6

1912 *continued*

May 11/May 24
Handel-Hubay, Larghetto from
Sonata no. 4 in D
Haydn-Auer, Vivace from Quartet
in D, op. 64, no. 5
Fauré, *Lullaby*
July 26
Tchaikovsky, *Melodie* from the cycle
Souvenir d'un lieu cher, op. 42, no.
3, ed. Auer
August 4
Handel, Largo [from Sonata no. 6
in E]
September 29/October 12
Bruch, Concerto no. 1 in G Minor,
op. 26
Bach-Auer, *Sicilienne* from Sonata
no. 2 for Flute and Harpsichord
Mozart-Auer, Gavotte from the
opera *Idomeneo*
Ernst, Variations on an Irish Theme
October 10/October 23
Tchaikovsky, *Sérénade mélancolique,*
op. 26
November 1/November 14
Sarasate, *Carmen Fantasy,* op. 25
November 24/December 7
Fiocco, Allegro
November 26/December 9
Cui, *Berceuse,* op. 20, no. 8
November 30/December 13
Conus, Concerto in E Minor
Tartini-Kreisler, Variations on a
Theme by Corelli

1913

March 27
Ernst, *Concerto pathétique* in
F-sharp Minor, op. 23
Sgambati, *Serenade,* op. 24, no. 2
Kreisler, Praeludium and Allegro
(in the style of Pugnani)
Wieniawski, Polonaise in A, op. 21
Paganini, Moto Perpetuo, op. 11
July 21
Bach, Concerto for Two Violins in
D Minor
September 17/September 30
Mozart-Burmester, Minuet in D
from Divertimento, no. 17
Beethoven, Romance no. 1 in G,
op. 40
September 19/October 2
Vitali-Charlier, Chaconne in G
Minor
Schumann-Auer, *The Prophet Bird,*
op. 82, no. 7
September 24/October 7
Aulin, *Humoresque* from the suite
Four Watercolors
Aulin, *Lullaby*
October 1/October 14
Lalo, *Symphonie Espagnole,* op. 21
Auer, *Concert Tarantella,* op. 2
December 4
Beethoven, Concerto in D, op. 61
December 20
Wieniawski, *Faust Fantasy*

1914

January 25/February 7

Goldmark, Concerto in A Minor,
op. 28

Handel, Sonata no. 6 in E

1915

March 1

Tartini-Kreisler, *Devil's Trill Sonata*
in G Minor

Grieg, Sonata no. 3 in C Minor,
op. 45

Aleksandr Taneyev, *Rêverie*, op. 23

Sarasate, *Malagueña* from the cycle
Spanish Dances, op. 21, no. 2

Sarasate, *Habanera* from the cycle
Spanish Dances, op. 21, no. 2

April 8

Corelli-David, *La Folia*, op. 5, no. 12

Mendelssohn-Achron, *Song Without
Words*, op. 19, no. 1

Elgar, *La Capricieuse*, op. 17

Drigo-Auer, *Valse Bluette* from the
ballet *Les Millions d'Arlequin*

April 14

Achron, *Dance Improvisation*, op. 37

Saminsky, *Lullaby*

April 25

Achron, *Hebrew Melody*, op. 33

Achron, *Hebrew Dance*, op. 35, no. 1

October 3

Achron, *Hebrew Lullaby*, op. 35, no. 2

December 20

Franck, Sonata in A

Bach, Andante in C and Allegro in
A Minor [from Sonata no. 2 in A
Minor for solo violin]

Tchaikovsky-Bezekirsky, *Valse-
Scherzo*, op. 34

1915 *continued*

Paganini-Kreisler, *I Palpiti*,
Introduction and Variations on
a theme from the aria 'Di tanti
palpiti' from Rossini's *Tancredi*,
op. 13

1916

January 27

Saint-Saëns, Concerto no. 3 in B
Minor, op. 61

Saint-Saëns, *Havanaise*, op. 83

Paganini-Kreisler, Caprice, op. 1,
no. 13

Paganini-Kreisler, Caprice, op. 1,
no. 20

Sarasate, Introduction and
Tarantella, op. 43

February 8

Kreisler, Sicilienne and Rigaudon
(in the style of Francoeur)

February 29

**Sinding, Suite in A Minor, op. 10

March 22

Debussy, *La plus que lente*

August 17/August 30

Kreisler, Minuet (in the style of
Porpora)

August 22/September 4

Juon, *Arva* (*Valse Mignonne*), op. 52,
no. 2

Aulin, Gavotte and Musette from
the cycle *Four poems in the form of
a suite*, op. 15, no. 4

September 12/September 25

Beethoven-Auer, *Turkish March*,
from *The Ruins of Athens*, op. 113

NOTES

AUTHOR'S PREFACE

1. Galina Kopytova, "Pervye shagi geniia: Iasha Kheifets [First steps of a genius: Jascha Heifetz]," *Sovetskaia muzyka,* no. 8 (1991): 91–95.

2. Deems Taylor, "Jascha, That's My Baby," *New York Times,* July 16, 1939.

3. Studio recordings of Heifetz, three films about him (1950, 1953, 1970), the 1938 movie *They Shall Have Music,* and the 1962 master class films all served as material for Pavel Sedov's 2002 dissertation at the Moscow Conservatory entitled, "Iskusstvo Iashi Kheifetsa v kontekste muzykal'no-ispolnitel'skoi kul'tury XX veka [The Art of Jascha Heifetz in the Context of Musical Performance Culture of the 20th Century]."

1. EARLY ROOTS OF THE HEIFETZ FAMILY

1. Herbert Axelrod, *Heifetz,* 3rd ed. (Neptune City, NJ: Paganiniana, 1990), 19.

2. This certificate and the employment documents of Aron Heifetz are preserved in the personal archive of Aleksandr Nemirovsky (Moscow). This source is henceforth described as the Nemirovsky Archive.

3. Shmuila Elyevich Heifetz, Imperial Warsaw University certificate, Nemirovsky Archive.

4. As context for currency values around this time in Russia, the following list is a selection of professions and their average annual wages in 1913: school teachers, 750 rubles; professors, no less than 2,000 rubles; doctors, 500–2,000 rubles; engineers, upward of 800 rubles; lawyers, upward of 2000 rubles; industrial workers, 240 rubles. In 1913 a chicken cost 0.45 rubles, boots for men cost between 2.50 and 6 rubles, and a

man's coat could cost between 10 and 55 rubles. The exchange rate in 1913 was 2 rubles to 1 U.S. dollar.

5. "A vunderkind bay yidn," *Gut-morgn* (Odessa), no. 474, 1911.

6. "A vunderkind," *Der Fraynd* (Warsaw), August 14, 1911.

7. Natan Heifetz, Personal Employment Record, December 12, 1943, Nemirovsky Archive.

8. An example from one mistake-filled letter in equivalent English: "I've very rarely have to correspond in Russian, simply to say because I even completely never learned it."

9. Lev Nikolaevich Raaben, *Zhizn' zamechatel'nykh skripachei* [*The Lives of Remarkable Violinists*] (Moscow, Leningrad: Muzyka, 1967), 222.

10. Natan Heifetz, three pages of handwritten personal memoirs, December 12, 1943, Moscow, Nemirovsky Archive.

11. Moisei Iakovlevich Beregovskii, *Evreiskaia narodnaia instrumental'naia muzyka* [*Jewish Folk Instrumental Music*] (Moscow: Sovetskii kompozitor, 1987), 18.

12. "A vunderkind bay yidn."

13. "Teaching Service Record for Heifetz, Aron Ilyich, educational worker of the Vitebsk Province of the Polotsk District 6th School," June 23, 1923, Nemirovsky Archive.

14. Beregovskii, *Evreiskaia narodnaia instrumental'naia muzyka*. Original typewritten source in KR RIII, f. 45, op. 1, no. 5, l. 88.

15. Nicole Hirsch, "Jascha Heifetz, l'empereur du violon," *Musica Disques,* no. 102, September 1962, 4.

16. Josefa Heifetz, stenogram of notes from phone conversations with Anna Sharfstein-Koch, Nov. 29 and Dec. 13, 1992 and Jan. 10, 1993, p1.

17. Ruvin Heifetz-Chaya Sharfstein wedding invitation, Nemirovsky Archive.

18. E. Iu. Petri and Iu. M. Shokal'skii, eds. *Bol'shoi vsemirnyi nastol'nyi atlas Marksa* [*Marx Big World Table Atlas*], 2nd ed. (St. Petersburg, 1910), no. 20 (Borovukh); Official Index of Railroad, Ship and other Passenger Services (St. Petersburg, 1911), 57 (Barovukh); *Atlas of Railroads of the USSR* (Moscow, 1988), 32 (Baravukh).

19. Samuel Chotzinoff, "Jascha Heifetz: The Early Years; Recollections of the celebrated violinist's early career (A selection by Robin Chotzinoff from the unpublished memoirs 'Till Death Us Do Part')," *Strad,* December 1988, 968.

20. Obituaries, *Musical America* (January 25, 1947), 26.

21. "A vunderkind bay yidn."

2. 1901–1906: VILNIUS

1. The original name of the street was derived from the Russian term *zhid,* or "Jew," and meant "Jewish Street." Over time, *zhid* took on a derogatory and anti-Semitic connotation in the Russian language. The term *yevrei,* or "Hebrew," became the accepted, non-derogatory term to refer to Jews in Russian. This is the source of the street's newer

name. *Zhid* remains an acceptable term without derogatory connotations in several other related Slavic languages.

2. The Vilnius register of Jewish births in 1901, LVIA, f. 728, op. 4, d. 77, l. 22 ob.–23. First reproduced in Genrikh Agranovsky, "The Childhood Years of the King of Violinists," *Jerusalem of Lithuania*, January 2001, 7–8. Notarized certification of the register is located in the TsGIA SPb, f. 361, op. 1, d. 4276, l. 2.

3. Jascha Heifetz, *The Heifetz Collection*, RCA, 1994, 46 vols., 65 compact discs, recorded 1917–1972.

4. Alexander Woollcott, "The Quest of a Lost Childhood," *Saturday Evening Post*, April 7, 1928.

5. Moisei Iakovlevich Beregovskii, *Evreiskaia narodnaia instrumental'naia muzyka* [*Jewish Folk Instrumental Music*] (Moscow: Sovetskii kompozitor, 1987), 32.

6. Herbert Axelrod, *Heifetz*, 3rd ed. (Neptune City, NJ: Paganiniana, 1990), 124.

7. Genrikh Agranovskii, "Korol' skripachei iz starogo Vil'niusa [King of Violinists from Old Vilnius]," *Vilnius*, no. 3, 1991, 181.

8. Genrikh Agranovsky, "The Childhood Years of the King of Violinists." Photo taken from Philip Taubman "In Lithuania Too, Nationalism Surges," *New York Times*, July 23, 1988, 3.

9. JHC LoC, box 280.

10. Plan goroda Vil'ny [Map of the City of Vilnius], Kartograficheskoe zavedenie Ia. Il'ina (St. Petersburg, 1892).

11. Josefa Heifetz, stenogram of notes from phone conversations with Anna Sharfstein-Koch, December 13, 1992, 3.

12. Aron's grandson Paul Olefsky recalled that his grandfather was a talented conductor. Telephone interview with Paul Olefsky, February 24, 2012. Anna Sharfstein-Koch recalled that Aron Olefsky was a cantor.

13. As with the debate over Jascha's true date of birth, some uncertainty surrounds Pauline's birth date, and there are two possible dates in 1903—either Jan. 15 (NS) or June 23 (OS). Vilna's Jewish birth register from 1903 contains the following information: "Date and Month of birth: Christian—June 23, Jewish—Tamuz 11. Class of father, names of father and mother: Polotsk *m*[*eshchanin*] Ruvin Elyev Heifetz, Chaya Israelevna. Who was born and his/her given name: Pesya" (TsGIA SPb, f. 361, op. 2, d. 7151, l. v2). A number of American documents pertaining to Pauline Heifetz (Pauline Chotzinoff), including the Social Security Death Index (N 080-38-2007), give her date of birth as January 15, 1903. Additionally, in a personal diary entry from 1919, Pauline wrote that she was to turn sixteen on January 15.

14. Axelrod, *Heifetz*, 124.

15. Alexander Woollcott, "The Quest of a Lost Childhood."

16. A. Dragomanov, "Iasha Kheifets v SSSR [Jascha Heifetz in the USSR]," *Russkii golos* (New York), May 13, 1934.

17. Leopold Auer, *Violin Playing As I Teach It* (1921; repr. New York: Dover Publications, 1980), 37–38.

18. *Biografia genial'nogo mal'chika* [*Biography of a boy genius*] (April 1911), handwritten manuscript in the file of Viktor Valter, KR RIII, f. 83, op. 1, no. 66, l. 1. This manuscript is not in Valter's handwriting, and almost certainly not in the handwriting of Heifetz's parents, who were unable to write such clear Russian, though it does appear to have been written from their recollections.

19. Axelrod, *Heifetz*, 138.

20. Hyman Gerber, "Thumb Trouble," *The Violinist*, December 1931, 87.

21. *Noveishaia shkola dlia skripki sochineniia K. Bériot* [*New School for Violin, Compositions by K. Bériot*], op. 102 (St. Petersburg: Bernard, 1870), part 1, 1.

22. Henrich Ernst Kayser, *36 Etudes elementaires et progressives pour violon*, 2 vols. (St. Petersburg: La Lyre du nord, s.a.).

23. Axelrod, *Heifetz*, 124.

24. Samuel and Sada Applebaum, *The Way They Play*, book 1 (Neptune City: Paganiniana, 1972), 75.

25. Letter of Y. M. Epstein (1902–1994) to Genrikh Agranovsky, 31 August 1989, in Genrikh Agranovskii, "Korol' skripachei iz starogo Vil'niusa [King of Violinists from Old Vilnius]," no. 3, *Vilnius*, 1991, 182. The Heifetz biographer Artur Weschler-Vered interviewed an elderly gentleman in Israel in 1977 who recalled an almost identical scene. Correspondence with the author, May 2012.

26. Uncertainty also surrounds the birth date of the third Heifetz sibling. Although a birth register record was not found, Elza's birth date is listed on her entrance examination form for the Petrograd Conservatory as September 10, 1905 (OS) (TsGIA SPb, f. 361, op. 6, d. 27, l. 751). Nevertheless, according to various official documents in the USA, including the Social Security Death Index record for Elza Behrman (Heifetz), the date of birth was September 5, 1905 (NS).

27. Recollections of Anna Sharfstein-Koch (November 29, 1992), 1.

28. A. Litvin, "A yidish vunderkind in Vilna," *Forverts*, no. 5 (1911).

29. Samuel Chotzinoff, "Jascha Heifetz: The Early Years; Recollections of the celebrated violinist's early career (A selection by Robin Chotzinoff from the unpublished memoirs 'Till Death Us Do Part')," *Strad*, December 1988, 970.

30. Alexander Woollcott, "The Quest of a Lost Childhood."

31. *Mestnaia khronika* [Local Chronicle], *Vilenskii vestnik*, May 11, 1906.

32. *Spravka o privitii ospy* [Certificate of smallpox vaccination], TsGIA SPb, f. 361, op. 1, d. 4276, l. 3.

3. 1906–1909: MUSIC SCHOOL

1. *Otchet direktskii Vilenskogo otdeleniia Russkogo muzykal'nogo obshchestva za 1873–74* [Report of the Board of the Vilnius Division of the Russian Musical Society for 1873–74] (Vilnius, 1874), 2–3; A. I. Puzyrevskii, "Imperatorskoe Russkoe muzykal'noe obshchestvo v pervye 50 let ego deiatel'nosti [Imperial Russian Music Society in the First 50 Years of its Activity]," (St. Petersburg, 1909), 33, 37.

2. Konstantin Mikhailovich Galkovskii (Galkauskas), "Vospominaniia [Memoirs]," LLMA, f. 58, op. 1, d. 23, l. 4–5. In the original, A. N. Spasskaya is mistakenly called L. Spasskaya.

3. A. I. Puzyrevskii, "Imperatorskoe Russkoe muzykal'noe obshchestvo," 37.

4. Otchet Vilenskogo otdeleniia Imperatorskogo Russkogo muzykal'nogo obshchestva i sostoiashchego pri nem muzykal'nogo uchilishcha za 1906–1907 uchebnyi god [Report of the Vilnius Division of the Imperial Russian Music Society and its Music School for the 1906–1907 Academic Year] (Vilnius, 1908), 3–5, 10.

5. Ustav muzykal'nykh uchilishch Imperatorskogo Russkogo muzykal'nogo obshchestva [Charter of the Music Schools of the Imperial Russian Music Society] (St. Petersburg, 1900), 12–13.

6. Malkin's biographical information was taken from his student record, preserved in the archive of the St. Petersburg Conservatory. TsGIA SPb, f. 361, op. 1, d. 2538, l. 1–22.

7. Artur Weschler-Vered, *Jascha Heifetz* (New York: Schirmer Books, 1986), 18.

8. A. Litvin, "A yidish vunderkind in Vilna," *Forverts*, no. 5 (1911).

9. Letter from Mikhail Gnesin to Alexander Siloti, August 22, 1916, in *Aleksandr Il'ich Ziloti: Vospominaniia i pis'ma* (Leningrad, 1963), 299–300.

10. Mestnaia Khronika [Local Chronicle], *Vilenskii vestnik*, September 12, 1906.

11. During the Soviet years this street bore the name of the Lithuanian poet Liudas Gira; presently, its former name is used, but in Lithuanian—Vilniaus.

12. Leopold Auer, *Violin Playing As I Teach It* (1921; repr. New York: Dover Publications, 1980), 96.

13. Programma uchenicheskogo vechera [Student recital evening program], taken from the Report of the Vilnius division of the IRMO and the Music School for the academic year 1906–1907, 13.

14. Vsia Vil'na: Adresnaia i spravochnaia kniga g. Vil'ny i putevoditel' po gorodu i ego okrestnostiam [All Vilna: Address and Information Book for the City of Vilna and Guide to the City and its Suburbs] (Vilnius, 1909), Otd. I. S. III.

15. M. V. Dobuzhinskii, *Vospominaniia* [*Memoirs*] (Moscow: Nauka, 1987), 94.

16. "Zemskii," "Uchenicheskii vecher v muzykal'nom uchilishche [Student Evening in the Music School]," *Vilenskii vestnik*, December 9, 1906.

17. Frederick H. Martens, *Violin Mastery: Talks with Master Violinists and Teachers* (New York: Frederick A. Stokes Company, 1919), 81.

18. Hugo Reimann, *Dictionary of Music*, 4th ed., trans. J. S. Shedlock (London: Augener, 1895), 737.

19. *Vilenskii vestnik*, May 13, 1907.

20. *Vilenskii vestnik*, June 9, 1907.

21. *Biografia genial'nogo mal'chika* [*Biography of a boy genius*] (April 1911), KR RIII, f. 83, op. 1, no. 66, l. 4.

22. *Vilenskii vestnik*, September 1, 1907.

23. Otchet Vilenskogo otdeleniia Imperatorskogo Russkogo muzykal'nogo ob-shchestva i sostoiashchego pri nem muzykal'nogo uchilishcha za 1907–1908 uchebnyi god [Report of the Vilnius Division of the Imperial Russian Music Society and its Music School for the 1907–1908 Academic Year] (Vilnius, 1909), 3.

24. Ibid., 14.

25. *Vilenskii vestnik*, December 11, 1907.

26. Auer was almost eighty when he married Wanda Bogutska-Stein. See: "Leopold Auer Marries," *New York Times*, June 27, 1924.

27. D. Bekar, Teatr i muzyka [Theater and Music], *Severo-zapadnyi golos*, February 14, 1908.

28. L. Shch, "V muzykal'nom uchilishche [In the Music School]," *Vilenskii vestnik*, May 30, 1908.

29. Alexander Woollcott, "The Quest of a Lost Childhood," *Saturday Evening Post*, April 7, 1928.

30. L. Shch, "V muzykal'nom uchilishche."

31. Auer, *Violin Playing As I Teach It*, 96–97.

32. This anecdote was cited in various unattributed newspaper clippings, including one with the handwritten note "4/14/1920 London." JHC LoC, box 248.

33. *Vilenskii vestnik*, May 2, 1908.

34. GARF, f. 1729, op. 1, ed. khr. 1502, l. 2.

35. KR RIII, f. 28, op. 2, no. 811, l. 1–2.

36. GARF, f. 1729, op. 1, ed. khr. 1502, l. 3.

37. Ibid. Letter dated September 8, 1908.

38. LLMA, f. 58, d. 23, l. 8.

39. Konstantin Mikhailovich Galkovskii (Galkauskas), "Publichnyi vecher uchash-chikhsia v muzykal'nom uchilishche IRMO [Public Evening of Students in the Music School of the IRMO]," *Severo-zapadnyi golos*, November 5, 1908.

40. Otchet Vilenskogo otdeleniia Imperatorskogo Russkogo muzykal'nogo ob-shchestva i sostoiashchego pri nem muzykal'nogo uchilishcha za 1908–1909 uchebnyi god [Report of the Vilnius Division of the Imperial Russian Music Society and its Music School for the 1908–1909 Academic Year] (Vilnius, 1909), 31.

41. P. M., Teatr i muzyka, *Severo-zapadnyi telegraf*, April 2, 1909.

42. TsGIA SPb, f. 361, op. 1, d. 1455, l. 1–4.

43. Teatr i muzyka, *Severo-zapadnyi telegraf*, April 28, 1909, 3.

44. D. Bekar, Teatr i muzyka, *Severo-zapadnyi telegraf*, May 2, 1909, 3.

45. D. Bekar, Teatr i muzyka, *Severo-zapadnyi telegraf*, May 10, 1909, 3.

46. Auer, *Violin Playing As I Teach It*, 97.

47. Martens, *Violin Mastery*, 81.

48. D. Bekar, Teatr i muzyka, May 10, 1909, 3.

49. *Russkaia muzykal'naia gazeta* (April 29, 1909): Stlb. 475.

50. A. I. "Vystavka—Iskusstvo v zhizni detei [Exhibit—Art in the Life of Children]," *Vilenskii vestnik*, April 2, 1909, 3.

51. *Vecherniaia gazeta* (Vilnius), December 5, 1913, 3.

52. To further confuse the situation, V. Grigoryev incorrectly associates Jascha's performance with the 1906 exhibit. See: V. Grigor'ev, "Kheifets, Iasha," *Russkoe zarubezh'e: Zolotaia kniga emigratsii, Entsiklopedicheskii biograficheskii slovar'* [*The Russian Abroad: Golden Book of Emigration, the Encyclopedic Biographical Dictionary*] (Moscow: ROSSPEN, 1997), 665.

53. *Vilenskii vestnik*, June 3, 1909.

54. Public exam program for May 29, 1909, in Otchet Vilenskogo otdeleniia Imperatorskogo Russkogo muzykal'nogo obshchestva i sostoiashchego pri nem muzykal'nogo uchilishcha za 1908–1909 uchebnyi god [Report of the Vilnius Division of the Imperial Russian Music Society and its Music School for the 1908–1909 Academic Year] (Vilnius, 1909), 43.

55. Heifetz kept the original certificate in a scrapbook in his collection. JHC LoC, box 251.

56. M-r M. S., "Muzykal'noe uchilishche Vilenskogo otdeleniia IRMO v 1908–1909 godu [Music School of the Vilnius Division of the IRMO in 1908–1909]," *Vilenskii vestnik,* June 3, 1909.

57. Program of the concert cited in Otchet Vilenskogo otdeleniia Imperatorskogo Russkogo muzykal'nogo obshchestva i sostoiashchego pri nem muzykal'nogo uchilishcha za 1908–1909 uchebnyi god [Report of the Vilnius Division of the Imperial Russian Music Society and its Music School for the 1908–1909 Academic Year] (Vilnius, 1909), 44–45.

58. M-r M. S., "Muzykal'noe uchilishche Vilenskogo otdeleniia IRMO."

59. Genrikh Agranovskii, "Udivitel'naia istoriia memorial'noi doski [Remarkable History of a Memorial Plaque]," *Litovskii Ierusalim* no. 1–2 (Vil'nius, 2001).

60. Ibid.

61. TsGIA SPb, f. 361, op. 1, d. 4276, l. 2–3.

62. Ibid., f. 361, op. 1, d. 4276, l. 1. Passport no. 2787, valid for five years.

63. JHC LoC, box 280.

64. Ibid.

65. I. Mor, "Kontsert Kheifetsa [Concert of Heifetz]," Nasha kopeika [Our Kopeck], *Vilenskii kur'er,* September 22, 1909.

66. *Vilenskii vestnik*, September 23, 1909.

67. *Vilenskii vestnik*, October 30, 1909.

68. Nasha kopeika, *Vilenskii kur'er,* December 25, 1909; *Severo-zapadnyi golos,* December 25, 1909.

69. KR RIII, f. 28, op. 2, no. 811, l. 3.

70. Nasha kopeika, *Vilenskii kur'er,* November 13, 1909.

71. "Heifetz welcomes one of his teachers," unidentified clipping. JHC LoC, box 253.

4. 1910: ST. PETERSBURG CONSERVATORY AND NALBANDIAN

1. Otchet S.-Peterburgskogo otdeleniia Imperatorskogo Russkogo muzykal'nogo obshchestva i konservatorii za 1909–1910 [Report of the S.-Petersburg Division of the Imperial Russian Music Society and Conservatory for 1909–1910] (St. Petersburg, 1912), 13–14.

2. Ustav konservatorii Imperatorskogo Russkogo muzykal'nogo obshchestva [Charter of the Conservatories of the Imperial Russian Music Society, St. Petersburg] (St. Petersburg, 1911), 20.

3. Polozheniia po Peterburgskoi konservatorii. Iz istorii Leningradskoi konservatorii: materialy i dokumenty [Regulations of the St. Petersburg Conservatory. From the History of the Leningrad Conservatory: Materials and Documents] (Leningrad, 1964), 68.

4. Ustav konservatorii [Charter of the Conservatories], 20. The term "progymnasium" refers to the initial classes of the gymnasium.

5. TsGIA SPb, f. 361, op. 6, d. 20, l. 680.

6. TsGIA SPb, f. 361, op. 1, d. 4276, l. 1.

7. TsGIA SPb, f. 361, op. 5, d. 36, l. 231.

8. M. K. Mikhailov, "A. K. Glazunov (Iz vospominanii) [A. K. Glazunov (From Recollections)]," in G. G. Tigranov, *Leningradskaia konservatoriia v vospominaniiakh* [*Leningrad Conservatory in Recollections*], Book 1 (Leningrad: Muzgiz, 1987), 99.

9. Sergei Prokofiev, "Iunye gody [Young Years]," in G. G. Tigranov, *Leningradskaia konservatoriia v vospominaniiakh,* Book 1, 51–52.

10. TsGIA SPb, f. 361, op. 6, d. 20, l. 681.

11. TsGIA SPb, f. 361, op. 5, d. 26, l. 574.

12. TsGIA SPb, f. 361, op. 1, d. 4276, l. 4.

13. Fyodor Dostoevsky, *Poor Folk & The Gambler,* trans. C. J. Hogarth (London: J. M. Dent, 1962), 5–6.

14. TsGIA SPb, f. 515, op. 1, d. 2380, l. 99–100.

15. An archaic Russian unit equivalent to 7 feet (2.13 meters).

16. GARF, f. DP 102, op. 5, ed. khr. 252, l. 6–12.

17. TsGIA SPb, f. 361, op. 5, d. 26, l. 26.

18. Roy Malan, *Efrem Zimbalist: A Life* (Cambridge: Amadeus Press, 2004), 8.

19. TsGIA SPb, f. 361, op. 1, d. 4276, l. 7.

20. Anushavan Grigor'evich Ter-Gevondian, "Nezabyvaemaia pora [Unforgettable Time]," in G. G. Tigranov, *Leningradskaia konservatoriia v vospominaniiakh,* Book 1, 45.

21. OR RNB, f. 187, no. 550, l. 46.

22. I. Zhi-v, "Deti-virtuozy [Child Virtuosos]," *Solntse Rossii,* October, 1911.

23. *Peterburgskaia gazeta* (April 18, 1911).

24. KR RIII, f. 8, razd. XI, no. 17, l. 1.

25. Cited in Lev Nikolaevich Raaben, *Leopol'd Semionovich Auer: Ocherk zhizni i deiatel'nosti* [*Leopold Auer: A Sketch of His Life and Career*] (Muzgiz, 1962), 119.

26. Ibid.

27. A. B. Derounian, "Heifetz Lauds Early Training by Nalbandian," *The Armenian Spectator* (New York), May 17, 1934.

28. Ibid.

29. Otchet S.-Peterburgskogo otdeleniia Imperatorskogo Russkogo muzykal'nogo obshchestva i konservatorii za 1909–1910 [Report of the St. Petersburg Division of the IRMO and Conservatory for 1909–1910] (St. Petersburg, 1912), 204–205, 211.

30. TsGIA SPb, f. 361, op. 8, d. 113, l. 568, ob. 569.

31. TsGIA SPb, f. 361, op. 1, d. 4276, l. 6.

32. Ibid., 1, 4.

33. JHC LoC, box 250.

34. Ibid.

35. The work record of I. R. Nalbandian. SPbGK, d. 164, l. 114.

36. M. M. Beliakov, "Ob I. R. Nalbandiane [On I. R. Nalbandian]," in G. G. Tigranov, *Leningradskaia konservatoriia v vospominaniiakh*, Book 2 (Leningrad: Muzgiz, 1988), 154–155.

37. JHC LoC, box 250.

38. JHC LoC, box 280.

39. Ibid.

40. Otchet S.-Peterburgskogo otdeleniia Imperatorskogo Russkogo muzykal'nogo obshchestva i konservatorii za 1909–1910 [Report of the St. Petersburg Division of the IRMO and Conservatory for 1909–1910], 193.

41. Leopold Auer, *My Long Life in Music* (London: Duckworth & Co., 1924), 157. Writing his memoirs in the early 1920s, it seems the elderly professor forgot that Glazunov had become director in 1905, long before Jascha's arrival.

42. Samuel and Sada Applebaum, *The Way They Play*, Book 5 (Neptune City: Paganiniana, 1978), 232.

43. TsGIA SPb, f. 361, op. 6, d. 21, l. 916.

44. TsGIA SPb, f. 361, op. 1, d. 4278, l. 1.

45. TsGIA SPb, f. 361, op. 6, d. 21, l. 915.

46. TsGIA SPb, f. 361, op. 1, d. 4278, l. 2.

47. TsGIA SPb, f. 361, op. 1, d. 4276, l. 8. In 1914 the street was renamed Lermontovsky Prospekt for the centenary of the poet Mikhail Lermontov.

48. Leopold Auer, *Violin Master Works and Their Interpretation* (New York: Carl Fischer, Inc., 1925), 55.

49. Leopold Auer, *Violin Playing As I Teach It* (1921; repr. New York: Dover Publications, 1980), 97.

50. Prilozhenie k otchetu SPb. otdeleniia Imperatorskogo Russkogo muzykal'nogo obshchestva za 1910–1911 god [Supplement to the report of the St. Petersburg Division of the IRMO and Conservatory for 1910–1911] (St. Petersburg, 1912), 34.

51. V. Grigor'ev, "Kheifets, Iasha [Heifetz, Jascha]," in *Russkoe zarubezh'e: Zolotaia kniga emigratsii, Entsiklopedicheskii biograficheskii slovar'* [*The Russian Abroad: Golden Book of Emigration, the Encyclopedic Biographical Dictionary*] (Moscow: ROSSPEN, 1997), 665.

52. Nadezhda Iosifovna Golubovskaia, "V Peterburgskoi konservatorii [In the Petersburg Conservatory]," in G. G. Tigranov, *Leningradskaia konservatoriia v vospominaniiakh,* Book 2, 58.

53. Ibid., 57.

54. La-mi [Nikolai Andreevich Mal'ko], "Kontsert Iashi Kheifetsa [Concert of Jascha Heifetz]," *Rech',* April 10, 1912.

55. TsGIA SPb, f. 361, op. 1, d. 178.

56. Nikolai Andreevich Mal'ko, *Vospominaniia* [*Memoirs*], Mashinopis' [Typewritten manuscript], KR RIII, f. 47, op. 1, no. 203, l. 115.

57. I. Knorozovskii, "Muzykal'nye zametki [Musical Notes]," *Teatr i iskusstvo,* no. 50 (1910): 978–979.

58. Izrail' Iampol'skii, *Frits Kreisler* (Moscow: Muzyka, 1975), 99.

59. "Kontserty Fritsa Kreislera [Concerts of Fritz Kreisler]," *Rech'* (December 10, 1910), 5.

60. See: Amy Biancolli, "Hoaxes All: Pugnani, Vivaldi, Martini, and Kreisler," in *Fritz Kreisler: Love's Sorrow, Love's Joy* (Portland: Amadeus Press, 1998), 154–182.

61. Prilozhenie k otchetu SPb. otdeleniia Imperatorskogo Russkogo muzykal'nogo obshchestva za 1910–1911 god, 41–42.

62. Aleksandra Dmitrievna Bushen, "Iz vospominanii o dalekom proshlom [Recollections of the Far Past]," in G. G. Tigranov, *Leningradskaia konservatoriia v vospominaniiakh,* Book 2, 63.

5. FIRST PERFORMANCES IN ST. PETERSBURG

1. JHC LoC, box 280.

2. TsGIA SPb, f. 361, op. 1, d. 4276, l. 11, d. 4278, l. 2.

3. Evidence for these two performances is vague; the source is the manuscript *Biography of a Boy Genius. Biografia genial'nogo mal'chika* [*Biography of a boy genius*] (April 1911), handwritten manuscript contained in the file of Valter, KR RIII, f. 83, op. 1, no. 66, l. 4, ob.

4. Aleksandra Iakovlevna Brushtein, *Stranitsy proshlogo* [*Pages of the Past*] (Moscow: Iskusstvo, 1956), 13.

5. JHC LoC, box 280.

6. JHC LoC, box 258.

7. B-n. Nik. [Nikolai D. Bernstein], "Novyi vunderkind [New wunderkind]," *Peterburgskaia gazeta,* April 18, 1911.

8. Grigorii T[imofeev], "Kontsert maloletnego skripacha Iosifa Kheifetsa [Concert of Young Violinist Joseph Heifetz]," *Rech',* April 19, 1911.

9. "Kontsert Iosifa Kheifetsa [Concert of Joseph Heifetz]," *Birzhevye vedomosti,* April 18, 1911.

10. Is-ev, "Kontsert Iosifa Kheifetsa [Concert of Joseph Heifetz]," *Teatr i sport,* April 19, 1911.

11. "Kontsert Iosifa Kheifetsa," *Birzhevye vedomosti.*

12. I. Mor-nik, "Kontsert Iosifa Kheifetsa [Concert of Jascha Heifetz]," *Obozrenie teatrov*, April 19, 1911.

13. B-n. Nik., "Novyi vunderkind [New wunderkind]."

14. Viktor Val'ter, Khronika: S.-Peterburg [Chronicle: S.-Petersburg], *RMG*, no. 17 (April 24, 1911): 429–430.

15. Cited in Lev Nikolaevich Raaben, *Leopol'd Semionovich Auer: Ocherk zhizni i deiatel'nosti [Leopold Auer: A Sketch of His Life and Career]* (Muzgiz, 1962), 135.

16. Viktor Val'ter, "Iasha Kheifets (Iz vospominanii) [Jascha Heifetz (From Recollections)]," *Zveno* (Paris), February 28, 1926.

17. Viktor Val'ter, "Kontsert I. Kheifetsa," *Rech'*, May 15, 1911.

18. Viktor Val'ter, "Iasha Kheifets (Iz vospominanii)."

19. JHC LoC, box 251. Ruvin addresses his brother with the title "E. V. B," an abbreviation for the term "His Most Honorable."

20. TsGIA SPb, 361, op. 8, d. 114, l. 660 ob.

21. Aleksandr Petrovich Aslanov (Aslanian), "Pervyi kontsert Iashi Kheifetsa (Posviashchaetsia ego otsu) [First Concert of Jascha Heifetz (Dedicated to his Father)]," *Novoe Russkoe Slovo* (New York), April 22, 1924. Although Aslanov states that this concert was in 1912, the actual concert program and countless newspaper reviews prove categorically that it took place in May 1911.

22. A. Koptiaev, "Kontsert I. Kheifetsa [Concert of J. Heifetz]," *Birzhevye vedomosti*, May 14, 1911.

23. "Maloletnii skripach [Young Violinist], *Severo-zapadnyi golos* (Vil'na), May 17, 1911.

24. Val'ter, "Kontsert I. Kheifetsa," *Rech'*.

25. Viktor Val'ter, "Kontsert Dmitriia Shostakovicha [Concert of Dmitrii Shostakovich]," *Teatr*, no. 12 (1923): 4.

26. *Grammofonnyi mir*, no. 12 (June 25, 1911).

27. No. 215, Schubert, *The Bee*; no. 216, Kreisler, *Caprice Viennois* (matrix no. 102); no. 217, Dvořák, *Humoresque*; no. 218, Auer, *Romance* (matrix no. 100); no. 219, Drdla, *Serenade* (matrix no. 105); no. 220, Drdla, *Souvenir* (matrix no. 104). This list has been compiled with information contained in correspondence from John A. Maltese to Galina Kopytova, February 24, 2002, and from V. Grigor'ev, "Kheifets, Iasha," *Russkoe zarubezh'e: Zolotaia kniga emigratsii, Entsiklopedicheskii biograficheskii slovar' [The Russian Abroad: Golden Book of Emigration, the Encyclopedic Biographical Dictionary]* (Moscow: ROSSPEN, 1997) (Moscow, 1997), 665.

28. *Grammofonnyi mir*, no. 8–9 (1911): 15.

29. *Grammofonnyi mir*, no. 10 (1911): 8.

30. RGAF, Archive of the "Zvukopis'" company, no. 17. No matrix number given.

31. Jascha Heifetz, *The Russian Recordings 1911*, Legendary Treasures: Jascha Heifetz Collection, vol. 5, 2000, Doremi Records, recorded 1911, 1945; Eric Wen, "Heifetz: a legend on record," *Strad*, January 1995, 38.

32. In full form: Mikhail, Yekaterina, and Aleksandra.

33. JHC LoC, box 280.

6. SUMMER 1911: CONCERTS IN PAVLOVSK AND ODESSA

1. Vsia Vil'na: Adresnaia i spravochnaia kniga g. Vil'ny i putevoditel' po gorodu i ego okrestnostiam [All Vilna: Address and Information Book for the City of Vilna and Guide to the City and its Suburbs] (Vilnius, 1909), Otd. I. C. XIII; A *verst* is an old Russian measurement of length equal to 3,500 feet.

2. Josefa Heifetz stenogram of notes from phone conversations with Anna Sharfstein-Koch, Jan. 10, 1993, 4.

3. KR RIII, f. 83, op. 1, no. 53, l. 1.

4. KR RIII, f. 83, op. 1, no. 53, l. 2, published in Galina Kopytova, "Pervye shagi geniia: Iasha Kheifets [First steps of a genius: Jascha Heifetz]," *Sovetskaia muzyka*, no. 8 (1991): 92–93.

5. Nasha kopeika [Our Kopeck], *Vilensky kur'er*, June 26, 1911.

6. Programs from Pavlovsk Station, 1911. Library of the St. Petersburg Academy Philharmonic.

7. V. G. Karatygin, "Benefis orkestra v Pavlovske [Benefit for the Orchestra in Pavlovsk]," *Rech'*, July 5, 1911.

8. Osip Mandelstam, trans. Clarence Brown and W. S. Merwin, *The Selected Poems of Osip Mandelstam* (New York: New York Review of Books, 1971, reprinted 2004), 39.

9. Some of these scenes were included in the documentary. See: *Jascha Heifetz: God's Fiddler*, directed by Peter Rosen (New York: Peter Rosen Productions, 2011), DVD.

10. KR RIII, f. 83, op. 1, no. 52, l. 1. Ruvin's "Erons Grois" probably refers to Heinrich W. Ernst's *Airs Hongrois*.

11. KR RIII, f. 83, op. 1, no. 52, l. 2. Postmarked in Vilna, July 14, 1911.

12. R. Engel, "Muzyka v provintsii: Odessa [Music in the Provinces: Odessa]," *RMG*, no. 36 (September 4, 1911): Stlb. 700.

13. Diavolo, Khronika [Chronicle], *Odesskaia pochta*, July 21, 1911.

14. R. Engel, "Muzyka v provintsii: Odessa [Music in the Provinces: Odessa]," *RMG*, no. 38 (September 18, 1911): Stlb. 762.

15. Dissonans, "Vystavochnye kontserty [Exhibit Concerts]," *Odesskie novosti*, July 23, 1911.

16. "Vystavka [Exhibit]," *Odesskie novosti*, July 23, 1911.

17. M. G. "Kontsert I. R. Kheifetsa [Concert of J. R. Heifetz]," *Odesskie novosti*, July 27, 1911.

18. Ibid.

19. "Vystavka," *Odesskie novosti*, July 27, 1911.

20. "Vystavka," *Odesskie novosti*, July 29, 1911.

21. "Vystavka," *Odesskie novosti*, August 2, 1911.

22. P. Nilus, "Zametki khudozhnika [Notes of an Artist]," *Odesskie novosti*, August 3, 1911.

23. I. Zhi-v, "Deti-virtuozy [Child Virtuosos]," *Solntse Rossii*, October 1911, 9.

24. "A vunderkind bay yidn," *Gut-morgn* (Odessa), no. 474, 1911.

25. Ibid.

26. Isaac Babel, "The Awakening," in *The Complete Works of Isaac Babel*, ed. Nathalie Babel, trans. Peter Constantine (London: W. W. Norton & Co., 2002), 628.

27. Ibid., 629.

28. Ibid., 633.

29. Nathan Milstein, with Solomon Volkov, *From Russia to the West* (New York: Limelight Editions, 1990), 2.

30. Ibid., 2–3.

31. Lisa K. Stein, *Syd Chaplin: A Biography* (Jefferson, N.C.: McFarland & Company, Inc., 2011), 86.

32. JHC LoC, box 250.

33. Ibid.

34. Ibid.

35. S. Vengerov, *Kritiko-biograficheskii slovar' russkikh pisatelei i uchenykh* [*Critical-Biographical Dictionary of Russian Writers and Scholars*] (Petrograd, 1915), 83.

36. JHC LoC, box 280.

37. "Kontsert 6 avgusta v Sventsianskom obshchestvennom sobranii [Concert 6 August in the Sventsiany Social Assembly]," *Sventsianskii listok*, August 10, 1911.

38. JHC LoC, box 258.

39. "Kontsert 6 avgusta [Concert 6 August]."

40. "V Sventsianakh [In Sventsiany]," *Vilenskii kur'er*, August 10, 1911.

41. KR RIII, f. 83 op. 1, published in Galina Kopytova "Pervye shagi geniia: Iasha Kheifets [First Steps of a Musical Genius]," 93.

42. "A vunderkind," *Der Fraynd* (Warsaw) (August 14, 1911).

43. A. Litvin, "A yidish vunderkind in Vilna," *Forverts*, no. 5 (1911).

44. Dissonans, "Kontsert na vystavke [Concert at the Exhibit]," *Odesskie novosti*, August 31, 1911.

45. "Vystavka," *Odesskie novosti*, September 1, 1911.

46. TsGIA SPb, f. 361, op. 1, d. 1443, l. 1–14.

47. Gdal Saleski, *Famous Musicians of Jewish Origin* (New York: Bloch Publishing Company, 1949), 346–347.

48. Ibid., 347.

49. Kto-to, "Didur i Kheifets [Didur and Heifetz]," *Iuzhnaia mysl'*, September 1, 1911.

50. Loengrin, "Benefis sluzhashchikh [Benefit for Workers]," *Odesskie novosti*, September 1, 1911.

51. "Vystavka: Benefis sluzhashchikh [Exhibit: Benefit for the Workers]," *Golos Odessy*, September 1, 1911.

52. Ar. A. "O publichnykh vystupleniiakh Iosifa Kheifetsa [On the Public Performances of Joseph Heifetz]" *Odesskie novosti*, September 3, 1911.

53. Kto-to, "Didur i Kheifets [Didur and Heifetz]."

7. FALL 1911: IN THE CLASS OF PROFESSOR AUER

1. Lev Nikolaevich Raaben, *Leopol'd Semionovich Auer: Ocherk zhizni i deiatel'nosti* [*Leopold Auer: A Sketch of His Life and Career*] (Muzgiz, 1962), 17.

2. JHC LoC, box 271. Note that the entry under November 1, 1872, includes a reference to 1873. It is unclear which of the years is correct.

3. O. Fon-Tidebel', "Shkola skripichnoi igry i ee znachenie dlia skripacha-ispolnitelia, kompozitora i pedagoga [School of Violin Playing and its Meaning for the Violinist-Performer, Composer, and Pedagogue]," *RMG*, no. 51–52 (December 19–26, 1910): Stlb. 1161–1162.

4. Carl Flesch, *The Memoirs of Carl Flesch* (London: Rockliff, 1957), 253.

5. Lev Nikolaevich Raaben, *Zhizn' zamechatel'nykh skripachei* [*The Lives of Remarkable Violinists*] (Moscow, Leningrad: Muzyka, 1967), 164–165.

6. Auer's eldest daughter Zoya died from typhus around 1918.

7. Raaben, *Zhizn' zamechatel'nykh skripachei* [*Remarkable Violinists*], 165.

8. TsGIA SPb, f. 361, op. 1, d. 4278, l. 3. ob.

9. Ibid.

10. The private collection of John Anthony Maltese. The calling card is reproduced in Herbert Axelrod, *Heifetz*, 3rd ed. (Neptune City, NJ: Paganiniana, 1990), 621.

11. KR RIII, f. 83, op. 1, no. 9, l. 1, published in Galina Kopytova "Pervye shagi geniia: Iasha Kheifets [First steps of a genius: Jascha Heifetz]," *Sovetskaia muzyka*, no. 8 (1991): 93.

12. Samarii Il'ich Savshinkii, "Vospominaniia o bylom [Recollections of the Past]," in G. G. Tigranov, *Leningradskaia konservatoriia v vospominaniiakh* [*Leningrad Conservatory in Recollections*], Book 2 (Leningrad: Muzgiz, 1988), 48.

13. Ibid., 46.

14. Noble Hollister, "Auer, The Mentor of Famous Violinists," *New York Times Magazine*, April 26, 1925, 3.

15. Nadezhda Iosifovna Golubovskaia, "V Peterburgskoi konservatorii [In the Petersburg Conservatory]," in G. G. Tigranov, *Leningradskaia konservatoriia v vospominaniiakh*, Book 2, 58.

16. Liudmila Vladimirovna Karagicheva, "Dalekoe i blizkoe [Far and Near]," *Sovetskaia muzyka*, no. 10 (1991): 70. In the cited text the "Kreutzer" studies are incorrectly identified as the "Kreisler" studies.

17. Mikhail Alekseevich Bikhter, "Telega zhizni [Cart of Life]." Bikhter's original manuscript is located in KR RIII, f. 96, op. 1, no. 4, and cited in Lev Raaben, *Leopol'd Semionovich Auer*, 152.

18. Hollister, "Auer, The Mentor of Famous Violinists," 3.

19. KR RIII, f. 96, op. 1, no. 4 (notebook 3), 21–22. Heifetz is not mentioned in the list because Bikhter accompanied the Auer class largely during the period before Heifetz entered the conservatory.

20. Axelrod, *Heifetz*, 126, 128.

21. Ibid., 129.

22. Hollister, "Auer, the Mentor of Famous Violinists," 22.

23. Golubovskaia, "In the Petersburg Conservatory," 58.

24. Hollister, "Auer, The Mentor of Famous Violinists," 3.

25. Ibid., 22.

26. Leopold Auer, *Violin Playing As I Teach It* (1921; repr. New York: Dover Publications, 1980), 83–84.

27. Aleksandr Iakovlevich Shtrimer, "Navsegda sokhraniu v pamiati [I Will Remember Forever]," in G. G. Tigranov, *Leningradskaia konservatoriia v vospominaniiakh,* Book 2 (Leningrad: Muzgiz, 1988), 152–153.

28. Prilozhenie k otchetu SPb. otdeleniia Imperatorskogo Russkogo muzykal'nogo obshchestva za 1911–1912 god [Supplement to the report of the St. Petersburg division of the Imperial Russian Music Society for 1911–1912], 61.

29. A. Litvin, "A yidish vunderkind in Vilna," *Forverts,* no. 5 (1911).

30. N. Golubev, "Obshchestvo 'Zvukopis' [Company 'Zvukopis']," *Grammofonnyi mir,* no. 18 (1911), 14.

31. Reproduced in Eric Wen, "Heifetz: a legend on record," *Strad,* January, 1995, 38.

32. "Deti-virtuozy [Child Virtuosos]," *Solntse Rossii,* October, 1911.

33. The article mistakenly names her Eleonora Donskaya. The harpist Eleonora Damskaya (1898–?) was a conservatory friend of Sergei Prokofiev and corresponded with him from 1912 until the end of the composer's life. For an English translation of a selection of the letters see: "Letters to Eleonora Damskaya" (Chapter Two) in *Selected Letters of Sergei,* ed. & trans. Harlow Robinson (Boston: Northeastern University Press, 1998).

34. Leopold Auer, *Violin Master Works and Their Interpretation* (New York: Carl Fischer, Inc., 1925), 31.

35. Ibid., 154.

36. Leopold Auer, *My Long Life in Music* (London: Duckworth & Co., 1924), 210.

37. Ibid., 210–211.

38. N. R. "Iasha Kheifets [Jascha Heifetz]," Nasha kopeika [Our Kopeck], *Vilenskii kur'er,* December 7, 1913. Although written in 1913, this article refers to an earlier performance when Jascha was eight years old.

39. Auer, *Violin Master Works and Their Interpretation,* 158.

40. "Vecher v pol'zu detskikh kolonii [Evening for the Benefit of Children's Colonies]," *Severo-zapadnyi golos,* December 31, 1911.

41. "Kolonial'nyi vecher [Colony Evening]," Nasha kopeika, *Vilenskii kur'er,* December 31, 1911.

42. JHC LoC, box 251.

43. TsGIA SPb, f. 361, op. 2, d. 7151, l. 3.

44. TsGIA SPb, f. 361, op. 2, d. 4276, l. 1.

45. TsGIA SPb, f. 361, op. 2, d. 7151, l. 1. Note the particular date of birth used here.

46. TsGIA SPb, f. 361, op. 6, d. 22, l. 967.

47. TsGIA SPb, f. 361, op. 6, d. 22, l. 968.

48. A. G. Ter-Gevondian, "Nezabyvaemaia pora [Unforgettable Time]," in G. G. Tigranov, *Leningradskaia konservatoriia v vospominaniiakh [Leningrad Conservatory in Recollections]*, Muzgiz, Book 1, 47.

49. Viktor Val'ter, "Iasha Kheifets (Iz vospominanii) [Jascha Heifetz (From Recollections)]," *Zveno* (Paris), February 28, 1926. For further information on Zinovy Kiselgof, including a number of photographs, see: Mikhail Beizer, *The Jews of St. Petersburg: Excursions Through a Noble Past*, ed. Martin Gilbert (Philadelphia: The Jewish Publication Society, 1989).

50. Val'ter, "Kheifets (Iz vospominanii)."

8. THE BEGINNING OF 1912

1. Ar. A., "U prof. Auera [With Professor Auer]," *Odesskie novosti*, January 13, 1912.

2. *Trudovaia gazeta*, January 6, 7, 11, 13, 14, 1912; *Nikolaevskaia gazeta*, January 11, 1912, 14.

3. *Trudovaia gazeta*, January 17, 1912.

4. *Nikolaevskaia gazeta*, January 17, 1912.

5. TsGIA SPb, f. 361, op. 1, d. 178.

6. *Trudovaia gazeta*, January 14, 1912.

7. Akkord, "Kontsert skripacha Iashi Kheifetsa [Concert of the Violinist Jascha Heifetz]."

8. L. Kopf, "Der kontsert fun der varshoyer filharmonye mit dem bateylikung fun 17-yorikn Yoysef Khayfets," *Lodzer tageblat*, January 31, 1912.

9. O. Thompson, *The International Encyclopedia of Music and Musicians* (New York, 1946), 190.

10. The piece identified only as a "Wieniawski Caprice" is probably the Wieniawski *Capriccio-Valse*, op. 7, which also appeared in the printed programs of Jascha's concerts in the summer of this same year.

11. A. Mukdoni, "Der kontsert fun Yoysef Khayfets," *Der Fraynd* (Warsaw), February 6 (19), 1912.

12. M. Kipnis, "A yidish vunderkind (Yoysef Khayfets)," *Haynt*, February 6 (19), 1912.

13. Wieniawska-Muromtseva was the daughter of Sergei Muromtsev, chairman of the First State Duma, and Maria Klimentova, a famous Moscow singer who played the part of Tatyana in the premiere of Tchaikovsky's *Eugene Onegin*. Wieniawska-Muromtseva was married to the composer Adam Wieniawski (nephew of the violinist Henryk Wieniawski) and during the 1910s she achieved some fame.

14. A. Z-ch, "Kontsert M. Veniavskoi i E. Izai [Concert of M. Wieniawska and E. Ysaÿe], *Varshavskii dnevnik*, January 31 (February 13), 1912.

15. A. Z-ch, "Skripach Kheifets [The Violinist Heifetz]," *Varshavskii dnevnik*, February 12 (25), 1912.

16. Ia. E. Korobkov, "Kontsert 10-letnego skripacha Iosifa Kheifetsa [Concert of 10-year old Violinist Jascha Heifetz]," *Varshavskoe slovo,* February, 11 (24), 1912.

17. A. Z-ch, "Skripach Kheifets."

18. *Varshavskoe slovo* (February 11 (24), 1912).

19. Natan Heifetz, Diploma from the Warsaw Musical Institute. Nemirovsky Archive.

20. TsA FSB, Criminal Case of F. A. Heifetz, no. 33716, l. 81.

21. JHC LoC, box 280. Jascha spells Fanny's name three ways in this postcard.

22. A. Z-ch, "Skripach Kheifets."

23. Published in English in Arthur M. Abell, "When Heifetz, Aged 11, Stormed Musical Berlin," *Musical Courier,* May 15, 1952, 6–7.

24. Leopold Auer, *Violin Master Works and Their Interpretation* (New York: Carl Fischer, Inc., 1925), 22.

25. Ibid., 23.

26. Leopold Auer, *Violin Playing As I Teach It* (1921; repr. New York: Dover Publications, 1980), 95.

27. -ev., "Kontsert Iashi Kheifetsa [Concert of Jascha Heifetz]," *Peterburgskii listok,* April 9, 1912.

28. "Kontsert Iashi Kheifetsa," *Vechernee vremia* (St. Petersburg), April 9, 1912.

29. Nikolai D. Bernstein, "Kontsert vunderkinda [Concert of a Wunderkind]," *Peterburgskaia gazeta,* April 9, 1912.

30. Nikolai D. Bernstein, "Maloletnii skripach [Young Violinist]," *Sankt-Peterburgskie vedomosti,* April 10, 1912.

31. I. J. "Konzert des kleinen Jascha Heifetz," *St. Petersburger Herold,* April 10 (OS April 23), 1912; for other reviews of the concert see O.N. Konzert des 11-jahriges Geigers Jascha Heifetz, *St. Petersburger Zeitung,* April 11 (24), 1912; and "D-d, "Kontsert Iashi Kheifetsa," *Obozrenie teatrov,* April 10, 1912.

32. La-mi [Nikolai Andreevich Mal'ko], "Kontsert Iashi Kheifetsa [Concert of Jascha Heifetz]" also appearing in *Rech',* April 10, 1912; *Sovremennoe slovo,* April 10, 1912.

33. V. Val'ter, "Concerts in Petersburg: Jascha Heifetz," *RMG,* no. 16 stlb. 393 (April 15, 1912).

34. *Peterburgskii listok,* April 9, 1912; *Peterburgskaia gazeta,* April 9, 1912.

35. JHC LoC, box 273.

36. TsGIA SPb, f. 361, op. 8, d. 115, l. 170.

37. TsGIA SPb, f. 361, op. 8, d. 115, l. 171.

38. TsGIA SPb, f. 361, op. 8, d. 115, l. 34, ob.—35. See also: TsGIA SPb, f. 361, d. 116, l. 38, ob.—39.

39. A passport for foreign travel (no. 4914) arrived on April 27. TsGIA SPb, f. 569, op. 16, d. 138, l. 339.

9. 1912: FIRST TRIP TO GERMANY

1. KR RIII, f. 28, op. 2, no. 722/83.

2. "Aus dem Leben eines Wunderkindes," *Prager Tagblatt,* October 25, 1912.

3. KR RIII, f. 83, op. 1, no. 52, l. 4, published in Russian in Galina Kopytova, "Pervye shagi geniia: Iasha Kheifets [First steps of a genius: Jascha Heifetz]," *Sovetskaia muzyka,* no. 8 (1991): 93. Originally in German.

4. Published in English translation in Arthur Abell, "When Heifetz, Aged 11, Stormed Musical Berlin," *Musical Courier,* May 15, 1952, 7; Abell informs his readers that "there were also perfervid testimonials from Willy Hess, Michael Press, Arrigo Serato, Theodore Spiering and Gustave Hollander, which because of space considerations can not be given in full."

5. Abell, "When Heifetz, aged 11, stormed musical Berlin," 6.

6. Selection from the journal *Musical Courier* with group photographs preserved in JHC LoC, box 251.

7. Abell, "When Heifetz, Aged 11, Stormed Musical Berlin," 7.

8. JHC LoC, box 259.

9. Louis P. Lochner, *Fritz Kreisler* (The Macmillan Company: New York, 1952), 128.

10. Harold C. Schonberg, *The Virtuosi* (Vintage Books: New York, 1988), 369–370.

11. Published in English translation in Abell, "When Heifetz, Aged 11, Stormed Musical Berlin," 7.

12. L. S. "Im Bechsteinsaal," *Berliner Tageblatt,* May 21, 1912.

13. G. G. "Konzerte," *Vossische Zeitung,* May 24, 1912.

14. *Volks-Zeitung,* May 25, 1912.

15. *Staatsbürger-Zeitung,* May 21, 1912.

16. Boris Schwarz, *Great Masters of the Violin: From Corelli and Vivaldi to Stern, Zukerman and Perlman* (New York: Simon & Schuster, 1983).

17. A copy of this item is preserved in the personal collection of Robert Heifetz, now located with Albina Starkova-Heifetz.

18. Abell, "When Heifetz, aged 11, stormed musical Berlin," 7.

19. *Berliner Tageblatt,* May 31, 1912. Also cited in F. v. H. "Konzerte," *Vossische Zeitung,* May 26, 1912; Dr. Karl Krebs, "Jascha Heifetz," *Der Tag,* May 26, 1912.

20. H. N. "Theater und Musik," *Berliner Lokal-Anzeiger,* May 26, 1912.

21. Hugo Rasch, "Aus Berliner Konzertsälen," *Allgemeine Musik-Zeitung,* June 7, 1912, 638.

22. Emil Liepe, "Konzert: Berlin," *Die Musik,* 1912, XI 18:2. Juniheft, 386.

23. Arthur M. Abell, "Berlin," *Musical Courier,* June 19, 1912.

24. "Po chuzhym kraiam: Iunyi skripach [Around Foreign Lands: Young Violinist]," *Putevodnyi ogoniok* (Moscow), no. 16 (1912): 477.

25. TsGIA SPb, f. 361, op. 1, d. 4276, l. 12; d. 4278, l. 5.

26. TsGIA SPb, f. 361, op. 1, d. 4278, l. 5 ob.

27. JHC LoC, box 250.

28. Ivin, "Benefis dubbel'nskogo orkestra [Benefit of the Dubbeln Orchestra]," *Rizhskaia mysl',* July 27, 1912.

29. N. A. Severskii, "Dubbel'n-Kurgauz [Dubbeln-Kurhaus]," *Rizhskii vestnik*, July 27, 1912.

30. "Konzert," *Rigaer Tageblatt*, July 27, 1912; A. M., "Dubbeln-Kurhaus," *Rigaschen Zeitung* (supplement), July 27 and August 6, 1912; Hans Schmidt, "Konzert," *Rigasche Rundschau*, August 6, 1912.

31. On August 20 Ruvin received a foreign passport (no. 17154). TsGIA SPb, f. 569, op. 16, d. 138, l. 342.

10. 1912: A GERMAN TOUR

1. TsGIA SPb, f. 361, op. 1, l. 4278, l. 6.

2. JHC LoC, box 280.

3. "Jascha Heifetz," *Berliner Lokal-Anzeiger*, Abendausgabe, October 11, 1912.

4. Otto Lessmann, "Aus Berliner Konzertsälen," *Allgemeine Musik-Zeitung*.

5. Paul Ertel, "Konzerte," *Berliner allgemeine Zeitung*, October 13, 1912.

6. *National-Zeitung*, October 13, 1912.

7. See: Saul Elman, *Memoirs of Mischa Elman's Father* (New York: Private printing, 1933), 159–169; and Allan Kozinn, *Mischa Elman and the Romantic Style* (New York: Harwood Academic Publishers, 1990). Biographical details about Waldemar Liachowsky also obtained from conversations with his sons, Henry and Rudolph Lea, USA, May 2011.

8. KR RIII, f. 83, op. 1, no. 52, 1, 5, published in Galina Kopytova, "Pervye shagi geniia: Iasha Kheifets [First steps of a genius: Jascha Heifetz]," *Sovetskaia muzyka*, no. 8 (1991): 93. Originally in German.

9. Berliner Konzerte, *Vossische Zeitung*, October 27, 1912; *Berliner Lokal-Anzeiger*, October 27, 1912.

10. E. E. Taubert, "Konzerte: Berlin," *Die Musik*. 1912. XII. 4:2 Novemberheft, 243.

11. *Berliner Tageblatt*, Morgenausgabe, November 1, 1912.

12. Musikalische Spaziergänge, *Berliner Zeitung am Mittag*, October 31, 1912.

13. *Märkische Volks-Zeitung*, Berlin, October 30, 1912.

14. W. K. Philharmonie, *Berliner Lokal-Anzeiger*, October 29, 1912. The same text was also published in *Der Tag*, October 29, 1912.

15. O. T. "Aus den Konzertsälen," Morgenausgabe *Berliner Börsen-Courier*, October 29, 1912.

16. H. W. D. II. Philharmonisches Konzert, *Berliner allgemeine Zeitung*, October 29, 1912.

17. Otto Lessmann, "Aus Berliner Konzertsälen," *Allgemeine Musik-Zeitung*, November 1, 1912, 1147.

18. M. M. "Konzerte," *Vossische Zeitung*, Morgenausgabe, October 30, 1912.

19. Postcard from Hyman Gerber to Jascha Heifetz, 8 October 1912, JHC LoC, box 280.

20. FreeBMD, England & Wales, FreeBMD Birth Index, 1837–1915, 1896, Q3-Jul-Aug-Sep, 466.

21. TsGIA SPb, f. 361, op. 2, l. 5889.

22. TsGIA SPb, f. 361, op. 8, d. 115, l. 756–757.

23. JHC LoC, box 280.

24. Ibid.

25. Ibid.

26. *The Dawn of Recording: The Julius Block Cylinders,* various performers, compact disc, 2008, Marston Records, recorded between 1891 and 1927. See: Daniel J. Wakin, "Classical Ghosts, Audible Once Again," *New York Times,* October 26, 2008.

27. Fonogramarkhiv Instituta russkoi literatury [IRLI Phonogram Archive], kollektsia Iu. I. Bloka [J. I. Block Collection], Jascha Heifetz: cylinders 192–197; Eddy Brown: cylinders 200–212.

28. JHC LoC, box 234.

29. Heinrich Chevally, "Konzert: Hamburg," *Die Musik.* 1912. XII. 6:2. Dezemberheft, 380.

30. Robert Müller-Hartmann, "Hamburg," *Allgemeine Musik-Zeitung,* November 6, 1912, 1306.

31. Jascha Heifetz *Germania* (Berlin), *Morgenausgabe,* November 30, 1912.

32. JHC LoC, box 273.

33. *Berliner Lokal-Anzeiger,* November 24, 1912; *Vossische Zeitung,* November 24, 1912.

34. Nemirovsky Archive.

35. Ibid.

36. *Sächsische Dorfzeitung und Elbgaupresse,* December 11, 1912.

37. JHC LoC, box 270.

38. *Berliner Lokal-Anzeiger,* December 1, 1912; *Vossische Zeitung,* December 1, 1912.

39. Viktor Val'ter, "Iasha Kheifets [Jascha Heifetz]," *Solntse Rossii [Sun of Russia],* no. 5, January, 1913, 16.

40. TsGIA SPb, f. 361, d. 4276, l. 13 ob.; d, 4278, l. 6 ob.

41. JHC LoC, box 280.

42. KR RIII, f. 3, op. 4, no. 203.

43. Taken from: Osip Mandelstam, "Noise of Time," trans. Clarence Brown. *The Prose of Osip Mandelstam: The Noise of Time, Theodosia, The Egyptian Stamp* (Princeton, N.J.: Princeton University Press, 1965), 94–95.

44. Samuel Chotzinoff, "Jascha Heifetz: The Early Years; Recollections of the celebrated violinist's early career (A selection by Robin Chotzinoff from the unpublished memoirs 'Till Death Us Do Part')," *Strad,* December 1988, 981.

11. THE BEGINNING OF 1913

1. JHC LoC, box 280.

2. TsGIA SPb, f. 361, op. 1, d. 4278, l. 7–7 ob.

3. Vsev. Ch-in, "2-i simfonicheskii kontsert Rizhskogo simfonicheskogo orkestra [2nd Symphony Concert of the Riga Symphonic Orchestra]," *Rizhskaia mysl'*, February 8, 1913.

4. A. N. Severskii, "2-i abonementnyi kontsert Rizhskogo simfonicheskogo orkestra [2nd Subscription Concert of the Riga Symphonic Orchestra]," *Rizhskii vestnik*, February 8, 1913.

5. JHC LoC, box 280.

6. Grigorii Nikolaevich Timofeev, "Kontsert A. Spol'ding [Concert of A. Spalding]," *Rech'*, February 13, 1913.

7. Albert Spalding, *Rise to Follow* (New York: Henry Holt & Co., 1943), 198–199.

8. Ibid., 202–203; Note that Jascha played on a three-quarter-size violin at the time, not a full-size as described in Spalding's story, "Class Lesson" from Spalding, *Rise to Follow;* Copyright © 1943 by Henry Holt and Company, © 1967 by Mary Pyle Spalding. Reprinted by permission of Henry Holt and Company, LLC.

9. André Benoist, *The Accompanist . . . and friends: An Autobiography of André Benoist,* ed. John Anthony Maltese (Neptune City, NJ: Paganiniana, 1978), 224.

10. Ibid., 223–6. Note that Thelma Given and Alexander Bloch never studied at the conservatory—they studied privately with Auer.

11. G. T[imofeev], "Kontsert G. O. Zalesskogo [Concert of G. O. Saleski]," *Rech'*, February 27, 1913.

12. Iulii Dmitrievich E[ngel'], Teatr i muzyka, *Russkie vedomosti*, March 7, 1913.

13. Grigorii Petrovich Pr[okof'ev], "Opera i kontserty v Peterburge [Opera and Concerts in S.-Petersburg]," *RMG*, no. 12 (March 24, 1913): Stlb. 303–304.

14. "Zal konservatorii," [Hall of the Conservatory]," *Sankt-Peterburgskie vedomosti*, March 31, 1913.

15. Ibid.

16. V. Ts., "Iasha Kheifets [Jascha Heifetz]," *Obozrenie teatrov*, March 29, 1913.

17. Viacheslav Gavrilovich Karatygin, "Kontsert Iashi Kheifetsa [Concert of Jascha Heifetz]," *Rech'*, March 30, 1913; Karatygin, "Kontsert Iashi Kheifetsa," *Sovremennoe slovo*, March 30, 1913.

18. Viktor Val'ter, "Kontserty v S.-Peterburge [Concerts in S.-Petersburg]," *RMG* (April 7, 1913): Stlb. 379–380.

19. Axelrod, *Heifetz*, 3rd ed. (Neptune City, NJ: Paganiniana, 1990), 604; A photograph of the bow appears in Kenway Lee, "Premier violinist," *Strad*, January 1995, 48–49.

20. JHC LoC, box 251.

21. *Odesskie novosti*, April 7, 1913; *Odesskii listok*, April 7, 1913.

22. *Odesskie novosti*, April 18, 1913; *Odesskii listok*, April 18, 1913.

23. "U Fritsa Kreislera [With Fritz Kreisler]," *Odesskie novosti*, April 18, 1913.

24. TsGIA SPb, f. 361, op. 8, d. 116, l. 38 ob.-39.

25. Ibid., l. 372 ob.-373.

26. Ibid.

12. SUMMER–FALL 1913: LOSCHWITZ

1. Leopold Auer, *My Long Life in Music* (London: Duckworth & Co., 1924), 338–339.

2. Ibid., 339.

3. TsGIA SPb, f. 361, op. 1, d. 1428, l. 1–12.

4. Auer, *My Long Life in Music*, 329.

5. According to a concert review from a few years later, Toscha initially began his studies not with Auer, but with Auer's former student and then assistant, Maria Gamovetskaya. See: *Rech'*, March 22, 1916.

6. KR RIII, f. 83, op. 1, no. 52, l. 6, published in Galina Kopytova, "Pervye shagi geniia: Iasha Kheifets [First steps of a genius: Jascha Heifetz]," *Sovetskaia muzyka*, no. 8 (1991): 93.

7. *Musical Courier* (October 23, 1912), 16.

8. KR RIII, f. 83, op. 1, no. 53, l. 3, published in Kopytova, "Pervye shagi geniia: Iasha Kheifets," 93.

9. JHC LoC, box 250.

10. Auer, *My Long Life in Music*, 339.

11. The Arthur Abell Archive, New York Public Library.

12. Auer, *My Long Life in Music*, 339–340.

13. A copy of the photograph is located in the Manuscript Research Division of the St. Petersburg State Conservatory, Illustration Archive (NIOR SPbGK, IF), no. 200.

14. Musical Celebrities, Broadway and Forty First Street, Commercial Trust Building, New York City. JHC LoC, box 251.

15. The Arthur Abell Archive, New York Public Library. Originally in German.

16. Iurii Aleksandrovich Shaporin, "Iz vospominanii ["From Recollections]," *Sovetskaia muzyka*, no. 3 (1961). Perepech. v sb. *Iurii Aleksandrovich Shaporin: Literaturnoe nasledie, stat'i, pis'ma* [Reprinted in the collection *Iurii Aleksandrovich Shaporin: Literary Legacy, Articles, Letters*] (Moscow: Sovetskii kompozitor, 1989), 70–71.

17. W. A., *Norddeutsche allgemeine Zeitung*, October 3, 1913; H. N. "Geigende Wunderkinder," *Berliner Lokal-Anzeiger* Abendausgabe, October 1, 1913; -ch. H. *Vossische Zeitung* (October 3, 1913); Konzerte, *Berliner Zeitung am Mittag*, October 3, 1913.

18. Leopold Auer, *Violin Master Works and Their Interpretation* (New York: Carl Fischer, Inc., 1925), 128.

19. Alexander Schmuller, "Chudo (ot nashego korrespondenta) [Miracle (from our correspondent)]," *Den'*, October 5, 1913. Note that Schmuller refers to a line written by the poet Heinrich Heine in a poem entitled "Yehuda ben Halevi," dedicated to the medieval Jewish poet and philosopher. Schmuller mistakenly ascribes these words to Halevi himself.

20. JHC LoC, box 251.

21. The Kopytova Collection.

22. TsGIA, SPb, f. 361, op. 1, d. 4276. A facsimile of the certificate is published in Kenway Lee, "Premier violinist," *Strad*, January 1995, 46.

23. *Novoe vremia*, November 22, 1913.

24. Nikolai D. Bernstein, "Kontsert trinadtsatiletnego Iashi Kheifetsa [Concert of Thirteen-year-old Jascha Heifetz]," *Peterburgskaia gazeta*, November 23, 1913.

25. V. Kolomiitsev, "Iasha Kheifets [Jascha Heifetz]," *Den'*, November 23, 1913.

26. V. L. "Kontsert Iashi Kheifetsa [Concert of Jascha Heifetz]," *Peterburgskii listok*, November 23, 1913.

27. "Kontsert Iashi Kheifetsa," *Teatr i zhizn'*, November 24, 1913.

28. Viktor Val'ter, "Kontserty v S.-Peterburge [Concerts in S.-Petersburg]," *RMG*, no. 48 (December 1, 1913): Stlb. 1103.

29. Viacheslav Gavrilovich Karatygin, "Kontsert Iashi Kheifetsa [Concert of Jascha Heifetz]," *Rech'*, November 24, 1913.

30. "Malen'kii kapel'maister [Little Conductor]," *Putevodnyi ogoniok*, no. 14 (1912): 421.

31. Nikolai D. Bernstein, "8-letnii dirizher pered simfonicheskim orkestrom [8-Year-Old Conductor Before the Orchestra]," *Peterburgskaia gazeta*, November 4, 1913.

32. Viacheslav Gavrilovich Karatygin, "Kontsert Villi Ferrero [Concert of Willy Ferrero]," *Rech'*, November 5, 1913.

33. "Josef Hofmann Celebrates a Golden Anniversary," *Life*, November 15, 1937, 71.

34. *Peterburgskii listok*, November 10, 1913.

35. "Teatral'nyi kur'er," *Peterburgskii listok*, November 13, 1913.

36. "Malen'kii dirizher na kontserte malen'kogo skripacha [Little Conductor at the Concert of the Little Violinist]," *Peterburgskaia gazeta*, November 23, 1913.

37. V. Ts., "Iasha Kheifets [Jascha Heifetz]," *Obozrenie teatrov*, November 23, 1913.

38. Aleksandr Borisovich Khessin, *Iz moikh vospominanii [From My Memories]* (Moscow: Vserossiiskoe teatral'noe obshchestvo, 1959), 219–220.

13. WINTER 1913–1914: BAR MITZVAH

1. *Vilenskii vestnik*, November 27–December 4, 191; *Vecherniaia gazeta*, November 27–December 4, 1913.

2. Herbert Axelrod, *Heifetz*, 3rd ed. (Neptune City, NJ: Paganiniana, 1990), 604.

3. TsGIA SPb, f. 361, op. 2, d. 1383. Only two pages concerning Cecilia Hansen survive in the conservatory archive. The first is a residency certificate, and the second page bears the note: "Removed all documents from here: B. Zakharov. 2 February 1920." This was written by the pianist Boris Zakharov, whom Cecilia married shortly after graduating from the conservatory. The couple performed frequently in pre- and post-revolutionary Russia.

4. I. Zhi-v "Deti-virtuozy [Child Virtuosos]," *Solntse Rossii*, October 1911.

5. "K kontsertu Iashi Kheifetsa [On the Concert of Jascha Heifetz]," *Vilenskii vestnik*, December 3, 1913.

6. Aleksandra Iakovlevna Brushtein, *Stranitsy proshlogo [Pages of the Past]* (Moscow: Iskusstvo, 1956), 262.

7. *Vilenskii vestnik*, December 5, 1913.

8. "Kontsert simfonicheskogo orkestra pri uchastii Iashi Kheifetsa [Concert of the Symphony Orchestra with the Participation of Jascha Heifetz], *Vecherniaia gazeta* (Vilnius), December 5, 1913.

9. N. R. "Iasha Kheifets [Jascha Heifetz]," Nasha kopeika [Our Kopeck], *Vilenskii kur'er,* December 7, 1913.

10. M., *Vilenskii vestnik,* December 6, 1913.

11. KR RIII, f. 83, no. 51, l. 1–2, published in Galina Kopytova, "Pervye shagi geniia: Iasha Kheifets [First steps of a genius: Jascha Heifetz]," *Sovetskaia muzyka,* no. 8 (1991): 93–94.

12. JHC LoC, box 280.

13. Ibid.

14. Uncle Samuil's reply to Jascha's postcard was dated December 30, 1913; JHC LoC, box 280.

15. V. O. "Kontsert Ia. Kheifetsa (Kupecheskoe sobranie) [Concert of J. Heifetz (Merchants' Club)]," *Kievskie novosti,* December 9, 1913.

16. "Kontsert Iashi Kheifetsa [Concert of Jascha Heifetz]," *Kievskaia mysl',* December 10, 1913.

17. Documents relating to the Achron brothers are held in the conservatory archive of Joseph Achron (TsGIA SPb, f. 361, op. 1, d. 163) and Isidor Achron (ibid., d. 164). During his life in St. Petersburg, their father went sometimes by Abram and sometimes by Yudel; as a patronymic the brothers took an altered form of their father's second name, becoming, as noted in Soviet and Russian musical books, Yosif Yulyevich and Isidor Yulyevich.

18. *Vilenskii vestnik,* December 15, 1913; *Vilenskii kur'er,* December 16, 1913.

19. M., "Simfonicheskii kontsert 20 dekabria s uchastiem Ia. Kheifetsa [Symphony Concert December 20th with the Participation of J. Heifetz]," *Vilenskii vestnik,* December 22, 1913.

20. Published in Artur Weschler-Vered, *Jascha Heifetz* (New York: Schirmer Books, 1986), 64.

21. JHC LoC, box 250.

22. TsGIA SPb, f. 361, op. 1, d. 2930, l. 1.

23. JHC LoC, box 280.

24. Ibid.

25. Ibid.

26. Postcard dated February 13, 1914. JHC LoC, box 280.

27. JHC LoC, box 273.

28. Postcard dated January 18, 1914. JHC LoC, box 273.

29. Postcard from January 16, 1914. JHC LoC, box 280.

30. OV (A. V. Ossovskii), "Kontserty v Peterburge: Kamernyi i simfonicheskii IRMO [Concerts in Petersburg: Chamber and Symphonic IRMO]," *RMG,* no. 4 (January 26, 1914): Stlb. 106.

31. JHC LoC, box 251.

32. This information was related to the author by the St. Petersburg philologist Arseny Smolevsky (1923–2003), a distant relative of Yuliya Abaza (née Stubbe).

33. JHC LoC, box 280.

34. Dr. Kurt Singer, "Im Berlin," *Allgemeine Musik-Zeitung*, February 13, 1914, 203.

35. JHC LoC, box 251.

36. JHC LoC, box 280.

37. Axelrod, *Heifetz*, 133. Although Heifetz places the concert in 1913, programs, posters, and newspaper reviews all point to 1914.

38. Viktor Val'ter, "Iasha Kheifets (Stranichka is istorii nashei kultury) [Jascha Heifetz (a page from our culture)]," *Den'*, March 22, 1914.

39. Max Unger, "Konzert: Leipzig," *Die Musik*. 1914. XIII. 12:2. Marzheft, 380.

40. JHC LoC, box 273.

41. F., "Konzert zugunsten des Deutschen Hilfsvereins," *Die Zeit*, February 15, 1914. Morgenblatt.

42. Ibid.

43. G. v. B., "Konzert," *Reichspost*, February 15, 1914.

44. E. B., "Kunst und Musik," *Neues Wiener Journal*, February 15, 1914, 15.

45. Richard Specht, "Konzert: Wien," *Die Musik* (1914). XIII. 14:2. Aprielheft, 128.

46. Postcard stamped in St. Petersburg on February 4, 1914. JHC LoC, box 280.

47. The letter is dated by the delivery stamp—February 26, 1914. JHC LoC, box 270.

48. E. B. "Konzert Jascha Heifetz," *Neues Wiener Journal*, February 28, 1914, 10.

49. Nicknames found in Abram Chasins, *Speaking of Pianists*, 2nd ed. (New York: Alfred A. Knopf, 1961), 27–39; and Genrikh Gustavovich Neigauz, *Razmyshlenia, vospominaniia, dnevniki. Izbrannye stat'i. Pis'ma k roditel'iam* [*Reflections, Recollections, Diaries. Collected Articles. Letters to Parents*] 2nd ed. (Moscow: Sovetskii kompozitor, 1983), 480.

50. Chasins, *Speaking of Pianists*, 27–29.

51. Dagmar Godowsky, *First Person Plural: The Lives of Dagmar Godowsky* (New York: The Viking Press, 1958), 52–53; *Peter Ibbetson* is the title character in a novel by George du Maurier.

52. Ibid., 53.

53. Postcard without a date or stamp (dated by the content). JHC LoC, box 280.

54. Prilozhenie k otchetu Petrogradskogo otdeleniia Imperatorskogo Russkogo muzykal'nogo obshchestva za 1913–1914 god [Supplement to the report of the Petrograd division of the IRMO for 1913–1914].

14. SPRING 1914

1. B. P. "Kontsert Iashi Kheifetsa [Concert of Jascha Heifetz]," *Golos Moskvy*, March 2, 1914.

2. Grigorii Petrovich Prokof'ev, "Kontserty v Moskve [Concerts in Moscow]," *RMG*, no. 11 (March 16, 1914): 303.

3. Postcard from March 7, 1914. JHC LoC, box 280.

4. *Odesskii listok,* April 5, 1914.

5. "Kontsert Iashi Kheifetsa [Concert of Jascha Heifetz]," *Odesskii listok,* April 9, 1914.

6. B. Iankovskii, "Kontsert Iashi Kheifetsa," *Odesskii listok,* April 10, 1914.

7. Teatral'nye listki [Theatrical Pages], *Odesskii listok,* April 10, 1914.

8. Bemol, "K kontsertu Iashi Kheifetsa [On the Concert of Jascha Heifetz]," *Bessarabskaia zhizn'* (Chișinău), April 10, 1914.

9. Deems Taylor, "Jascha, That's My Baby," *New York Times,* July 16, 1939.

10. Teatr i muzyka [Theater and Music], *Odesskaia pochta* (April 10, 1914).

11. JHC LoC, box 280.

12. Ibid.

13. "Kontsert Iashi Kheifetsa," *Vitebskii vestnik,* April 10, 1914.

14. "Kontsert Iashi Kheifetsa," *Vitebskii vestnik,* April 22, 1914.

15. Letter from N. V. Artsybushev to Alexander Glazunov, 26 June 1914, OR SPbGK, no. 2784, l. 2.

16. Ibid., l. 1.

17. Prilozhenie k otchetu SPb. otdeleniia Imperatorskogo Russkogo muzykal'nogo obshchestva za 1911–1912 god [Supplement to the report of the St. Petersburg division of the Imperial Russian Music Society for 1911–1912], 30.

18. TsGIA SPb, f. 361, op. 8, d. 117, l. 447 ob.-448.

19. TsGIA SPb, f. 361, op. 8, d. 117, l. 43 ob.-44.

20. Carl Flesch, *The Memoirs of Carl Flesch* (London: Rockliff, 1957), 253.

21. Ibid.

22. Ibid., 254.

23. I. Lesman, *Skripichnaia tekhnika i ee razvitie v shkole prof. L. S. Auera* [Violin Technique and its Development in the School of Prof. L. S. Auer], 2nd ed. (St. Petersburg, 1910), v.

24. Leopold Auer, *Violin Playing As I Teach It* (1921; repr. New York: Dover Publications, 1980), 83.

25. Staff member of the St. Petersburg Musical Library, interview by author, 2001.

26. JHC LoC, box 251.

27. JHC LoC, box 273.

15. SUMMER–FALL 1914: WAR

1. JHC LoC, box 280. *Piter* is a commonly used nickname for St. Petersburg-Petrograd.

2. One of the photographs appears in Herbert Axelrod, *Heifetz,* 3rd ed. (Neptune City, NJ: Paganiniana, 1990), 38, but is incorrectly labeled.

3. JHC LoC, box 250.

4. *Musical America,* November 10, 1917.

5. "Remembrance of Things Past," *Strad,* February, 1986, 776.

6. JHC LoC, box 280.

7. "Remembrance of Things Past," 776.

8. KR RIII, f. 28, no. 1100 (zapisnaia knizhka [record book] no. 2), l. 20 ob.

9. Kenway Lee, "Jascha Heifetz's Carlo Tononi violin, 1736," *Strad,* January 1995, 50–51.

10. Michel Mok, "Only Mad People Go Out and Steal Strads," *New York Post,* December 13, 1937, 15.

11. Leopold Auer, *My Long Life in Music* (London: Duckworth & Co., 1924), 340–342.

12. Letter from A. K. Glazunov to I. A. Shkarovskaia, 14 August 1914, OR SPbGK, no. 6107.

13. Auer, *My Long Life in Music,* 342.

14. Letter from the personal collection of John A. Maltese.

15. JHC LoC, box 270.

16. Ibid.

17. Boris Schwarz, *Great Masters of the Violin* (New York, 1983), 434–435.

18. Samuel Chotzinoff, *A Little Nightmusic* (London: Hamish Hamilton, 1964), 23.

19. Ibid.

20. Henry Roth, interview with Paul Olefsky, "The Complete Cellist," *Strad,* November 1989, 973.

21. TsGIA SPb, f. 361, op. 11, d. 594.

22. "Vozvrashchenie iz plena [Return from Captivity]," *Zadushevnoe slovo* (Petrograd), January 4, 1915, 3.

16. JANUARY–SEPTEMBER 1915

1. *Rech',* January 1, 1915.

2. "A. Skriabin o voine [A. Scriabin on the War]," *RMG,* no. 14 (April 5, 1915): 252.

3. TsGIA SPb, f. 515, op. 1, d. 8309, l. 118.

4. Architectural description of Building 115 on Yekateringofsky Prospekt, TsGIA SPb, f. 515, op. 1, d. 8309, l. 97.

5. Ibid., l. 107 ob.

6. JHC LoC, box 273.

7. TsGIA SPb, f. 361, op. 8, d. 119, l. 562 ob. 563. For a report on Mina's work in Maksimilian Steinberg's class see: TsGIA SPb, f. 361, op. 8, d. 120, l. 1353 ob.—1354.

8. Letter from February 1, 1930. Published in *A. K. Glazunov: Pis'ma, stat'i, vospominaniia [A. K. Glazunov: Letters, Articles, Memoirs]* (Moscow: Muzgiz, 1958), 398.

9. Card postmarked January 19, 1915. JHC LoC, box 280.

10. Letter from Anna Sharfstein-Koch to Albina Starkova-Heifetz, October 16, 2000.

11. Samuel Chotzinoff, "Jascha Heifetz: The Early Years; Recollections of the celebrated violinist's early career (A selection by Robin Chotzinoff from the unpublished memoirs 'Till Death Us Do Part')," *Strad,* December 1988, 970–971.

12. Vladimir Il'ich Muzalevskii, *Zapiski muzykanta* [*Notes of a Musician*] (Leningrad: Muzyka, 1969), 24. Muzalevsky mistakenly names Jascha's sister as "Nina."

13. Ibid., 23.

14. JHC LoC, box 280.

15. Ibid.

16. JHC LoC, box 250.

17. See: *Jascha Heifetz: God's Fiddler,* directed by Peter Rosen (New York: Peter Rosen Productions, 2011), DVD.

18. See: Mikhail Beizer, *The Jews of St. Petersburg: Excursions Through a Noble Past,* ed. Martin Gilbert (Philadelphia: The Jewish Publication Society, 1989), 98.

19. Noble Hollister, "Auer, The Mentor Of Famous Violinists," *New York Times Magazine,* April 26, 1925, 3, 22.

20. Alexander Woollcott, "The Quest of a Lost Childhood," *Saturday Evening Post,* April 7, 1928, 14.

21. KR RIII, f. 83, op. 1, no. 66, 9–10.

22. B., "Kontsert Iashi Kheifetsa [Concert of Jascha Heifetz]," *Petrogradskie vedomosti,* March 3, 1915; A. I., "Maly zal konservatorii [Small Hall of the Conservatory]," *Petrogradskii listok,* March 2, 1915; and "Kontsert Iashi Kheifetsa [Concert of Jascha Heifetz]," *Vechernee vremia,* March 2, 1915.

23. V. Ch., "Kontsert Iashi Kheifetsa [Concert of Jascha Heifetz]," *Obozrenie teatrov,* March 4, 1915.

24. A. Koptiaev, "Kontsert Iashi Kheifetsa," *Birzhevye vedomosti,* March 2, 1915.

25. Grigorii Timofeev, "Kontsert Iashi Kheifetsa [Concert of Jascha Heifetz]," *Rech',* March 3, 1915.

26. Viktor Val'ter, "Kontsert Iashi Kheifetsa [Concert of Jascha Heifetz]," *Den',* March 3, 1915.

27. JHC LoC, box 251.

28. KR RIII, f. 83, op. 1, no. 66, 11–12.

29. "Maly zal konservatorii [Small Hall of the Conservatory]." *Petrogradskii listok,* April 9, 1915.

30. V. G. Val'ter, "Vtoroi kontsert Iashi Kheifetsa [Second Concert of Jascha Heifetz]," Rukopis' [Manuscript], KR RIII, f. 83, op. 1, no. 15.

31. JHC LoC, box 251. Letter dated April 9, 1915.

32. Viktor Val'ter, "Kontsert Iashi Kheifetsa [Concert of Jascha Heifetz]," *Den',* March 3, 1915.

33. Information from Vladimir Grigoryev, who met Tamara Chapro.

34. Leopold Auer, *My Long Life in Music* (London: Duckworth & Co., 1924), 351.

35. KR RIII, f. 83, op. 1, no. 66, 13.

36. TsGIA SPb, f. 361, op. 8, d. 119, l. 458 ob.—459.

37. TsGIA SPb, f. 361, op. 16, d. 2, l. 31 ob.

38. JHC LoC, box 280.

39. Teatr i muzyka [Theater and Music], *Odesskie novosti,* April 26, 1915.

40. Largo, "Kontsert Iashi Kheifetsa [Concert of Jascha Heifetz]," *Odesskie novosti,* April 27, 1915.

41. M. R., "Premia Mikhalovskogo Dvortsa—14-letnemu mal'chiku [Mikhailovsky Palace Prize—to a 14-Year Old Boy]" *Petrogradskaia gazeta,* May 11, 1915.

42. TsGIA SPb, f. 361, op. 1, d. 4278, l. 8.

43. TsGIA SPb, f. 361, op. 1, d. 4278, l. 8 ob.

44. JHC LoC, box 250.

45. Josefa Heifetz, stenogram of notes from phone conversations with Anna Sharf-stein-Koch, Jan. 10, 1993, 4.

46. JHC LoC, box 280.

17. THE END OF 1915

1. TsGIA SPb, f. 361, op. 1, d. 4278, l. 9–9 ob.

2. Letter from A. K. Glazunov to I. A. Shkarovskaia, OR SPbGK, no. 6103.

3. "Bezhentsy v Petrograde [Refugees in Petrograd]," *Den',* October 15, 1915.

4. KR RIII, f. 83, op. 1, no. 47.

5. V. Kolomiitsov, "Iubileinyi vecher V. G. Val'tera [Jubilee Evening for V. G. Val-ter]," *Den',* November 3, 1915.

6. KR RIII, f. 83, op. 1, no. 59.

7. Grigorii Petrovich Prokof'ev, "Moskovskie kontserty [Moscow Concerts]," *RMG,* no. 49 (December 6, 1915): Stlb. 799.

8. Viktor Val'ter, "Iasha Kheifets [Jascha Heifetz]," *Den',* March 22, 1914.

9. Viktor Val'ter, "Tretii simfonicheskii kontsert S. Kusevitskogo [Third Symphony Concert of S. Koussevitzky]," *Den',* December 17, 1915.

10. Viacheslav Gavrilovich Karatygin, "Tretii kontsert S. Kusevitskogo [Third Con-cert of S. Koussevitzky]," *Rech',* December 16, 1915.

11. "Kontsert v chest' A. K. Glazunov pod upravleniem S. Kusevitskogo [Concert in Honor of A. K. Glazunov under the Direction of S. Koussevitzky]," *Petrogradskaia gazeta,* December 16, 1915.

12. *Petrogradskaia gazeta,* December 20, 1915.

13. Viktor Val'ter, "Pervyi kontsert Iashi Kheifets [Jascha Heifetz]," *Den',* December 21, 1915.

14. Leopold Auer, *Violin Master Works and Their Interpretation* (New York: Carl Fischer, Inc., 1925), 152.

15. Val'ter, "Pervyi kontsert Iashi Kheifetsa."

16. *Petrogradskaia gazeta,* January 7, 1916.

17. Grigorii N. Timofeev, "Kontsert M. Poliakina [Concert of M. Polyakin]," *Rech',* April 24, 1916.

18. JHC LoC, box 251.

18. THE FIRST HALF OF 1916

1. TsGIA SPb, f. 361, op. 8, d. 120, l. 197 ob; ibid., l. 195.

2. *Petrogradskaia gazeta,* January 17, 1916.

3. Kar. [Viacheslav Gavrilovich Karatygin], "Kontsert Iashi Kheifetsa [Concert of Jascha Heifetz]," *Rech',* January 29, 1916.

4. Story recounted by Robert Heifetz, in conversation with Galina Kopytova and Albina Starkova-Heifetz.

5. Iulii Dmitrievich E[ngel'], Teatr i muzyka, *Russkie vedomosti,* January 31, 1916.

6. Grigorii Petrovich Prokofiev, "Kontserty i opera v Moskve [Concerts and Opera in Moscow]," *RMG,* no. 7 (February 14, 1916): Stlb. 163. See: L. Sabaneev, "Muzyka v Moskve [Music in Moscow]," Khronika zhurnala *Muzykal'nyi sovremennik* [Chronicles of the journal *Musical Contemporary*], no. 18, 1916.

7. Leopold Auer, *Violin Master Works and Their Interpretation* (New York: Carl Fischer, Inc., 1925), 137.

8. Sabaneev, "Muzyka v Moskve," 30.

9. E[ngel'], *Teatr i muzyka.*

10. JHC LoC, box 280.

11. *Kievskii teatral'nyi kur'er,* January 28, 1916.

12. Dz., "Kontsert Iashi Kheifetsa," *Kievskaia mysl',* February 4, 1916.

13. Red N., "Kontsert Iashi Kheifetsa," *Kievskii teatral'nyi kur'er,* February 4, 1916. See also: Iu. Kister, "Zal Kupecheskogo sobraniia: Kontsert Iashi Kheifetsa [Hall of the Merchants' Assembly: Concert of Jascha Heifetz]," *Vecherniaia gazeta* (Kiev), February 4, 1916.

14. Iu. Kister, "Zal Kupecheskogo sobraniia: Vtoroi kontsert Iashi Kheifetsa [Hall of the Merchants' Assembly: Second Concert of Jascha Heifetz]," *Vecherniaia gazeta,* February 7, 1916.

15. A. Kanevtsov, "Kontsert skripacha Ia. Kheifetsa [Concert of the Violinist J. Heifetz]," *Kievlianin,* February 7, 1916.

16. JHC LoC, box 280; Jascha's spelling of the Russian word *kak* (*as* or *how*) as "kk" in this letter is not a chance mistake; similar abbreviations with missing vowels appear in subsequent letters. This was something of a fashion at the time—the letters of Sergei Prokofiev contain lines of consonants—for example "Srg Prkf."

17. Noted in the conservatory record of Isidor Achron. TsGIA SPb, f. 361, op. 1, d. 164, l. 19 ob.

18. JHC LoC, box 280.

19. A. Gorovits, "Kontsert Iashi Kheifetsa [Concert of Jascha Heifetz]," *Iuzhnyi krai* (Khar'kov), February 11, 1916.

20. Rigoletto, "Kontsert Ia. Kheifetsa [Concert of J. Heifetz]," *Utro* (Khar'kov), February 9, 1916.

21. R. Genika, "Khar'kov (korrespondentsia) [Kharkov (Correspondence)]," *RMG,* no. 19 (March 6, 1916): Stlb. 226.

22. *Rech',* February 2, 1916.

23. JHC LoC, box 280.

24. Evidence is found in the autobiography and in the work record of Natan Heifetz. Nemirovsky Archive.

25. "O Iashe Kheifetse [On Jascha Heifetz]," *Tiflisskii listok*, February 10, 1916; B. An-ii, "O 'vunderkindakh' [On 'Wunderkinder']," *Tiflisskii listok* (February 7, 1916).

26. "K kontsertu Iashi Kheifetsa," *Tiflisskii listok*, February 14, 1916; Teatr i muzyka [Theater and Music], *Kavkazskoe slovo*, February 16, 1916.

27. Lia-do, Teatr i muzyka, *Kavkaz*, February 18, 1916.

28. Khronika [Chronicles], *RMG*, no. 2 (January 8, 1912): Stlb. 55.

29. V. A. "Kazennyi teatr: 4-e simfonicheskoe sobranie pod upravleniem L. Pyshnov pri uchastii Ia. Kheifetsa [State Theater: 4th Symphony Gathering under the Direction of L. Pouishnoff with the Participation of J. Heifetz]," *Kavkazskoe slovo*, February 18, 1916.

30. Lazar Iosifovich Saminskii, "Simfonicheskii kontsert (pri uchastii Iashi Kheifetsa) [Symphony Concert (with the Participation of Jascha Heifetz)]," *Zakavkazskoe rech'*, February 19, 1916.

31. JHC LoC, box 251.

32. Ibid.

33. Lia-do. "Kontsert Ia. Kheifetsa [Concert of J. Heifetz]," *Kavkaz*, February 20, 1916.

34. V. A. "Iasha Kheifets (18 fevralia. Zal Artisticheskogo obshchestva) [Jascha Heifetz (18 February. Hall of the Artistic Society)]," *Kavkazskoe slovo*, February 20, 1916.

35. JHC LoC, box 251.

36. JHC LoC, box 273.

37. "Elias Malkin Dies; Heifetz Teacher," *New York Times*, July 19, 1953.

38. K-ii. "Kontsert Ia. Kheifetsa [Concert of Jascha Heifetz]," *Kavkaz*, February 23, 1916.

39. V. A. "Iasha Kheifets [Jascha Heifetz]," *Kavkazskoe slovo*, February 23, 1916.

40. A letter stamped in Tbilisi on February 25, 1916. JHC LoC, box 251.

41. Samuel Chotzinoff, "Jascha Heifetz: The Early Years," 989.

42. Lazar Iosifovich Saminskii, "Evreiskie muzykanty i ikh 'estradnyi ekzotizm' (Po povodu kontsertov Iashi Kheifetsa) [Jewish Musicians and their 'Stage Exoticism' (on the concerts of Jascha Heifetz)]," *Evreiskaia nedelia* (Petrograd), no. 14–15 (1916).

43. Vol'fing [Emil K. Medtner], *Modernizm i muzyka: Stat'i kriticheskie i polemicheskie [Modernism and Music: Critical and Polemical Articles]* (1907–1910) (Moscow, 1912).

44. Ibid.

45. Leonid Leonidovich Sabaneev, "Muzyka i patriotizm [Music and Patriotism]," *Muzyka*, no. 107 (1912).

46. Vol'fing [Medtner], *Modernizm i muzyka*, 395.

47. Saminskii, "Evreiskie muzykanty i ikh 'estradnyi ekzotizm,'" 54.

48. Lyrics reprinted in Ira Gershwin, *Lyrics On Several Occasions* (New York: Alfred A. Knopf, 1959), 177.

49. KR RIII, f. 83, op. 1, no. 59.

50. A copy of this letter is kept in the archive of V. Grigoryev.

51. Maksim Gor'kii, "Russkii—evreiu [A Russian—to a Jew]," *Evreiskaia nedelia*, no. 6, 1916.

52. Kar. [V. G. Karatygin], "Vecher Obshchestva dlia izucheniia evreiskoi zhizni [Evening of the Society for the Study of Jewish Life]," *Rech'*, March 24, 1916.

53. This Joseph (Yosif) Heifitz submitted an entrance application in 1913 as an auditor of the violin class but was finally accepted into the French horn class; TsGIA SPb, f. 361, op. 1, d. 4281, l. 1 and 7.

54. TsGIA SPb, f. 361, op. 8, d. 120, l. 201 ob.

55. JHC LoC, books; Aleksei Petrov was an experienced professor and theoretician who had taught in the conservatory since 1887. Three years later, Petrov worked with thirteen-year-old Dmitry Shostakovich, coaching him in musical theory in preparation for his entry into the Petrograd Conservatory.

56. TsGIA SPb, f. 361, op. 8, d. 120, l. 76 ob.-77.

57. Isidor Achron, Jascha's favored accompanist at the time, received a conservatory certificate of vacation leave from May 5 through September 15, 1916. TsGIA SPb, f. 361, op. 1, d. 164, l. 16.

58. *Odesskii listok,* May 27, 1916.

59. L-ii, "Kontsert Iashi Kheifetsa [Concert of Jascha Heifetz]," *Odesskii listok,* May 28, 1916.

60. JHC LoC, box 251.

19. THE SECOND HALF OF 1916: NORWAY AND DENMARK

1. As noted in Ruvin's conservatory record: foreign passport, no. 9915, received 21 April 1916. TsGIA SPb, f. 361, d. 4278, l. 1 ob.

2. Leopold Auer, *My Long Life in Music* (London: Duckworth & Co., 1924), 347–348.

3. *Rech'*, March 17, 1916.

4. Auer, *My Long Life in Music,* 351–352.

5. "Jascha Heifetz," *Dagbladet,* August 29, 1916.

6. Hjalmar Borgstrøm. "Konsert" *Aftenposten,* August 29, 1916.

7. "Violinaften," *Morgenbladet,* August 31, 1916.

8. "Jascha Heifetz" (Pencil Sketch), *Morgenbladet,* September 5, 1916.

9. Auer, *My Long Life in Music,* 352.

10. "Jascha Heifetz," *Dagbladet.*

11. Not "M. De Goulkevitsch" as Auer wrote in his memoirs.

12. Auer, *My Long Life in Music,* 353.

13. Ibid.

14. Ibid.

15. JHC LoC, box 251.

16. "Raznye Izvestiia [Various News]," Khronika zhurnala *Muzykal'nyi sovremennik* [Chronicles of the journal *Musical Contemporary*], no. 1 (September 20, 1916): 17.

17. TsGIA SPb, f. 361, op. 1, d. 4869.

18. Information derived from a talk by L. A. Novikov, at a conference dedicated to the memory of Vladimir Grigoryev (Moscow Conservatory, April 14, 1999). Novikov drew the information about the link between Jascha Heifetz and Darya Chasovitina (1896–1996?) from personal interviews with her.

19. Samuil Samosud (1884–1964) later became a prominent conductor during the Soviet era.

20. "Pervyi kontsert simfonicheskogo orkestra 1.-gv. Preobrazhenskogo polka [First Concert of the Symphony Orchestra of the L-Guard of the Preobrazhensky Regiment]," Khronika zhurnala *Muzykal'nyi sovremennik*, no. 9–10 (December 9, 1916): 7–8.

21. Ibid., 8.

22. Viktor Val'ter, "Simfonicheskii kontsert orkestra leib-gv. Volynskogo polka [Symphony Concert of the Orchestra of the Lifeguard of the Volyn Regiment]," *Den'*, December 13, 1916.

23. "Simfonicheskii kontsert orkestra 1.-gv. Volynskogo polka [First Concert of the Symphony Orchestra of the L-Guard of the Volyn Regiment]," *Muzykal'nyi sovremennik*, 8.

24. Val'ter, "Simfonicheskii kontsert orkestra leib-gv. Volynskogo polka."

25. "Kontsert Iashi Kheifetsa [Concert of Jascha Heifetz]," Khronika zhurnala *Muzykal'nyi sovremennik* [Chronicle of the Journal *Musical Contemporary*], no. 13–14 (January 17, 1917): 11.

26. Ibid.

27. Ibid.

28. V. K. [V. P. Kolomiitsev], "Kontsert Ia. Kheifetsa [Concert of Jascha Heifetz]," *Rech'*, December 24, 1916.

29. Viktor Val'ter, "Kontsert Iashi Kheifetsa [Concert of Jascha Heifetz]," *Den'*, December 24, 1916.

20. THE FIRST HALF OF 1917: FEBRUARY REVOLUTION

1. Pr., "'Vanemuine': Kontsert Iashi Kheifetsa ['Vanemuine:' Concert of Jascha Heifetz]," *Rizhskii vestnik*, January 14, 1917; like many other institutions in Riga, the *Rizhskii vestnik* had been evacuated from the front lines and relocated to Tartu, Estonia.

2. *Rech'*, January 31, 1917; *Novoe vremia*, January 31, 1917.

3. JHC LoC, box 270. Note: in Russian it is clear the author is female.

4. TsGIA SPb, f. 361, op. 5, d. 35, l. 16 ob.—17.

5. TsGIA SPb, f. 361, op. 6, d. 27, l. 751.

6. KR RIII, f. 83, op. 1, no. 66.

7. JHC LoC, box 251.

8. KR RIII, f. 83, op. 1, no. 66.

9. *Rech'*, March 9, 1917.

10. JHC LoC, box 251.

11. "Jascha Heifetz: The Great Violin Virtuoso," *The Daily News* (Perth, Australia), June 17, 1927.

12. JHC LoC, box 251; *oprichniki*—A term first used during the sixteenth-century reign of Tsar Ivan the Terrible, which referred to the close circle of his loyal followers and bodyguards, who sometimes operated as a brutal secret police force. Clad in black, riding black horses, and known for cruelty, the *oprichniki* became a symbol of oppression.

13. JHC LoC, box 251.

14. See: *Kievskaia mysl'*, April 9, 1917; and *Poslednie novosti* (Kiev), April 9, 1917.

15. JHC LoC, box 280.

16. Nicole Hirsch, "Jascha Heifetz, l'empereur du violon," *Musica Disques*, no. 102, September 1962, 7.

17. E., "Kontsert Iashi Kheifetsa [Concert of Jascha Heifetz]," *Pridneprovskii krai*, April 14, 1917.

18. *Pridneprovskii krai*, April 15, 1917; the concert was canceled due to the absence of lighting in the theater.

19. *Pridneprovskii krai*, April 22, 1917.

20. Vladimir Galaktionovich Korolenko, "Otechestvo v opasnosti [Fatherland in Danger]," *Izvestiia Petrogradskogo soveta rabochikh i soldatskikh deputatov* [*News of the Petrograd Council (Soviet) of Workers' and Soldiers' Deputies*], March 14, 1917.

21. JHC LoC, box 280.

22. Announcements as well as advertisements and events pages in the newspaper *Gomel'skaia kopeika*, April 11, 15, 22, and 24, 1917.

23. "Khronika: Otchet po ustroistvu kontserta Iashi Kheifetsa 24 aprelia sego goda [Chronicle: Account of the Organization of the Concert of Jascha Heifetz]," *Gomel'skaia kopeika*, April 29, 1917.

24. JHC LoC, box 280.

25. Ibid.

26. "Kontsert Iashi Kheifetsa [Concert of Jascha Heifetz]," *Rostovskaia rech'*, April 22, 1917.

27. V. "Kontsert Iashi Kheifetsa," *Rostovskaia rech'*, April 29, 1917.

28. "Publichnyi akt v Petrogradskoi konservatorii [Public Ceremony at the Petrograd Conservatory]," *Petrogradskii listok*, May 10, 1917.

29. Spiski predsedatelia ekzamenatsionnoi komissii za 1916/17 uchebnyi god [Records of the Chairman of the Examination Committee for the 1916–1917 Academic Year], TsGIA SPb, f. 361, op. 5, d. 39, 40.

30. *Rech'*, May 14, 1917.

31. JHC LoC, box 240. Program for the concert-rally.

32. *Rech'*, May 14, 1917.

33. Ibid.

34. *Saratovskii listok,* March 28, 1917.

35. JHC LoC, box 240.

21. SUMMER 1917: DEPARTURE FOR AMERICA

1. Edward H. Smith, "A Boyish Genius Who Makes Musicians Marvel," *The World Magazine,* November 25, 1917, 5. The author explains in the full-page article that this interview with the Heifetzes was conducted in a "treasonable and, I fear, a wretched German."

2. "Jascha Heifetz Soon to Arrive in America," *Musical America,* September 1, 1917.

3. "Heifetz Here After a Perilous Journey," *Musical America,* September 1917.

4. KR RIII, f. 83, op. 1, no. 53, 4–5, published in Galina Kopytova, "Pervye shagi geniia: Iasha Kheifets [First steps of a genius: Jascha Heifetz]," *Sovetskaia muzyka,* no. 8 (1991): 94.

5. *Delo naroda,* June 13, 1917; *Rech',* June 17, 1917.

6. Letter from Anna Sharfstein-Koch to Albina Starkova-Heifetz, October 16, 2000.

7. Josefa Heifetz, stenogram of notes from phone conversations with Anna Sharfstein-Koch, January 10, 1992, 5.

8. Howard Taubman, "Heifetz Urges Ritard in Tempo of Musician's Life," *New York Times,* December 13, 1968.

9. KR RIII, 83, 1, no. 53, 6, published in "Pervye shagi geniia: Iasha Kheifets."

10. Some of these photographs, from Pauline Heifetz's personal photograph album, were reprinted in Samuel Chotzinoff, "Jascha Heifetz: The Early Years; Recollections of the celebrated violinist's early career (A selection by Robin Chotzinoff from the unpublished memoirs 'Till Death Us Do Part')," *Strad,* December 1988, 969.

11. Smith, "A Boyish Genius Who Makes Musicians Marvel."

12. Ibid.

13. See for example: "Picturing the Home Life of Jascha Heifetz," *Musical America,* November 10, 1917.

14. Record group 85, San Francisco, 1893–1953, no. 16468, sheet 19, National Archives, Washington, DC.

15. For information about Sir Henry Heyman see: "King Kalākaua and Mr. Heyman," *Strad,* October 1890, 107–108; *The Bay of San Francisco: A History,* vol. 2 (Chicago: The Lewis Publishing Company, 1892), 511; "Sir Henry Heyman, Violinist, Is Dead," *Los Angeles Times,* March 29, 1924; Cheerio, *The Story of Cheerio,* New York: Garden City Publishing Co., 1936, 146–148.

16. See: Sabina Teller Ratner, *Camille Saint-Saëns, 1835–1921: A Thematic Catalogue of his Complete Works. Volume 1: The Instrumental Works* (New York: Oxford University Press, 2002), 224.

17. Photograph (dated November 17, 1919) held in the de Young Museum, San Francisco. This item is part of a large collection of autographed photographs owned by

Sir Henry Heyman and gifted to the museum by his brother Alexander Heyman, "in memory of Sir Henry Heyman."

18. "Heifetz Here After a Perilous Journey," *Musical America.*

19. Information from Robert Heifetz in conversation with Galina Kopytova.

20. "Remembrance of Things Past," *Strad*, February 1986, 777.

21. André Benoist, *The Accompanist . . . and friends: An Autobiography of André Benoist*, ed. John Anthony Maltese (Neptune City, NJ: Paganiniana, 1978), 268.

22. Ibid., 274.

23. "Boy's Head Isn't Turned," *Kansas City Star*, November 3, 1917. First printed in the *New York World.*

24. Pitts Sanborn, "Enter a Genius: Jascha Heifetz," *Commercial Advertiser and Globe*, October 29, 1917.

25. "Who's Who and Why," *Violinist*, vol. 21 (November 1917): 447.

26. Benoist, *The Accompanist*, 268.

27. Pierre V. R. Key, "Jascha Heifetz Scores Triumph," *The World*, October 28, 1917.

28. Ibid.

29. Many people have reported this story in many different forms. For the story as told by Godowsky's daughter, see: Dagmar Godowsky, *First Person Plural: The Lives of Dagmar Godowsky* (New York: The Viking Press, 1958), 52–53.

SELECTED SOURCES

Abell, Arthur M. "Berlin." *Musical Courier.* June 19, 1912.

———. "When Heifetz, Aged 11, Stormed Musical Berlin." *Musical Courier.* May 15, 1952.

Agranovskii (Agranovsky), Genrikh. "Korol' skripachei iz starogo Vil'niusa [King of Violinists from Old Vilnius]." *Vilnius,* no. 3. 1991.

———. "The Childhood Years of the King of Violinists." *Jerusalem of Lithuania,* January, 2001.

———. "Udivitel'naia istoriia memorial'noi doski [Remarkable History of a Memorial Plaque]," *Litovskii Ierusalim [Lithuanian Jerusalem]* (Vil'nius) no. 1–2. 2001.

Agus, Ayke. *Heifetz As I Knew Him.* Pompton Plains, New Jersey: Amadeus Press, 2001.

Applebaum, Samuel and Sada. *The Way They Play.* Book 1. Neptune City, NJ: Paganiniana, 1972.

———. *The Way They Play.* Book 5. Neptune City, NJ: Paganiniana, 1978.

Aslanov, A. "Pervyi kontsert Iashi Kheifetsa (Posviashchaetsia ego otsu) [First Concert of Jascha Heifetz (Dedicated to his Father)]." *Novoe Russkoe Slovo [New Russian Word]* (New York). April 22, 1924.

Auer, Leopold. *Violin Playing As I Teach It.* New York: Frederick A. Stokes Company, 1921. Reprint, New York: Dover Publications, 1980.

———. *My Long Life in Music.* London: Duckworth & Co., 1924. The American edition was published in 1923 by Frederick A. Stokes Company.

———. *Violin Master Works and Their Interpretation.* New York: Carl Fischer, Inc., 1925.

———. *Sredi muzykantov [Among Musicians].* Moscow: M. and S. Sabashnikov, 1927.

————. *Moia shkola igry na skripki. Interpretatsiia proizvedenii skripichnoi klassiki* [*My School of Violin Playing. Interpretation of the Works of the Violin Classics*]. Edited by Ia. Iampol'skii. Moscow: Muzyka, 1965.

Auer, Leopold, and various authors. "Leopold Auer Special Edition." *Violinist*, XLVA, no. 2 (September 1930), 190–227.

Axelrod, Herbert R. *Heifetz*. 3rd ed. Neptune City, NJ: Paganiniana, 1990.

Babel, Isaac. *The Complete Works of Isaac Babel*. Edited by Nathalie Babel. Translated by Peter Constantine. London: W. W. Norton & Co., 2002.

Beizer, Mikhail. *The Jews of St. Petersburg: Excursions Through a Noble Past*. Edited by Martin Gilbert. Philadelphia: The Jewish Publication Society, 1989.

Beliakov, M. M. "Ob I. R. Nalbandiane [On I. R. Nalbandian]." In Tigranov, *Leningradskaia konservatoriia v vospominaniiakh* [*Leningrad Conservatory in Recollections*]. Book 2.

Benoist, André. *The Accompanist . . . and friends. An Autobiography of André Benoist*. Edited by John Anthony Maltese. Neptune City, NJ: Paganiniana, 1978.

Beregovskii, Moisei. *Evreiskaia narodnaia instrumental'naia muzyka* [*Jewish Folk Instrumental Music*]. Moscow: Sovetskii kompozitor, 1987.

Biancolli, Amy. *Fritz Kreisler. Love's Sorrow, Love's Joy*. Portland, Oregon: Amadeus Press, 1999.

Brushtein, Aleksandra Iakovlevna. *Stranitsy proshlogo* [*Pages of the Past*]. Moscow: Iskusstvo, 1956.

Bushen, Aleksandra Dmitrievna. " Iz vospominanii o dalekom proshlom [Recollections of the Far Past]." In Tigranov, *Leningradskaia konservatoriia v vospominaniiakh* [*Leningrad Conservatory in Recollections*]. Book 2.

Cantú, Alberto. *Jascha Heifetz l'Imperatore Solo*. Varese, Italy: Zecchini Editore, 2007.

Chasins, Abram. *Speaking of Pianists*. 2nd Edition. New York: Alfred A. Knopf, 1961.

Chotzinoff, Samuel. *A Little Nightmusic*. London: Hamish Hamilton, 1964.

————. "Jascha Heifetz: The Early Years; Recollections of the celebrated violinist's early career (A selection by Robin Chotzinoff from the unpublished memoirs 'Till Death Us Do Part.')" *Strad*, December 1988.

Creighton, James. *Discopaedia of the Violin, 1889–1971*. Toronto: University of Toronto Press, 1974.

————. "Voyage of Discovery." *Strad*, February 1986, 751.

————. *Discopaedia of the Violin*. 2nd Edition. 4 vols. Ontario, Canada: Records Past Publishing, 1994.

Crimp, Bryan. "Obituary: Heifetz (1901–1988)." *Gramophone*, March 1988, 1289.

————. "The Auer Legacy." *Strad*, April 1990.

Derounian, A. B. "Heifetz Lauds Early Training by Nalbandian." *The Armenian Spectator* (New York), May 17, 1934.

Dobuzhinskii, M. V. *Vospominaniia* [*Memoirs*]. Moscow: Nauka, 1987.

Dostoevsky, Fyodor. *Poor Folk & The Gambler*. Translated by C. J. Hogarth. London: J. M. Dent, 1962.

Elman, Saul. *Memoirs of Mischa Elman's Father.* New York: Private printing, 1933.

Flesch, Carl. *The Memoirs of Carl Flesch.* London: Rockliff Publishing Co., 1957.

———. "Vospominaniia skripacha." *Ispolnitel'skoe iskusstvo zarubezhnykh stran* ["Memoirs of a Violinist." *Performance Art of Foreign Countries*]. 8th Edition. Moscow: Muzyka, 1977.

Galkovskii (Galkauskas), Konstantin Mikhailovich. "Vospominaniia [Memoirs]." LLMA f. 58, op. 1, d. 23, l. 4–5.

Gerber, Hyman. "Thumb Trouble." *The Violinist,* December 1931.

Gershwin, Ira. *Lyrics On Several Occasions.* New York: Alfred A. Knopf, 1959.

A. K. Glazunov: Pis'ma, stat'i, vospominaniia [*A. K. Glazunov: Letters, Articles, Memoirs*]. Moscow: Muzgiz, 1958.

Godowsky, Dagmar. *First Person Plural: The Lives of Dagmar Godowsky.* New York: Viking Press, 1958.

Golubovskaia, Nadezhda Iosifovna. "V Peterburgskoi konservatorii [In the Petersburg Conservatory]." In Tigranov, *Leningradskaia konservatoriia v vospominaniiakh* [*Leningrad Conservatory in Recollections*]. Book 2.

Grigor'ev, V. "Kheifets, Iasha [Heifetz, Jascha]." *Russkoe zarubezh'e: Zolotaia kniga emigratsii, Entsiklopedicheskii biograficheskii slovar'* [*The Russian Abroad: Golden Book of Emigration, the Encyclopedic Biographical Dictionary*]. Moscow: ROSSPEN, 1997.

Hirsch, Nicole. "Jascha Heifetz, l'empereur du violon." *Musica Disques* no. 102, September 1962.

Hollister, Noble. "Auer, The Mentor of Famous Violinists." *New York Times Magazine,* April 26, 1925.

Iampol'skii, Izrail' Markovich. *Frits Kreisler* [*Fritz Kreisler*]. Moscow: Muzyka, 1975.

Karagicheva, Liudmila Vladimirovna. "Dalekoe i blizkoe [Far and Near]." *Sovetskaia muzyka* [*Soviet Music*], no. 10, 1991.

Karatygin, Viacheslav Gavrilovich. "Benefis orkestra v Pavlovske [Benefit of the Orchestra in Pavlovsk]." *Rech'* [*Speech*], July 5, 1911.

———. "Kontsert Iashi Kheifetsa [Concert of Jascha Heifetz]." *Rech'* [*Speech*], March 30, 1913.

———. "Kontsert Iashi Kheifetsa [Concert of Jascha Heifetz]." *Sovremennoe slovo* [*Contemporary Word*], March 30, 1913.

———. "Kontsert Villi Ferrero [Concert of Willi Ferrero]." *Rech'* [*Speech*], November 5, 1913.

———. "Kontsert Iashi Kheifetsa [Concert of Jascha Heifetz]." *Rech'* [*Speech*], November 24, 1913.

———. "Tretii kontsert S. Kusevitskogo [Third Concert of S. Koussevitzky]." *Rech'* [*Speech*], December 16, 1915.

———. "Kontsert Iashi Kheifetsa [Concert of Jascha Heifetz]." *Rech'* [*Speech*], January 29, 1916.

———. "Vecher Obshchestva dlia izucheniia evreiskoi zhizni [Evening of the Society for the Study of Jewish Life]." *Rech' [Speech]*, March 24, 1916.

Key, Pierre V. R. "Jascha Heifetz Scores Triumph." *The World*, October 28, 1917.

Khessin, Aleksandr Borisovich. *Iz moikh vospominanii [From My Memories]*. Moscow: Vserossiiskoe teatral'noe obshchestvo, 1959.

Kipnis, M. "A yidish vunderkind (Yoysef Khayfets)." *Haynt*, February 6 (19), 1912.

Kloss, Sherry. "Remembering Mr. Heifetz." *Strad*, January 1995, 52–55.

———. *Jascha Heifetz Through My Eyes*. Muncie, Indiana: Kloss Classics, 2000.

Kopf, L. "Der kontsert fun der varshoyer filharmonye mit dem bateylikung fun 17-yorikn Yoysef Khayfets." *Lodzer tageblat*, January 31, 1912.

Kopytova, Galina. "Pervye shagi geniia: Iasha Kheifets [First steps of a genius: Jascha Heifetz]." *Sovetskaia muzyka [Soviet Music]* no. 8 (1991): 91–95.

Kozinn, Allan. *Mischa Elman and the Romantic Style*. New York: Harwood Academic Publishers, 1990.

Kushnariov, Khristofor Stepanovich. "K novym beregam [To New Shores]." In Tigranov, *Leningradskaia konservatoriia v vospominaniiakh [Leningrad Conservatory in Recollections]*. Book 1.

Lee, Kenway. "Premier Violinist." *Strad*, January 1995.

———. "Jascha Heifetz's Carlo Tononi Violin, 1736." *Strad*, January 1995.

Lesman, I. *Skripichnaia tekhnika i ee razvitie v shkole prof. L. S. Auera [Violin Technique and its Development in the School of Prof. L. S. Auer]*. 2nd Edition. St. Petersburg, 1910.

Litvin, A. "A yidish vunderkind in Vilna." *Forverts*, no. 5 (1911).

Lochner, Louis P. *Fritz Kreisler*. The Macmillan Company: New York, 1952.

Malan, Roy. *Efrem Zimbalist: A Life*. Cambridge: Amadeus Press, 2004.

Mal'ko, Nikolai Andreevich. *Vospominaniia [Memoirs]*. Mashinopis' [Typewritten manuscript]. KR RIII. f. 47, op. 1, no. 203, l. 115.

Maltese, John. "Rare Jewels: John Maltese compiles Heifetz's non-commercial recordings." *Strad*, September 1986, 329–336.

Mandelstam, Osip. "Noise of Time." *The Prose of Osip Mandelstam: The Noise of Time, Theodosia, The Egyptian Stamp*. Translated by Clarence Brown. New Jersey: Princeton University Press, 1965.

———. "Concert at the Railway Station," in *The Selected Poems of Osip Mandelstam*. Translated by Clarence Brown and W. S. Merwin. New York Review of Books. New York, 1971.

Martens, Frederick H. *Violin Mastery: Talks with Master Violinists and Teachers*. New York: Frederick A. Stokes Company, 1919.

Medtner, Emil K. *See Vol'fing*.

Mikhailov, M. K. "A. K. Glazunov (Iz vospominanii) [A. K. Glazunov (From Recollections)]." In Tigranov, *Leningradskaia konservatoriia v vospominaniiakh [Leningrad Conservatory in Recollections]*. Book 1.

Milstein, Nathan, with Solomon Volkov. *From Russia to the West*. New York: Limelight Editions, 1991.

Molkhou, Jean-Michel. "Heifetz on disc and film." *Strad,* January 1995, 90–97.

Muzalevskii, Vladimir Il'ich. *Zapiski muzykanta* [*Notes of a Musician*]. Leningrad: Muzyka, 1969.

Neigauz, Genrikh Gustavovich. *Razmyshlenia, vospominaniia, dnevniki. Izbrannye stat'i. Pis'ma k roditel'iam* [*Reflections, Recollections, Diaries. Collected Articles. Letters to Parents*]. Moscow: Sovetskii kompozitor, 1983.

New York Post. "Only Mad People Go Out and Steal Strads." December 13, 1937.

New York Times. "Elias Malkin Dies; Heifetz Teacher." July 19, 1953.

Oistrakh, Igor. "Pamiati Iashi Kheifetsa [To the Memory of Jascha Heifetz]." *Sovetskaia muzyka* [*Soviet Music*] no. 4 (1988).

Pfeiffer, John. "Perfect Record." *Strad,* February 1986, 754–756.

Prokof'ev, Grigorii Petrovich. "Opera i kontserty v S.-Peterburge [Opera and Concerts in S.-Petersburg]." *RMG* [*Russian Musical Gazette*], no. 12 (March 24, 1913).

———. "Kontserty v Moskve [Concerts in Moscow]." *RMG* [*Russian Musical Gazette*], no. 11 (March 16, 1914).

———. "Moskovskie kontserty [Moscow Concerts]." *RMG* [*Russian Musical Gazette*] no. 49 (December 6, 1915).

———. "Kontserty i opera v Moskve [Concerts and Opera in Moscow]." *RMG* [*Russian Musical Gazette*] No. 7 (February 14, 1916).

Prokof'ev, Sergei Sergeevich. "Iunye gody [Young Years]." In Tigranov, *Leningradskaia konservatoriia v vospominaniiakh* [*Leningrad Conservatory in Recollections*]. Book 1.

Prokofiev, Sergei. *Selected Letters of Sergei.* Edited and translated by Harlow Robinson. Boston: Northeastern University Press, 1998.

Puzyrevskii, A. I. *Imperatorskoe Russkoe muzykal'noe obshchestvo v pervye 50 let ego deiatel'nosti* [*Imperial Russian Music Society in the First 50 Years of its Activity*]. St. Petersburg, 1909.

Raaben, L. N. *Zhizn' zamechatel'nykh skripachei* [*The Lives of Remarkable Violinists*]. Moscow, Leningrad: Muzyka, 1967.

———. *Leopol'd Semionovich Auer: Ocherk zhizni i deiatel'nosti* [*Leopold Auer: A Sketch of His Life and Career*]. Muzgiz, 1962.

Ratner, Sabina Teller. *Camille Saint-Saëns, 1835–1921: A Thematic Catalogue of his Complete Works. Volume 1: The instrumental works.* New York: Oxford University Press, 2002.

Rosen, Peter. *Jascha Heifetz: God's Fiddler,* DVD. Directed and produced by Peter Rosen. New York: Peter Rosen Productions, 2011.

Roth, Henry. Interview with Paul Olefsky, "The Complete Cellist." *Strad,* November 1989.

Sabaneev, Leonid Leonidovich. "Muzyka i patriotizm [Music and Patriotism]." *Muzyka* [*Music*], no. 107, 1912.

———. "Muzyka v Moskve [Music in Moscow]." Khronika zhurnala *Muzykal'nyi sovremennik* [Chronicles of the journal *Musical Contemporary*], no. 18, 1916.

Saleski, Gdal. *Famous Musicians of a Wandering Race.* New York: Bloch Publishing Company, 1927.

———. *Famous Musicians of Jewish Origin*. New York: Bloch Publishing Company, 1949.

Saminskii, Lazar Iosifovich. "Simfonicheskii kontsert (pri uchastii Iashi Kheifetsa) [Symphony Concert (with the Participation of Jascha Heifetz)]." *Zakavkazskaia rech'* [*Transcaucasian Speech*], February 19, 1916.

———. "Evreiskie muzykanty i ikh 'estradnyi ekzotizm' (Po povodu kontsertov Iashi Kheifetsa) [Jewish Musicians and their 'Stage Exoticism' (on the concerts of Jascha Heifetz)]." *Evreiskaia nedelia (Petrograd)* [*Jewish Week* (Petrograd)], no. 14–15, 1916.

Sanborn, Pitts. "Enter a Genius: Jascha Heifetz." *Commercial Advertiser and Globe*, October 29, 1917.

Sarlo, Dario. "Investigating Performer Uniqueness: The Case of Jascha Heifetz," PhD diss., Goldsmiths, University of London, 2010.

Savshinkii, Samarii Il'ich. "Vospominaniia o bylom [Recollections of the Past]." In Tigranov, *Leningradskaia konservatoriia v vospominaniiakh* [*Leningrad Conservatory in Recollections*]. Book 2.

Schonberg, Harold C. *The Virtuosi*. New York: Vintage Books, 1988.

———. "Jascha Heifetz is dead at 86; A virtuoso since childhood." *New York Times*, December 12, 1987.

Schwarz, Boris. *Great Masters of the Violin: From Corelli and Vivaldi to Stern, Zukerman and Perlman*. New York: Simon & Schuster, 1983.

Sedov, Pavel. "Iskusstvo Iashi Kheifetsa v kontekste muzykal'no-ispolnitel'skoi kul'tury XX veka [The Art of Jascha Heifetz in the Context of Musical Performance Culture of the 20th Century]." PhD diss., Moscow Conservatory, 2002.

Shaporin, Iurii Aleksandrovich. "Iz vospominanii." *Sovetskaia muzyka* ["From Recollections," *Soviet Music*] no. 3, 1961. Perepech. v sb. *Iurii Aleksandrovich Shaporin: Literaturnoe nasledie, stat'i, pis'ma* [Reprinted in the collection *Iurii Aleksandrovich Shaporin: Literary Legacy, Articles, Letters*]. Moscow: Sovetskii kompozitor, 1989.

Shtrimer, Aleksandr Iakovlevich. "Navsegda sokhraniu v pamiati [I Will Remember Forever]." In Tigranov, *Leningradskaia konservatoriia v vospominaniiakh* [*Leningrad Conservatory in Recollections*]. Book 2.

Smith, Edward H. "A Boyish Genius Who Makes Musicians Marvel." *The World Magazine*, November 25, 1917.

Spaeth, Sigmund. "Perfect Violin Playing at Last." *Evening Mail*, October 29, 1917.

Spalding, Albert. *Rise to Follow*. New York: Henry Holt & Co., 1943.

Stein, Lisa K. *Syd Chaplin: A Biography*. Jefferson, North Carolina: McFarland & Company, Inc., 2011.

Strad. "Remembrance of Things Past," February, 1986, 758–779.

Taylor, Deems. "Jascha, That's My Baby." *New York Times*, July 16, 1939.

Taubman, Howard. "Heifetz Urges Ritard In Tempo Of Musician's Life." *New York Times*, December 13, 1968.

Ter-Gevondian, Anushavan Grigor'evich. "Nezabyvaemaia pora [Unforgettable Time]." In Tigranov, *Leningradskaia konservatoriia v vospominaniiakh* [*Leningrad Conservatory in Recollections*]. Book 1.

The Bay of San Francisco: A History, vol. 2. Chicago: The Lewis Publishing Company, 1892.

Tigranov, G. G., ed. *Leningradskaia konservatoriia v vospominaniiakh* [*Leningrad Conservatory in Recollections*]. 2 books. Leningrad: Muzgiz, 1987.

Val'ter, Viktor. "Vtoroi kontsert Iashi Kheifetsa [Second Concert of Jascha Heifetz]," Rukopis' [Manuscript]. KR RIII, f. 83, op. 1, no. 15.

———. "Khronika: S.-Peterburg [Chronicle: S.-Petersburg]" *RMG* [*Russian Musical Gazette*] no. 17, April 24, 1911.

———. "Kontserty v Peterburge: Iasha Kheifets [Concerts in Petersburg: Jascha Heifetz]." *RMG* [*Russian Musical Gazette*] no. 16 stlb. 393, April 15, 1912.

———. "Iasha Kheifets [Jascha Heifetz]." *Solntse Rossii* [*Sun of Russia*] no. 5, January, 1913.

———. "Kontserty v S.-Peterburge [Concerts in S.-Petersburg]." *RMG* [*Russian Musical Gazette*] April 7, 1913.

———. "Kontserty v S.-Peterburge [Concerts in S.-Petersburg]." *RMG* [*Russian Musical Gazette*] no. 48, December 1, 1913.

———. "Iasha Kheifets [Jascha Heifetz]." *Den'* [*Day*], March 22, 1914.

———. "Kontsert Iashi Kheifetsa [Concert of Jascha Heifetz]." *Den'* [*Day*], March 3, 1915.

———. "Tretii simfonicheskii kontsert S. Kusevitskogo [Third Symphony Concert of S. Koussevitzky]." *Den'* [*Day*], December 17, 1915.

———. "Pervyi kontsert Iashi Kheifets [Jascha Heifetz]." *Den'* [*Day*], December 21, 1915.

———. "Simfonicheskii kontsert orkestra leib-gv. Volynskogo polka [Symphony Concert of the Orchestra of the Lifeguard of the Volyn Regiment]." *Den'* [*Day*], December 13, 1916.

———. "Kontsert Iashi Kheifetsa [Jascha Heifetz]." *Den'* [*Day*], December 24, 1916.

———. "Kontsert Dmitriia Shostakovicha [Concert of Dmitrii Shostakovich]." *Teatr* [*Theater*] no. 12, 1923.

———. "Iasha Kheifets (Iz vospominanii) [Jascha Heifetz (From Recollections)]." *Zveno* (Paris) [*Link* (Paris)], February 28, 1926.

Vol'fing [Emil K. Medtner], *Modernizm i muzyka: Stat'i kriticheskie i polemicheskie* [*Modernism and Music: Critical and Polemic Articles*] (1907–1910), Moscow, 1912.

Wen, Eric. "Heifetz: a legend on record." *Strad*, January 1995.

Weschler-Vered, Artur. *Jascha Heifetz*. New York: Schirmer Books, 1986.

Woollcott, Alexander. "The Quest of a Lost Childhood." *Saturday Evening Post*, April 7, 1928.

Zhi-v, I. "Deti-virtuozy [Child Virtuosos]." *Solntse Rossii* [*Sun of Russia*]. October, 1911.

INDEX

observance of, 63; residency permits of, 51–52, 54, 70, 119, 320; St. Petersburg addresses of, 52–53, 62–63, 107, 189, 229, 302–303; summer vacations of, 60, 82–83, 186, 221–222, 273, 275, 290, 317–318, 350–351; United States arrival of, 388–390; United States journey of, 382–383, 384, 385, 386, 387; Vilnius addresses of, 16–18

Heifitz, Joseph (Yosif), 347, 347n53

Helsinki Philharmonic Orchestra, 188

Herrmann, Emil, 295

Hess, Willy, 162, 181, 181n4

Heyman, Sir Henry, 388–389

Hin-Goldovskaya, Rachel M., 106

Hirsch, Nicole, 8, 21

Hochstein, David, 393

Hofmann, Josef, 45, 198, 205–206, 233, 254, 308, 336–337

Hollaender, Gustav, 162, 181, 181n4

Horner Photography Company (Boston), 391

Hotel Palace (Vilnius), 15, 27

Hotel Passage (Odessa), 88, 157

Hřímalý, Jan, 19, 20, 199

Hubay, Jenő, 178, 184, 252

Huberman, Bronislaw, 45, 182

Hülsen-Haeseler, Count von, 297–298

Imperial Russian Music Society (IRMO), 104, 247, 301, 335; Auer, 102, 103, 104, 105, 124; background of, 24; charter and rules, 26, 47–48; Kharkov division, 334; Kiev and Odessa divisions, 124; Moscow division, 251; St. Petersburg conservatory, 266; St. Petersburg division, 47–48, 104, 359; Tbilisi division, 337, 338; Vilnius division, 25, 26, 28, 29, 31, 32, 33, 35, 36, 40, 41, 43, 144

Imperial Russian Opera, 37, 91

Ipolyi, László, 162, 180–182

Ippolitov-Ivanov, Mikhail Mikhailovich, 321

Iretskaya, Natalia Aleksandrovna, 64

IRMO. See Imperial Russian Music Society (IRMO)

Israel, xi, 1, 8, 15

Ivan the Terrible (tsar), 3, 371n12

Izmailovsky Lifeguard Regiment Symphony Orchestra, 359

Izvestia, 372, 381, 384

Jacobsen, Sascha, 345

Jewish Chamber Theater, 3

Joachim, Joseph, 57, 105, 128, 178, 181, 191, 242, 250, 252

Johnston, R. E., 225–226, 234, 269, 303–304, 382

Jollos Foundation, 203

Jugel-Janson, 188

Juon, Paul Fyodorovich, 199, 353, 364

Juon, Konstantin Fyodorovich, 199

Jurjāns, Andrejs, 321

Kadets, 347, 364, 371, 378

Kahn, Roger, xi

Kalafati, Vasily Pavlovich, 304, 328

Kalākaua (king), 389

Kalantarova, Olga Kalantarovna, 109

Kapp, Artur, 321

Karatygin, Vyacheslav Gavrilovich, 86, 217, 231–232, 325, 329, 346

Karkaria, Navroz, xviii

Karmilov, V. S., 26, 40

Katulskaya, Yelena Klimentyevna, 91

Katz, Gustav, 85, 96, 143

Kaufman, Maurice, 393

Kaunas (Kovno), 33, 37–39, 64, 72, 321, 332

Kaunas City Theater, 38–39

Kayser, Heinrich Ernst, 19, 20

Kerensky, Aleksandr Fyodorovich, 379, 383, 386

performs Gavotte, 190, 198; Heifetz performs Minuet in D (Burmester), 226, 230, 231, 240, 254, 256, 257, 261, 266, 380, 394, 401; Heifetz performs Rondo, 209; as inspiration for Heifetz, 60;
Mtskheta, 336
Musaget, 343
Musical America, 10, 275, 291, 389
Musical Celebrities, 225
Musical Courier, 162, 180, 181, 182, 185
Muzalevsky, Vladimir Ilyich, 307

Napoleon, 3, 13
Nalbandian (Nalbandov), Anton Arakelovich, 57–58
Nalbandian, Anna Akimovna (mother of Ioannes), 57–58
Nalbandian, Anna Stepanovna (wife of Ioannes), 57–58
Nalbandian, Ioannes, 105, 109, 115, 146, 147, 178, 317; biographical details of, 57–58, 59; concerts of, 32, 69, 71–72, 77, 210, 321, 328; enrolling Ruvin as a student, 61–62; Mina's opinion of, 196–197; newspaper commentary on teaching Heifetz, 73, 79, 134; public exams, 58, 76; teaching Heifetz, 50, 51, 56–57, 58–59, 60, 63, 64, 78, 116
Nápravnik, Vladimir Eduardovich, 36
National Postal Museum, Washington, D.C., 98
Nemirovsky (accompanist), A. M., 91
Nemirovsky, Aleksandr Yosifovich, xiii
Nenarokomova, L. I., 40
Neris River (Viliya), 38
Netcke und Dr. Löser, 225
New York: early Heifetz reviews appear in, 97, 185–186; Heifetz family arrival in, 389, 392–395; Metropolitan Opera, 100; Philharmonic Society, 251; Symphony Orchestra, 89, 210

Newton Classical High School, 392–393
Newtonville, 286, 390–392
Nicholas I (tsar), 2, 3, 218
Nicholas II (tsar), 25, 101, 363, 364, 366, 368, 369, 371
Nicholas Konstantinovich, Grand Duke, 358–359
Niedzielski, 8
Nikisch, Arthur, 71, 165, 178, 198, 200, 219, 323; Berlin Philharmonic 1912 with Heifetz, 166, 184, 193–194, 252, 352; on Heifetz, 192, 193; Leipzig Gewandhaus 1914 with Heifetz, 242, 250, 259, 352; reaction to Ferrero tour, 233
Nikolaev (Mykolaiv), 124–125
Nikolaev, Leonid Vladimirovich, 120, 196, 304
Nikolaev, Nikolai Dmitrievich, 338
Nabokov, Vladimir Vladimirovich, 263
Norway, King and Queen of, 354
Noskowski, Zygmunt, 127
Novikov, L. A., 359n18
Novo-Alexandria, 1–2

Odessa, 157, 158, 159; City Orchestra, 88; City Theater, 260; Exhibit of 1911, 83, 84, 87, 88, 90, 91, 93, 94, 317; Heifetz described as from, 191, 197; Heifetz legend (Babel), 92–94; Heifetz rescued from crowd, 98–99; history and description of, 12, 88, 261; issue of presenting child prodigies discussed in local press, 100–101; Opera Theater, 88; Opera Troupe, 99; unfulfilled contract, 218–219
Odesskie novosti, 90, 92, 219, 316; Heifetz visits offices of, 95
Oistrakh, David Fyodorovich, 93
Oistrakh, Igor Davidovich, xi
Olav, Prince, 354–355
Olefsky, Aron Solomonovich, 17–18, 50, 243, 244, 245, 293

performs *Sérénade mélancolique*, 190, 193, 227; Heifetz performs *Valse-Scherzo*, 326, 332; lessons with Auer on the concerto of, 117; Nikisch affinity for, 193, 323; performances of, 15, 32, 72, 89, 128, 346, 379; personal life, 47; voice recording of, 198

Tcherepnin, Nikolai Nikolaevich, 58, 113, 120, 134, 233

tefillin, 245

Telmányi, Emil, 252

Ter-Gevondian, Anushavan Grigoryevich, 55–56, 108, 121

Thackeray, William Makepeace, 342

Theater of Musical Drama (St. Petersburg). *See* St. Petersburg Conservatory, Bolshoi Hall of

Thibaud, Jacques, 128

Thornberg, Julius, 162, 181

Tiflis. *See* Tbilisi (Tiflis)

Timofeev, Grigory Nikolaevich, 72, 210, 311

Titanic, 133

Tkhorzh, Franz Ivanovich, 44

Tolstoy, Leo Nikolaevich, 65, 66, 198, 342

Tomars, Joseph Semyonovich, 315

Tononi, Carlo, 295, 300, 310, 327

Tourte, François, 218

Tovbin, Mr., 101

Trans-Siberian Railroad, 385, 386

Trepov, Alexander Fyodorovich, 364

Treskin, Mikhail Ivanovich, 25, 26, 29, 34, 36, 40, 43

Trofimovna, Olga, 244, 247, 253

Tseitlin, Lev Markovich, 243

Tsereteli, Irakli Georgievich, 379

Tsitron, Isidor Lvovich, 249–250

Twain, Mark, 342

Ufa, 385

Unger, Max, 251

University of California, Los Angeles, 112

University of Southern California, 112

University of the Peoples of the West, 3

Urstein, Ludwik, 256

Ushkov family, 323

Utochkin, Sergei Isaevich, 83, 94, 327

Valentinova, Ms., 44

Valter, Aleksandr (Shura) Viktorovich, 108, 383

Valter, Tosya Viktorovna, 108, 383

Valter, Viktor Grigoryevich, ix, x, *151*; assisting the Heifetzes, 78, 90; Auer Violin Competition, 116; biographical details of, 73, 74, 107–108; broadening Heifetz's horizons, 314, 317, 325, 342, 347, 371; contesting the bad review for Malkin, 238–239, 241–243; correspondence with Heifetz about American trip, 382–383, 385; correspondence with the Heifetzes, 84, 87, 96, *156*, 180, 192, 193, 223, 345; criticizes Heifetz, 231; friendship with the Heifetzes, 107, 108, 121, 123, 247, 262, 395; review comparing Shostakovich with Heifetz, 79; revolution program annotation, 369; twenty-fifth work anniversary celebration, 277, 322; unpublished criticism of Heifetz program, 312–313; writing about Heifetz, 75, 79, 97, 135, 204, 217, 250–251, 258–260, 311, 324, 326, 362

Valter, Vladimir (Volodya) Viktorovich, 108, 383

Valter, Yekaterina (Kitty), 107–108, 383

Van Der Schkroof, Mr., 90

Vandervelde, Émile, 379

Varon, Isay Faivishevich, 40

Vasilyevsky Island, 308

Vecsey, Franz von, 178, 185, 252

Vengerova, Izabella Afanasyevna, 37, 109, 296

GALINA KOPYTOVA is a scholar and an archivist who specializes in the history of Russian musical culture. She heads the Office of Manuscripts of the Russian Institute for the History of the Arts in St. Petersburg and has authored numerous books and articles on major figures in Russian music (Glinka, Rubinstein, Shostakovich, Tchaikovsky), and on the relationship between foreign musicians and Russia (Rossini, Sarti). Her research also includes the history of Jewish music in Russia at the beginning of the twentieth century.

ALBINA STARKOVA-HEIFETZ, who assisted Kopytova in her research, is a professional architect in Moscow. Her husband, Robert Heifetz (1932–2001), was the initiator and inspiration for Kopytova and Starkova-Heifetz's collaboration on the Russian biography of his great father.

ALEXANDRA SARLO has a degree in Russian from Cornell University, in Russian and East European Studies from Georgetown University, and in Political Science from the University of Pennsylvania. An enthusiastic amateur violinist herself, she has also conducted research in Central and Eastern Europe.

Born in England, DARIO SARLO has earned degrees in music studies from Kings College London and Goldsmiths, University of London. He was a post-doctoral fellow at the John W. Kluge Center, Library of Congress, in Washington D.C., where he worked closely with the Jascha Heifetz Collection. Sarlo participated as a researcher in the documentary film, *Jascha Heifetz: God's Fiddler* (2011, Peter Rosen Productions). He plays the violin and also writes for *The Strad*. He lives in the United States with his wife, Alexandra, the translator and co-editor of this book.

www.ingramcontent.com/pod-product-compliance
Lightning Source LLC
Chambersburg PA
CBHW070405100426
42812CB00005B/1646

9 780253 010766